Globalisation and its Economic Consequences

Given the rising criticisms of and growing doubts about globalisation, this timely edited volume looks at globalisation and its economic impact on eight countries in Asia and the Pacific region, namely Australia, China, Indonesia, Japan, Malaysia, Thailand, the United States (US), and Vietnam. The eight selected countries are members of the Asia-Pacific Economic Cooperation (APEC) forum and yet the economies of these member countries have benefited differently from globalisation.

This book summarises findings from existing academic literature in a coherent framework and reviews them critically to provide a balanced analysis. It also identifies the mechanisms through which globalisation impacts economies and explains how understanding of such mechanisms can be useful for formulating policies, which would benefit from globalisation while achieving inclusive economic growth in the context of rising nationalism and protectionism.

Shujiro Urata is Professor Emeritus, at Waseda University, Japan and a Senior Research Advisor at Economic Research Institute for ASEAN and East Asia, Indonesia.

Ha Thi Thanh Doan is an Economist at Economic Research Institute for ASEAN and East Asia, Indonesia.

Routledge-ERIA Studies in Development Economics

Social Protection Goals in East Asia
Strategies and Methods to Generate Fiscal Space
Edited by Mukul G. Asher, Fauziah Zen and Astrid Dita

World Trade Evolution
Growth, Productivity and Employment
Edited by Lili Yan Ing and Miaojie Yu

Emerging Global Trade Governance
Mega Free Trade Agreements and Implications for ASEAN
Edited by Lurong Chen, Shujiro Urata, Junji Nakagawa and Masahito Ambashi

East Asian Integration
Goods, Services and Investment
Edited by Lili Yan Ing, Martin Richardson and Shujiro Urata

Developing the Digital Economy in ASEAN
Edited by Lurong Chen and Fukunari Kimura

The Effects of Globalisation on Firm and Labour Performance
Edited by Chin Hee Hahn, Dionisius Narjoko, Ha Thi Thanh Doan and Shujiro Urata

Financial Inclusion in Asia and Beyond
Measurement, Development Gaps, and Economic Consequences
Edited by Tony Cavoli and Rashesh Shrestha

Globalisation and its Economic Consequences
Looking at APEC Economies
Edited by Shujiro Urata and Ha Thi Thanh Doan

For more information about this series, please visit: www.routledge.com/Routledge-ERIA-Studies-in-Development-Economics/book-series/ERIA

Globalisation and its Economic Consequences

Looking at APEC Economies

Edited by Shujiro Urata and Ha Thi Thanh Doan

Routledge
Taylor & Francis Group
LONDON AND NEW YORK

ERIA
Economic Research Institute for ASEAN and East Asia

JIIA

First published 2022
by Routledge
2 Park Square, Milton Park, Abingdon, Oxon OX14 4RN

and by Routledge
605 Third Avenue, New York, NY 10158

Routledge is an imprint of the Taylor & Francis Group, an informa business

British Library Cataloguing-in-Publication Data
A catalogue record for this book is available from the British Library

Library of Congress Cataloging-in-Publication Data
A catalog record has been requested for this book

ISBN: 978-0-367-68266-8 (hbk)
ISBN: 978-0-367-68668-0 (pbk)
ISBN: 978-1-003-13850-1 (ebk)

DOI: 10.4324/9781003138501

Typeset in Galliard
by MPS Limited, Dehradun

Contents

Figures

Tables

Contributors

Meenal Banga is Ph.D. student in Management at the University of Texas at Austin, the United States.

Thi Nhan Thien Do is Researcher, Department for General Economic Issues and Integration Studies, Central Institute for Economic Management, Vietnam.

Ha Thi Thanh Doan is Economist at the ERIA.

Christopher Findlay is Honorary Professor at the Australian National University and Emeritus Professor at University of Adelaide, Australia.

Keiko Ito is Professor at the Faculty of Commerce, Chuo University, Japan.

Juthathip Jongwanich is Associate Professor at the Faculty of Economics, Thammasat University, Thailand.

Cassey Lee Hong Kim is Senior Fellow at Institute of Southeast Asian Studies (ISEAS) – Yusof Ishak Institute, Singapore.

Archanun Kohpaiboon is Associate Professor in the Faculty of Economics, Thammasat University, Thailand.

Kostas Mavromaras is Director and Professor, Future Employment and Skills Research Centre at University of Adelaide, Australia.

Anh Duong Nguyen is Director, Department for General Economic Issues and Integration Studies, Central Institute for Economic Management, Vietnam.

Mari Elka Pangestu is Professor of International Economics at University of Indonesia, Indonesia.

Peter A. Petri is Professor of International Finance at the Brandeis International Business School, the United States.

Shujiro Urata is Professor Emeritus at Waseda University, Japan and Senior Research Advisor to the President of the ERIA.

Kiki Verico is Assistant Professor at the Faculty of Economics and Business, University of Indonesia, Indonesia.

Thanh Tri Vo is the President, Institute for Brand and Competitiveness Strategy, Vietnam.

Zhang Wei is Senior Research Fellow, Future Employment and Skills Research Centre at University of Adelaide, Australia.

Miaojie Yu is Professor at China Center for Economic Research, National School of Development, Peking University, China.

Huihuang Zhu is Ph.D. student at Department of Economics, University of California, Los Angeles, the United States.

Foreword

The project "Fostering Free Trade and Overcoming its Challenges in ASEAN and East Asia Region" supported by ERIA, was presented at the symposium in Tokyo on 22 and 23 April 2019, organised by the Japan Institute of International Affairs (JIIA). This project treats an issue of current significance, namely the effects of globalisation accelerated by liberalisation and facilitation of trade and investment on the economic structure and society in the Asia-Pacific region, through providing historical analyses and empirical studies. I highly value this project and express my deep respect for the efforts made by the honourable professors led by Professor URATA Shujiro and the JIIA who took part in the project.

As each chapter shows, the globalisation contributes to improving society and economy in various means, which consequently highlights the importance of pursuing liberalisation and facilitation of trade and investment as one of the key enablers of the economic growth. As Japan is keen on supporting the rules-based multilateral trading system and deepening global and regional economic integration, it is determined to continuously work on the eventual realisation of the Free Trade Area of the Asia-Pacific. Its effort has recently seen significant progress including the entering into force of the Comprehensive and Progressive Agreement for Trans-Pacific Partnership (CPTPP) and the successful signing of the Regional Comprehensive Economic Partnership (RCEP) Agreement. Simultaneously, Japan has been taking initiatives in the reform of the WTO as a pressing issue for maintaining and strengthening the multilateral trading system and promoting the stability and predictability of international trade flows.

Through pursuing the globalisation, it is important to recognise that the world today, especially the COVID-19 pandemic reminds us again of the importance of fostering sustainable and inclusive growth. This unprecedented crisis might add to already existing sceptical perspectives against trade liberalisation, influenced by its negative aspects such as job bi-polarisation and wage inequality that are rightly argued in the book. I, therefore, believe that it will become increasingly crucial to discuss various economic policies to realise 'quality growth that brings palpable benefits and greater health and wellbeing to all, including MSMEs, women and others with untapped economic potential,' as set out as one of the long-term objectives of our region in the APEC Putrajaya Vision 2040 launched by the APEC Economic Leaders. Japan will continue to work together with partners in the region to achieve this objective through various international fora such as APEC.

From this perspective, this valuable analytical work will contribute not only to further understanding on the economic aspect of the globalisation but also to being a source of inspiration to potential policies to be taken by the governments in the awake the crisis. I sincerely hope this book will be referred to by a wide range of readers.

TAJIMA Hiroshi,
APEC Senior Official of Japan,
Ambassador in charge of Economic Diplomacy,
Deputy Assistant Minister, Economic Affairs Bureau,
Ministry of Foreign Affairs of Japan

Acknowledgements

This book is based on the findings of the ERIA's research project "Fostering Free Trade and Overcoming Its Challenges in ASEAN and the East Asia Region" (July 2018–May 2019), conducted at the Japan Institute of International Affairs (JIIA). The project, which was led by Professor Shujiro Urata, invited prominent experts from Australia, China, Indonesia, Japan, Malaysia, Thailand, the United States, and Vietnam. In the course of the project, the JIIA held an international symposium in collaboration with the Ministry of Foreign Affairs of Japan on 22–23 April 2019 in Tokyo.

The possible adverse effects of globalization accelerated by rapid technological progress and the movement of people are not limited to the economy but cut across society. Today, we are witnessing spread of populism and anti-globalism around the world. We see an erosion of public trust in politics and weakened social cohesion in many countries. States have become more prone to pursue their self-interest, leading to the rise of protectionism and nationalism. The politics of blame and divisive social norms are seen at the forefront of our daily lives. Multilateral liberal institutions are being threatened and eroded from within and without.

To tackle these problems, there are at least two essential approaches. First, we need to curb adverse effects stemming from rapid structural changes by promoting sustainable and inclusive growth through various policies. These include investment in both human and physical capital. Second, there needs to be a coordinated and integrated policy framework across different entities that involves diverse stakeholders in the policy-making process.

This book provides information and analysis on what contributions free trade has made to improve people's quality of life, especially employment, and what policies are possible to tackle the negative aspects of globalisation using the lessons learnt from the experience of various countries in the Asia-Pacific.

I sincerely thank Professor Shujiro Urata for his leadership in bringing international experts together for this project and for making it possible to publish the project's findings as a book. I am confident that readers will find valuable information and insightful policy proposals that help advance sound globalisation in the Asia-Pacific.

Kenichiro Sasae,
President and Director General,
The Japan Institute of International Affairs (JIIA)

1 Introduction and overview

Shujiro Urata and Ha Thi Thanh Doan

1 Introduction

In 2020, the coronavirus disease (COVID-19) pandemic changed the world so remarkably that few believe a return to the pre-COVID-19 economic and social situation is possible. Since January 2020, when the first COVID-19 infection was officially detected in Wuhan, China, more than 49.0 million cases – including more than 1.2 million deaths – have been reported worldwide as of 7 November 2020. The economic impacts of the COVID-19 pandemic have been devastating; various lockdown and stay-at-home policies, implemented by many countries to deal with the situation, have virtually stopped economic activities for several months. Indeed, the International Monetary Fund (IMF) projected global economic growth rate for 2020 is –4.4%, down from 2.8% for 2019 (IMF, 2020). This marks the worst economic situation since the Great Depression of the 1920 and 1930.

A view has emerged that globalisation, which brought high economic growth before the pandemic, will be reversed. Indeed, governments around the world have intervened in the market to secure sufficient supplies of medical and health products, such as face masks and medical gowns, by restricting exports and by promoting domestic production of these goods, against the recommendations of international organisations such as the World Trade Organization (WTO) and international fora such as the G20. Moreover, it is undeniable that the rapid and sizeable movement of people, which became possible thanks to globalisation, has contributed to the spread of the coronavirus.

Anti-globalisation views did not emerge as a result of the COVID-19 pandemic, however; protectionist movements began to trend after the Global Financial Crisis in 2008 and 2009. The pace and magnitude of protectionism then grew after United States (US) President Donald Trump began to apply such measures mainly by raising import tariff rates. It has been argued that an increasing number of his constituents, such as unemployed workers who did not benefit from globalisation, are supporting this trend.

It has been well-established, however, that globalisation, which had been propelled by the liberalisation of trade and foreign direct investment (FDI) policies as well as technological progress that reduced trade and FDI costs, has

DOI: 10.4324/9781003138501-1

contributed to rapid global economic growth – especially in East Asia, which has grown more rapidly compared to the rest of the world. Protectionism, therefore, could have serious impacts on this region, as important engines of economic growth (i.e. trade and FDI expansion) could be slowed or stopped.

In light of protectionist policies resulting from the growing anti-globalisation sentiment, the Japan Institute of International Affairs (JIIA), with financial assistance from the Economic Research Institute for ASEAN and East Asia (ERIA), conducted a study of the economic consequences of globalisation for eight selected members of the Asia-Pacific Economic Cooperation (APEC) – Australia, China, Indonesia, Japan, Malaysia, Thailand, the US, and Vietnam – in 2018–19. As there are many lessons to be learned from these countries that have experienced globalisation through trade and FDI liberalisation, the study aimed to deepen the understanding of the benefits and costs of globalisation to provide insight for policy makers in formulating foreign economic policy. Today, as many countries are rapidly adopting protectionist policies in response to the COVID-19 pandemic, it is hoped that this study brings about new insights that will help overcome the economic crisis spurred by the pandemic as well as achieve economic growth in the post-pandemic era.

As many studies already exist on this subject, it was decided that this study would collate and analyse important findings and lessons from past literature rather than conduct original research. The authors of each chapter have aimed to draw policy implications from examining past studies, focusing on impacts on productivity, employment, inequality, and innovation.

This chapter is organised as follows. Section 2 presents a brief overview of globalisation, with a focus on the study's sample countries. Section 3 reviews previous studies on the economic impacts of globalisation in the forms of trade and FDI. Section 4 presents major findings from this study, while Section 5 provides policy implications. Section 6 presents a synopsis of each chapter.

2 Economic globalisation: an overview

Several indicators can be used to examine the extent of economic globalisation, a phenomenon in which economic activities, such as trade and investment, are conducted on a global basis to result in active cross-border movement of goods, services, capital, people, and data. The most popular indicators are trade and FDI, because they have been important international economic activities for decades, and data on these activities are generally collected. The international movement of people, labour, capital other than FDI, services, and data are also important activities contributing to globalisation, but they suffer from a lack of reliable data.

Figures 1.1 and 1.2 show the changes in trade–gross domestic product (GDP) and inward FDI stock–GDP ratios for the world and APEC member economies from 1989 (i.e. the year of APEC establishment) to 2018 (i.e. the year for the most up-to-data available at the time of writing). The upward trend of these indicators shows the advancement of globalisation of the world economy and

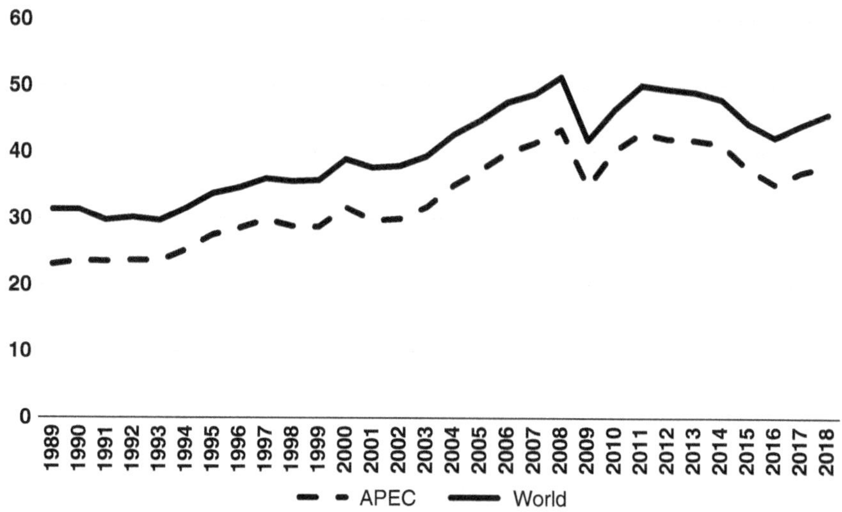

Figure 1.1 Trade–GDP Ratios of Selected APEC Member Countries and the World (%).
Source: APEC, *StatsAPEC*, http://statistics.apec.org/ (accessed 7 November 2020).
Note: APEC = Asia-Pacific Economic Cooperation, GDP = gross domestic product.

APEC member economies, because international economic activities indicated by trade and FDI increased faster than domestic economic activities indicated by GDP. Both indicators declined in 2008–09, however, because of the Global Financial Crisis. It should also be pointed out that the trade–GDP ratio did not increase after 2011, with only a slight increase after 2016. This was due to several reasons, including growing protectionism, the reshoring of Chinese production, the global shift in demand away from goods and towards less tradable services, and the possible saturation of the development of global value chains (GVCs) (Rodrik, 2018). Moreover, the level of globalisation for APEC member economies is lower compared to that of the rest of the world, because the three largest economies in the world – China, Japan, and the US – are APEC members and exhibited relatively low levels of globalisation. Generally speaking, dependence on international economic activities is low for large economies, although trade and FDI have made significant contributions to these countries' economic growth.

In recent decades, there has been an active interaction amongst – and rapid expansion of – different types of international economic activities, especially regarding trade and FDI. A typical pattern of their interaction may be described as follows. Think of a multinational corporation (MNC) that is operating various activities, processes, or tasks in an integrated form in the same location. Faced with a reduction in transport and communication costs, it recognises the benefit of breaking up the operation into various tasks, putting them in different locations through FDI, and linking these production bases by trade in components

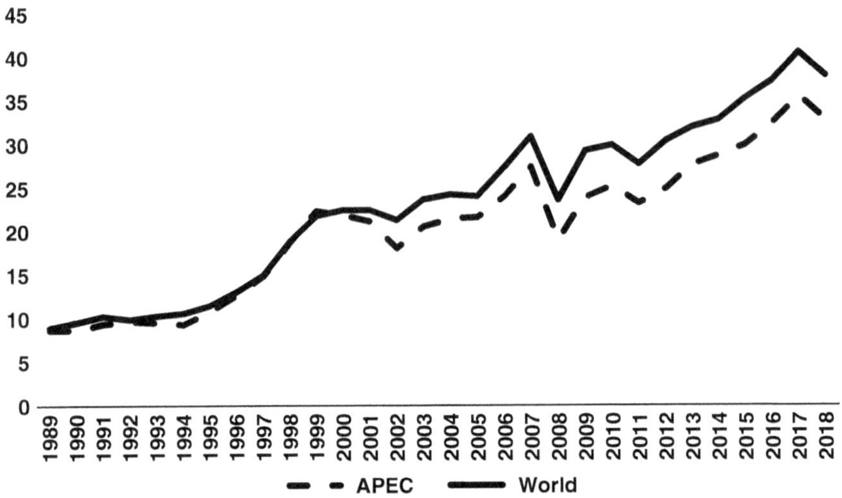

Figure 1.2 Inward FDI Stock–GDP Ratios of Selected APEC Member Countries and the World (%).
Source: APEC, *StatsAPEC*, http://statistics.apec.org/ (accessed 7 November 2020).
Note: APEC = Asia-Pacific Economic Cooperation, FDI = foreign direct investment, GDP = gross domestic product.

to achieve efficient production systems. Adoption of such a fragmentation strategy leads to the formation of a GVC, promoting trade in components between the affiliates set up by FDI. Indeed, as noted earlier, the rapid economic growth of East Asian economies can be attributed to the remarkable expansion of trade and FDI.[1] Other international economic activities also interact with trade and FDI; for example, a Chinese student in Japan finds a business opportunity in exporting high-quality Japanese products to China, and sets up a trading company. This is a case where movement of people results in FDI and trade.

Several factors have contributed to the rapid expansion of globalisation. One was a sharp reduction in the cost of undertaking trade and FDI.[2] Many countries – especially developing countries – undertook trade and FDI liberalisation unilaterally during economic difficulty under the pressure of international organisations, such as the IMF and World Bank, to receive financial assistance. Some countries liberalised trade and FDI regimes bilaterally and regionally with like-minded countries in the form of free-trade agreements (FTAs) to promote economic growth. In addition, the members of the General Agreement on Tariffs and Trade (GATT) and WTO carried out trade and FDI liberalisation multilaterally by implementing commitments made under various international agreements. A reduction in trade and FDI costs occurred through decreasing transport and communication costs, which, in turn, resulted from rapid technological progress and deregulation in such services.

Table 1.1 Trade and FDI for Sample Countries

	Exports/GDP		*Imports/GDP*		*Outward FDI Stock/GDP*		*Inward FDI Stock/GDP*	
	1989	*2018*	*1989*	*2018*	*1989*	*2018*	*1989*	*2018*
Australia	12.4	17.9	15.0	16.4	11.3	34.1	24.0	47.4
China	15.1	18.3	17.0	15.7	0.8	14.3	3.8	12.0
Indonesia	23.5	17.3	17.4	18.1	0.1	6.9	6.4	21.7
Japan	9.0	14.8	6.9	15.1	5.1	33.4	0.3	4.3
Malaysia	64.5	69.0	57.9	60.7	2.5	33.6	20.8	43.0
Thailand	27.8	50.1	35.7	49.1	0.3	24.0	7.4	44.1
US	6.4	8.1	8.7	12.7	14.7	31.4	9.4	36.2
Vietnam	30.9	99.4	40.8	96.6	--	4.4	1.0	59.3
APEC	10.7	18.7	11.3	19.3	10.3	32.2	8.7	32.9
World	15.4	22.7	16.0	23.1	--	36.7	9.0	37.9

Note: APEC = Asia-Pacific Economic Cooperation, FDI = foreign direct investment, GDP = gross domestic product, US = United States.Source: APEC, *StatsAPEC*, http://statistics.apec.org/ (accessed 7 November 2020).

Most countries saw the acceleration of globalisation in the forms of trade and FDI, as trade–GDP and FDI stock–GDP ratios increased from 1989 to 2018 (Table 1.1). Two exceptions are Indonesia in its export–GDP ratio and China in its import–GDP ratio. Indonesia's export–GDP ratio fell due to the declining value of oil exports, partly due to a drop in oil prices. In China, the import–GDP ratio did increase from 17.0% in 1989 to 28.9% in 2005 but then declined to 15.7% in 2018, due to a shift in the country's development strategy from an outward to an inward orientation, reflecting the government's attempt to reduce external dependence. Trade friction with the US also caused a substantial decline in imports from that country. It must be noted, however, that the presence of foreign companies increased in China from 1989 to 2018, indicating their growing importance in China's economic activities. Based on these findings, it is not clear if external dependence declined for the Chinese economy.

The extent of globalisation widely varies amongst the eight countries examined in this study. The degree of globalisation is high in Malaysia, Thailand, and Vietnam; amongst these three countries, all of which are ASEAN members, Vietnam globalised its economic activities at a remarkably high rate, transforming its economic system from a centrally planned to a market economy. However, Australia, China, Indonesia, Japan, and the US show low trade ratios, mainly because of their large economic size.

The patterns are different for FDI stock–GDP ratios. All eight countries, except Indonesia and Vietnam, increased outward FDI stock–GDP ratios, indicating that firms in these countries were active in expanding their operations in foreign countries, also reflecting that the number of successful firms with capable management increased in these countries. Regarding the inward FDI stock–GDP ratio, China and Japan are exceptions with low ratios – despite an increase in these ratios. As noted earlier, adaptation of an inward-oriented development strategy may be behind China's low ratio; for Japan, multiple factors, including high wages and office rental costs, have discouraged FDI by foreign companies there, despite the fact that the government has been eager to promote inward FDI.

3 Economic impacts of globalisation: a brief literature review

This section reviews previous studies on the economic impacts of globalisation. It is divided into two sections: economic growth, and unemployment and inequality. Within the discussion of the impacts of globalisation on economic growth, trade and FDI are examined separately.

3.1 Economic growth

3.1.1 Trade

Expansion of trade can contribute to economic growth by improving resource allocation, known as the resource allocation effect, which may be realised at the sector and firm levels. At the sector level, foreign trade leads to a shift of resources, such as labour and capital, from low-productivity sectors (i.e. those with a comparative disadvantage) to high-productivity sectors (i.e. those with a comparative advantage), resulting in improved use of resources (Alessandrini et al., 2011; McCaig and Pavcnik, 2018). At the firm level, trade-induced competition forces low-productive firms to contract or to exit from the market, reshuffling resources to more productive ones (Pavcnik, 2002; Ha and Kiyota, 2014). For a multi-product firm, trade can also trigger resource reallocation within the firm through adjustment of product structure (Goldberg et al., 2010; Bernard, Redding, and Schott, 2011; Lopresti, 2016).

An expansion of trade, both exports and imports, is also likely to improve the productivity of the countries involved. Exporting firms are shown to have higher productivity compared to domestic firms (Melitz, 2003). Exporting requires firms to overcome various barriers or fixed costs, such as obtaining market information and setting up distribution channels, which may be overcome by high-productivity firms (i.e. a self-selection effect). In addition, exporting firms improve productivity if they acquire technical and managerial knowledge by being exposed to foreign markets and competition (i.e. a learning-by-exporting effect). A similar argument on a productivity-enhancing export effect has been made; exporting enables firms to exploit a benefit-of-scale effect, as exporting leads to expanded production (i.e. a scale effect).

Empirical evidence supports these predictions. For example, Bernard and Jensen (1999) found robust evidence of a self-selection effect for US exporters, although the learning impact was less clear. Alvarez and Lopez (2005) found supporting evidence for both self-selection and learning-by-exporting hypotheses amongst Chilean firms. Using data from Slovenia, De Loecker (2013) showed substantial productivity gains associated with export entry, ranging up to 7.35%. Kim (2000) found that trade liberalisation improved productivity performance, increased competition, and promoted scale efficiency in Korean manufacturing industries.

Increased imports can contribute to the improved productivity of importing and import-competing firms. For importing firms, an increase in imported intermediate goods may improve their productivity, because this enables them to use high-quality intermediate goods (i.e. a high-quality import input effect), especially in developing countries. This effect was observed by Amiti and Konings (2007), who showed that input tariff reduction increased productivity in Indonesia.

An increase in final good imports can lead to improved productivity of import-competing domestic firms, as they face greater competitive pressure from increased imports (i.e. the import-discipline effect). Increased imports may force out inefficient domestic firms, which cannot compete against increased imports. The exit of inefficient firms from the market is, of course, undesirable from the exiting firm's point of view, but it leads to improved productivity for the industry and economy. The negative impacts of increased imports on importing countries can occur through declining employment and incomes. Two studies, de Melo and Urata (1986) and Levinsohn (1993), found support for the import-discipline hypothesis in Chile and Turkey, respectively.[3]

Although the role of innovation in promoting productivity is implicitly assumed in the discussions of the impacts of trade on productivity, some studies have emphasised the importance of a trade–innovation link for promoting productivity. Specifically, a firm may acquire technological knowledge through its international contacts and demand–supply links with foreign firms through trade. In addition to opportunities to learn from foreign firms, a firm exposed to foreign competition through trade faces competitive pressure, providing an incentive to carry out innovation. Damijan and Kostevc (2015) found that firms, learning from both imports and exports, innovated in Spain. Furthermore, they found a sequence in the relationship between trade and innovation to follow from imports to innovation to exports.

3.1.2 Foreign direct investment

FDI is shown to have different impacts on investing (i.e. home) countries and receiving (i.e. host) countries in a simple static theory. In the home country, the amount of capital declines, leading to a drop in output, while in the host country, the opposite situation arises, leading to economic growth. The host country can achieve additional economic growth if technology is transferred from foreign investors or MNCs to the host country.

For a host country of FDI, successful technology transfer from MNCs is key to achieving economic growth. Technology transfer takes place in two steps: (i) intra-firm technology transfer, where technology is transferred from MNCs to their foreign affiliates in the host country by on-the-job training and the exchange of workers between the parent office and affiliates; and (ii) inter-firm or technology spillover, where technology is transferred from foreign affiliates to domestic firms through the business environment, such as sales and procurement. Domestic firms may also obtain technology by hiring workers who used to work for foreign affiliates.

Horizontal technology spillover takes place within the same industry, while vertical technology spillover takes place between different sectors. Vertical technology spillover is further divided into backward and forward technology spillover, depending on the nature of inter-industry relationships. Backward technology spillover takes place through procurement of intermediate goods from the procurer (i.e. buyer) to the supplier, while forward technology spillover occurs from the supplier to the buyer. The success or failure of technology acquisition by domestic firms largely depends on their absorptive capability. Specifically, domestic firms can successfully acquire technology if they have capable workers and conducive environments for adopting new technology.

Early empirical studies of the impacts of FDI on economic growth have been conducted using country- and sector-level analyses. Many studies found positive impacts of FDI on economic growth. By analysing 124 cross-country data sets for 1971–2010, Iamsiraroj (2016) found that FDI and economic growth positively affect each other. Several studies also found that FDI contributes to the economic growth of FDI-receiving countries when certain conditions, such as the availability of human resources and openness in trade, are satisfied (Borensztein, De Gregorio, and Lee, 1998; Balasubramanyam, Salisu, and Sapsford, 1996). Unfortunately, country- and sector-level studies did not explicitly consider technology transfer in their analyses of the impacts of FDI on economic growth.

Few studies have been conducted on intra-firm technology transfer, although several exist on inter-firm technology transfer. Some studies also did not distinguish between these two types of technology transfer. Urata and Kawai (2000) studied intra-firm technology transfer using data on parent firms and foreign affiliates of Japanese firms. They found that, on average, approximately 89% of technology was transferred from parent firms to their foreign affiliates, and that absorptive capability was most important for obtaining technology.

Regarding technology spillover, empirical findings showed positive, neutral, and negative effects. According to Rojec and Knell (2018), in a comprehensive survey of the literature on technology spillover, this lack of a consensus is due to a variety of reasons. They pointed out possible problems in the empirical studies, which include inappropriate methodology and lack of adequate data. They found greater similarity in the results from the studies; backward vertical technology spillover was found in many but not horizontal or forward vertical technology spillovers.

As discussed above, outward FDI may have a negative impact on economic growth of the home country as capital moves out. However, outward FDI may contribute to economic growth of the home country, particularly in the medium to long term, if outward FDI improves the productivity of FDI firms or MNCs. Possible reasons for productivity improvement for MNCs are similar to those discussed for exporting, such as acquiring technology and management know-how from recipient countries. This impact is significant, particularly when outward FDI takes the form of acquisition of foreign companies owning high-quality technology.

Empirical analyses of the impacts of outward FDI on MNCs and home countries showed mixed results.[4] Based on the literature survey, Hayakawa, Kimura, and Machikita (2010) argued that such results can be attributed to the differences in the types of outward FDI, which were not considered in many studies. When classifying outward FDI into vertical and horizontal types, previous studies only found a positive impact on the productivity of vertical FDI. Vertical FDI is undertaken to seek efficiency, while horizontal FDI captures the market. These differences in motives or mechanisms can lead to different impacts.

3.2 Unemployment and inequality

Globalisation is often accused of creating unemployment and increasing inequality within countries. It has been argued that the inflow of imports that are in competition with domestic production replaces domestic production, which, in turn, leads to reduced employment. Moreover, outward FDI relocates production from the home country to a host (i.e. foreign) country, leading to reduced employment in the home country. These reasonings rest on the validity of certain assumptions, however, such as the perfect substitutability between imports or foreign production and domestic production.

Many empirical studies have examined the impacts of increased imports on unemployment. Autor, Dorn, and Hanson (2013) studied the impacts of increased imports from China on US employment (i.e. 'the China shock'). By considering not only the direct effect but also the indirect effect through input–output links, Acemoglu et al. (2016) found that import growth from China between 1999 and 2011 reduced the employment of 2.4 million US workers.[5] Similarly, Hayakawa, Ito, and Urata (2019) examined the impacts of increased Chinese imports on Japan's labour market, finding that these imports had a negative impact on total employment, especially for industries that produced competing products, as well as a positive impact on industries that purchased Chinese imports as intermediate inputs.

Studies on the impacts of outward FDI on home employment exhibited mixed results. In one on US manufacturing firms, Harrison and McMillan (2011) showed how the motive of outward FDI and its location affected the impact of FDI on parent firms' employment. Overseas operation in low-wage countries substituted for home employment, but overseas operation conducting different tasks from parent firms complemented home employment. They showed the net effect of FDI to only be a small decline in employment at home.[6] Moreover, several studies on Japanese manufacturing firms, such as those by Ando and

Kimura (2015) and Kodama and Inui (2015), did not find negative impacts of outward FDI or foreign operations on employment in Japan. Indeed, many studies found positive impacts of outward FDI on home employment, particularly for MNCs that expanded their overseas operations.

Many studies have also been conducted on globalisation and inequality.[7] An important theoretical explanation of the impacts of globalisation on income distribution is based on the Stolper-Samuelson Theorem within the Heckscher-Ohlin trade model. According to the Stolper-Samuelson Theorem, globalisation expands the production and exports of abundant factor-intensive products while reducing the production of scarce factor-intensive products by increasing imports of scarce factor-intensive products. Consequently, trade liberalisation leads to an increase in the price of abundant factors relative to the price of scarce factors. Assuming that skilled and unskilled labour exist and that developing (developed) countries are relatively well endowed with unskilled (skilled) labour, an application of this theorem indicates that an increase in trade by trade liberalisation leads to an improvement (deterioration) in income distribution or a narrowing (widening) of the wage gap between unskilled and skilled labour in developing (developed) countries.

A survey of empirical studies on the impacts of trade on inequality by Urata and Narjoko (2017) found that country and cross-country studies, conducted on the relationship between trade and income distribution, showed different patterns. Some country-level studies showed that an increase in trade–GDP ratios worsened inequality, while others did not detect significant impacts of trade on income distribution. Yet cross-country studies found that trade improved income distribution, although the impacts were small. These mixed results indicate the need for more analyses.

The impacts of FDI from developed to developing countries on income inequality are basically the same if FDI promotes trade. However, income inequality may deteriorate even in developing countries if the demand for high-skilled workers increases, because MNCs hire high-skilled workers to adopt to high-skilled worker-intensive management styles, for which they have an advantage. Few rigorous studies have been conducted on this issue, but Jaumotte, Lall, and Parageorgiou (2013) found an inequality-deteriorating effect of inward FDI in a cross-country econometric analysis.

Many empirical studies found that technological progress has negative impacts on income inequality as well. Specifically, Jaumotte, Lall, and Parageorgiou (2013) found that the introduction of skill-biased technologies, or labour-saving technologies, contributed to worsening income inequality. Having noted the negative impact of technological progress on income distribution, a bidirectional relationship between technological progress on one hand and trade and investment on the other should also be noted. For example, an exporting firm facing intensive competition in foreign markets will conduct research and development to create new technologies to improve competitiveness. Recognition of this point shows the difficulty in separating the impacts of trade and FDI as well as technological progress.

4 Major findings of this study

4.1 Foreign trade

Regarding the impacts of international trade on economic growth, all of the eight country studies find positive impacts, mainly attributable to the resource allocation and productivity-enhancing effects of international trade. A growth-enhancing resource allocation effect is evident as well because trade expansion was accompanied by structural changes from low value- to high value-added sectors in Australia, Malaysia, Thailand, the US, and Vietnam.

Moreover, all of the country studies find a productivity-enhancing effect of international trade. Export expansion is found to improve productivity in all of the sample countries. As to the mechanism behind the positive impacts of exports on productivity, the self-selection effect is identified for Australia, China, Japan, Malaysia, and the US, while the learning-by-exporting effect is found in Australia, Japan, Malaysia, and the US. For Australia, broad policy reform, under which trade liberalisation was pursued, played an important role in promoting productivity.

Ito (2021), in her study of Japan, makes two key observations: not all high-productivity firms exported, and new exporters had lower productivity compared to established successful exporters. She argues that the former finding indicates the lack of information on exporting opportunities for potential exporters and calls for policy support from governments in providing information on market opportunities and situations in foreign countries. She posits that the latter finding indicates the difficulty in continuing to export; thus, many new exporters stop exporting. She points out a need for the government to support new exporters to continue exporting in the long term to enjoy learning effects.

Lee (2021), however, observes the opposite in Malaysia; new exporters are more productive than surviving exporters. Based on this finding, Lee argues that the churning of exporters makes larger contributions to productivity growth. Although a comparative analysis of the reasons for the different outcomes is difficult due to, for instance, variances in the methodologies, these contrasting findings call for further analysis on the dynamic effects of exporting.

Yu and Zhu (2021) report another interesting finding on the relationship between exporting and productivity in China, inconsistent with findings from the previous studies. Processing trade was actively conducted by Chinese firms in the pre-millennium period. Usually, a Chinese firm obtained raw materials and parts from a foreign trading partner without any payment, and then sold its products to the same foreign trading partner by charging an assembly fee. Yu and Zhu, however, find that firms engaged in such processing trade had lower productivity compared to firms engaged in non-processing trade and those engaged only in the domestic market. Based on these findings, they argue that processing trade does not contribute to economic growth through improving productivity because of its unskilled labour-intensive operation. Yet it did enable Chinese firms to accumulate experience in international trade, probably contributing to the rapid expansion of trade in the succeeding periods.

Imports of intermediate goods or inputs are found to promote the productivity of importing firms in China and Thailand. A similar finding is observed in Japan, as Ito (2021) reports positive impacts of offshoring on the productivity of such firms. The import discipline hypothesis, which is mainly applied to the import of final goods, is supported in Thailand, with a condition that the industries to which imported final goods belong were liberalised. An interesting relationship is found between increased imports and productivity in China; increased imports had positive impacts on productivity for firms producing complex goods, while they had the opposite effect for the producers of simple goods.

Several of the studies, including those on China, Japan, Malaysia, and the US, find a close, bidirectional relationship between trade and innovation, both of which are important sources of productivity and economic growth. Lee (2021) finds the innovation-inducing effect of exports in Malaysia, while Yu and Zhu (2021) and Ito (2021) report the innovation-inducing effect of both exports and imports in China and Japan, respectively. Exporting firms, which are faced with foreign competition and are knowledgeable about technologies and new products, were likely to increase innovative activities – a kind of learning by exporting. Yu and Zhu find that innovation in the pre-exporting period in China had a substantial, positive impact on productivity after a firm began exporting. Importing firms were also likely to increase their innovative effort to compete against import competition, likely improving productivity.

Unemployment and widening income inequality due to globalisation were reported in Australia and the US. Widening wage gaps were also reported in China and Malaysia, while unemployment in non-competitive sectors was seen in Indonesia. The study on the US (Petri and Banga, 2021) points out that there is no convincing evidence that trade increases unemployment or inequality in a long-term, economy-wide context; however, technological change, reflected in increased productivity, was shown to have more significant impacts on unemployment and inequality. Petri and Banga (2021) argue that even if technological change and globalisation have caused adverse labour market trends, it does not follow that the erection of barriers against them is a useful solution, as they reduce the size of the economic pie without necessarily improving its distribution. Instead, they recommend that the government focus on redistributing gains from growth, increasing the productivity of all workers, and helping affected communities adapt socially and economically to the rapid change.

On the benefits and costs of globalisation, Verico and Pangestu (2021), in their study of Indonesia, emphasise that the positive impact of globalisation is dynamic and only felt in the medium term, whereas costs and potential negative impacts are often felt more immediately. Since globalisation creates net benefits in the long run, managing the costs of globalisation during the transition process, before reaping long-term benefits, is a challenge.

4.2 Foreign direct investment

Beginning with inward FDI, all of the eight country studies find positive impacts on economic growth through its contribution to capital formation and/or productivity improvement. Findings on technology spillover, however, are mixed. Technology spillover is reported in Australia. For Malaysia, horizontal spillovers from FDI are found to be weak and backward, and forward spillovers are found to be negative. Regarding Thailand, a horizontal spillover is detected when industries operated under an open trade regime, while vertical backward spillover is found when the link was formed by economic concerns as well as motivated by the capability of domestic suppliers rather than by policy measures such as local content requirement. For Vietnam, mixed results are found, but a greater level of spillover is observed in the cases of joint-venture firms or firms partially owned by domestic firms than wholly foreign-owned firms.

Regarding outward FDI, the case studies of Australia, China, and Japan report positive impacts on the productivity of investing firms. One study on Chinese outward FDI found that Chinese MNCs without state ownership but with stronger absorptive capability gained higher and more sustainable productivity effects. Moreover, such gains were higher for MNCs investing in countries belonging to the Organisation for Economic Co-operation and Development (OECD). The studies in the Japanese case found the learning effect of outward FDI to be a source of high productivity of FDI firms but not the selection effect.

5 Policy recommendations

Several important policy recommendations can be drawn from the studies in this project.

First, on international trade, liberalisation policies should be pursued to achieve economic growth, as they promote both exports and imports. Trade liberalisation promotes exports, because it shifts firms' incentives from domestic sales to export sales, as increased imports from trade liberalisation reduce the profitability of domestic sales. In addition, firms have an incentive to expand exports, because they can benefit from economies of scale and market diversification.

Although trade liberalisation has an export-promoting effect, governments should also assist potential exporting firms, because exporting entails fixed costs such as obtaining market information in foreign countries. Government assistance, in the form of disseminating information on foreign markets (e.g. product standards), can be helpful for firms, particularly for small and medium-sized enterprises.

Increasing imports of both intermediate and final goods contributes to economic growth by improving productivity, as discussed in the previous section. Although most studies in this project examined reduced tariff rates in the discussion of trade liberalisation, non-tariff measures in various forms, such as technical barriers to trade and sanitary and phytosanitary measures, are becoming important. Application of these measures can be justified for safety purposes, but they can be also used for protective purposes or in the form of 'disguised' protection. To avoid protection and to facilitate trade, mutual recognition or harmonisation of these measures should be pursued.

Measures should be adopted to deal with the opposition against trade liberalisation. One is assisting those negatively affected, known as trade adjustment assistance, which has been implemented in Australia and the US. This usually includes temporary income compensation and education or training programmes, which should be formulated to facilitate change to higher-paid jobs by improving workers' skills. Theoretically, there is no reason to treat those negatively affected by trade liberalisation differently from those negatively affected for other reasons, such as technological progress. However, trade adjustment assistance may also be justified for promoting trade liberalisation, which would bring various economic and political benefits, as previously discussed. Other measures for dealing with the opposition to trade liberalisation include enacting bilateral or regional FTAs and/or promoting multilateral trade negotiations, which will not only open the market in the country in question but also markets in trading partners.[8] A country can then expect to increase exports, which would grow job opportunities for the negatively affected workers.

Pursuing liberalisation, in the cases of both inward and outward FDI policies, is recommended. Many countries, especially developing countries, have restricted inward FDI due to a fear of dominance of MNCs over domestic firms; however, in recent decades, more have begun liberalising their inward FDI regimes to attract inward FDI as they realise the various benefits from hosting MNCs. Nevertheless, some continue to restrict activities of MNCs by applying various measures. Trade-related investment measures, such as local content requirements and export restrictions, are banned under the WTO, while other restrictions on MNC activities, such as repatriation of profits and employment of expatriates, are legal. Developing countries often restrict outward direct investment to save scarce investment funds or foreign exchange, whereas for developed countries maintaining job opportunities for local workers is a popular motive. These restrictions cannot be justified under the efficient use of investment funds and other resources, such as technology and management know-how. Countries should thus remove all restrictions to attract FDI, with exceptions for legitimate reasons, such as national security.

Liberalisation of FDI policies can be pursued more easily if liberalisation policies are implemented jointly with partner countries rather than unilaterally, as they expand opportunities for domestic firms to increase outward FDI. Specific forms of joint policies include bilateral investment treaties and FTAs with investment chapters. It should be noted that there are no multilateral rules on investment other than the Agreement on Trade-Related Investment Measures (TRIMs) Agreement under the WTO, which covers only a small part of FDI-related activities.

FDI should be attracted and promoted, but preferential measures, such as subsidies, are not recommended. Although preferential measures may be effective in attracting FDI, they create market distortions, possibly resulting in loss of economic welfare. A case in point is 'the race to the bottom,' where competition between countries using subsidies for attracting FDI is bound to end up in a situation where both countries suffer from lost government revenue. Rather, countries should develop business environments under which MNCs can operate efficiently. Specifically, the development of hard (e.g. transport and communication networks and electricity generation) and soft (e.g. legal and education systems) infrastructure is crucial for attracting inward FDI; ensuring their effective functioning is also critical. For this, capable human resources must be developed.

Policies to improve technological capability should also be developed, which would contribute to the maximisation of benefits from trade and FDI expansion for firms and countries, including information on advanced technology and management know-how. To assimilate technology so that domestic firms can improve productivity, domestic firms must have the appropriate capacity to learn and to utilise technology and management know-how. To develop this capability, governments can help provide education and training.

Finally, governments should support innovation activities by firms. With successful innovation, firms can become involved in exporting and outward FDI by improving their competitiveness, so that they may enjoy the benefits from the interaction with foreign firms and countries. Improved competitiveness also helps firms become involved with MNCs operating in the domestic market through joint-venture partnerships, sales, and/or procurement partnerships so that firms can obtain technology and management know-how. To promote innovation, governments should ensure the protection of intellectual property rights in addition to provision of various support measures, such as technical and financial assistance. One effective way to provide intellectual property right protection is to participate in FTAs with intellectual property right provisions, because international agreements on intellectual property right protection, such as those provided by the WTO and World Intellectual Property Organization, are viewed as insufficient.

6 Synopses of chapters

6.1 Australia

Globalisation of the Australian economy has proceeded rapidly since the 1970, as the share of trade and FDI in GDP has increased substantially. According to Findlay, Mavromaras, and Wei (2021), rapid globalisation of the economy is attributed to the changes in international economic policy from inward-oriented protectionist policies to outward-oriented liberalisation policies, including reduced import tariffs and relaxed restrictions on inward FDI and the movement of people. The shift in international economic policies occurred as the government was trying to overcome unfavourable economic performance. A liberalisation of international economic policy was thus implemented as part of broader economic reform, comprising reforms in the labour market, financial market, and tax system. A series of domestic reforms in various sectors, including the financial sector, labour market, as well as private and public sectors, also contributed to Australia's globalisation.

The economic impacts of globalisation have been both positive and negative in Australia. Globalisation has contributed to favourable economic performance; indeed, Australia is the only OECD country that has not experienced a recession in the last 27 years. Globalisation has also contributed to increased productivity through the expansion of trade and FDI as well as the promotion of innovation. Participation in trade contributed to increasing productivity through learning-by-doing channels and market-size effects. Trade has provided access to technology, and the competition associated with trade has added to incentives to innovate. FDI has improved productivity through the transfer of technology and the promotion of competition. Migrants are likely to have contributed to an increase in productivity with their skills as well.

A negative impact of globalisation in Australia, due to the expansion of trade and FDI, is unemployment resulting from increased imports and widening income inequality. Various labour-adjustment programmes have been implemented to deal with unemployment, but evaluation of the programmes is mixed. Increasing income inequality has been reduced by a progressive income tax system and transfer system.

The chapter provides important policy lessons from the Australia experience, referencing Banks (2005). First, 'external liberalisation' is a good manner in which to begin reform. Second, Australia reformed unilaterally in the 1980, and not in exchange for market access offered by trading partners. Third, reform did not follow a 'big bang' approach but an incremental one, and the reform programme was wide-ranging. Fourth, institutional reform was crucial to promote and to sustain the reform. Fifth, political leadership was critical for carrying out institutional reform and entrenching the right institutions.

6.2 China

China's rapid economic growth since 1978 is attributable to various factors, including globalisation of its economy. Yu and Zhu (2021) observe that the characteristics of China's involvement in international trade changed during its process of economic development. The chapter identifies four stages in China's engagement in international trade.

The first, an extensive margin of opening up, comparative advantage following, and processing trade, occurred from 1986 to 2001. After experiencing slow economic growth by adopting the comparative advantage-defying strategy of heavy industry promotion with import protection, the government implemented reform and an opening-up strategy in 1979, under which comparative advantage following processing trade was expanded through government policies such as the preferential trade policy of importing intermediate goods with zero tariffs. Through processing trade, China began integrating into GVCs by taking advantage of its abundant labour force.

The years 2001–08 then marked an intensive margin of opening up. In the process of and after WTO accession in 2001, China reduced import tariffs substantially, leading to improved productivity and promotion of innovation, which in turn contributed to increased productivity. Another important consequence was an increase in the wage gap between low- and high-skilled labour. Access to the WTO benefited Chinese exports, as it provided certainty in China's access to foreign markets.

The third period, from 2008 to 2017, demonstrated a deeper opening up against financial crisis. Triggered by the Global Financial Crisis, increasing labour costs, and renminbi appreciation, Chinese exporters were in a difficult situation for export expansion. Faced with an increasingly competitive export market, exporters adopted several strategies, including innovation, upgrading product quality, and outward FDI. Since 2017, faced with growing protectionist policies spearheaded by the US, China is introducing various measures, such as the construction of free-trade ports, introduction of the Belt and Road Initiative, internationalisation of the renminbi, and development of the Pearl River Greater Bay Area, with an objective of further opening up.

An important lesson from China's experience is that China's evolving comparative advantage must be fully exploited and its industry and trade policy be fully implemented to facilitate the exploitation.

6.3 Indonesia

Globalisation of the Indonesian economy has proceeded through the expansion of trade and FDI. An important factor has been the adoption of trade and FDI liberalisation, which was realised by implementing the commitments under multilateral frameworks of the GATT and WTO, regional and bilateral FTAs including the ASEAN Free Trade Area and ASEAN Plus FTAs, and obligations for obtaining economic assistance from international organisations such as the IMF and World Bank.

Verico and Pangestu (2021) find that globalisation generated a positive impact on Indonesia's economic growth through the trade and investment channel. Through the trade channel, globalisation contributed to Indonesia's productivity and structural economic transformation, benefited small and medium-sized enterprises, aided poverty alleviation, and reduced inequality. Trade liberalisation had a negative impact on employment in non-competitive sectors, however. Through the investment channel, there is evidence of a spillover effect of technology transfer, technology progress, improvement of the role of small and medium-sized enterprises, and poverty alleviation. They note that the positive impact of globalisation is felt in the medium term, whereas a negative impact is often felt more immediately.

A challenge for Indonesia is to ensure that its globalisation strategy stays focused on long-term net positive benefits, because in the past, its external economic strategies have swung between outward- and inward-looking policy, depending on economic circumstances. Towards this objective, Indonesia needs public support for globalisation, which may be generated by presenting convincing narratives based on rigorous empirical research.

6.4 Japan

Globalisation of the economy has been attracting attention in Japan because it is discussed in relation to the prolonged sluggishness of the domestic economy. However, Ito (2021) finds that globalisation has contributed to economic growth through increased firm productivity. Indeed, Japanese firms that are engaged in international trade and FDI have higher productivity than domestic firms, although only a few firms are directly engaged in international business.

Two effects, the selection effect and learning effect, explain the high productivity of exporting firms. Not all highly productive firms are engaged in exporting, indicating the presence of obstacles such as difficulty in obtaining market information and uncertainty in overseas markets. This finding calls for government assistance in providing market information and mitigating risk.

As for the impact of globalisation on the labour market, many studies have shown that competition from imports as well as offshoring have shifted labour demand towards skilled workers, resulting in a widening wage gap between skilled and unskilled workers. However, the contribution of globalisation to this gap is limited in Japan.

To understand the impacts of globalisation on firm performance and the labour market, the close relationship between globalisation and innovation is identified. While innovative firms are more likely to become exporters, firms serving international markets are also more likely to increase innovation activities. Both globalisation and innovation tend to benefit skilled workers, while unskilled workers are likely to be worse off. Given that the importance of globalisation and innovation is likely to increase in the future, it is important for Japanese firms to invest in new technology and human capital to respond to the structural changes brought about by globalisation and technological change. Policy support should be provided to increase investment, particularly in intangible assets, for firms that are striving to succeed in the global market.

6.5 Malaysia

Globalisation in the forms of trade, FDI, and foreign workers has had significant impacts on Malaysia's economy and society. Lee (2021) posits that the impacts of globalisation on economic growth have been shown to be positive from macroeconomic as well as microeconomic studies. Macroeconomic studies, employing time-series econometrics, demonstrated the positive relationship between exports and economic growth, while microdata studies found that globalisation had positive impacts on productivity in Malaysia.

Foreign labour has had significant economic and social impacts in Malaysia. Before Malaysia's independence, the massive inflow of foreign workers from China and India contributed to the development of its export-oriented, labour-intensive tin and rubber industries, as well as Malaysia's multi-ethnic society. Then, after the successful development of FDI-driven, export-oriented manufacturing in the 1980, the country began to experience labour shortages in the early 1990, leading to rapid growth in the number of foreign workers. Relatively cheap and low-skilled foreign labour helped sustain the country's manufacturing competitiveness in the 1990; however, this later became an obstacle to efforts to upgrade the manufacturing and other economic sectors.

Globalisation also contributed to the reduction of poverty and income inequality, as it enabled an expansion of labour-intensive, export-oriented manufacturing. However, there is growing concern that the country's addiction to cheap foreign labour could suppress the wages of low-skilled workers, possibly increasing income inequality. An important issue related to inequality in Malaysia is inter-ethnic income and wealth distribution. The government has thus introduced various policies, such as increasing government ownership in key sectors, on behalf of the Bumiputra (i.e. indigenous) community. These policies could limit the country's ability to deepen its participation in the GVC in manufacturing and services.

The negative impact of globalisation in Malaysia is its vulnerability to global economic shocks. Prior to the 1990, crises were mainly transmitted through the trade sector; however, since liberalising its financial sector in the 1990, the economy has become vulnerable to external shocks to both the trade and financial sectors.

An important policy issue related to globalisation is corruption in trading activities. If institutional reforms occur regarding corruption, Malaysia's competitiveness as an export-oriented manufacturing base and as a trading nation is likely to improve. Good governance is thus important for obtaining benefits from globalisation.

6.6 Thailand

Industrialisation in Thailand began with an import-substitution policy in the 1960, which comprised an escalating tariff structure that achieved relatively high economic growth but led to successive balance-of-payments problems due to increased imports of intermediate goods. Its trade policy gradually shifted towards an export orientation in the mid-1980, when tariff rates were relatively high compared to other Southeast Asian countries, but export promotion was pursued by policies such as import tariff-exemption schemes. During the past two decades, FTAs have played an important role in expanding export opportunities.

Thailand has always been open and successful in attracting FDI. As a consequence, the shares of trade and FDI in GDP have increased to relatively high levels. Labour mobility has also played an increasing role as a driver of economic globalisation. A large number of foreign workers have come to Thailand, which had been suffering from a labour shortage.

As the Thai economy has begun to slow down and fall into the 'middle-income trap,' the government has been formulating policies to achieve high economic growth. Kohpaiboon and Jongwanich (2021) point to globalisation's potential to create a favourable economic impact. Opening up to international trade promotes productivity by improving resource allocation and encouraging research and development. Participation in GVCs and provision of a competitive market environment play key roles in the efficient use of resources. Large FDI inflows generate horizontal technological spillovers within a given industry, although vertical spillovers through links in Thailand are insignificant.

Studies examined also pointed to the importance of a liberal trade policy to promote technology spillovers. Another favourable impact of MNCs is to promote export and research and development by domestic firms. There is no evidence that employing foreign workers retards firm productivity, and global production sharing does not necessarily mean that participating countries are trapped at the low end of the quality ladder. Indeed, mutual benefits from participation in the GVC network can be shared between developed and developing countries. Thus, Thailand's past experience supports the case for further globalising its economy, as any possible side effects of globalisation can be mitigated by other policies such as strengthening the country's social safety net.

6.7 United States

Petri and Banga (2021) examine the consequences of globalisation in the US by focusing on three issues: (i) overall gains from trade, (ii) adverse labour market trends and causal effects of trade on the labour market, and (iii) the results of changes in trade policy.

The US has benefited from globalisation, as it has enhanced productivity by improving resource allocation, especially by participating in GVCs and by promoting innovation through the inflow of ideas and money. Indeed, Petri and Banga provide an estimate of gains from globalisation, accounting for 11%–19% of the country's GDP, comprising increased opportunities for purchasing a variety of imports and exporting US products to foreign markets. However, the general US public discussion does not fully recognise these benefits, and instead focuses on the costs in the form of job losses, which may be actually caused by trade or technological progress.

Labour market effects, which have dominated recent critiques of globalisation in the US, have focused on unemployment, wage inequality, and labour force participation. Some studies found significant impacts from trade on unemployment under specific circumstances, such as declining industries in some localities. However, there is no convincing evidence that trade increased unemployment in a long-term, economy-wide context. Indeed, an empirical study found that technological change, reflected in increased productivity, had much more significant impacts on unemployment. Regarding increased inequality, trade may have had a significant impact; as a high-wage country, the US tends to import products from countries with lower wages, but the evidence mainly pointed to technological change rather than import competition as the source of pressure.

The gains from trade likely exceed – potentially by orders of magnitude – the costs of fighting inequality attributable to trade. Nevertheless, the economic, as well as political, costs of worsening distributional trends are substantial and demand urgent solutions. Policies should focus on redistributing gains from growth, increasing the productivity of all workers, and helping affected communities adapt socially and economically to the rapid change.

6.8 Vietnam

Since Đổi Mới in 1986, Vietnam has gradually opened its economy to foreign trade and investment and has become integrated into the global economy. Its economic integration had four milestones: (i) accession to the ASEAN Free Trade Area in 1996 and an array of FTAs under ASEAN Plus frameworks; (ii) signing of the Vietnam–US Bilateral Trade Agreement in 2000; (iii) accession to the WTO in 2007; and (iv) signing of bilateral and multilateral FTAs, including those with Chile, the CPTPP, the Eurasian Economic Union, European Union, Japan, and Republic of Korea. Thanks to these milestones, trade and FDI in the Vietnamese economy became increasingly important.

Vo, Nguyen, and Do (2021) find that globalisation based on trade and FDI contributed to the rapid growth of the Vietnamese economy and expanded employment. However, they also find that the economy has not fully exploited globalisation's potential benefits. Mainly foreign firms, established in Vietnam through FDI, contributed to export expansion, but their presence has not contributed much to improved productivity nor the technological capability of domestic firms. One problem is poor links between foreign and domestic firms; as such, the technology spillover has been limited. Moreover, the inadequate ability of domestic firms has trapped them in low value-added production stages in GVCs.

Globalisation in the form of trade, however, has contributed to expanded employment and improved resource allocation. Trade has enabled Vietnam to exploit its comparative advantage, that is, its labour-intensive production. Indeed, its poverty situation has improved under the liberalised regime with the help of social programmes, although income inequality has not changed much in recent decades.

Vo, Nguyen, and Do present several policy recommendations for Vietnam to achieve deeper global integration and associated benefits, including implementing domestic economic reforms, building hard and soft infrastructure, and consulting actively with the business community.

Notes

1 See, for example, Urata (2012).
2 See, for example, Hummels (2007) on the decline in trade cost.
3 Although not directly investigating the increased impacts of imports on economic growth, several studies empirically examined the impacts of trade liberalisation,

which promote imports, on economic growth. Irwin (2019) provided a comprehensive survey of such studies and concluded that trade liberalisation, in the form of reduced import tariffs, has a positive impact on economic growth, on average, although the effect is heterogeneous across countries.

4 See Hayakawa, Kimura and Machikita (2010) for a survey of the literature on this point.

5 Autor (2018) provided a summary of the studies on the impacts of increased Chinese imports on the US employment.

6 Brainard and Riker (1997) obtained similar findings in the case of US MNCs. A study on Korean MNCs by Debaere, Lee, and Lee (2010) found that investment in less-advanced countries decreased companies' employment growth, especially in the short run.

7 Inequality is discussed from various perspectives, which include gender, generation, region, and others. See Urata and Narjoko (2017) for a review.

8 Regarding regional FTAs in the Asia-Pacific, the Comprehensive and Progressive Agreement for Trans-Pacific Partnership (CPTPP) and the Regional Comprehensive Economic Partnership (RCEP) are two important regional FTAs working towards the eventual establishment of the Free Trade Area of the Asia-Pacific (FTAAP), involving all APEC economies. The CPTPP entered into force in December 2018, and seven countries have joined. Expanding membership, however, is a major challenge. The RCEP negotiation, began in May 2013, is still under negotiation. First proposed by the US in 2006, the FTAAP has undergone a formal feasibility study, but negotiations have not yet started because of the differences in the opinions of the APEC members. The most important driving force for promoting FTAs is national leaders' determination, which comes from a strong belief in regional economic integration for achieving economic growth.

References

Acemoglu, D., D. Autor, D. Dorn, G.H. Hanson, and B. Price (2016), 'Import Competition and the Great US Employment Sag of the 2000s', *Journal of Labor Economics*, 34(S1), pp.S141–S198.

Alessandrini, M., B. Fattouh, B. Ferrarini, and P. Scaramozzino (2011), 'Tariff Liberalization and Trade Specialization: Lessons from India', *Journal of Comparative Economics*, 39(40), pp.499–513.

Alvarez, R., and R.A. Lopez (2005), 'Exporting and Performance: Evidence from Chilean Plants', *Canadian Journal of Economics/Revue canadienne d'économique*, 38(4), pp.1384–1400.

Amiti, M., and J. Konings (2007), 'Trade Liberalization, Intermediate Inputs, and Productivity: Evidence from Indonesia', *American Economic Review*, 97(5), pp.1611–1638.

Ando, M., and F. Kimura (2015), 'Globalization and Domestic Operations: Applying the JC/JD Method to Japanese Manufacturing Firms', *Asian Economic Papers*, 14(2), pp.1–35.

Autor, D.H. (2018), 'Trade and Labor Markets: Lessons from China's Rise', *IZA World of Labor*, February. https://wol.iza.org/uploads/articles/431/pdfs/trade-and-labor-makets-lessons-from-chinas-rise.pdf?v=1 (accessed 27September2020).

Autor, D.H., D. Dorn, and G.H. Hanson (2013), 'The China Syndrome: Local Labor Market Effects of Import Competition in the United States', *American Economic Review*, 103(6), pp.2121–2168.

Balasubramanyam, V.N., M. Salisu, and D. Sapsford (1996), 'Foreign Direct Investment and Growth in EP and IS Countries', *Economic Journal*, 106(434), pp.92–105.

Banks, G. (2005), 'Structural Reform Australian-style: Lessons for Others?', Presentation to the International Monetary Fund, World Bank, and Organisation for Economic Co-operation and Development, May. https://www.pc.gov.au/news-media/speeches/cs20050601/cs20050601.pdf (accessed 22October2019).

Bernard, A.B., and J.B. Jensen (1999), 'Exceptional Exporter Performance: Cause, Effect, or Both?' *Journal of International Economics*, 47(1), pp.1–25.

Bernard, A.B., S.J. Redding, and P.K. Schott (2011), 'Multiproduct Firms and Trade Liberalization', *Quarterly Journal of Economics*, 126(3), pp.1271–1318.

Borensztein, E., J. De Gregorio, J.-W. Lee (1998), 'How Does Foreign Direct Investment Affect Economic Growth?' *Journal of International Economics*, 45(1), pp.115–135.

Brainard, S.L., and D.A. Riker (1997), 'Are US Multinationals Exporting US Jobs?' *NBER Working Paper Series*, No. 5958, Cambridge, MA: NBER.

Damijan, J.P., and C. Kostevc (2015), 'Learning from Trade through Innovation', *Oxford Bulletin of Economics and Statistics*, 77(3), pp.408–436.

De Loecker, J. (2013), 'Detecting Learning by Exporting', *American Economic Journal: Microeconomics*, 5(3), pp.1–21.

Debaere, P., H. Lee, and J. Lee (2010), 'It Matters Where You Go: Outward Foreign Direct Investment and Multinational Employment Growth at Home', *Journal of Development Economics*, 91, pp.301–309.

Findlay C., K. Mavromaras, and Z. Wei (2021), 'Economic Consequences of Globalisation: The Australian Framework for Reforms', this volume, pp.26–56.

Goldberg, P.K., A.K. Khandelwal, N. Pavcnik, and P. Topalova (2010), 'Multiproduct Firms and Product Turnover in the Developing World: Evidence from India', *Review of Economics and Statistics*, 92(4), pp.1042–1049.

Ha, D.T.T., and K. Kiyota (2014), 'Firm-Level Evidence on Productivity Differentials and Turnover in Vietnamese Manufacturing', *Japanese Economic Review*, 65, pp.193–217.

Harrison, A., and M. McMillan (2011), 'Offshoring Jobs? Multinationals and US Manufacturing Employment', *Review of Economics and Statistics*, 93(3), pp.857–875.

Hayakawa, K., T. Ito, and S. Urata (2019), 'Impacts of Increased Chinese Imports on Japan's Labor Market', *RIETI Discussion Paper Series*, No. 19-E-098, Tokyo: RIETI.

Hayakawa, K., F. Kimura, and T. Machikita (2010), 'Firm-level Analysis of Globalization: A Survey of the Eight Literatures', *ERIA Discussion Paper Series*, No. 5, Jakarta: ERIA.

Hummels, D. (2007), 'Transportation Costs and International Trade in the Second Era of Globalization', *Journal of Economic Perspectives*, 21(3), pp.131–154.

Iamsiraroj, S. (2016), 'The Foreign Direct Investment–Economic Growth Nexus', *International Review of Economics and Finance*, 42, pp.116–133.

IMF (2020), *World Economic Outlook, October 2020: A Long and Difficult Ascent*. Washington, DC: International Monetary Fund.

Irwin, D.A. (2019), 'Does Trade Reform Promote Economic Growth? A Review of Recent Evidence', *PIIE Working Paper Series*, No. 19-9, Washington, DC: PIIE.

Ito, K. (2021), 'The Impact of Economic Globalisation on Firm Performance and the Labour Market: Evidence from Japan', this volume, pp.103-128.

Jaumotte, F., S. Lall, and C. Parageorgiou (2013), 'Rising Income Inequality: Technology, or Trade and Financial Globalization?' *IMF Economic Review*, 61(2), pp.271–309.

Kim, E. (2000), 'Trade Liberalization and Productivity Growth in Korean Manufacturing Industries: Price Protection, Market Power, and Scale Efficiency', *Journal of Development Economics*, 62(1), pp.55–83.

Kodama, N., and T. Inui (2015), 'The Impact of Globalization on Establishment-level Employment Dynamics in Japan', *Asian Economic Papers*, 14(2), pp.41–65.

Kohpaiboon, A., and J. Jongwanich (2021), 'Economic Consequences of Globalisation: Case Study of Thailand', this volume, pp.164-191.

Krishna, P., and D. Mitra (1998), 'Trade Liberalization, Market Discipline and Productivity Growth: New Evidence from India', *Journal of Development Economics*, 56(2), pp.447–462.

Lee, C. (2021), 'Globalisation and Economic Development: Malaysia's Experience', this volume, pp.129-163.

Levinsohn, J. (1993), 'Testing the Imports-as-Market-Discipline Hypothesis', *Journal of International Economics*, 35(1–2), pp.1–22.

Lopresti, J. (2016), 'Multiproduct Firms and Product Scope Adjustment in Trade', *Journal of International Economics*, 100, pp.160–173.

McCaig, B., and N. Pavcnik (2018), 'Export Markets and Labor Allocation in a Low-Income Country', *American Economic Review*, 108(7), pp.1899–1941.

Melitz, M.J. (2003), 'The Impact of Trade on Intra-Industry Reallocations and Aggregate Industry Productivity', *Econometrica*, 71(6), pp.1695–1725.

de Melo, J., and S. Urata (1986), 'The Influence of Increased Foreign Competition on Industrial Concentration and Profitability', *International Journal of Industrial Organization*, 4(3), pp.287–304.

Pavcnik, N. (2002), 'Trade Liberalization, Exit, and Productivity Improvements: Evidence from Chilean Plants', *Review of Economic Studies*, 69(1), pp.245–276.

Petri, P.A., and M. Banga (2021), 'The Economic Consequences of Globalisation in the United States', this volume, pp.192-213.

Rodrik, D. (2018), 'New Technologies, Global Value Chains, and the Developing Economies', *Pathways for Prosperity Commission Background Paper Series*, No. 1, Oxford: P4P Commission.

Rojec, M., and M. Knell (2018), 'Why Is There a Lack of Evidence on Knowledge Spillovers from Foreign Direct Investment?' *Journal of Economic Surveys*, 32(3), pp.579–612.

Urata, S. (2012), 'Dynamic Gains of Trade and Foreign Direct Investment in East Asia', in T. Henckel (ed.), *Sustaining Development and Growth in East Asia*, Abingdon, UK: Routledge, pp. 99–153.

Urata, S., and H. Kawai (2000), 'Intrafirm Technology Transfer by Japanese Manufacturing Firms in Asia', in T. Ito and A.O. Krueger (eds.), *The Role of Foreign Direct Investment in East Asian Economic Development*, Chicago: University of Chicago Press, pp.49–74.

Urata, S., and D. Narjoko (2017), 'International Trade and Inequality', in M. Helble and B. Shepherd (eds.), *Win–Win: How International Trade Can Help Meet the Sustainable Development Goals*, Tokyo: ADB Institute, pp.175–204.

Verico, K., and M.E. Pangestu (2021), 'The Economic Impact of Globalization in Indonesia', this volume, pp.76-102.

Vo, T.T., D.A. Nguyen, and T.T. Nhan Do (2021), 'Economic Consequences of Trade and Investment Liberalisation: The Case of Vietnam', this volume, pp.214-240.

Yu, M., and H. Zhu (2021), 'Processing Trade, Trade Liberalisation, and Opening Up: China's Miracle of International Trade', this volume, pp.57-75.

2 Economic consequences of globalisation: the Australian framework for reforms

Christopher Findlay, Kostas Mavromaras, and Zhang Wei

1 Introduction

This paper reviews various elements of the Australian experience of globalisation and its consequences. Australia's experience has many positive elements, but involves challenges, and both are valuable to share in the context of the current debate about the value of international economic integration.

The approach adopted in this paper is to review existing studies, rather than conduct new research. Existing work on relevant topics is synthesised and policy implications are identified.

The focus of this paper is the period since the 1970s, where a significant shift out of an era of protection begins with a policy of significant tariff cuts in 1973. Section 2 outlines some of the drivers that led to this policy shift.

Section 3 provides more detail on the movement across borders of goods, services, capital, and people. The evolution of Australian policy in these areas is reviewed. The broader context of microeconomic and macroeconomic reform is outlined there too. Some of this material can be put into context by reference to a much longer time period, and in other cases only more recent data are available, or even a snapshot, depending on the scope of existing studies.

Section 4 identifies some of the consequences of these changes in terms of structural change (including labour market adjustment), productivity, and incomes.

The final part of the paper, Section 5, reviews some of the policy lessons and identifies elements of the future reform agenda.

2 Drivers of change

Several studies have reviewed the origins of the shift from the 1970s in Australian policy towards globalisation. These drivers include natural circumstances, policy shifts in trading partners, specific events, and the impact of particular people and of ways of thinking.

To place this change in context, Anderson and Garnaut (1987) reviewed the origins of the policy of protection before the 1970s. The motivations were to

DOI: 10.4324/9781003138501-2

redistribute income towards workers, attract more migrants from Europe in that context, maintain employment especially in import competing sectors, and develop a diversified industrial economy. Banks (2005) (also drawing on Kelly, 1992) explained that Australian policy was part of the 'Australian settlement', which involved using trade barriers to protect manufacturing while employing migrant labour at relatively high wages. These were set Australia-wide by a regulatory body, associated with which was a rigid set of workplace arrangements. Public utilities were created to provide services at 'fair' (but which turned out to be high) prices. Agriculture bore the costs of protection to manufacturing, which led to its own demands for assistance, especially from the less internationally competitive producers. Ergas and Pincus (2016) referred to the 'panoply of schemes', including those to subsidise inputs and to disconnect domestic and international prices. The goal of this system was reflected in the description of 'protection all round' but overall it was 'highly regulated, anti-competitive and distributive' (Banks, 2005, p. 2).

The system was sustained in the early post World War II period by the growth of national income, not generated by manufacturing but by the high-performing agricultural sector. This sector also generated exports required to meet the constraints of an external balance. Its performance was driven by its favourable terms of trade, as well as productivity growth (Ergas and Pincus, 2016), and occurred despite the discrimination against it through the differences in the relative rates of assistance.

Australia had not participated in multilateral tariff reduction negotiations in the 1950s and 1960s under the General Agreement on Tariffs and Trade (Snape, 1984; Adams, Brown, and Wickes, 2013). It had argued a special case on development grounds for not being classified as an industrial country, based on its export mix. Also, its export interests were not included in the scope of the negotiations and dealing with manufacturing tariffs would have been 'unfair' and would have undermined its model of development. As a result, Australia retained very high manufacturing tariffs up to 1970, the highest amongst the so-called 'advanced industrial countries' (Anderson, 2020).

Relative to other economies, Australia's performance started to decline (Anderson and Garnaut, 1987). Australia's world gross domestic product (GDP) per capita ranking dropped from fifth in 1950 to ninth in 1973 and 15th in the late 1980s (Banks, 2005). This decline was the result of 70 years of import substituting industrialisation alongside the other complementary policy measures operating in the labour market, which supported extensive growth (including immigration). It did not support intensive growth, which would have increased productivity and thereby income (Ergas and Pincus, 2016; Anderson, 2020). The policy model was challenged as a result (Berger-Thomson, Breusch, and Lilley, 2018). At the same time, Ergas and Pincus (2016) argued that the regime also provided the foundations that supported the subsequent reforms (for example, the orientation to Asia, the large size of the private sector, access to foreign capital, conservative fiscal policy settings, a narrower base of social transfers, and a role for independent entities in policymaking).

Another important challenge emerged from the shift in the patterns of Australia's trade, both actual and potential. Australia was naturally resource rich and lightly populated so its main trading partners would always be economies which were heavily populated and resource poor (Anderson, 2020). Initially this was the United Kingdom (UK), and by the late 1940s, half of Australia's imports came from the UK and nearly 40% of exports went to the UK, with more than 20% going to other western European countries (Pomfret, 2015). However, the UK in the 1960s began its own reorientation to Europe, finally joining what is now the European Union in 1973. Opportunities in Europe were then denied to Australia through trading arrangements which discriminated against farm exports. Yet they were the bulwark of the 'settlement'.

Following these changes by the UK, the orientation of Australia switched to East Asia, another resource poor and heavily populated region, which had begun to industrialise and to export manufactured products. Mineral discoveries added to the complementarity of Australia and East Asia. Australian policy leaders sought new ways to deepen the integration with the region (Adams, Brown, and Wickes, 2013, ch.3). However, they found that the existing patterns of protection of Australian manufacturing and impediments to migration and investment were inconsistent with doing so. A significant policy shift was required to capture the opportunities, and for mutual benefit both in economic and national security terms. Garnaut (1989) articulated the case for this orientation.

Another factor noted by Corden (1996) was the reinforcement of the standing and capacity of the institution which reviewed and made recommendations on tariff policy (this is now called the Productivity Commission, originally the Tariff Board, which in 1974 became the Industries Assistance Commission). This body operated with transparency and with great effect, taking a focus on national efficiency. Other influences of this type were changes in the ways of thinking, including the translation to Australia of a 'new liberalisation', which emerged from events in other countries. One element was the lack of success of mainly developing countries with the protectionist alternative, and the success of export-oriented growth in East Asia: analysis provided by staff of multilateral agencies reinforced these assessments of failure and success, respectively. Another element was the set of reforms which were also in progress in the 1980s in the UK (under Prime Minister Thatcher) and in the United States (US) (under President Reagan). Anderson (2020) observes that in this context Australia's conservative parties gave up their 'populist and negative opposition' to reductions in protection.

Other events and circumstances contributed to policy change in Australia (Corden, 1996). The Whitlam government (elected in 1972) faced high inflation and a balance of payments surplus, with a fixed exchange rate. There were significant reductions in tariffs in 1973 (of 25% across the board), a motivation for which was to increase the supply of imports for inflation relief. This was a false start (Adams, Brown, and Wickes, 2013) since there was subsequently a reintroduction of protectionist measures shortly afterwards, linked to the perception of the consequences for employment. However, by 1983, the continuing economic crisis (high inflation, high unemployment, large current account deficit, and rising external debt) brought together a variety of other forces for reform.[1]

Finally, Gruen (2009) characterises the strategy of the prime minister (Bob Hawke,[2] prime minister at the time of the substantial changes in policy, as explained below) as that of 'triangulation'.[3] The leader in this strategy finds a bundle of policies drawing on both the left and right wings of politics, to create a new bundle that responds to the motivations of all sides of politics and which is also coherent. Because it appeals to the fundamental motivations of a range of opinions, it creates winning political support. An example is the combination of social equity alongside economic liberalism in this period in Australia (Kelly, 2000). Another consequence on this way of thinking was a focus on reaching consensus and taking a gradual approach. As Kelly (2000) explained, there were some 'big bang' events in Australia but generally that method was not followed. The alternative to triangulation presented by Gruen is 'wedge politics', which he says frustrates the development of coherent policy. It may be electorally appealing, but he argues it does not provide the basis for good policy design. He also observes that the lack of a coherent reform strategy in later decades, as discussed below, is linked to the adoption of the strategy of wedge politics.

3 Policy change

This section provides more details of the changes in the various elements of policy affecting Australia's experience of globalisation. The indicators show a significant reduction in barriers to merchandise trade, including in highly protected sectors. Foreign direct investment (FDI) flows have also been liberalised, but the degree of restriction on those flows remains high relative to the Organisation for Economic Co-operation and Development (OECD) average. A snapshot of services markets shows they are relatively open compared to the OECD average, although Australian policy is generally more restrictive than the most open regimes in the OECD. Longer-run studies of domestic regulatory reform show a significant degree of reform. The movement of people has also made a significant contribution to the growth of the workforce in Australia. These changes have taken place in the context of a broader reform agenda.

3.1 Barriers to trade in goods

Figure 2.1 shows the changes in the rate of protection applied to goods (manufacturing and agriculture) trade since 1903–04 in Australia. The very long-term trend is that of a decline, but with significant spikes in the 1930s and after World War II (see Lloyd, 2008 for a detailed discussion of these events). As noted, there was a significant tariff cut in 1973 which, following a couple of reversals, is sustained from the late 1980s from which time the average rate fell from 10% for manufacturing and 4% for agriculture, to 2% and 1%, respectively. The fall in the rate of assistance to manufacturing closed the gap to the rate applied to

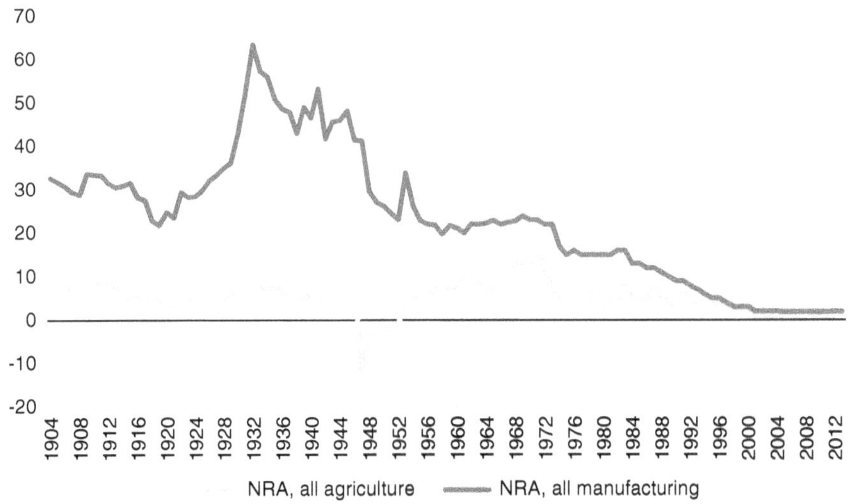

Figure 2.1 Nominal Rates of Assistance, Agriculture and Manufacturing, 1904–2013.
Source: Anderson and Aryal (2015), Table A9.
Note: NRA = nominal rates of assistance.

agriculture. Adams, Brown, and Wickes (2013) pointed out these reforms were fundamental to Australia being more active in the multilateral trading system: Australia could be active in the Uruguay Round (from 1986), binding the increasing openness while asking for better market access from others.

The Centre for International Economics (Centre for International Economics CIE, 2017, Box A.1) provides more detail of the changes. Between 1988 and 1992, all tariffs over 15% were reduced to 15% and those between 10% and 15% were reduced to 10%. Then between 1992 and 1996 all tariffs were reduced to 5%. Textiles, clothing, and footwear as well as motor vehicles followed their own schedule, falling to at most 5% by 2015. Even at 5%, the Productivity Commission (2018a) observed that these tariffs raise costs and reduce the competitiveness of Australian exporters (p. 13).[4]

There is considerable variation in tariff rates at the sectoral level. In 1986, the import weighted average tariff ranged from 0.5% for forestry products to 89% for apparel (CIE, 2017). By 2016, this range had narrowed, so that the minimum was 0% for a number of agricultural products and the maximum was 2.4% for apparel.[5]

The Centre for International Economics (CIE, 2017) found that trade liberalisation between 1986 and 2016 increased real GDP by 5.4% (national income by slightly less reflecting the growth of FDI and income transferred offshore). Investment grew by nearly 12%, trade by nearly 30%, and real wages by over 7%. The average family income was about $8,500 higher because of liberalisation.[6]

Pomfret (2015) pointed out that in the late twentieth century, apart from its agreement with New Zealand (Scollay, Findlay, and Kaufmann, 2011) and the preferences for developing countries, Australia did not discriminate amongst partners. Australia remains a key advocate of the multilateral system[7] but in the context of its failure to progress, and given the global shift in strategy towards preferential agreements, Australia has mobilised its own strategy. Pomfret (2015) also argued that in an era of low tariffs, other barriers to trade are relatively more important and reform in an international setting becomes connected to (non-discriminatory) deregulation more generally, a process which is managed in agreements with fewer members.[8] Adams, Brown, and Wickes (2013) reviewed the debate about the transition to free trade agreements (pp. 116–118) and they refer to motivations for changes, including the value of covering new issues and of responding to events in East Asia, plus business sector pressure. Having signed four agreements in the first decade of the century, Australia has already signed 10 agreements this decade with prospects of more to come. The 'genie was ... out of the bottle' (Adams, Brown, and Wickes, 2013, p. 119). Over 60% of Australia's two-way trade is covered potentially by these agreements (excluding the Comprehensive and Progressive Agreement for Trans-Pacific Partnership or

CPTPP

which covers 22% by itself).

The Asia-Pacific Economic Cooperation (APEC) process was launched in 1989, and its leaders included the Hawke government. Australian economists were also leaders in the design of the process (see for example Drysdale, 2009) and adoption of its principles of open regionalism. The APEC made a critical contribution to the evolution of trade in the region and between the region and the rest of the world, and to Australia's participation in that development (Armstrong and Drysdale, 2009).

A variety of other measures affect trade in goods, including anti-dumping measures. Information in the Global Trade Alert Data Base shows a rise in the use of measures of this (and other) types affecting trade (see also Kirchner, 2018). The average duty imposed over the period 2009–15 was 17%, which is high relative to the current maximum tariff of 5% and the measures applied mainly (86%) to the steel industry (Productivity Commission, 2018a).

Industries benefit from budget assistance and tax concessions. Examples of the latter are often cross-cutting, such as those for small business and for research and development expenditure. Expenditure is mostly related to programmes for specific industries. The Productivity Commission (2018a, ch.2) calculates that in 2016–17 these items were $5.3 billion and $7.2 billion, respectively. The value of tariff assistance was $6.8 billion in that year. Allowing for the offset of the effects of tariffs on industry inputs (a cost of $5.9 billion) the net assistance to all industry was $13.4 billion. The Productivity Commission observes that the bulk of the input penalty from tariffs was borne by the services sector and also by mining while manufacturing was the beneficiary.

The Productivity Commission (2018a) calculated the trend in the effective rate of assistance (the combination of tariff and budget assistance, allowing for the input penalty, which is an indication of the change in the ability of an industry to attract resources from the rest of the economy). Agriculture had been disadvantaged by the relatively high rate of nominal assistance for manufacturing. But the effective rate has since fallen to below 5% for both agriculture and manufacturing.

Anderson, Lloyd, and MacLaren (2007) provided further commentary on the relative rates of assistance to manufacturing and agriculture. The average nominal rate of assistance for agriculture fell from 16% in the early 1970s, to less than 2% in the first decade of the 2000s (Figure 2.1). The authors report that no other OECD country other than New Zealand has made such a dramatic change in assistance for agriculture. As they also show, previously there had been a bias against agriculture which was removed as assistance to manufacturing fell. Consumers too benefited from lower prices: they paid an average equivalent of 2% on food purchases in the decade to 2004 compared to a tax between 23% and 36% for the OECD on average (p. 474). Anderson (2020) notes that Australia is one of the few industrial countries that has not increased assistance to agriculture as per capita incomes increased.

3.2 Services trade and investment restrictions

There is little data available in consistent terms on trends in policy applying to the services sector. Figure 2.2 reproduces the OECD (2018a) estimates of the services trade restrictiveness index (STRI) for Australia in 2017. The STRI examines policy which affects both competition in domestic services markets and also the ability of foreign providers to enter those markets. Australia has more open services sectors for all but one sector (courier services), compared to the OECD average. Other sectors with relatively high scores (above 0.2 out of 1) are air transport, logistics, and accounting. However very few sectors are at the minimum OECD score, the exceptions including rail freight. There are relatively high restrictions on some business services, such as accounting, logistics, courier, and distribution services. The OECD (2018b), in a Trade Policy Brief summarising a more detailed review of Australian policy, observed that there is 'scope for beneficial policy reforms in all sectors' (p. 2). The OECD (2018a) also pointed out that Australia has several cross-cutting (or horizontal) measures that apply to services: these include labour market needs tests, rules on foreigners buying land, restrictions on residency of corporate board members, and costs of obtaining a business visa.

The OECD provides a series of indicators of changes in regulation of various markets (Koske et al., 2015). Table 2.1 shows the values of these indicators for the network sectors, retail, and professional services between 1998 and 2013 (scores can range from 0 to 6, higher scores are more restrictive). Generally, they show significant declines for Australia. Professional services are an exception primarily due to the higher entry barriers for lawyers. Australia's score in the network sectors is in the bottom three of the OECD. Australia is ranked fifth lowest in retail and sixth lowest in professional services.

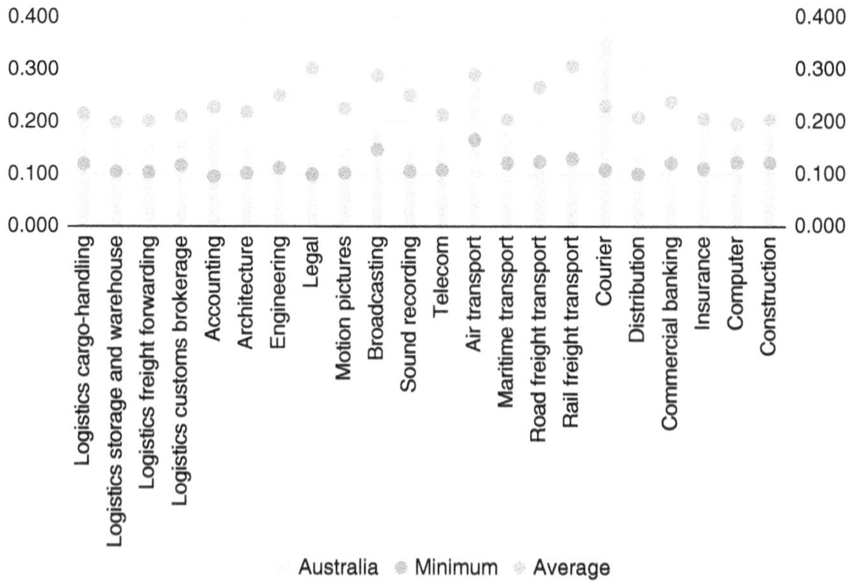

Figure 2.2 OECD Services Trade Restrictiveness Index: Australia, 2018.
Source: OECD (2018a).

Table 2.1 Indicators of Regulation, Australia, 1998–2013

	Network Sectors	*Retail*	*Professional Services*
1998	2.24	1.44	1.58
2003	1.98	1.35	0.79
2008	1.60	1.35	0.79
2013	1.50	0.70	0.92

Source: OECD. Indicators of Product Market Regulation. http://www.oecd.org/eco/growth/indicatorsofproductmarketregulationhomepage.htm (accessed 22 Oct. 2019).

Ferencz (2019) compiled cross-sectoral measures from the STRI database to estimate an indicator of restrictions applying to digital transactions, which are increasingly important in the services sector. Relevant policies are those applying to infrastructure and connectivity, electronic transactions, payment systems, and other barriers relevant to digitally enabled services. Australia's score is relatively low. However, the principles for the design of policy in this area continue to be debated (Voon and Mitchell, 2019; Findlay, 2019).

3.3 *Foreign direct investment policy*[9]

Pomfret (2015) identified different stages of the development of foreign investment in Australia. The first stage involved investment primarily from the US and the UK, to 'jump' the tariff wall. Then followed investment in the minerals sector in the 1960s. Ergas and Pincus (2016) stressed the openness of the economy to capital inflow in the 1950s and 1960s.

A screening process was introduced in 1972 to monitor foreign direct investment and to 'protect' Australian companies if a public interest case could be made for doing so. The rate of rejection of investment proposals rose over the period to the early 1980s. Then a process of liberalisation began, partly driven by the treatment of investment matters in the World Trade Organization and its treatment in Australia's free trade agreements. Armstrong, Reinhardt, and Westland (2017) asked whether free trade agreements are making 'swiss cheese' of Australian policy. The issue became the levels of discrimination amongst trading partners, and China in particular when new criteria related to state-owned enterprises were introduced (Drysdale and Findlay, 2009).

An indicator of the change in the regime applying to inbound foreign investment is the measure of FDI restrictiveness developed by the OECD (with scores out of 1, higher values indicating a more restrictive regime). For Australia, the index fell from 0.27 in 1997 to 0.15, indicating a significant change in policy (Table 2.2). But the score for Australia remains high relative to the OECD average (which was less than half that of Australia in 2017). Significant contributors to Australia's relatively high scores are its screening procedures (Thangavelu and Findlay, 2018).

3.4 People movement regime

Australia has been a country of migration but its early history is one of discrimination in the sources of the inflows. Since the origin of the country in 1901,

Table 2.2 OECD FDI Restrictiveness Index, Australia and OECD Average 1997–2017

	Australia	*OECD Average*
1997	0.266	0.127
2003	0.246	0.098
2006	0.237	0.084
2010	0.128	0.068
2011	0.128	0.068
2012	0.128	0.067
2013	0.128	0.066
2014	0.127	0.066
2015	0.140	0.066
2016	0.146	0.066
2017	0.147	0.066

Source: OECD.FDI Regulatory Restrictiveness Index. https://stats.oecd.org/Index.aspx?datasetcode=FDIINDEX# (accessed 22 Oct. 2019).

FDI = foreign direct investment, OECD = Organisation for Economic Co-operation and Development.

there were tight constraints on those of non-European descent (Pomfret, 2015). Various events broke down this discrimination, including the experience of World War II, and the acceptance of displaced people. The demand for skills was another driver of change, as was the interest in integration with Asia. But it was not until 1973 that race was removed in formal terms as a factor in migration.

Hugo (2014) referred to the introduction in 1996 of options for temporary migration. Before this, Australia had focussed on permanent migration. Other major changes from this time were the greater attention to the skills of migrants and their distribution across the regions of Australia. Other major changes were removing limits (in 1985) on enrolments of international students, who then had the right to work and later the introduction of visas, which allowed graduates to remain in Australia for employment. The current arrangement allows graduates to remain for 18 months and postgraduates for up to four years (Wright et al., 2016). Another example of more liberal policy is that working holiday visa holders could apply for longer-term visas (up to three years) if they worked for various periods in regional areas.[10] On the other hand, temporary migration for skilled workers was tightened from March 2018 onwards with shorter visa issue periods, more testing, and less likelihood of leading to permanent residency.

3.5 Context of microeconomic and macroeconomic reform

Other policy measures affect the impact of globalisation in Australia. Berger-Thomson, Breusch, and Lilley (2018) pointed to three waves of reforms. The first wave they say began in the 1970s with the deregulation of the financial sector and led to the floating of the exchange rate and the removal of capital controls in 1983. Foreign banks also then were able to enter the market. Another part of the first phase was an agreement between the government and labour unions, in which unions agreed to limit wage demands while the government undertook to support workers through tax reform, retirement policy, and spending programmes.

The second wave from the mid-1980s included the tariff reforms already discussed. The second wave also included a more decentralised wage bargaining system, which led to a more flexible labour market, which was more able to respond to shocks. Various reforms of regulation and changes promoting competition were also included in this stage. These had the effect of lowering input costs to business, which assisted in the adjustment to the reductions in tariff rates.

Banks (2005) also referred to the interaction of packages of reform, especially in the second phase. Scheduled tariff reductions, as noted above, were introduced from 1988. An important consequence was that the traded goods sector faced more intense international competition. Businesses then pressed not for a reinstatement of protection (reflecting the change in thinking about policy options) but for reductions in input costs, especially in labour markets and utility services' markets. Government policies and institutions were impeding this outcome and Banks says that this situation led to a wide range of domestic reforms in product and factor markets and in the public and private sectors.[11]

The third wave according to Berger-Thomson, Breusch, and Lilley (2018) was mainly focussed on fiscal and monetary policy. The key element of interest in this context was the movement to constrain the federal budget deficit, which is important later in the context of a discussion about the sustainability of the tax-transfer system.

3.6 Trade, capital, and people flows

Australia's policy settings before the 1970s were anti-trade, and the share of trade in GDP was smaller than might be expected (Anderson, 2020). Following reform, there has been a remarkable reorientation to the world economy.

First, the ratio of exports plus imports of both goods and services to GDP rose from 25% in 1975 to 42% in 2016. However, the traded share of GDP is low compared to the OECD average, which is closer to 60%.[12] Guttmann and Richards (2004) argue a relatively low traded share for Australia is to be expected given its location and geography, including its distance from international markets (Pomfret, 2015). Armstrong, Drysdale, and Kalirajan (2008) found that for the period 2002–04, Australia's export performance in terms of meeting its potential exceeds the world average: they also find that Australia exports to East Asia very efficiently (p. 12).

Second, there has been a remarkable redirection of Australian trade, initially towards Japan, which became Australia's largest export market in 1966–67,[13] then to others in northeast Asia. China became the largest export market in 2009–10 and by 2017–18 accounted for 24% of Australia's two-way trade. Japan accounted for 10%, followed by the US, the Republic of Korea, and India. Overall, Asia accounted for 65% of total trade and Europe for 15% (Department of Foreign Affairs and Trade DFAT, 2019). The UK share plunged to only 3.5% of two-way trade, the same share as New Zealand.

Third, another interest is the management of trade and the impact of preferential agreements on trade flows. A study by PwC (2018) using a business survey, reports the utilisation rates in the order of 80% for merchandise trade in Australia's northeast Asian agreements. Crook and Gordon (2017) using customs data, found lower rates (26% of total trade or 47% of eligible trade (p. 11)). They also report considerable variation in utilisation across agreements. Utilisation depends on being able to meet the rules of origin of these agreements, which the Productivity Commission (2018a) advocates be relaxed. The CPTPP, signed in 2018 allows for the accumulation across members in meeting the conditions of the rules of origin and it involves easier administrative processes.[14] Some countries are referred to in more than one agreement, so traders have decisions to make about which agreement to use.[15]

Fourth, with respect to foreign direct investment, the stock as a ratio to GDP averaged around 13% in the 1950s and 1960s, falling to under 10% in the 1970s, but after the reform period grew towards 50% (Bingham, 2016). This growth is remarkable, but Kirchner (2018) expressed concern that the growth of this ratio has levelled off in the last few years. In terms of FDI flows, Australia attracted an inflow of $62 billion in 2018, a 40% increase on the previous year, which put Australia at number eight in the world as a destination (UNCTAD, 2019). Capital flows into the non-financial private sector in Australia have consistently been of the order of 2%–3% of GDP since 1998 (Debelle, 2017, Table 2.1). The world average is 2.3% and for the Asia-Pacific it is 2.1%.[16] The mining sector has become increasingly important as a host of this investment (2.4% of GDP in 2014–16 compared to 3.0% in total). Bingham (2016) reported that Australia's outward FDI was only 1.3% of GDP on average from the 1950s to the end of the 1970s. This ratio increased after the reform period, reaching 38% in 2006–07. Following a decline during the global financial crisis in 2008–09 and then recovery, Australia has had a small net equity position in recent years.

Sales by Australian affiliates offshore are high relative to the gross value of exports. Bingham (2016) quoted a study by the Australian Bureau of Statistics (ABS) in 2002–03 that found that 48% of the provision of Australian goods and services to the world came from an Australian commercial presence abroad. DFAT (2019), using the statistics of partner countries found for 2015 that Australian-owned affiliates in Canada, the European Union, and the United States had sales of goods and services of about $124 billion, which was more than double the value of direct exports from Australia to these economies of $49.4 billion.

The ratio of affiliate sales to cross-border exports is higher for services (two-thirds) than for goods (DFAT, 2018). Bingham (2016) quoted other studies to show that this ratio varies by sector, being high for financial and insurance services, balanced for legal services, and low for education. However, only 40% of the stock of offshore investment is in the services sector (Bingham, 2018), which is low relative to the world average of about two-thirds. Also, Australia is low in terms of the services share of foreign-owned value-added generated in the home economy (OECD, 2017).

Finally, with respect to people flows, the consequences of the relevant policy changes have been significant. The proportion of Australians who were born overseas in 2016 hit the highest point in over 120 years, with 28% of Australia's population born overseas (ABS, 2016). That percentage has also increased every year for the last 15 years. About half the Australian population is born overseas or has one parent born overseas (The Guardian, 2017). The growth of migration has made a significant contribution to the growth of the Australian population (Wright et al., 2016, Figure 2.1). It was since 2006 more important than the natural population increase. The main components are classified as economic migrants (Table 2.3), with faster growth in the skilled categories compared to those on working holidays. Migrants arriving since 2012 accounted for 65% of the growth of the workforce between 2012 and 2017.[17]

The permanent migration programme is expected to be 160,000 per year (previously at 190,000) (ABC News, 2019). On the other hand, the number of temporary visa holders (such as international students and working holiday visits) is much larger than this, and its growth has been relatively fast (Australian Government, 2019). The number of such visa holders in Australia as at June

Table 2.3 Annual Intakes for Selected Visa Categories, Australia, 1996–97 to 2014–15

	1996–97	*2000–01*	*2004–05*	*2008–09*	*2012–13*	*2014–15*	*% increase 1996–97 to 2014–15*
Skilled '457' (temporary)	25,368	36,900	48,590	101,280	126,350	96,080	279
Working holiday (temporary)	52,700	76,600	104,400	194,582	258,248	226,812	330
International student (temporary)	68,611	146,565	175,825	319,632	259,278	299,540	337
Skilled (permanent)	19,697	44,730	77,878	114,777	128,973	127,774	549
Family (permanent)	36,490	33,470	41,736	56,366	60,185	61,085	67
Humanitarian (permanent)	11,902	13,733	13,078	13,373	19,985	13,756	16

Source: Wright et al. (2016), Table 1.

2018 was 878,912 people, which was over 300,000 higher than that number 10 years earlier, an increase of 54% over that decade. Students make up about half the number and temporary skilled visa and working holiday visa holders account for about 15% each.

Another result was a significant change in the direction of migration. The rate of migration from Asia increased, especially after the Vietnam war from 1975. England remains the number one country of origin, but now China and India are ranked two and three (Table 2.4). The main source of growth of temporary visa holders was East and South Asia. China was also the largest source of temporary visa holders, followed by India, then the UK, Nepal, and the Republic of Korea.

4 Consequences of reform

Overall, a key indicator of the outcome of this package of reforms has been the growth of the Australian economy, in which there have not been two quarters of negative growth (that is, no recession) for the last 27 years. Australia is now

Table 2.4 Australia's Population by Country of Birth, 2018

Country of Birth	*No.*	*%*
England	992,000	4.0
China	651,000	2.6
India	592,000	2.4
New Zealand	568,000	2.3
Philippines	278,000	1.1
Vietnam	256,000	1.0
South Africa	189,000	0.8
Italy	187,000	0.7
Malaysia	174,000	0.7
Scotland	135,000	0.5
All overseas-born	**7,343,000**	**29.4**
Australian-born	**17,650,000**	**70.6**

Source: Australian Bureau of Statistics (2016), '7.3 Million Migrants Call Australia Home', Media Release, 3 April. http://www.abs.gov.au/ausstats/abs@.nsf/Latestproducts/3412.0Media%20Release12017-18?opendocument&tabname=Summary&prodno=3412.0&issue=2017-18&num=&view= (accessed 22 Oct. 2019).

the only OECD country with this record, despite a series of external shocks. The drivers of this resilience (Berger-Thomson, Breusch, and Lilley, 2018) are the packages of reforms outlined so far, including with respect to migration, as well as the flexibility of the exchange rate, the flexibility of the labour market, fiscal management, and monetary policy parameters.

Another driver of performance has been the shift in the terms of trade (Figure 2.3). There had been a long decline in Australia's terms of trade from the early 1950s. This trend turned around from 2003 until 2011, with rising demand from China for resources. This boom had many important consequences, which are also outlined below, including the ability to sustain reform. The following sections discuss several more specific indicators of the performance of the Australian economy.

4.1 Structural change

The reforms have been associated with a significant change in the structure of the economy. The share of manufacturing in GDP by 1960 was about the same as the OECD average, although Australia's relatively low population meant that it could not have a strong comparative advantage in that sector (Anderson, 2020). Since the first tariff cut in 1973, the share of manufacturing fell from 16% to close to 6% by 2017–18 (Berger-Thomson, Breusch, and Lilley, 2018, Chart 6; see also Figure 2.4).

The services sector share of output grew to over 70% by 2016. Adeney (2018) highlights the growth of the business services sector (Figure 2.4). This is part of a process in Australia in which domestic supply chains have become more

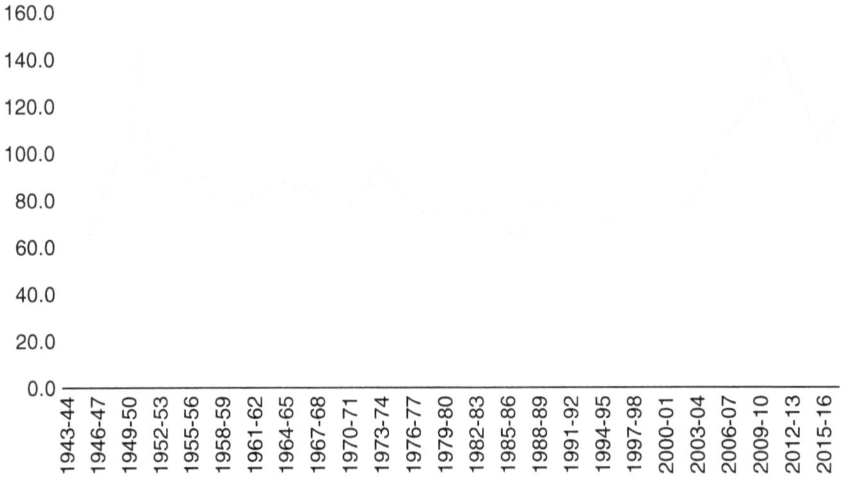

Figure 2.3 Terms of Trade, Australia, 1943–44 to 2016–17 (2015–16 = 100).
Source: *Australia's Trade and Economic Indicators.* https://dfat.gov.au/trade/resources/trade-statistics/Pages/trade-time-series-data.aspx

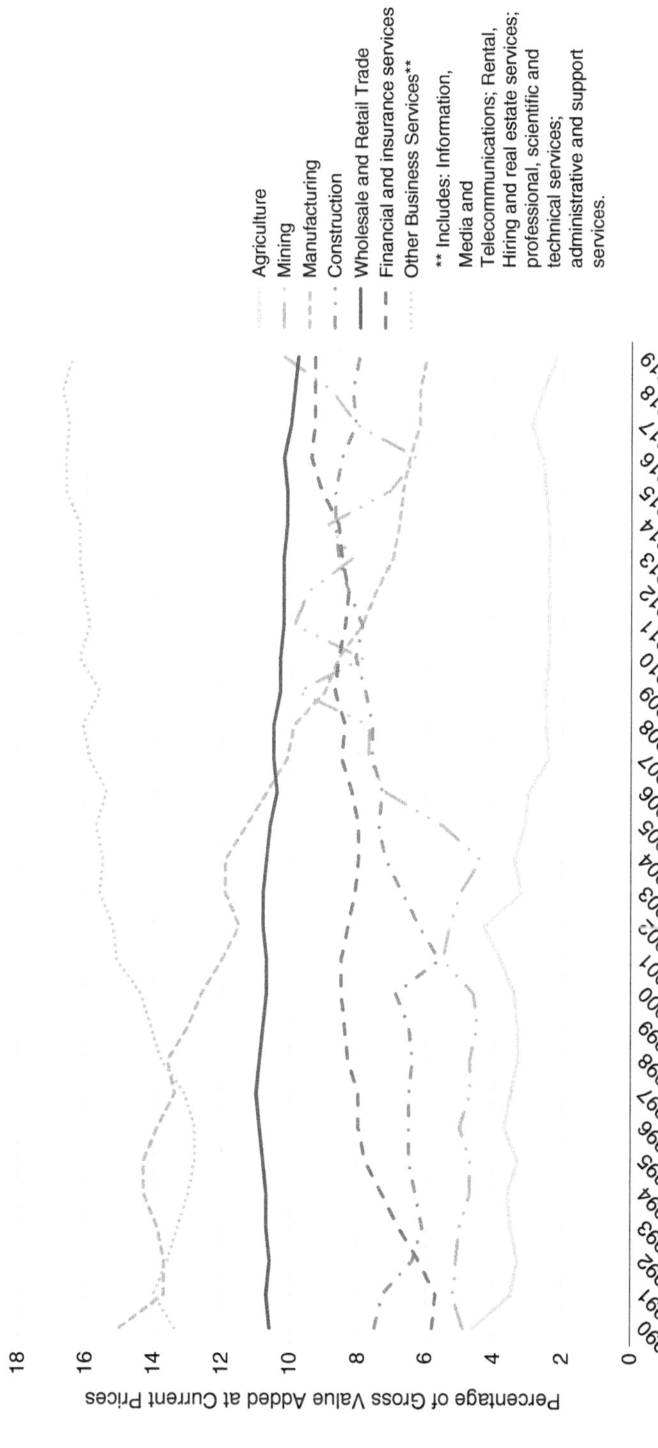

Figure 2.4 Structure of Production, Australia, 1987–88 to 2017–18.
Source: *The Australian Economy and Financial Markets: Chart Pack.* https://www.rba.gov.au/chart-pack/pdf/chart-pack.pdf?v=2019-04-03-10-14-19

fragmented and where various sectors are located. This process is especially evident in goods production since the first tariff cut of 1973 (Adeney, 2018, Graph 5). It is also an Australian example of 'servicification', which others have observed (Lodefalk, 2015).

Anderson (2018) examined the question of why the agricultural sector has been so resilient, with a long period up to the 1950s where it continued to account for 20%–30% of output and then in the recent period when (at a much lower share) it was far less relatively affected by reform than manufacturing. First, Anderson pointed out that agricultural prices rose almost as much as mineral prices. Second, other factors were reductions in trade costs, good investment in and returns to spending on research and development. The flexible exchange rate also meant that the economy could adjust more smoothly to the resource boom without a rise in inflation, which would have been more disruptive. Third, Australian resource endowments matter, since there is a relatively large endowment of land in the country.

The growth of trade and structural change combined to produce significant shifts in the composition of Australian exports, although less so with respect to imports (Anderson, 2014). Up to the early 1980s, exports were dominated by wool and wheat – Australia 'rode on the sheep's back' (Cashin and McDermott, 2002). From the 1970s, there was a shift to minerals and fuel exports, originally iron ore and coal, and later gas. From the 1980s, services exports became more significant, particularly tourism and education. For a long period, imports were dominated by capital goods, but as tariffs were cut consumer goods imports increased, also reflecting a rise in their quality as a result of access to international markets.[18] Tourism imports also increased.

The adjustment within the previously relatively highly-protected manufacturing sector has been a topic of interest. In a study of the period since 1990, ANZ (2017) found that exports of processed primary products grew by (about) a factor of 5, elaborately transformed manufactured (ETM) goods by a factor of 3 (including the value of re-exports), and simply transformed manufactured (STM) products by a factor of 2 (but with little change since 2000).[19] The composition of these changes aligns with expectations based on Australian resource endowments, but the growth is relatively slow: over the same period Australia's total exports of goods and services grew by more than six times.

The growth of ETM exports might be an indicator of an increase in Australia's participation in global value chains. But in relative terms, Australia's global value chain participation remains low, in terms of forward and backward linkages, and lower than any other OECD country in terms of the foreign value-added share of exports, in part due to Australia's location at the start of the value chain for most products (e.g. mining) and its distance from potential foreign suppliers.[20]

4.2 Labour market adjustment programmes

The structural change of the Australian economy in the recent decades driven by globalisation has significant impacts on the labour market. Displaced workers from the declining firms and sectors must move to the expanding ones. Australia has mainly relied on a flexible labour market during this labour movement process and thus it is common that displaced workers receive limited public support in transiting to new jobs. However, displaced workers in certain sectors and regions have access to special support through various labour adjustment programmes (LAPs), which operate within the broader structural and regional adjustment programmes (OECD, 2016). These programmes aim to support affected workers, businesses, industries, and regions through a time of change. Support has been provided to a diverse range of sectors, but most expenditure and programme effort has been concentrated in the manufacturing (the automotive industry and the textile, clothing, and footwear industry) and agricultural sectors.

Beer (2015) reviewed structural adjustment programmes in Australia between 2000 and 2012. During that period, 135 structural adjustment programmes were operating, with the total value of commitments over $80 billion of prospective outlays, the vast majority of which was federal expenditure. The scale of funding varies substantially across programmes. A few of them are enormous. For instance, The Dairy Structural Adjustment Program had a total budget of $1.63 billion and the Automotive Competitive investment Scheme was budgeted for $7 billion. It is more common that a programme costs between $5 million and $500 million. There are also programmes which are very small.[21]

LAPs are a crucial component of structural and regional adjustment assistance in Australia. LAPs are designed to assist displaced workers transition to new jobs during a plant closure or economic shock. Until July 2015, retrenched workers in the sectors of the automobile industry, textile, clothing and footwear, steel and the forest industry in Tasmania had been offered automatic access to the LAPs. In addition, four new programmes have been recently established for displaced workers in four companies.[22]

Some reviewers argue that the LAPs work well. Beer (2015) identifies the benefits of the LAPs to workers and to regions. Others are more critical. Daley and Lancy (2011) found that these programmes only include a modest amount of funding for job search and training assistance for directly affected workers. They further suggest that these programmes have a high cost per job (the one-off cost per expected job from structural adjustment programmes ranges from $20,000 to $60,000), do not have a significant effect on long-term employment trends and do not lead to better performance than other regions that lose a major employer but without government assistance. Daley and Lancy (2011) only focused on the direct labour market outcomes of affected workers while Beer (2015) considers both social and economic outcomes.

The OECD (2016) also criticised the LAP programmes in Australia mainly for their limited coverage compared with the overall figure of displaced employees in

Australia. It is suggested that the total number of employees possibly concerned by the LAPs is less than 1% of total employees in Australia, while on average 2.3% of employees with tenure of at least one year were displaced each year over the period 2002–13. Other OECD countries have programmes with wider coverage (e.g. the Trade Adjustment Assistance programme in the United States). The OECD report also suggests that the services provided through the LAPs could be improved by aiding displaced workers occur earlier and offering better training.

O'Neil (2014), based on the experience of adjustment in a regional city in South Australia, argued that the most important component is the provision of training for the development of human capital. The Productivity Commission (2014) reviewed the global context and Australian policy changes that led to the demise of the automotive industry, which occurred by the end of 2017 (Beer, 2018). The Commission stressed that decades of transitional assistance had forestalled but not prevented the closure of the industry. It observed that in the order of 40,000 people would lose their jobs over the transition period, compared to about 355,000 that had been retrenched in the year to February 2013 in all sectors. In other words, labour market processes were accommodating much larger adjustments in aggregate. The Commission noted that the costs of adjustment may be higher for workers retrenched from this industry (as noted by the Australian Government, 2014) and that the costs could be regionally concentrated. But the Commission argued that regional adjustment funds and industry specific programmes were inefficient and an inequitable way of providing support. The generally available 'welfare, training, and employment services' should be used.

4.3 Productivity

Labour productivity growth is linked to growth in wages and incomes, and therefore is a key channel by which the benefits of globalisation are distributed. The drivers of labour productivity growth include capital deepening and multifactor productivity growth, the latter indicating the effects of changes in technology and of economic efficiency. Both capital deepening and multifactor productivity (MFP) growth are affected by exposure to globalisation.

The Productivity Commission (2017a; 2019, Table 1) decomposes the growth of labour productivity from 1973 to 2018 in these two sources. Over that period, MFP growth accounts for about 40% of labour productivity growth. The exceptions are firstly in the 1990s, when MFP accounted for two-thirds of the growth. The other is the period since 2003 when MFP growth had been zero or small, at least up until 2011–12 (see also Campbell and Withers, 2017).[23]

The shift in the contribution of MFP growth before, during, and after the 1990s is also a feature of other OECD economies (Mann, 2016; Productivity Commission, 2019). Various explanations are offered for the slowdown, which preceded the global financial crisis. There appears to be a paradox since this slowdown has occurred alongside the emergence of new technologies.

Crafts (2018) concluded the issue is not a result of measurement errors. He expects powerful effects of new technologies but with a lag. In any case, the commentators (e.g. Mann, 2016) focused on the contributions of the government to resolving the slowdown, which is the interest here with respect to the Australian experience.

The starting point is to examine the link from reform to productivity and the rise in productivity in the 1990s compared to the earlier period. Kent and Simon (2007) found that reforms have a consequence for productivity in later years. The Productivity Commission (2017a) also argued that there is a link between the performance of the 1990s and the earlier reforms, but that this effect should be considered in conjunction with the impact of the application of information and communication technology (ICT). However, access to ICT may itself be a consequence of the openness of the economy. The productivity growth of the 1990s, the Productivity Commission reports, was led by the application of this technology in the services sector, which also depended on the performance of input-supplying services sectors like telecommunications, which also underwent reform. Anderson, Lloyd, and MacLaren (2007) also concluded that the reduction in assistance to agriculture has been associated with a rise in farm MFP.

Participation in trade, which followed reform, is a driver of productivity, through learning by doing channels and market size effects, for example. Using firm-level data for Australia, Tuhin, and Swanepoel (2017) found that exporters generally are larger than non-exporters and will have grown faster than non-exporters. They also find that exporting increases labour productivity and the average wage paid by exporters, and that exporting increases the chance of business survival. Trade (and factor movements, see below in this section) provides access to technology and the competition associated with trade adds to the incentives to innovate.

Firm-level selection and performance in open markets will also drive sectoral productivity growth. For example, as new international markets become available due to liberalisation, relatively more productive firms are attracted to exporting (they can more easily cover the set up costs of doing so), more productive firms then also expand, and less productive firms contract (Melitz, 2003). This will change productivity measured at the sectoral level, and should also lead to a reduction in the degree of dispersion of productivity amongst firms in a sector.[24] Anderson, Lloyd, and MacLaren (2007) also suggested that the Melitz effect of raising average productivity and narrowing its dispersion applied in agriculture, and contributed to better export performance by some sub-sectors, which reinforced the commitment to openness.

There are other observations contrary to the Melitz outcome. One of the explanations of the slowdown in productivity is the survival of 'zombie firms', which means the Melitz effect has not been as effective as otherwise. Various explanations are offered, including conditions in the financial sector (especially banking) and insolvency regimes. Quinn (2019) reported that the Australian technological frontier has not kept up with the global frontier (except in the mineral and energy sectors) and that amongst laggard firms, productivity has not improved. The Productivity Commission (2019, p. 47) also noted the dispersion across productivity levels amongst Australian firms and promotes the concept of improving the diffusion of existing technologies and knowledge.

FDI is important for growth, through its contribution to the capital stock and in mining in particular. Through the transfer of technology and the promotion of competition, FDI can also have the effect of adding to productivity in the domestic economy. Another channel is the transfer of the income and experience generated by offshore investment (which as reported is of a similar magnitude to the domestic stock).

Parham et al. (2015) discussed the ways in which migration, also a source of growth in terms of the labour force, might contribute to productivity. The channels they identify are the selection of migrants, policies that affect the work of migrants after their arrival, and the broader environment that affects the connectivity of the migrants with others. They found positive effects on productivity from changes in policy relevant to these matters. They also found that migrants have been more productive (according to earnings) and have increased their productivity faster than non-migrants. They note that migration has played an important role in meeting the requirements for various skills.

Structural change, also driven by globalisation, combined with different productivity levels between expanding and declining sectors, could be an important explanation for the change in overall productivity growth rates. The Productivity Commission (2107b) highlighted the structural change towards the services sector, which it asserts has a lower level of productivity, and which might thereby reduce labour productivity growth in future. Campbell and Withers (2017) on the other hand concluded that there is 'little cause for alarm over the effect of structural change' since the productivity levels in the services sector are similar to all other sectors of the economy. Adeney (2018) suggested that the reorganisation of production processes in Australia, and the lengthening of supply chains, including the processes of contracting, generate gains for productivity.

Several factors have been linked to this slowdown in MFP growth in Australia, especially up until 2011–12, which has contributed to the lower labour productivity growth. These include the effects of drought on productivity in agriculture and an acceleration of the use of inputs which preceded the growth in output. The growth in inputs followed from increased profits in the past and expectations of further increases (Parham, 2012). An example is the construction phase in the mining boom; however the mining sector was not the only factor.

Another explanation is that the effects of the reforms were significant but also exhausted or that reform fatigue and backtracking have set in. The Productivity Commission (2017a) reported that productivity levels in Australia are below the frontier observed in the same sectors in other economies (see their Figure 2.10, where only for an aggregate of mining, agriculture utilities, and construction is Australia at the frontier). Further improvements are possible. The Productivity Commission said there is a clear role for a policy change to close this gap. A similar point was made by the OECD in relation to the services policy. Garnaut (2005, 2013) argued that there is substantial scope for reform.

4.4 Inequality

The next question is how the developments in industry structure and productivity feed into income inequality in Australia. Leigh (2013) identified a process of a 'great compression' of income distribution (ch. 2) in Australia from the 1920s to the 1970s, which was also observed in other economies, and a 'great divergence' (ch. 3) from the 1980s until now. Over that time the share of what Leigh calls the affluent and the opulent doubled from 6% to 12%. Australia is now twice as unequal as it was in the 1980s, according to these data. But Leigh also points out that the US is twice as unequal as Australia, and that in Australia over this period those at low- and middle income-levels have all gained, although those at the top have gained by more.

The Productivity Commission (2018b) reported that while incomes in Australia rose in every decile in the last 27 years, the Gini coefficient related to market incomes has increased. The Commission then also found that the tax system, which is progressive and the transfer system which is highly targeted has offset this increase (reducing the Gini coefficient by 30%). The Commission noted, however that the application of these measures may have had effects on the supply of labour. Households in Australia also receive in-kind transfers from the government in health, education, housing, and childcare. Considering these, the Gini coefficient is lowered by another 30%. The Commission concluded that policies and institutions can affect the levels of inequality. However, the Productivity Commission (2017a) also expressed concern that the growth of the social insurance system is 20% faster than the growth of GDP, which suggests there is a risk that it will be difficult to maintain. Leigh (2013, ch.4) argued that, allowing for tax-transfer systems and the provision of services, developments in 'technology and globalisation' contribute about one-third of the divergence in incomes (other factors include a fall in the degree of unionisation of the work force, cuts in taxes, and the provision of education services).

Apart from taxes, transfers, and in-kind transfers, the Commission also discusses the role of policies for specific issues. For example, the Commission noted the movement of people through deciles of the income distribution in the course of their life, but reports that some are stuck and remain 'entrenched'. About 3% of households remain in the lowest two deciles over their lifetime. The Commission discussed measures relevant to these groups, related to health and housing. One of Leigh's (2013) concerns was that higher inequality slows down social mobility (ch.6).

5 Conclusion

In the manufacturing, agriculture, and several services sectors, policy reform in Australia has been significant. Issues remain with respect to some services sectors and to factor flows. These changes are associated with outcomes that have been significant in terms of indicators of the openness and growth of the economy, the direction of trade, and the structure of output and trade. At the same time, the perception of the community to trade appears to be positive.[25]

Banks (2005) drew lessons from this experience. First, he argued that 'external liberalisation' is a good place to start reform. This might be contrary to expectations, based on the idea that improving domestic efficiency first is important to help adjust to a change in external openness but in Australia, the latter drove the former.

Banks' second observation was that Australia reformed unilaterally in the 1980s, not in exchange for market access offered by trading partners. Partly, as both he and Corden (1996) explained, this was because the multilateral system was not initially dealing with markets of interest to Australia, which then had to consider the nature of the gains from reform regardless of the actions of others.

The third observation by Banks was that reform in Australia was not a 'big bang' approach but an incremental one. It was also a programme that was wide-ranging. The experience of the original 25% tariff cut might have influenced the design of the later programme, he proposes. He suggested that the approach adopted brought about the benefits that might have been found in the big bang approach but without the costs. It was important that losses from reform in some sectors were offset by benefits to that sector from reform in others.[26] Specific measures were, however, introduced into the most sensitive sectors. There were also examples of direct compensation for losses due to reform and regions where costs of reform were concentrated were also supported.

Fourth, Banks stressed two institutional reforms. They were designed to promote and sustain reform, to build wider community support, and to offset the influence of private interests in the design of policy. These were the reliance on the role of the Productivity Commission and the adoption of a framework for competition policy, which applied across the whole economy. Banks linked the use of these institutions and the design of their processes and systems to the response to obstacles to reform including its diffuse benefits, the lack of incentives for winners to mobilise to support reform, bureaucratic constraints, and multiple jurisdictions.

Banks' final observation was that while political leadership is critical for reform (see the earlier discussion of triangulation, for example), 'its most enduring legacy' may be to entrench the right institutions.

Anderson, Lloyd, and MacLaren (2007) provided a more specific case of how policies across sectors matter. For example, the cuts to assistance for non-agricultural sectors was important for the success of the reforms of agriculture. They said other microeconomic and macroeconomic reforms made it easier for farmers to adjust and to raise their productivity. Farmer resistance to reform in their own sector was thereby reduced.

Lloyd (2008) discussed the experience of the 1973 reductions in tariffs and the longer-term changes dating from the late 1980s. The lesson he takes from those experiences is that phased reductions can work, since they apply across the board and they occur each year, which helps to maintain momentum and predictability. Corden (1996) also made the point that the operation of tariff systems based on clear principles are less likely to be eroded by private interests and lobbying. The commitment to reform and the nature of the policymaking process also meant that lobbying for special assistance was made less worthwhile in the reform period (Anderson, 2020).

The reform agenda is not over, and a number of issues are identified in the material reviewed here. The drop in productivity growth in the 2000s was also highlighted, and Australian per capita incomes continuing to grow in spite of that development as the terms of trade improved. Garnaut (2013) identified a great complacency in Australia and argued for further reform to sustain productivity growth. The culture of policymaking in this respect, however, demands constant attention, he said. Garnaut's (2013) assessment is that in this century the role of private interests in policymaking has increased. Garnaut (2018) also argued that

> we will not get back to policy-making in the public interest without reform to reduce the influence of vested business interests in the political process, to strengthen independent centres of policy research, and to nurture a more competitive and better resourced media.

There are many issues now worthy of attention for policymaking in the public interest. Barriers at the border remain important. For example, the scope of the services sector issues that might be addressed is evident in the discussion of policy in Australia in that sector. For agriculture, although writing a decade ago, Anderson, Lloyd, and Maclaren (2007) identified priorities that remain relevant, including reviewing import restrictions applied on the grounds of human health, removing remaining restrictions on the use of genetically modified varieties of farm products, and the adoption of more efficient water pricing policies. In manufacturing, items for attention include the use of the anti-dumping system and the removal of remaining tariffs (as well as binding them). New issues will continue to emerge as technology changes and world markets evolve; already restrictions related to data flows are more prominent. With respect to factor flows, significant degrees of discrimination remain in investment policy and elements of migration policy have been tightening.

A feature of the Australian approach to reform as noted already has been its wide-ranging coverage. Attention to barriers to international engagement remains important but according to the Australian experience doing so in the context of a package of reforms will be more effective (that is, the outcome will be more extensive and more likely to be sustained). Examples are the following.

- The Productivity Commission (2017b) developed a new agenda for microeconomic reform more generally, which includes attention to the health and education systems, to the performance of cities (including the management of infrastructure projects and land use), energy markets, and the innovation ecosystem, as well as the relationships between federal and state governments.
- Garnaut's action list (2013, ch.6) included firstly a focus on competition, including audits for monopoly power and high profit margins and reviews of

pricing of natural monopolies in utilities, airports and roads. His second main area was barriers to international transactions. His third main area was taxation reform.

Notes

1 Anderson (2020) and Brennan and Pincus (2002) presented different views on the positive and neutral contributions (respectively) of key economists to the implementation of reform.
2 Bob Hawke died in May 2019. For another assessment of the elements of success of the Hawke government reforms, see Adam Creighton (2019), 'He Came, He Saw, He Fixed the Economy', *The Australian*, 18–19 May, p. 41. https://www.theaustralian.com.au/inquirer/he-came-he-saw-he-fixed-the-economy/news-story/60a50b164d3aa98751e1a6bf13fb33b5
3 This concept is attributed to President Clinton adviser Dick Morris. See https://politicaldictionary.com/words/triangulation/
4 The World Trade Organization in its trade policy of review of Australia in 2015 stresses that these tariff reductions have not been bound and that there is a significant gap between applied and bound rates (World Trade Organization WTO, 2015).
5 As Treasury says, 'Over recent decades the importance of tariffs as a revenue source has declined dramatically. This is expected to continue into the future.' Its share in total tax revenue was of the order of 2% by 2008–09, compared to 6% in 1973–74. See *Australia's Future Tax System*, ch E. http://taxreview.treasury.gov.au/content/FinalReport.aspx?doc=html/publications/Papers/Final_Report_Part_2/chapter_e8-3.htm
6 Dollar values in this paper refer to Australian dollars.
7 See for a recent example the speech in September 2018 by the Secretary of the Department of Foreign Affairs and Trade. https://dfat.gov.au/news/speeches/Pages/defending-the-rules-based-trading-system-the-role-of-business.aspx
8 The Productivity Commission continues to argue for precautions in the application of a preferential strategy – see section 5.2 of Productivity Commission (2018a). See also Armstrong (2012).
9 This section concentrates on barriers to direct investment. See Thangavelu and Findlay (2018) for a more detailed discussion of issues related to portfolio flows of capital.
10 A significant number of people also breach their visa conditions and stay in Australia longer than originally approved, estimated to be about 63,000 in 2017. See *Australian Migration Statistics 2016–17.*https://data.gov.au/data/dataset/australian-migration-statistics/resource/9e5ffab9-81dd-4e34-81b4-71a920da4d98 (accessed 22 Oct. 2019), Table 4.0. See also Australian Government (2019, pp. 24–25).
11 Banks (2005) in Box 1 summarised the reforms in tariffs, capital markets, infrastructure, labour markets, human services, competition policy, macroeconomic policy, and taxation.
12 OECD Data. *Trade in Goods and Services.* https://data.oecd.org/trade/trade-in-goods-and-services.htm#indicator-chart (accessed 22 Oct. 2019).
13 Dates in this format refer to Australian financial years, which start on 1 July and end on 30 June.
14 See White and Case (2019). Some commentary however is that the self-certification process, which the CPTPP offers will also create different risks for business. See Pitcher Partners (2018).

15 The Department of Foreign Affairs and Trade provides a portal to free trade agreements: https://ftaportal.dfat.gov.au/ (accessed 22 Oct. 2019).
16 World Bank, *Foreign Direct Investment, Net Inflows* (% of GDP). https://data.worldbank.org/indicator/BX.KLT.DINV.WD.GD.ZS (accessed 22 Oct. 2019).
17 Australian Government, *Australian Migration Statistics, 2016–17*. https://data.gov.au/data/dataset/australian-migration-statistics/resource/9e5ffab9-81dd-4e34-81b4-71a920da4d98, Table 7.0 (accessed 22 Oct. 2019).
18 See examples presented by DFAT (clothing, footwear, motor vehicles, household appliances, and audio visual equipment) at https://dfat.gov.au/trade/resources/publications/Pages/benefits-of-trade-and-investment.aspx (accessed 22 Oct. 2019).
19 According to the ABS: 'STM consist mainly of basic metal manufactures, chemicals and other intermediate manufactured goods which will be used as inputs into other goods. Examples include flat-rolled steel products, chemicals, leather and cotton yarn. ETM are generally what would be termed 'finished goods'. ETM covers a vast range of goods, including machinery, whitegoods and other household wares, motor vehicles, clothing and footwear.' See https://www.abs.gov.au/ausstats/abs@.nsf/Lookup/by%20Subject/5489.0~2015~Main%20Features~Trade%20Import%20and%20Export%20Classification~10029
20 OECD/WTO Trade in Value-added Database (TIVA): Australia. http://www.oecd.org/sti/ind/TiVA%20Australia.pdf
21 Examples of mid-size programmes are the Moreton Bay Marine Park Structural Adjustment Package ($15.1 million), the Structural Adjustment Fund for South Australia ($45 million from the Commonwealth and $10 million from the State), the Illawarra Advantage Fund ($10 million), and the Regional Food Producers Innovation and Productivity Program ($35 million). With respect to small programmes, two individuals received assistance of around $50,000 as a result of the creation of Marine Protected Areas in Tasmania.
22 Alinta Energy is an Australian electricity generating and gas retailing company with around 700 employees. In May 2016, it permanently closed Playford A Power Station, Playford B Power Station, and Northern Power Station in South Australia. Arrium was an Australian mining and materials company. The company employed nearly 10,000 workers. In April 2016 the company went into voluntary administration with debts of more than $2 billion. In September 2017, it was acquired by British-owned GFG Alliance. Caterpillar is a mining equipment manufacturer. In 2015, it closed its north-west Tasmanian factory, making 280 workers redundant as it moved to its new facility in Thailand. Queensland Nickel is a company owned by businessman and former politician Clive Palmer in the sector of refinery. In January 2016 the company entered into voluntary administration. In April 2016, the company's creditors voted for liquidation.
23 See Parham's website (http://www.deanparham.com/australia-s-productivity-trends/recent-developments) for a discussion of the growth and then decline of MFP growth since 2011–12 and also the collapse of labour productivity growth in recent years (negative in 2017–18: Productivity Commission, 2019).
24 Various explanations are offered, including conditions in the financial sector (especially banking) and insolvency regimes. See http://www.oecd.org/eco/growth/exit-policies-and-productivity-growth.htm.
25 Lowy Institute. 2017 Poll. https://www.lowyinstitute.org/publications/2017-lowy-institute-poll
26 An important contribution by the Productivity Commission and its predecessors was investment in general equilibrium modelling methodologies which could be used to capture the significance of reform at the industry and regional levels. See Anderson (2003) and Dixon (2008) for a discussion of these contributions.

References

ABC News (2019), 'Scott Morrison's Population Plan Aims to Draw Migrants to Country Towns to Ease Congestion', 20 March. https://www.abc.net.au/news/2019-03-20/scott-morrison-population-plan-migration-program/10921258 (accessed 22 Oct. 2019).

Adams, M., N. Brown, and R. Wickes (2013), *Trading Nation: Advancing Australia's Interests in World Markets*. Sydney: UNSW Press.

Adeney, R. (2018), 'Structural Change in the Australian Economy', *Bulletin*, March, Reserve Bank of Australia.

Anderson, D. (2014), *Fifty Years of Australian Trade*. Canberra: Department of Foreign Affairs and Trade. https://dfat.gov.au/about-us/publications/Documents/fifty-years-of-Australias-trade.pdf (accessed 22 Oct. 2019).

Anderson, K. and R. Garnaut (1987), *Australian Protectionism: Extent Causes and Effects*. Sydney: Allen and Unwin.

Anderson, K. (2003), 'International Trade and Industry Policies', in I. McAllister, S. Dowrick, and R. Hassan (eds), *The Cambridge Handbook of Social Sciences in Australia*. Cambridge: Cambridge University Press, pp. 168–185.

Anderson, K. (2018), 'Mining's Impact on the Competitiveness of Other Sectors in a Resource-rich Economy: Australia Since the 1840s', *Mineral Economics*, 31, pp. 141–153.

Anderson, K. (2020), 'Introduction and Overview', in K. Anderson (ed.), *World Scientific Reference on Asia-Pacific Trade Policies: Volume 2: Agricultural and Manufacturing Protection in Australia*. Singapore: World Scientific.

Anderson, K., P. Lloyd, and D. MacLaren (2007), 'Distortions to Agricultural Incentives in Australia Since World War II', *The Economic Record*, 83(263), pp. 461–482.

Anderson, K. and N. Aryal (2015), *Australian Grape and Wine Industry Database, 1843 to 2013*, Wine Economics Research Centre, University of Adelaide. https://www.adelaide.edu.au/wine-econ/databases/winehistory/ (accessed 30 Oct. 2019).

ANZ (2017), 'Australian Made', *Infocus*, May. https://bluenotes.anz.com/content/dam/bluenotes/documents/ANZ_Manufacturing_AustralianMade.pdf

Armstrong, S. (2012), 'Australian Trade Policy Strategy Contradictions', *The World Economy*, 35, pp. 1633–1644.

Armstrong, S.P. and P. Drysdale (2009), 'The Influence of Economics and Politics on the Structure of World Trade and Investment Flows', *East Asia Bureau of Economic Research Working Paper*, No. 61.

Armstrong, S.P., P. Drysdale, and K. Kalirajan (2008), 'Asian Trade Structures and Trade Potential: An Initial Analysis of South and East Asian Trade'. Paper presented at the Conference on the Micro-Economic Foundations of Economic Policy Performance in Asia, co-hosted by NCAER and EABER, 3–4 April, New Delhi. https://crawford.anu.edu.au/pdf/phd/armstrong/s3p1.pdf (accessed 22 Oct. 2019).

Armstrong, S., S. Reinhardt, and T. Westland (2017), 'Are Free Trade Agreements Making Swiss Cheese of Australia's Foreign Investment Regime?', *International Journal of Public Policy*, 13(3–5), pp. 290–303.

Australian Bureau of Statistics (2016), 'Overseas Born Aussies Highest in Over A Century', Media Release. http://www.abs.gov.au/ausstats/abs@.nsf/lookup/3412.0Media%20Release12014-15 (accessed 22 Oct. 2019).

Australian Government (2014), *Growing Opportunities: South Australian and Victorian Comparative Advantages. Report of the Panels for the Reviews of the South Australian and Victorian Economies.* Canberra: Department of Industry.

Australian Government (2019), *Report of the Migrant Workers' Taskforce.* Canberra: Commonwealth of Australia.

Banks, G. (2005), 'Structural Reform Australian-style: Lessons for Others?' Presentation to the IMF, World Bank, and OECD, May. https://www.pc.gov.au/news-media/speeches/cs20050601/cs20050601.pdf (accessed 22 Oct. 2019).

Beer, A. (2015), 'Structural Adjustment Programmes and Regional Development in Australia', *Local Economy*, 30(1), pp. 21–40.

Beer, A. (2018) 'The Closure of the Australian Car Manufacturing Industry: Redundancy, Policy and Community Impacts', *Australian Geographer*, 49(3), pp. 419–438.

Berger-Thomson, L., J. Breusch, and L. Lilley (2018), 'Australia's Experience with Economic Reform', *Treasury Working Paper*, October. https://treasury.gov.au/publication/p2018-t332486 (accessed 22 Oct. 2019).

Bingham, F. (2016), *Australia's Trade Since Federation.* Canberra: Department of Foreign Affairs and Trade. https://dfat.gov.au/about-us/publications/Documents/australias-trade-since-federation.pdf (accessed 22 Oct. 2019).

Bingham, F. (2018), *Australia's Foreign Affiliates Trade in Services.* Canberra: Department of Foreign Affairs and Trade. https://dfat.gov.au/about-us/publications/Documents/australias-foreign-affiliates-trade-in-services.pdf (accessed 22 Oct. 2019).

Brennan, G. and J. Pincus (2002), 'Australia's Economic Institutions', in G. Brennan and F.G. Castles (eds.), *Australia Reshaped: 200 Years of Institutional Transformation.* Cambridge, UK: Cambridge University Press, pp. 53–85.

Campbell, S. and H. Withers (2017), 'Australian Productivity Trends and the Effect of Structural Change', *Economic Round-up.* https://treasury.gov.au/publication/p2017-t213722c (accessed 22 Oct. 2019).

Cashin, P. and C.J. McDermott (2002), '"Riding on the Sheep's Back": Examining Australia's Dependence on Wool Exports' *Economic Record*, 78, pp. 249–263.

Centre for International Economics (CIE) (2017), *Australian Trade Liberalisation: Analysis of Economic Impacts – Final Report. Prepared for Australian Department of Foreign Affairs and Trade.* Canberra: CIE. https://dfat.gov.au/about-us/publications/trade-investment/Pages/cie-report-on-australian-trade-liberalisation.aspx (accessed 22 Oct. 2019).

Corden, W.M. (1996), 'Protection and Liberalization in Australia and Abroad', *Australian Economic Review*, 29(2), June, pp. 141–154.

Crafts, N. (2018), 'The Productivity Slowdown: Is It the "New Normal"?', *Oxford Review of Economic Policy*, 34(3), pp. 443–460.

Crook, W. and J. Gordon (2017), 'Rules of Origin: Can the Noodle Bowl of Trade Agreements be Untangled?', *Productivity Commission Staff Research Note*, Canberra: Productivity Commission. May.

Daley, J. and A. Lancy (2011), *Investing in Regions: Making a Difference.* Melbourne: Grattan Institute.

Debelle, G. (2017), 'Recent Trends in Australian Capital Flows', Presentation to the Australian Financial Review Banking and Wealth Summit, April.

Department of Foreign Affairs and Trade (DFAT) (2018), 'Australia's Foreign Affiliates Trade in Services'. https://dfat.gov.au/about-us/publications/Documents/australias-foreign-affiliates-trade-in-services.pdf (accessed 22 Oct. 2019).

Department of Foreign Affairs and Trade (DFAT) (2019), Composition of Trade Australia 2017–18. https://dfat.gov.au/about-us/publications/Documents/cot-2017-18.pdf (accessed 22 Oct. 2019).

Dixon, P.B. (2008), 'Trade Policy in Australia and the Development of Computable General Equilibrium Modelling', *Journal of Economic Integration*, 23(3), pp. 605–630.

Drysdale, P. (2009), 'APEC: Achievements and Challenges in International Diplomacy', http://www2.jiia.or.jp/kokusaimondai_archive/2000/2009-10_003e.pdf?noprint Accessed (22 Oct. 2019)

Drysdale, P. and C. Findlay (2009), 'Chinese Foreign Direct Investment in Australia: Policy Issues for the Resource Sector', *China Economic Journal*, 2(2), pp. 133–158.

Ergas, H. and J. Pincus (2016), 'The Wealth of the Nation', in J.R. Nethercote (ed.), *Menzies: The Shaping of Modern Australia*. Brisbane, Qld, Australia: Connor Court Publishing.

Ferencz, J. (2019), 'The OECD Digital Services Trade Restrictiveness Index', *OECD Trade Policy Papers*, No. 221. Paris: OECD Publishing.

Findlay, C. (2019), 'Can Cooperation Prevent a Digital Iron Curtain', *East Asian Forum Quarterly*, 11(3), July–September, pp. 15–18.

Garnaut, R. (1989), *Australia and the Northeast Asian Ascendancy: Report to the Prime Minister and Minister for Foreign Affairs and Trade*. Canberra: Australian Government Public Service.

Garnaut, R. (2005), 'Breaking the Great Complacency of the Early Twenty First Century', Paper presented at the conference, Sustaining Prosperity, New Reform Opportunities for Australia, 2005 Economic and Social Outlook Conference, Melbourne Institute and The Australian, Melbourne, 31 March.

Garnaut, R. (2013), *Dog Days: Australia After the Boom*. Collingwood, Vic, Australia: Redback.

Garnaut, R. (2018), 'Plenary Speech at the 2018 Social and Economic Outlook Conference'. https://cpb-apse2.wpmucdn.com/blogs.unimelb.edu.au/dist/a/142/files/2016/03/11.10.18-Politicians-Delivering-Change-11adasg.pdf (accessed 22 Oct. 2019).

Gruen, N. (2009), 'The Contrast Could Not Have Been Greater', in E. Beecher (ed.), *Best Australian Political Writing 2009*. Melbourne: Melbourne University Publishing. https://www.themandarin.com.au/108619-lessons-from-the-hawke-and-howard-years-of-australian-governance/ (accessed 22 Oct. 2019).

The Guardian (2017), 'Barely Half of Population Born in Australia to Australian-born Parents', 27 June. https://www.theguardian.com/australia-news/2017/jun/27/australia-reaches-tipping-point-with-quarter-of-population-born-overseas (accessed 22 Oct. 2019).

Guttmann, S. and A. Richards (2004), 'Trade Openness: An Australian Perspective', *Research Discussion Paper* 2004-11, December. Sydney: Economic Group Reserve Bank of Australia.

Hugo, G. (2014), 'Change and Continuity in Australian International Migration Policy', *International Migration Review*, 48, pp. 868–890.

Kelly, P. (1992), *The End of Certainty: The Story of the 1980s*. Sydney, NSW, Australia: Allen and Unwin.

Kelly, P. (2000), 'The Politics of Economic Change in Australia in the 1980s and 1990s', *RBA Annual Conference Volume*. Sydney: Reserve Bank of Australia.

Kent, C. and J. Simon (2007), 'Productivity Growth: The Effect of Market Regulations', *Research Discussion Paper* – RDP 2007-04. Sydney: Reserve Bank of Australia.

Koske, I., I.Wanner, R. Bitetti, and O. Barbiero (2015), 'The 2013 Update of the OECD Product Market Regulation Indicators: Policy Insights for OECD and non-OECD Countries', *OECD Economics Department Working Papers*, No. 1200. Paris: OECD.

Kirchner, S. (2013), 'Time to Dump Australia's Anti-dumping System', *Issue Analysis*, 141. Sydney:Centre for Independent Studies,.

Kirchner, S. (2018), *An Open Door: How Globalised Are the Australian and US Economies.* Sydney:The United States Studies Centre, University of Sydney.

Leigh, A. (2013), *Battlers and Billionaires: The Story of Inequality in Australia*, Melbourne, Vic, Australia: Redback.

Lodefalk, M. (2015). 'Servicification of Manufacturing Firms Makes Divides in Trade Policy-making Antiquated', *Working Paper* 2015:1. Örebro, Sweden: Örebro University.

Lloyd, P. (2008), '100 Years of Tariff Protection in Australia', *Australian Economic History Review*, 48, pp. 99–145.

Mann, C.L. (2016), *The Twin Challenges of Promoting Productivity and Inclusive Growth.* Paris: OECD.

Melitz, M. (2003), 'The Impact of Trade on Intra-industry Reallocations and Aggregate Industry Productivity', *Econometrica*, 71(6), pp. 1695–1725.

OECD (2016), *Back to Work: Australia: Improving the Re-employment Prospects of Displaced Workers.* Paris: OECD Publishing.

OECD (2017), 'Australia: Trade and Statistical Note'. http://www.oecd.org/investment/Australia-trade-investment-statistical-country-note.pdf (accessed 22 Oct. 2019).

OECD (2018a), 'OECD Services Trade Restrictiveness Index (STRI): Australia'. http://www.oecd.org/trade/topics/services-trade/documents/oecd-stri-country-note-australia.pdf (accessed 22 Oct. 2019).

OECD, (2018b), 'Australian Services Trade in the Global Economy', *Trade Policy Brief*, October. http://australianservicesroundtable.com.au/wp-content/uploads/2018/11/Australian-services-trade-in-the-global-economy.pdf (accessed 22 Oct. 2019).

O'Neil, M. (2014) 'Structural Change: Lessons from Port Augusta's Experience in the 1990s'. Economic Issues Paper No. 42, SA Centre for Economic Studies, Adelaide, https://www.adelaide.edu.au/saces/docs/issues-papers/saces-economic-issues-42.pdf access date 22 October 2019

Parham, D. (2012), 'Australia's Productivity Growth Slump: Signs of Crisis, Adjustment or Both?' Canberra: Productivity Commission.

Parham, D., H. To, N. Ratna, S. Regan, and Q. Grafton (2015), *Migration and Productivity in Australia.* Canberra: Crawford School of Public Policy, ANU.

Pitcher Partners (2018), 'What Does the New Trans-Pacific Partnership Mean For you?' http://www.pitcher.com.au/news/what-does-new-trans-pacific-partnership-mean-you (accessed 22 Oct. 2019).

Pomfret, R. (2015), 'Reorientation of Trade, Investment and Migration', in S. Ville S. and G. Withers, (eds.), *The Cambridge Economic History of Australia*, Port Melbounre: Cambridge University Press, pp. 397–418.

Productivity Commission (2014), 'Australia's Automotive Manufacturing Industry', *Inquiry Report* No. 70, Productivity Commission, Canberra.

Productivity Commission (2017a), 'Productivity and Income – The Australian Story, Shifting the Dial: 5 Year Productivity Review', *Supporting Paper* No. 1, Productivity Commission, Canberra.

Productivity Commission (2017b), 'Shifting the Dial: 5 Year Productivity Review', *Report* No. 84, Productivity Commission, Canberra.

Productivity Commission (2018a), *Trade and Assistance Review 2016–2017.* Canberra: Productivity Commission.

Productivity Commission (2018b), Rising Inequality? A Stocktake of the Evidence, *Commission Research Paper*, Productivity Commission, Canberra.

Productivity Commission (2019), *PC Productivity Bulletin*, May, Productivity Commission, Canberra.

PwC (2018), *Free Trade Utilisation Study.* PwC. https://www.pwc.com.au/trade/free-trade-agreement-survey.html (accessed 22 Oct. 2019).

Quinn, M. (2019), 'Keeping Pace with Technological Change: The Role of Capabilities and Dynamism', Speech to the OECD Global Forum on Productivity, Sydney. https://treasury.gov.au/speech/s2019-390085 (accessed 22 Oct. 2019).

Scollay, R., C.C. Findlay, and U. Kaufmann (2011), *Australia New Zealand Closer Economic Relations Trade Agreement (ANZCERTA) and Regional Integration.* Singapore: Institute of Southeast Asian Studies.

Snape, R.H. (1984), 'Australia's Relations with GATT', *Economic Record*, 60, pp. 16–27.

Thangavelu, S. and C. Findlay (2018), 'Foreign Investment and Innovation', in J. Drake-Brockman, and P.A. Messerlin (eds.), *Potential Benefits of an Australia-EU Free Trade Agreement: Key Issues and Options.* Adelaide: University of Adelaide Press, ch.1.

Tuhin, R. and J.A. Swanepoel (2017), 'Export Behaviour and Business Performance: Evidence from Australian Microdata', *Department of Industry, Innovation and Science Research Paper* 7/2016. https://industry.gov.au/Office-of-the-Chief-Economist/Research-Papers/Documents/ (accessed 22 Oct. 2019).

UNCTAD (2019), 'Global FDI Continue Their Slide in 2018', Investment Trends Monitor, 31. https://unctad.org/en/PublicationsLibrary/diaeiainf2019d1_en.pdf (accessed 22 Oct. 2019).

Voon, T. and A. Mitchell (2019), 'Australia's Huawei Ban Raises Difficult Questions for the WTO', East Asia Forum, 22 April. https://www.eastasiaforum.org/2019/04/22/australias-huawei-ban-raises-difficult-questions-for-the-wto/ (accessed 22 Oct. 2019).

White and Case (2019), 'The CPTPP Enters Into Force: What Does it Mean for Global Trade?' https://www.whitecase.com/publications/alert/cptpp-enters-force-what-does-it-mean-global-trade (accessed 22 Oct. 2019).

Wright, C.F., S. Clibborn, N. Piper, and N. Cini (2016), *Economic Migration and Australia in the 21st Century.* Sydney, Australia: Lowy Institute.

World Trade Organization (WTO) (2015), *Australia. Trade Policy Review.* Report by the Secretariat. WT/TPR/S/312, 3 March. Geneva: WTO.

3 Processing trade, trade liberalisation, and opening up: China's miracle of international trade

Yu Miaojie and Zhu Huihuang

1 Introduction

China began to reform its economy in 1978, and that economy has continued to grow rapidly over the past four decades. That such a large economy can achieve such long-term sustainable development has been seen as a miracle. One obvious feature of this miracle is that China has participated deeply and extensively in the global international trading system. Due to its opening-up policies, China has become the largest trading country in the world. In 2018, its foreign trade was valued at $4.62 trillion, with exports of $2.48 trillion and imports of $2.14 trillion. China replaced Germany as the largest exporter in the world in 2009, and the United States (US) as the largest importer in 2015. Over the past four decades, China's foreign trade volume has increased 204-fold, whereas its gross domestic product has only increased 34-fold. In this regard, China has already successfully achieved a miracle of foreign trade. Thus, to understand the miracle of China's economic growth, it is necessary to understand what role international trade has played in this process.

The realisation of this foreign trade miracle can be broken into four steps: the extensive margin of opening up (before 2001), the intensive margin of opening up (2001–08), deeper opening up against financial crises (2008–17), and all-around opening up (since 2017) after China's Communist Party announced the establishment of a new era of all-around opening up in China in its 19th National Congress.

The first stage was the extensive margin of opening up. During this period, the main feature of China's international trade was the utilisation of the country's huge labour force, which provides China with comparative advantages in labour-intensive industries and processing trade. Along with the decline of trade barriers between countries all over the world, the development of transportation and communication technologies, and the separation of production processes, China began integrating into the global value chain and taking advantage of its abundant labour force. A typical example of this integration was China's preferential trade policy of importing intermediate goods with zero tariffs to encourage processing trade production. Firms who participated in processing trade specialised in tasks requiring labour-intensive

DOI: 10.4324/9781003138501-3

production. At the same time, by participating in processing trade and importing intermediate goods and capital goods, Chinese firms gradually became familiar with production technology and gained experience from foreign companies, which further improved their production and operation efficiency.

The second stage was the intensive margin of opening up. The main feature of this period was trade liberalisation in China and dramatic changes in Chinese firms' performance, product market, and intermediate market. On the one hand, opening up brought intensive import competition, compelling domestic firms and companies to reduce inefficiency and improve product quality to become more competitive. On the other hand, the reduction of import tariffs allowed domestic companies to purchase high-quality intermediate goods and capital goods, allowing them to save costs and upgrade technology. At the same time, export trade liberalisation (for example, the removal of the Multi-Fiber Arrangement) expanded Chinese firms' foreign markets. These market-scale effects can stimulate enterprises to increase investment, research and development (R&D), innovation, and export. Furthermore, along with the increased labour costs, the proportion of processing trade (a relatively low value-added trade mode) gradually decreased, and ordinary trade began to dominate.

The third stage was deeper opening up against the financial crisis. The global financial crisis in 2008 had significant negative impacts on the economic development of the global economy, especially in developed economies. Demand from major developed economies was weak, and the mode of relying mainly on exports to drive China's economic growth was no longer feasible. Thus, Chinese firms began to find new advantages, including quality, brand, service, and so on. On the other hand, the Government of China also implemented several actions to encourage local firms to improve product quality, provide first-class service to their customers, and, at the same time, attract multinational companies to invest in China.

The fourth stage is the all-around opening up. In 2017, the 19th National Congress of the Communist Party of China pointed out that China's economy has shifted from a high-speed increase stage to a high-quality development stage, and improving the supply quality has become a top priority. At the same time, trade protectionism and anti-globalisation forces are on the rise. Against this background, the government proposes to build a new pattern featuring all-around opening up, thus promoting the development of both the Chinese and global economies. Specific measures to be undertaken include (i) further widening market access, (ii) improving the investment environment for foreign investors, (iii) strengthening protection of intellectual property rights, and (iv) taking the initiative to expand imports. In doing so, China will send a message to the world that China's door will not be closed and will only open even wider.

2 Comparative-advantage-following and processing trade

Before opening up its policy, China adopted a heavy industry-oriented development strategy – a comparative-advantage-defying development strategy. Lin and Yu (2015) found that a development strategy that prioritised heavy industry (which is a comparative-advantage-defying strategy) distorted product and factor prices, and had to rely on a highly centralised planned resource allocation mechanism. Thus, before the reform China adopted a distorted macroeconomic policy, which included suppressing interest rates, over-valuing domestic currency, adopting an import-substitution strategy, setting up 'price-scissors' against peasants, and restricting labour migration. After the 1978 economic reform, China abandoned the heavy industry-oriented development strategy, adopting the comparative-advantage-following (CAF) development strategy based on its factor endowments.

Where does China's comparative advantage lie? Yao and Yu (2009) found that a low dependent rate[1] and low urbanisation rate contribute significantly to China's large labour force and low wages. This provides China with a long-term advantage in labour-intensive industries. Tian et al. (2013) used cross-country data and a gravity model to show that a large labour population has a positive effect on a country's imports and exports. Ma, Tang, and Zhang (2014) found that firms become less capital-intensive but more productive after exporting, compared to non-exporters with similar ex-ante characteristics.

After its economic reform, China adopted a CAF development strategy. The government realised that processing trade is an ideal way to implement the CAF strategy given that China is a labour-abundant country. Indeed, processing trade is one of the main causes of the high level of intra-industry trade among the capital-intensive industries mentioned above (Lin and Yu, 2015). The General Administration of Customs reports 16 specific types of processing trade in China. Of these, the two most important are processing with assembly and processing with inputs. Both types of processing trade are duty-free but they are characterised by an important difference. For processing with assembly, a domestic Chinese firm obtains raw materials and parts from its foreign trading partners without any payment. However, after local processing, the firm must sell its products to the same foreign trading partner by charging an assembly fee. By contrast, for processing with inputs, a domestic Chinese firm pays for raw materials from a foreign seller. After local processing, the Chinese firm can then sell its final goods to other foreign countries (Yu, 2015).

Compared with ordinary imports, processing imports in China accounted for just a small proportion of total imports in the early 1980s. However, as shown in Figure 3.1, China's processing imports increased dramatically in the early 1990s and began to dominate ordinary imports in 1992, when China officially announced the adoption of a market economy. In 1995, processing imports accounted for more than 50% of the country's total imports (now decreased to

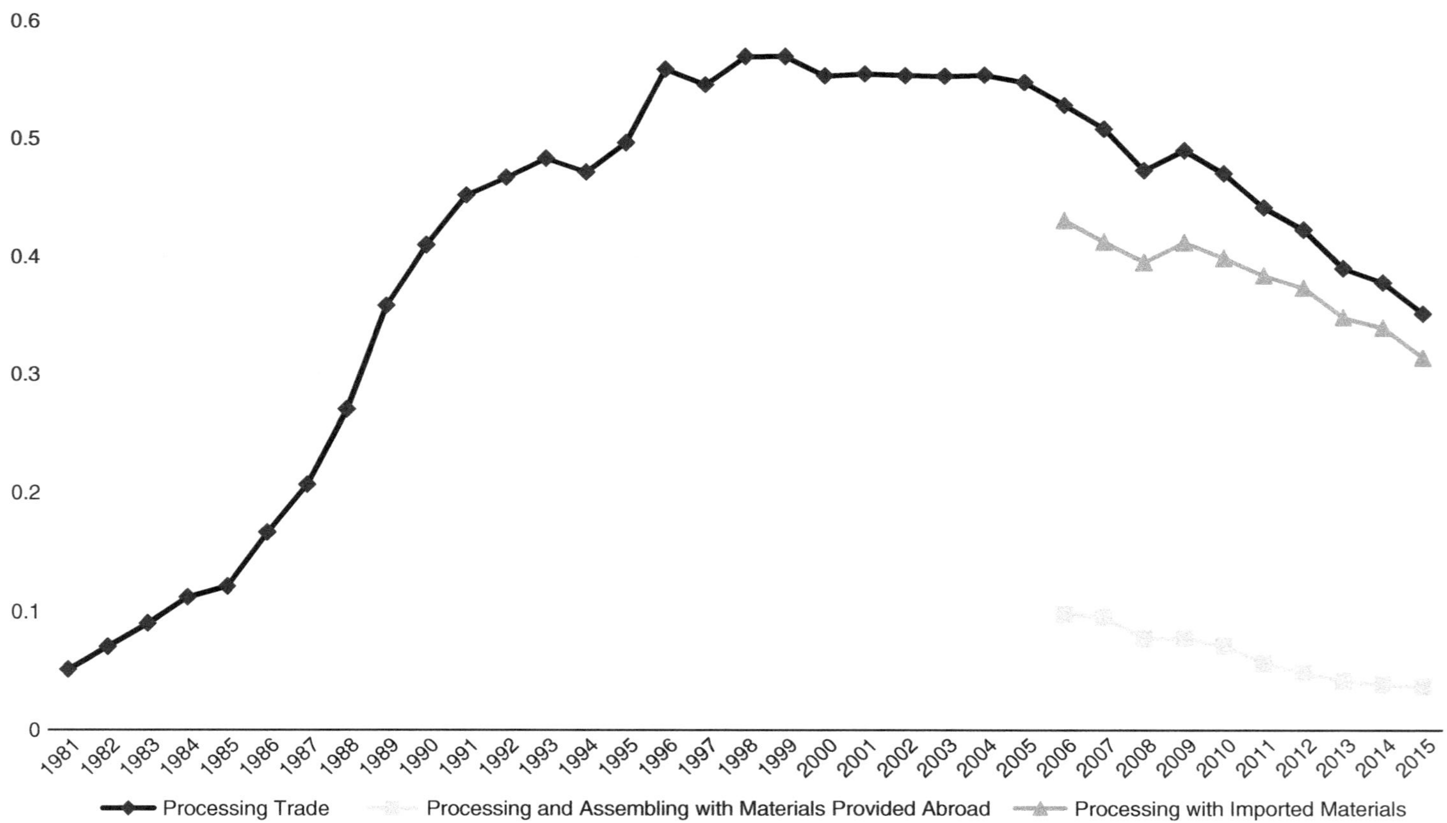

Figure 3.1 Ratio of Processing Trade Export in Total Export.
Source: National Bureau of Statistics, Department of Trade and External Economic Relations Statistics (2017), *China Trade and External Economic Statistical Yearbook*. Beijing: China Statistics Press.

one-third of total trade). Interestingly, processing imports with assembly were more popular in the 1980s because most Chinese firms lacked the capital needed to import. Since the 1990s, processing imports with inputs have become more prevalent.

Due to the prevalence of processing trade, the literature has revisited some international trade theory, one of the main findings of which is the paradox of Chinese exporters' productivity. The firm-level trade literature finds that exporters are exceptional performers for a wide range of countries and measures (Melitz, 2003). Paradoxically, the one documented exception is the world's largest exporter, China. Dai, Maitra, and Yu (2016) showed that this puzzling finding is entirely driven by firms that engage only in export processing – the activity of assembling tariff-exempted imported inputs into final goods for resale in foreign markets. They document that processing exporters are less productive than non-processing exporters and non-exporters, and perform more poorly in many other aspects such as profitability, wages, R&D, and skill intensity. Furthermore, accounting for processing exporters explains the abnormality in exporter performance in China documented in the previous literature. Although processing trade accounts for half of China's exports, processing firm productivity is lower than that of non-processing (i.e. ordinary) firms and even lower than that of non-exporters. Once they drop processing firms, Chinese exporters are more productive than non-exporters, meaning that the paradox disappears. Low fixed costs of processing exporting and trade and industrial policies favouring processing exporters are both responsible for the low productivity of processing exporters. Tian and Yu (2015) found rich evidence that a reduction in input trade costs for large trading firms leads to an increase in export intensity (i.e. exports over total sales). This impact is more pronounced for ordinary firms than for hybrid firms that engage in both processing and ordinary trade since ordinary imports enjoy duty-free treatment in China. Declining input trade costs not only increase the probability of a firm's being a new exporter (i.e. extensive margin) but also lead to higher export intensity (i.e. intensive margin).

Another main finding is how input and output tariffs affect a firm's productivity. Yu (2015) showed that reducing output tariffs has had a greater effect on productivity improvement than has reducing input tariffs for large Chinese trading firms in the 21st century. Such results are primarily attributable to the special tariff treatment afforded to imported inputs by processing firms as opposed to non-processing firms in China. Processing imports, which account for half of the total imports in China, have zero tariffs. He documents that further tariff reductions on imported intermediate inputs have no impact on firms that engage entirely in processing trade but still have some impact on firms that engage in both processing and non-processing trade. As the firm's processing share grows, input tariff reductions have a smaller impact on productivity gains. Similarly, as a firm's processing share increases, the share of domestic sales decreases accordingly; and the pro-competition effects from the reductions in output tariffs are hence weaker.

3 Trade liberalisation and firm performance

China's accession to the World Trade Organization (WTO) has had a profound influence on the world economy. However, this step took China far longer than it did other economies. As one of the 23 contracting parties to the General Agreement on Tariffs and Trade (GATT), it took China 15 years, from 1986 to 2001, to accede to the WTO. Wong and Yu (2015) observe this interesting phenomenon and argue that the level of democracy of an applicant country affects the time it takes to gain GATT/WTO accession. They find that most GATT/WTO members are democratic. More interestingly, democratic regimes seem to take less time to accede to the GATT/WTO than do non-democratic regimes. For example, Hong Kong acceded to GATT in 1986 immediately after its application. In contrast, Congo took more than 26 years to accede to the WTO. In addition, democratising countries also suffer from the length of time spent in attempting to accede to this large global trading organisation.

Democracy also has an impact on economic performance and export. Giavazzi and Tabellini (2005) provided evidence that countries that liberalise and then democratise perform much better than countries that do the reverse. Eichengreen and Leblang (2008) argued the existence of two-way positive causality between trade openness and democracy using historical data from 1870 to 2000. Yu (2010a) documents that democracy affects trade through different channels. First, democratisation in the exporting country can improve product quality and reduce trade costs, increasing bilateral trade. Second, democratisation in the importing country may increase trade barriers and thus reduce imports.

After China's accession to the WTO, along with the significant reduction in applied tariff rate (Figure 3.2), China's exports, firm performance, industrial structure, and factor market have undergone huge developments. According to the empirical findings of other countries, import trade liberalisation mainly affects firms in one country through two following channels: one is the intense competition caused by trade liberalisation in the final goods market; the other is the effect of tariff reductions on imported intermediate inputs (Amiti and Konings, 2007; Goldberg et al., 2010; Topalova and Khandelwal, 2011). On the one hand, import trade liberalisation and tariff reductions make it easier for foreign companies and their products to enter the domestic market, leading to greater competition for domestic companies and products. This will force domestic firms to reduce inefficiency in operations, markup and product price to better cope with the competition. On the other hand, tariff cuts have enabled many companies to purchase better quality intermediates at lower prices, which permits cost savings and quality upgrades.

Amiti and Konings (2007) analysed Indonesian firm-level data and find that firms gain at least twice as much from the reduction of input tariffs as from the reduction of output tariffs. Furthermore, Topalova and Khandelwal (2011) found that Indian firms could gain 10 times as much from input tariff reduction as from output tariff reduction in several industries. They argue forcefully that the primary reason for this result is that access to better intermediate inputs through the reduction of input tariffs is more important than the procompetitive effect of the reduction of output tariffs.

In addition to the commonality with the trade liberalisation process in other developing countries, many studies use Chinese firm-level data to study how trade liberalisation affects firm productivity. Firstly, trade liberalisation can boost firm productivity through different channels. Yu, Ye, and Qu (2013) investigated the linkage between firm productivity and product complexity. First, they adopt the Olley-Pakes (1996) approach to address two empirical challenges: simultaneity bias and selection bias caused by ordinary least squares. Then, the estimation results suggest that trade liberalisation significantly increases productivity for firms that produce complex goods. In contrast, they find that trade liberalisation has the opposite effect on the productivity of producers of simple goods.

Secondly, trade liberalisation can boost firm total factor productivity through R&D and innovation. Dai and Yu (2013) argue that absorptive capacity developed through pre-export R&D investment is crucial for learning to occur. They estimate the instantaneous and long-term productivity effects of starting to export on the universe of Chinese manufacturing firms during 2001–07 using propensity score-matching techniques. The baseline results show that, while the productivity effect of exporting is weak and transient for all firms on average, it is large and lasting for firms with pre-export R&D. For firms without pre-export R&D, exporting has no significant productivity effect, even instantaneously. In

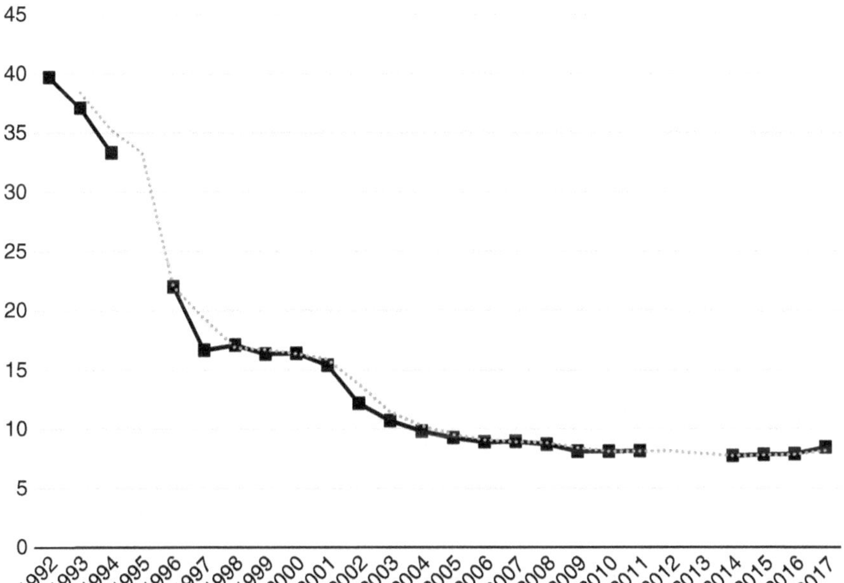

Figure 3.2 Applied Tariff Rate, Simple Mean, All Products (%).
Source: The World Bank, World Bank Open Data, retrieved 15 November 2019 from: https://data.worldbank.org/indicator/TM.TAX.MRCH.SM.AR.ZS

addition, the productivity effect of exporting increases with the number of years of pre-export R&D investment, suggesting that firms involved in intentional and persistent R&D activities enjoy greater learning effects than do firms only accidentally involved in R&D activities. They suggest that policies that encourage firm R&D and other absorptive capacity-building activities should be combined with trade liberalisation to reap the full growth benefits of openness. Tian and Yu (2017) also find strong evidence that input trade liberalisation due to the WTO accession significantly fosters firm R&D activity.

Furthermore, trade liberalisation can boost firm total factor productivity by increasing import variety. Feenstra, Li, and Yu (2014) use Chinese firm-level data to confirm the positive effect of imported intermediate goods on firm productivity. The results are primarily attributable to spillover and competition effects from imported goods. However, they find that the impact of imported intermediate inputs on firm productivity becomes weaker as firms produce more complex products. Differentiated products, which account for four-fifths of total products, to some extent bear less pressure from severe competition but enjoy fewer benefits from foreign imports penetrating the domestic market than do homogeneous products. However, the growth in productivity of firms that produce heterogeneous goods is slower than that of firms that produce homogeneous goods when product complexity requires more imported intermediate goods. If a homogeneous intermediate input is imported, firms will find it easier to adopt its up-to-date technology because homogeneous products are less technology-specific than heterogeneous products.

Finally, Yu and Yuan (2016) have also found that the reduction of final tariffs has led to a decline in firms' production cost, and the reduction of tariffs on intermediate goods has led to an increase in firms' production cost. As a firm's processing share increases, the impact of the reduction in tariffs on firms' markup will be smaller. Yu and Li (2016) investigate the impact of trade liberalisation on the quality of imported inputs within narrow product categories. They follow the model in Khandelwal (2010) to estimate the quality of inputs imported to China. To estimate the impact of both input tariff reductions and output tariff reductions, they choose processing trade, which is free from both tariffs, as a control group. By implementing the difference-in-difference method, they find evidence to support the argument that trade liberalisation promotes the quality of imported inputs in ordinary trade relative to processing trade. Yu and Jin (2015) study the impact of imported intermediate inputs and imports of final goods on the firm by taking product complexity into account. After controlling for the endogeneity of imported intermediate inputs, they confirm that firms could benefit from imports. Further, they find that imports could improve the productivity of firms that produce homogeneous goods, but have little effect on those produce complex goods. To explain this heterogeneous effect, market concentration is introduced, and the result reveals that the import competition effect weighs more in homogeneous industry while the import spillover effect is more important to heterogeneous industry. The low impact of imports on firm productivity in heterogeneous industry could be explained by a weak import spillover effect due to low R&D efficiency. Yu and Zhi (2016) find that, in the short term, import liberalisation of final goods allows more foreign firms to export to the domestic market, intensifying domestic market competition and thus reducing the profitability of pure domestic selling firms. However, in the long term, since firms can choose whether to enter or exit the market, some domestic reigning firms will choose to exit, allowing the firms that remain in the market to enjoy higher profitability in equilibrium.

Trade liberalisation also affects within-firm income inequality. Chen, Yu, and Yu (2017) develop a Mincer (1974)-type approach to investigate the impact of input trade liberalisation on firms' wage inequality between skilled and unskilled workers (or skill premium). When controlling for product-market tariffs in a firm's industry, they find robust evidence that reduced input tariffs in a firm's industry are associated with a higher skill premium at firms with more skilled workforces. This effect is more pronounced at ordinary (non-processing) firms. They also provide evidence that reduced input tariffs in a firm's industry are associated with higher value added and profits at firms with more skilled workforces. Rodriguez-Lopez and Yu (2017) also find a link between trade liberalisation and firm employment. They document a phenomenon where reductions in Chinese and foreign final-good tariffs are associated with job destruction in low-productivity firms and job creation in high-productivity firms. In contrast, the net effect of reductions in Chinese input tariffs is limited to job destruction in low-productivity ordinary exporters.

Moreover, Loren et al. (2017) observe the effects of the trade liberalisation that accompanied China's WTO accession on the evolution of markups and productivity of Chinese manufacturing firms. They show that cuts in output tariffs reduce markups but raise productivity, while cuts in input tariffs raise both markups and productivity. They highlight several mechanisms operating in liberalised sectors that help explain our findings in the Chinese context. Liberalised sectors saw an increase in the exit of private firms and more frequent replacement of management in badly performing state-owned firms. Lim, Trefler, and Yu (2019) use both econometrics and a calibrated structural model to disentangle the mechanisms via which trade affects innovation, focusing on scale effects (impact on market size) and competition effects (impact on markups). They find that both scale and competition effects are important for understanding how trade affects innovation in China. In particular, scale effects of trade on innovation are positive in the aggregate, whereas competition effects are negative. However, when firms can innovate to escape competition, greater competition induced by lower trade barriers can lead firms to increase innovation rather than reduce it.

In addition to trade liberalisation and reductions in import tariffs, Chinese firms also experienced export trade liberalisation, which has greatly expanded the international market faced by Chinese firms. Khandelwal, Schott, and Wei (2013) examine Chinese textile and clothing exports before and after the elimination of externally imposed export quotas. Both the surge in export volume and the decline in export prices following quota removal are driven by net entry.

This outcome is inconsistent with a model in which quotas are allocated based on firm productivity, implying the misallocation of resources. Removing this misallocation accounts for a substantial share of the overall gain in productivity associated with quota removal. Feng, Li, and Swenson (2017) study how a reduction in trade policy uncertainty affects firm export decisions. Using a firm-product level dataset on Chinese exports to the US and the European Union in the years surrounding China's WTO accession, they provide strong evidence that the reduction in trade policy uncertainty simultaneously induced firm entries to and exits from export activity within fine product-level markets. In addition, they uncover accompanying changes in export product prices and quality that coincided with this reallocation: firms that provided higher quality products at lower prices entered the export market, while firms that provided lower quality products at higher prices prior to the changes exited. To explain the simultaneous export entries and exits, as well as the fact that new entrants are more productive than exiters, they provide a model of heterogeneous firms that incorporates trade policy uncertainty, tracing the effects of the changes in policy uncertainty on firm-level payoffs and the resulting selection effects.

Despite the substantial reduction in tariff rates, recent literature notices a new aspect – non-tariff measures (NTMs) – that is gaining more importance than ever before, sometimes hampering the flow of international trade. NTMs are defined as 'policy measures, other than ordinary customs tariffs, that can potentially have an economic effect on international trade in goods, changing quality traded, or prices or both' (United Nations Conference on Trade and Development [UNCTAD], 2013). Ing, Li, and Yu (2019) have identified and collected all currently enforced NTMs in China, and provide a brief overview of the diverse types of NTMs that exist in China based on national laws and regulations.

4 Deeper opening up against financial crisis

The global financial crisis has had far-reaching repercussions on cross-border economic activity. After a sharp and sudden collapse in international trade in the last quarter of 2008, world trade flows declined by about 12% in 2009 according to the WTO (Chor and Manova, 2012). This exceeded the estimated loss of 5.4% of world gross domestic product during the same period. The contraction in exports was especially acute for small open economies, several of whom saw their trade volumes in the second half of 2008 fall by up to 30% year-on-year.

This trade decline contributed to the spread of recessionary pressures to countries which had little direct exposure to the US subprime mortgage market where the crisis originated. By exploiting the variation in the cost of capital across countries and over time, as well as the variation in financial vulnerability across sectors, Chor and Manova (2012) show that credit conditions were an important channel through which the crisis affected trade volumes. They notice that countries with higher interbank rates and thus tighter credit markets exported less to the US at the peak of the crisis. This effect was especially pronounced in sectors that require extensive external financing, have limited access to trade credit, or have few collateralisable assets. Exports of financially vulnerable industries were thus more sensitive to the cost of external capital than exports of less vulnerable industries, and this sensitivity rose during the financial crisis.

In the context of China, credit constraints faced by exporters played a significant role in the fall in exports. Manova, Wei, and Zhang (2015) use China's customs data to provide firm-level evidence that credit constraints restrict international trade and affect the pattern of multinational activity. They show that foreign affiliates and joint ventures in China have better export performance than private domestic firms in sectors that are more financially vulnerable. These results are stronger for destinations with higher trade costs, and are not driven by firm size or other sector characteristics. These findings are consistent with multinational subsidiaries being less constrained by liquidity because they can access foreign capital markets or funding from their parent company.

Feenstra, Li, and Yu (2014) examine why credit constraints for domestic and exporting firms arise in a setting where banks do not observe firms' productivities. To maintain incentive compatibility, banks lend below the amount that firms need for optimal production. The longer time needed for export shipments induces a tighter credit constraint on exporters than on purely domestic firms. Using Chinese firm-level data, they find that the credit constraint becomes more stringent as a firm's export share grows, as the time to ship for exports is lengthened, and as there is greater dispersion of firms' productivities, reflecting more incomplete information.

Accompanied by the export pressure caused by the global financial crisis, the increase in China's labour cost and appreciation of the renminbi also eroded China's export competitiveness significantly, especially in labour-intensive industries. We focus on three main solutions to expand trade volume. The first of these is to increase the firm's R&D. Dai, Yu, and Zhao (2018) find that competition plays an important role in providing incentives for firm innovation. They use the appreciation of the renminbi exchange rate during 2005–07 as a natural experiment and exploit its differential impact on Chinese manufacturing firms with different export exposures. The appreciation reduced exports and imposed greater competitive pressure on exporters relative to non-exporters. In response, exporters increased innovation activities more than did non-exporters. Using a difference-in-difference approach, they find that the R&D expenditure of exporters increased by 11% more than that of non-exporters during the appreciation period, and the new product development of exporters increased by nearly 1.5 times more than that of non-exporters.

The second solution is to upgrade the quality of exported goods. First, it is necessary to examine how Chinese manufacturers' export quality has evolved since 2000. Yu and Zhang (2017) developed a new method to estimate export quality and avoid pitfalls in the literature. Using China's manufacturing firm data and customs data from 2000 to 2006, they estimate firm-product-destination-year level export quality and find that the overall export quality of Chinese manufacturers has increased by 15%. The quality gap between foreign and domestic firms has narrowed, with domestic firms exhibiting quality convergence.

Table 3.1 Quality Distribution, China 2000–13

Year	*Mean*	*Median*	*75th Percentile*	*25th Percentile*
2000	1.217	1.072	1.677	0.550
2001	1.242	1.111	1.714	0.579
2002	1.242	1.105	1.704	0.588
2003	1.247	1.111	1.724	0.587
2004	1.293	1.151	1.772	0.621
2005	1.335	1.191	1.817	0.664
2006	1.383	1.232	1.882	0.684
2007	1.371	1.210	1.881	0.650
2008	1.444	1.267	1.968	0.689
2009	1.449	1.275	2.007	0.666
2010	1.470	1.297	2.038	0.689
2011	1.493	1.303	2.063	0.684
2012	1.558	1.351	2.184	0.687
2013	1.588	1.360	2.218	0.702

Source: Ing, Yu, and Zhang (2018).

Export quality increases for most industries are higher in high-income destinations and are negatively associated with both export and import tariffs. Surviving varieties contribute to most of the aggregate export quality upgrading, while low-quality existing varieties facilitate the aggregate export quality upgrading. Ing, Yu, and Zhang (2018) estimated micro-level firm-product-destination-year export quality for China (2000–13).

As shown in Table 3.1, from 2000 to 2013, the quality of Chinese exports increased by 30%. Their findings show that a firm will produce and export a higher quality product to a place with higher consumer preferences when the relative cost of shipping is higher than the unit production costs. They also show that better quality goods are more likely to be sold to high-income destinations. When they decompose the aggregate weighted-average export quality into the intensive and extensive margins, they find that the intensive margin plays a major role in Indonesia's exports, while the extensive margin plays a major role in China's exports. Cui and Yu (2018) studied the effect of the exchange rate on the domestic value-added ratios of processing exports via two channels: substitution and markup. First, home currency depreciation leads to an increase in domestic value-added ratios by affecting each firm's imported and domestic intermediate inputs (the substitution channel). Second, home currency depreciation improves exporters' profitability and results in higher domestic value-added ratios of processing firms (the markup channel), as exports become more competitive with depreciation. Using Chinese firm-level production data and product-level trade transaction data, they find that processing firms' domestic value-added ratios increase significantly through the two channels in response to firm-level nominal effective exchange rate depreciation. The markup channel contributes almost 39% of the variation in domestic value-added ratios in response to changes in the exchange rate.

The third solution is to increase outward foreign direct investment (FDI). Since 2010, the sharp increase in outward FDI from developing countries has been phenomenal, and this is especially true for China. The UNCTAD World Investment Report (UNCTAD, 2015) shows that outward FDI flows from developing economies have already accounted for more than 33% of overall FDI flows, up from 13% in 2007. Furthermore, despite the fact that global FDI flows plummeted by 16% in 2014, multinational corporations (MNCs) from developing economies invested almost $468 billion abroad in 2014, an increase of 23% over the previous year. As the largest developing country in the world, China has seen an astonishing increase in its outward FDI flows. In 2015, China's outward FDI reached the level of 9.9% of the world's total FDI flows, making China the second largest home country of FDI outflows globally. In addition, manufacturing outward FDI from China is becoming more important in China's total outward FDI flows, having increased from 9.9% in 2012 to 18.3% in 2016.

Chen, Tian, and Yu (2019) examine how domestic distortions affect firms' production strategies abroad by documenting two puzzling findings using Chinese firm-level data from manufacturing firms. First, private MNCs are less productive than state-owned MNCs, but more productive than state-owned enterprises overall. Second, there are disproportionately fewer state-owned MNCs than private MNCs. They also built a model to rationalise these findings by showing that domestic discrimination against private firms incentivises them to produce abroad. The model shows that selection reversal is more pronounced in industries with more severe discrimination against private firms, a theory that receives empirical support. Liu et al. (2017) use unique data on Chinese manufacturing firms over the sample period 2002–08. They find that MNCs are generally more productive after they conduct outward FDI, but this productivity effect varies depending on the parent firm and investment strategy heterogeneity. Their results suggest that MNCs without state ownership but with stronger absorptive capability gain higher and more sustainable productivity effects, and such gains are higher for MNCs investing in countries in the Organisation for Economic Co-operation and Development than elsewhere.

5 All-around opening up and trade globalisation

Since the 2008 global financial crisis, there has been a new wave of trade protectionism headed by the US, casting a shadow on the world economy. The current situation arises from the stagnation of the Doha negotiations, the failure of the Transatlantic Trade and Investment Partnership, negotiations among Western countries, the Brexit negotiations, the Trump regime's abolition of the Trans-Pacific Partnership, renegotiation of the North American Free Trade Agreement, and the recent trade war between the US and China, which has resulted in a tremendous shock to world markets. Widespread protectionism could lower global output, making worldwide economic recovery difficult.

One the one hand, Trump's trade war will have a huge impact on the world economy. Guo et al. (2018) used Eaton and Kortum's 2002 multi-sector, multi-country general equilibrium model with inter-sectional linkages to forecast how exports, imports, output, and real wages would change if Trump's threat of 45% tariffs is carried out. To consider plausible scenarios, they evaluate the case of unilateral action on the part of the US, as well as a scenario where China retaliates by imposing an equally high 45% tariff on its imports from the US. In all of the scenarios, the calibration exercise suggests that a trade war triggered by high US import tariffs will lead to a collapse in US–China bilateral trade. In all of the scenarios, the US will experience large social welfare losses, while China may lose or gain slightly depending on the effect of the trade war on the US–China trade balance. Globally, some small open economies may experience small benefits, while other countries may suffer collateral damage.

On the other hand, China has implemented multiple methods to minimise the impact of Trump's trade war and to continue to open up to the outside world. The first of these is the construction of free trade ports. By definition, a free trade port is a port area within the territory of a country or region that is not subject to the usual customs control, with free access to overseas goods and funds. The main feature of a free trade port is that it is outside the control of the customs authority of a country. It has the features of a port and a free trade zone, with many trade-related functions, including product processing, logistics, and warehousing.

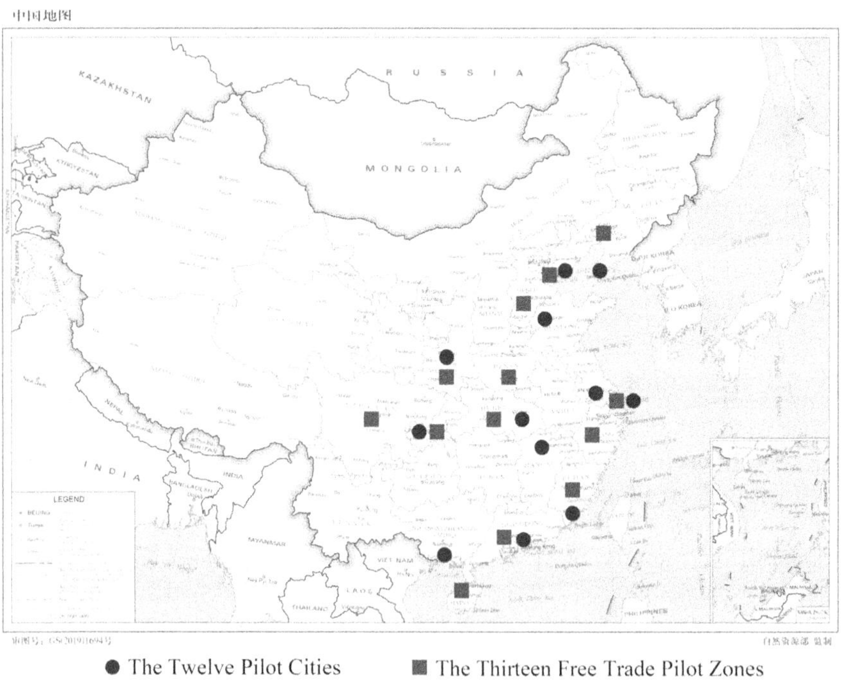

Figure 3.3 Map of the Free Trade Pilot Zones and Pilot Cities.
Source: authors.

Geographically, a free trade port is part of the territory of a country, but from the perspective of administrative supervision, it is outside the customs jurisdiction of the country. As shown in Figure 3.3, there are 13 free trade pilot zones and twelve pilot cities in China. Tian et al. (2018) suggested three areas to promote the development of free trade ports. First, it is necessary to improve convenience for businesses engaging in trade in the ports. Second, the ports must take steps to improve the fluidity of personnel as well as their ability to attract talent. Finally, the process of improving the ports' financial systems presents an opportunity to deepen financial reform and improve market openness. Moreover, the government should establish a financial leasing system, so that it can provide sufficient capital support for all businesses in ports and encourage more international companies to establish headquarters in the free trade ports.

The second method is the One Belt, One Road initiative (BRI). The BRI, which was initiated by the Chinese government in 2013, is devoted to improving regional cooperation and connectivity on a transcontinental scale. The initiative aims to strengthen infrastructure, trade, and investment links between China and the other BRI countries. Currently, 64 countries are actively involved in the BRI. These include 10 Association of Southeast Asian Nations countries, 18 countries in Western Asia, 8 in South Asia, 5 in Central Asia, 7 in the Commonwealth of Independent States, and 16 in Central and Eastern Europe. Yu (2018a) found

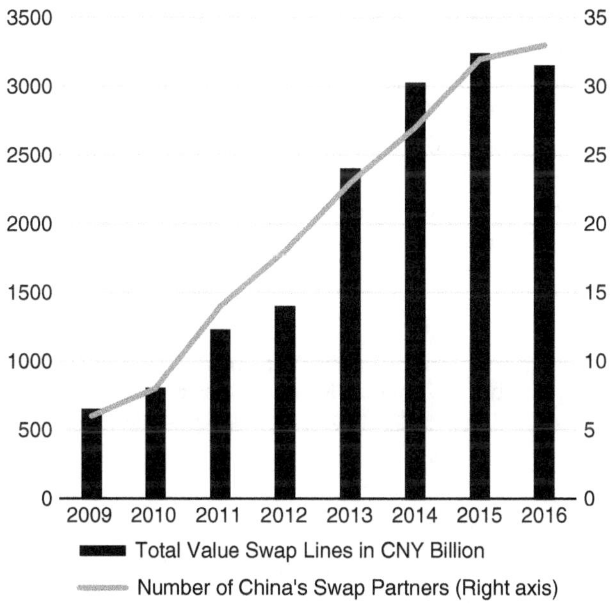

Figure 3.4 China's Bilateral Swap Values and Numbers.
Source: People's Bank of China.
Note: Data of swaps are from the People's Bank of China (2016). This graph does not include swaps under the Chiang Mai Initiative.

that if China chooses to import more intermediate goods from the European Union and Association of Southeast Asian Nations countries, or countries alongside the BRI instead, the price of the intermediate goods would be more competitive, and the Chinese people can also access cheaper finished goods.

The third method is the internationalisation of the renminbi. Since around 2005, the Government of China has pursued a variety of initiatives designed to encourage wider use of the renminbi. As shown in Figure 3.4, these efforts sped up after the global financial crisis in 2008 and have made great progress since 2009. This progress peaked in 2015 and has slowed in some aspects since 2016. The progress of renminbi internationalisation can be categorised into four fields: renminbi trade settlement, renminbi-denominated investment, renminbi bond issuance, and renminbi currency swaps and direct trading (Eichengreen and Kawai, 2014). Zhang et al. (2018) found a significant positive effect of swap agreements on trade. In their benchmark model, the negotiations of the swap agreement would improve 30.4% of bilateral trade values between China and its partners. For BRI countries, the effect is even stronger. This effect is both statistically and economically significant. They believe that renminbi swap agreements support economic integration between China and BRI countries by facilitating bilateral trade.

The fourth method is the construction of the Pearl River Greater Bay Area (GBA). If the BRI and Regional Comprehensive Economic Partnership constructions are treated as the key content of the new pattern of all-around opening up, the Guangdong–Hong Kong–Macau GBA indeed is an important domestic carrier of the BRI. Thus, the construction of the Guangdong–Hong Kong–Macau GBA is the most urgent task of China's opening up. Yu (2018b) suggests that the development of the GBA should focus on the following perspectives. First, it is essential for the GBA to focus on manufacturing industries rather than services industries only. Second, the construction of the GBA should focus on innovation. The third objective is to achieve institutional innovation. Fourth, the GBA should pay more attention to its ecological environment.

Note

1 According to the Chinese statistical yearbook (2008), the dependent rate of China in 2007 was only 0.4. This number was not only lower than the average dependent rate in east Asia, but also one of the lowest dependent rates all over the world (Yao and Yu, 2009).

References

Amiti, M. and J. Konings (2007), 'Trade Liberalization, Intermediate Inputs, and Productivity: Evidence from Indonesia', *American Economic Review*, 97(5), pp.1611–1638.

Chen, B., M. Yu, and Z. Yu (2017), 'Measured Skill Premia and Trade Liberalization: Evidence from Chinese Firms', *Journal of International Economics*, 109, pp.31–42.

Chen, C., W. Tian, and M. Yu (2019), 'Outward FDI and Domestic Input Distortions: Evidence from Chinese Firms', *The Economic Journal*, 129(624), pp.3025–3057.

Chor, D. and K. Manova (2012), 'Off the Cliff and Back: Credit Conditions and International Trade During the Global Financial Crisis', *Journal of International Economics*, 87(2012), pp.117–133.

Cui, X. and M. Yu (2018), 'Exchange Rate and Domestic Value Added in Processing Exports: Evidence from Chinese Firms', *China Center for Economic Research Working Paper*, 2018.

Dai, M. and M. Yu (2013), 'Firm R&D, Absorptive Capacity, and Learning by Exporting: Firm-Level Evidence from China', *The World Economy*, 2013, pp.1131–1145.

Dai, M., M. Maitra, and M. Yu (2016), 'Unexceptional Exporter Performance in China? Role of Processing Trade', *Journal of Development Economics*, 2016, 121, pp.177–189.

Dai, M., M. Yu, and C. Zhao (2018), 'Export Tightening, Competition and Firm Innovation: Evidence from the Renminbi Appreciation', *Review of Development Economics*, 22(1), pp.263–286.

Eichengreen, B. and D. Leblang (2008), 'Democracy and Globalization', *Economics and Politics*, 20(3), pp.289–334.

Eichengreen, B. and M. Kawai (2014), 'Issues for Renminbi Internationalization: An Overview', *Asian Development Bank Institute Working Paper Series*, No. 454. https://papers.ssrn.com/sol3/papers.cfm?abstract_id=2382420 (accessed 4 Sept. 2019).

Feenstra, R., Z. Li, and M. Yu (2014), 'Exports and Credit Constraints Under Incomplete Information: Theory and Application to China', *Review of Economics and Statistics*, 96(4), pp.729–744.

Feng, L., Z. Li, and D.L. Swenson (2017), 'Trade Policy Uncertainty and Exports: Evidence from China's WTO Accession', *Journal of International Economics*, 106, pp.20–36.

Giavazzi, F. and G. Tabellini (2005), 'Economic and Political Liberalization', *Journal of Monetary Economics*, 52, pp.1297–1340.

Goldberg, P., A. Khandelwal, N. Pavcnik, and P. Topalova (2010), 'Imported Intermediate Inputs and Domestic Product Growth: Evidence from India', *Quarterly Journal of Economics*, 125(4), pp.1727–1767.

Guo, M., L. Lu, L. Sheng, and M. Yu (2018), 'The Day After Tomorrow: Evaluating the Burden of Trump's Trade War', *Asian Economic Papers*, 17(1), pp.101–120.

Ing, L.Y., M. Yu, and R. Zhang (2018), 'The Evolution of Export Quality: China and Indonesia', in L.Y. Ing and M. Yu (eds.) *World Trade Evolution*. Abingdon; New York, NY: Routledge, pp.261–302.

Ing, L.Y., M. Li, and M. Yu (2019), 'Non-Tariff Measure in China', Working paper.

Khandelwal, A.K., P.K. Schott, and S.J. Wei (2013), 'Trade Liberalization and Embedded Institutional Reform: Evidence from Chinese Exporters', *American Economic Review*, 103(6), pp.2169–2195.

Khandelwal, A. (2010), 'The Long and Short Quality Ladders', *Review of Economic Studies*, 77, pp.1450–1476.

Loren, B., J. Van Biesebroeck, L. Wang, and Y. Zhang (2017), 'WTO Accession and Performance of Chinese Manufacturing Firms', *American Economic Review*, 107(9), pp.2784–2820.

Lim, K., D. Trefler, and M. Yu (2019), 'Trade and Innovation: The Role of Scale and Competition', *University of Toronto Working Paper.*

Lin, J.Y. and M. Yu (2015), 'Industrial Structural Upgrading and Poverty Reduction in China', in A. Szirmai (ed.) *Structural Change and Industrial Development in the BRICS.* Oxford, UK: Oxford University Press, pp.93–118.

Liu, X., L. Li, M. Yu, and D. Yuan (2017), 'Does Outward FDI Generate Higher Productivity for Emerging Economy MNEs? Micro-Level Evidence from Chinese Manufacturing Firms', *International Business Review*, 2017(26), pp.839–854.

Ma, Y., H. Tang, and Y. Zhang (2014), 'Factor Intensity, Product Switching, and Productivity: Evidence from Chinese Exporters', *Journal of International Economics*, 92(2), pp.349–362.

Manova, K., S.J. Wei, and Z. Zhang (2015), 'Firm Exports and Multinational Activity Under Credit Constraints', *Review of Economics and Statistics*, 97(3), pp.574–588.

Melitz, M.J. (2003), 'The Impact of Trade on Intra-Industry Reallocations and Aggregate Industry Productivity', *Econometrica*, 71(6), pp.1695–1725.

Mincer, J. (1974), 'Schooling, Experience, and Earnings', *Human Behavior and Social Institutions*, 2.

Olley, S. and A. Pakes (1996), 'The Dynamics of Productivity in the Telecommunications Equipment Industry', *Econometrica*, 64(6), pp.1263–1297.

Rodriguez-Lopez, A. and M. Yu (2017), 'All-Around Trade Liberation and Firm Employment: Theory and Evidence from China', *University of California, Irvine Working Paper.*

Tian, W., I.Y. Yao, M. Yu, and Y. Zhou (2013), 'Structure of Population and International Trade', *Jingjiyanjiu*, 2013(11), pp.87–99.

Tian, W. and M. Yu (2015), 'Processing Trade, Export Intensity, and Input Trade Liberalization: Evidence from Chinese Firms', *Journal of Asia-Pacific Economy*, 20(3), pp.444–464.

Tian, W. and M. Yu (2017), 'Firm R&D, Processing Trade and Input Trade Liberalisation: Evidence from Chinese Firms', *The World Economy*, 40(2), pp.297–313.

Tian, W., Z. Xu, M. Yu, and H. Zhu (2018), 'China's Free Trade Ports: Effective Actions Against the Threat of De-Globalization', *China and the World Economy*, 26(4), pp.62–81.

Topalova, P. and A. Khandelwal (2011), 'Trade Liberalization and Firm Productivity: The Case of India', *Review of Economics and Statistics*, 93(3), pp.995–1009.

UNCTAD. (2015). World Investment Report 2015. https://unctad.org/webflyer/world-investment-report-2015.

United Nations Conference on Trade and Development (2013), *Classification of Non-Tariff Measures, February 2012 Version.* Geneva: United Nations Conference on Trade and Development.

Wong, K.-F. and M. Yu (2015), 'Democracy and the GATT/WTO Accession Duration', *Review of Development Economics*, 19(4), pp.843–859.

Yao, Y. and M. Yu (2009), 'Labor Force, Population and Chinese Export-Oriented Growth Pattern', *Jinrongyanjiu*, 2009(9), pp.1–13.

Yu, M. (2010a), 'Trade, Democracy, and the Gravity Equation', *Journal of Development Economics*, 91(2), pp.289–300.

Yu, M. (2010b), 'Trade Liberalization and the Productivity of Manufacturing Firms', *Jingjiyanjiu*, 2010(12), pp.97–110.

Yu, M., G. Ye, and B. Qu (2013), 'Trade Liberalization, Product Complexity, and Productivity Improvement: Evidence from Chinese Firms', *The World Economy*, 36(7), pp.913–934.

Yu, M. and L. Jin (2014), 'Import, Firm Productivity, and Product Complexity', *Japanese Economic Review*, 65(2), pp.178–192 .

Yu, M. (2015), 'Processing Trade, Tariff Reductions, and Firm Productivity: Evidence from Chinese Firms', *Economic Journal*, 125(585), pp.943–988.

Yu, M. and L. Jin (2015), 'Imports, Heterogeneous Industry and Improvement of Firm Productivity', *Jinjiyanjiu*, 2015(8), pp.85–97.

Yu, M. and D. Yuan (2016), 'Trade Liberalization, Processing Trade and Markup', *Guanlishijie*, 2016(9), pp.33–43.

Yu, M. and L. Li (2016), 'Trade Liberalization and Quality Upgrading of Intermediate Inputs: Evidence from Chinese Customs Data', *China Economic Quarterly*, 2016(3), pp.1011–1029.

Yu, M. and K. Zhi (2016), 'Import Liberalization and Firm Profitability', *Jingjiyanjiu*, 2016(8), pp.57–71.

Yu, M, and R. Zhang (2017). 'Estimating China's manufacturing export quality: pitfalls and remedy', *China Economic Quarterly*, 1, pp.463–484.

Yu, M. (2018a), 'Expanding Opening Up: China's Olive Branch to Globalization', *China Economic Transition*, 1(3), pp.66–75.

Yu, M. (2018b), 'China's International Trade Development and Opening-up Policy Design', *China Economic Journal*, 11(3), pp.301–318.

Zhang, F., M. Yu, J. Yu, and Y. Jin (2018), 'The Effect of RMB Internationalization on Belt and Road Initiative', *Emerging Markets Finance & Trade*, 53(12), pp.2845–2857.

4 The economic impact of globalisation in Indonesia

Kiki Verico and Mari Elka Pangestu

1 Background

Trade and foreign direct investment (FDI) are essential instruments for economic growth. Theoretically, the combination of the Solow growth model, Cobb–Douglas production function, and Harrod–Domar model show that trade and investment are the primary sources of economic growth. Trade allows all countries to consume cheaper goods and services from other countries based on their comparative advantage. FDI promotes technological transfer as well as human capital and institutional improvement from developed to developing countries. Developing countries typically face a savings–investment gap, whereas FDI inflows allow them to receive technological transfer from developed countries. This transfer stimulates both human capital and institutional improvement in developing countries.[1]

As trade and investment are the major sources of economic growth, Indonesia must remain on track by continuing the process of globalisation and openness. The openness experienced by Indonesia, particularly in the 1990s, has benefited its development in the last few decades. Globalisation and an open economy create economic benefits in the form of economic growth and welfare. However, economic globalisation entails costs, as trade increases competition for domestic producers and workers. Globalisation creates trade with other countries, but implies loss for non-competitive domestic producers because their products have to compete with imported products.

Trade liberalisation at bilateral, regional, and multilateral fora increases trade creation with the countries involved in the agreements (Viner, 1950; Verico, 2017; Mattoo, Mulabdic, and Ruta, 2019). Trade creation allows Indonesia to export its products to other countries, but increases import products from other countries. Increasing imports is immediate and classified as the cost of liberalisation. Increasing exports requires supply-side improvement, which takes longer than increasing imports from the demand side.

Stiglitz (2007) showed that globalisation creates costs in the short run and benefits in the medium to long run. Nevertheless, the short-run cost is always less than the long-run benefit, and several empirical studies have supported this statement.[2]

DOI: 10.4324/9781003138501-4

Economic theory and empirical results have shown that globalisation yields positive net benefits, but policymakers have to mitigate the short-run costs. The biggest challenge for Indonesia in continuing its globalisation process is finding the balance between the long-run net benefits of globalisation and managing the adverse effects in the short run. In a democratic Indonesia, this has political implications. Thus, like many other countries, Indonesia has to balance the political economy of the long-term benefits of globalisation and the short-term negative impact of the continued globalisation.

This paper has two primary objectives: firstly, to understand the globalisation trends in Indonesia – both in trade and investment liberalisation – over the last four decades, from the period before the reform era until now. Section 3 discusses the factors behind Indonesia's process of globalisation. An understanding of these underlying factors is essential to see how Indonesia needs to deal with globalisation factors in the short term to bring it to the next stage of development and structural transformation. Section 4 provides an overview of Indonesia's recent trade policy and globalisation, followed by a description of the underlying phenomenon in the different periods of globalisation. It also details the government's trade and investment policies, including forms of protection.

The second objective is to understand the impact of globalisation on Indonesia's economy in order to provide the longer-term case for economic globalisation. Section 5 focuses on the impacts of trade liberalisation on growth, productivity, labour, poverty, inequality, small and medium-sized enterprises (SMEs), and tourism. Section 6 focuses on the impact of investment liberalisation on economic growth, technological transfer, and progress. The last section provides conclusions and policy recommendations.

2 Trends of globalisation in Indonesia

2.1 Trade liberalisation in Indonesia

The legal basis of the international trade and investment regime was established through international commitments and domestic laws and regulations. Indonesia was a member of the General Agreement on Tariffs and Trade (GATT) from 24 February 1950, and participated in the Uruguay Round of multilateral trade negotiations, which saw the creation of the World Trade Organization (WTO) in 1995. It also ratified WTO commitments in its national legislation in 1994, including laws related to the use of trade remedies and the setting up of the necessary institutions.

In addition to the WTO, Indonesia was a founding member of the Asia-Pacific Economic Cooperation (APEC), and the host of the 1994 APEC meeting which created the Bogor Goals for free trade and investment flows in the Asia-Pacific region no later than 2010 for developed economies and 2020 for developing economies. Indonesia announced a number of critical reforms, especially removing restrictions on foreign investment, such as allowing 100% foreign ownership and linking it to export orientation. The APEC principles support the elimination of trade restrictions, voluntary liberalisation, and non-exclusive regionalism; and have provided benefits for member economies (Seng et al., 2002). The Bogor Goals were the forerunner of the proposed Free Trade Area of the Asia Pacific.

Indonesia experienced several periods of liberalisation as part of its globalisation process to integrate with the world economy. The beginning of the New Order[3] brought a series of reforms such as FDI liberalisation, the removal of foreign exchange restrictions, and tariff rationalisation. In subsequent years and during the oil boom years, the import substitution industrialisation strategy resulted in high tariffs, quantitative restrictions, and high effective rates of protection (ERP). However, the decline in oil prices in the mid-1980s and the need to reduce dependence on oil affected some bold deregulatory policies in Indonesia. Notably, the 6 May Policy Package issued in 1986 abolished many tariff levels; and corrupt customs were replaced by SGS, a Swiss surveyor company. In 2007, the foreign and domestic investment law was merged and managed by the Indonesian Investment Coordinating Board (BKPM) and showed much improvement.

Empirically, based on the World Bank's World Development Indicators, Indonesia's tariff rates (applied and most favoured nation) declined from an average of 15% in the 1990s to an average of 2% of applied and 6% of most favoured nation weighted tariffs in 2018 (World Bank, 2019).

In 1992, Indonesia agreed to the Association of Southeast Asian Nations (ASEAN) Free Trade Area (AFTA), which set intra-ASEAN tariff rates at zero. The AFTA involved two stages of implementation: the Common Effective Preferential Tariff for the ASEAN Six (Brunei Darussalam, Indonesia, Malaysia, the Philippines, Singapore, and Thailand) in 2010; and its extension to the remaining ASEAN Four (Cambodia, the Lao People's Democratic Republic, Myanmar, and Vietnam) in 2015.[4] Since then, Indonesia has applied a 0% tariff for all ASEAN members (Common Effective Preferential Tariff).

In 1995, Indonesia committed to implementing tariff deregulation, which was followed by a series of reforms due to commitments under the WTO. Indonesia complied with its WTO commitments in terms of import tariffs not exceeding its bound tariffs. It also fulfilled several other commitments, such as eliminating local content regulations. Studies have shown that global economic liberalisation in trade and investment contributed to a positive and significant effect on the economic growth of the member states of the WTO (Ying, Chang, and Lee, 2014).

In terms of regional cooperation, Indonesia is one of ASEAN's founding members. It is very active in the deepening and widening of ASEAN economic integration, starting with AFTA in 1992 and the broader and deeper ASEAN Economic Community in 2003. Indonesia was also active in the formation of the ASEAN Economic Community Blueprint in 2006 and the development of free trade agreements (FTAs) between ASEAN and China; the Republic of Korea (henceforth, Korea); Japan; Australia and New Zealand; and India. ASEAN is like 'battleground training' for Indonesia before facing global trade competition.

Indonesia only has two major bilateral agreements: (i) the Indonesia–Japan Economic Partnership Agreement, completed and signed in 2006; and (ii) the Indonesia–Pakistan Preferential Trade Agreement, signed and in effect since September 2013. Several bilateral trade negotiations with major partners such as the European Union, Korea, Australia, and Chile, were started around 2008–09 but stopped due to the global financial crisis and the retreat from the openness that occurred from 2012.

Besides tariff reductions, non-tariff measures (NTMs) were deregulated, and the number of items covered by such barriers fell by 15 percentage points from 31% to around 16% (Wymenga, 1991). Indonesia's liberalisation of trade and investment policies was basically shaped by various rounds of international agreements of which Indonesia was a participant or chair, leading to a further series of unilateral liberalisations in Indonesia.[5]

The most obvious example was Indonesia's 'Timor' national car, where a joint venture with Kia and President Suharto's son was given the privilege of duty-free imports of 'completely knocked down' vehicles. This was in contrast to the conditions for existing automotive companies, which could only import 'knocked down' cars and assemble them in Indonesia with relatively high tariffs. Japan, supported by the United States (US) and the European Union, brought this case to the WTO's dispute settlement mechanism. It was one of the first cases to be brought to the mechanism and the first for Indonesia. Indonesia lost the case because the policy violated the most fundamental principle in the GATT/WTO – non-discrimination.

Another phenomenon that affects the liberalisation and reform of countries such as Indonesia is 'competitive liberalisation,' where countries open up trade and investment as their competitor countries liberalise their markets (the Nash equilibrium or reciprocal action). In general, this took place during the 1990s in East Asia, as countries undertook liberalisation and reforms to attract FDI and diversify their sources of growth.[6] Concerted unilateral liberalisation was also part of the spirit of APEC, undertaken under agreed non-binding principles and examples of other countries, as showcased by the regular announcements of individual action plans.

Another impact of competitive liberalisation is competitive trade pacts, leading to a snowball effect. The Trans-Pacific Partnership (TPP) was launched in 2006 with the original four small countries (Brunei Darussalam, Chile, New Zealand, and Singapore). In the beginning, it was named the Trans-Pacific Strategic Economic Partnership Agreement (TPSEP). In 2008, Australia, Peru, and Vietnam joined as non-members and associate members of the TPSEP. The TPSEP got a boost in 2010 when the US, along with Malaysia, joined and tried to entice larger countries to join, and the name was changed to the TPP. The TPP gained much ground when Canada and Mexico joined in 2012, and most importantly, Japan joined in 2013, and with US leadership, the negotiations were completed in 2015 and signed by all 12 members in early 2016. Vietnam is a member of the TPP and has been on the record as using the TPP to shape its domestic reforms. Under pressure from its exporters, which would be at a competitive disadvantage in the US market and could face trade diversion, Indonesia announced its intention to join the TPP in 2015. Since the US withdrew from the TPP in January 2017, the TPP changed to 11 members and is known as the TPP11 or the Comprehensive and Progressive Agreement for Trans-Pacific Partnership (CPTPP).

Meanwhile, with Indonesia as chair, ASEAN launched the Regional Comprehensive Economic Partnership (RCEP) in 2011 to consolidate the ASEAN Plus One FTAs with China, Japan, Korea, Australia and New Zealand, and India. The RCEP is much more significant in terms of population but similar in size to the TPP in terms of gross domestic product (GDP) and trade. Negotiations started in 2012 and are ongoing, although the completion of the TPP and the CPTPP, as well as global uncertainties, heightened the importance of completing negotiations in 2019. Six of the 11 countries (Australia, Canada, Japan, Mexico, New Zealand, and Singapore) ratified the agreement on 30 December 2018, followed by Vietnam in January 2019, and the CPTPP agreements came into force in these countries. The RCEP agreement is to be signed in 2020, according to the commitment made at the ASEAN Summit on 2 November 2019, but will not include India, which decided not to move forward.

Warr (1992) argued that Indonesia's competitiveness remains stagnant because the reduction in tariff and import restrictions had only liberalised Indonesia's economy, without serious efforts to improve the competitiveness of its domestic supply. Permani (2011) supported this finding that Indonesia took more in terms of tariff protection (demand side) and showed little effort to boost economic growth from the improvement of its supply side.

2.2 Investment liberalisation in Indonesia

Since 1986, Indonesia had waived some of the restrictions on foreign investment. Right after independence and under the 'old order' period of Sukarno, there was massive nationalisation and a very restrictive and nationalistic approach to foreign investment, e.g. Law No. 78/1958 on Foreign Direct Investment. Following the collapse of the economy and under the New Order era of President Suharto, the technocrats in government recognised the need to attract foreign investment to lift Indonesia out of its economic crisis. Thus, they introduced Indonesia's first foreign investment law (Law No. 1/1967), which adopted an open-door policy, as well as a parallel domestic investment law (Law No. 6/1968). Indonesia's investment liberalisation was one of the major reforms under the New Order Government and was intended to attract FDI after the economic crisis under the old order period. Law No. 1/1967 allowed for the first FDI joint ventures, which was followed by waves of foreign investment restrictions during the oil boom years and relaxation during bad times and economic crisis.

The Coordinating Investment Board was also created in 1973 to facilitate investment and become a one-stop shop – a centralised, top–down government approach where the authority to issue related licensing and regulations was given to the officials at the Investment Board. These laws and policies led to a vast increase in FDI in mining, oil and gas, and manufacturing, as well as domestic investments. There was a wave of Japanese investments in the manufacturing sector, notably the electronics and automotive segments.

After some resistance to foreign investment, an amendment and supplement to Law No. 1/1967 on Foreign Direct Investment (Law No. 11/1970) was passed, marking the introduction of restrictions on foreign ownership and divestment. With the objective of increasing investment in the aftermath of the Asian financial crisis, Indonesia reformed its investment regulation in 2007 and the domestic and foreign investment laws were merged under Law No. 25/2007 on Investment of both Foreign and Domestic Direct Investment. The intention was to create greater certainty and introduce the best practices of investment laws such as national treatment, non-discrimination, transparency, a negative list approach, removal of the divestment requirements, and streamlining of investment processes, with an integrated investment system similar to the notion of the one-stop service of the past. The passage of the law and subsequent institutional and regulatory improvements succeeded in increasing FDI inflows to Indonesia around threefold from an annual average of $5.5 billion (2004–2007) to $15.7 billion (2007–2017).

As a result, FDI inflows to Indonesia have turned from negative and slow growth during 1999–2004 (Asian financial crisis period)[7] to positive and increasing growth from 2005 onwards (Figure 4.1). This significant progress began with the implementation of the new investment law in 2007 and a clear signal from the government on its intention to improve the investment climate. From 2015, however, the proportion of FDI to Indonesia's GDP has been declining, suggesting that Indonesia needs further reform to attract more FDI inflows from abroad.

Otsuka, Thomsen, and Goldstein (2011) found that Indonesia had significantly liberalised its investment regulation in 2007 by applying one-stop integrated services (PTSP) to reduce red tape, granting fiscal incentives for investment regardless of a firm's ownership, and establishing transparent procedures for investment. These actions increased FDI inflows to Indonesia, in particular in 2008 and 2010. Nevertheless, the investment climate has been affected by various other issues such as the proliferation of NTMs, rigid labour laws and lack of clarity regarding the minimum wage, and legal uncertainties. A survey of Japanese foreign investment by JETRO (2019) showed that Indonesia has become the most challenging country in terms of NTMs, in particular on import restriction, standards and conformity assessment systems, and local content requirement regulations.

Regarding movement of people, Indonesia sends more people to work overseas than the number of foreign workers it receives from abroad. Data from Bank Indonesia show that 3.51 million Indonesians were working abroad in 2016, increasing to 3.65 million people in 2018. This resulted in remittances of $10 billion in 2016 (10% of the foreign exchange reserve) and $12 billion in 2018 (11% of the foreign exchange reserve).[8] The total value of remittances from foreign workers is $12 billion (2019), highlighting the importance of the

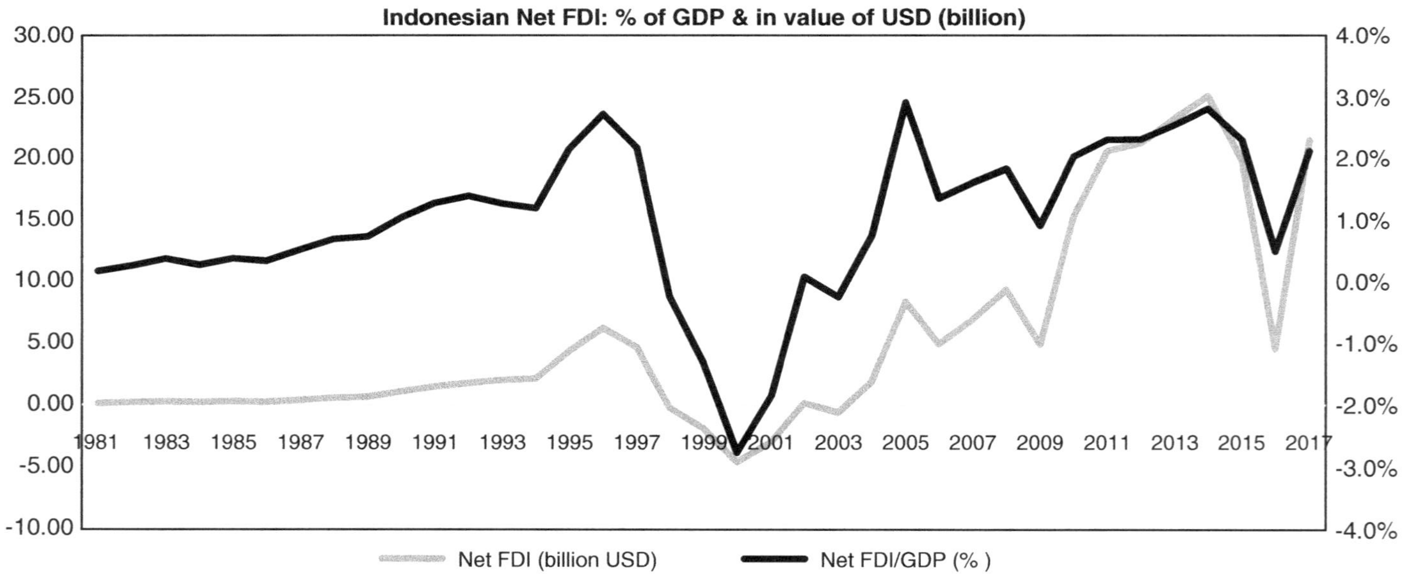

Figure 4.1 FDI Inflows to Indonesia and Net Value, 1981–2017 ($ billion and % of GDP).
Source: World Bank (2019).
Note: FDI = foreign direct investment, GDP = gross domestic product.

contribution of worker remittances to foreign exchange reserves. In comparison, the number of foreign workers in Indonesia decreased from 97,000 in 2016 to 94,000 in 2018. In terms of skills, most of Indonesia's migrant workers are low-skilled domestic workers, while the foreign workers in Indonesia working in foreign companies come from the home country of the FDI. Expatriates in Indonesia are skilled workers who mostly work for foreign companies or international organisations. Indonesia has restrictive policies on foreign workers and talent. A recent estimate showed that foreign immigrants comprise only 0.1% of Indonesia's population – the lowest in the region – compared with 6% in Malaysia, 8% in Thailand, and 45% in Singapore (United Nations Department of Economic and Social Affairs, Population Division, 2015).

3 Factors behind Indonesia's options in globalising its economy

In the context of Indonesia's unilateral economic liberalisation, many political economic analyses point to Sadli's Law: 'bad economic conditions drive good policy and good economic conditions drive bad (*inward looking*) policy.'[9] The different episodes of economic openness are depicted in Figure 4.2. Historically, bad economic conditions during the old order regime and the transition to the new order regime in 1966 led to massive regulatory reform and unilateral economic liberalisation, with a significant positive impact.

During the oil boom years or the Dutch disease period in the 1970s and 1980s, Indonesia had a trade surplus and the real gross national product growth rates were considerably high, at 7.5% in 1978 and 8.6% in 1980 (Juoro, 1993). During this period, Indonesia continued to pursue an import substitution policy to support industrialisation by increasing the tariff rate of final goods more than that of inputs – leading to high levels of effective protection – whereas consumers and producers had to pay a higher price due to the increasing rate of protection.[10] An increased role was given to state-owned enterprises and certain well-connected private sector enterprises linked to the inner circle of the New Order,[11] which received special business privileges, access to financing, and monopoly over the import of strategic goods. By the mid-1980s, more than 200 enterprises were state-owned, many of which were being used for rent-seeking by cronies (Robertson-Snape, 1999). The policy stance was somewhat mixed because some measures were also undertaken to increase non-oil exports, such as subsidies for exports and the relaxation of foreign investment restrictions for the promotion of exports.

The collapse in oil prices in 1986 led to major reforms and deregulation to diversify away from dependence on the oil sector. The government undertook rationalisation of tariffs; a concerted focus to increase exports by removing obstacles to the movement of goods, such as the closure of the corrupt customs department and a substantial improvement in the restitution mechanism to allow duty- and tax-free access to international inputs; and relaxation of restrictions on export-oriented investments. The result was an increase in export-oriented

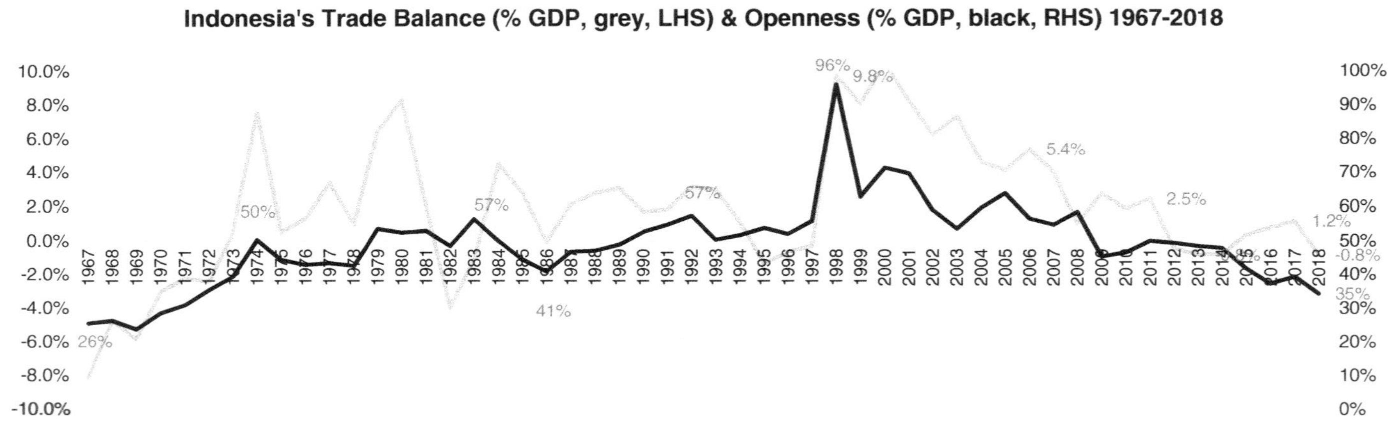

Figure 4.2 Indonesia's Trade Balance and Trade Openness, 1967–2018 ($ billion and (export + import)/GDP (%)).

Source: World Bank (2019).

Note: The grey line indicates trade balance while the black line indicates trade openness (TO). TO is the total of the value of exports and the value of imports per GDP: TO = $\frac{(X_{nt} + M_{nt})}{GDP_{nt}}$; TO is trade openness; X is the value of export; M is the value of import; n is country space; t is the time dimension; and GDP is the value of gross domestic product. A good economy indicates a surplus trade balance while the opposite (a bad economy) indicates a deficit trade balance. Inward-looking policy denotes a closed-door policy while outward-looking policy is an open-door policy.

investments and Indonesia's exports of manufactured goods in labour-intensive products such as garments and footwear, as well as electronics. By the 1990s, Indonesia had reduced its dependence on oil exports from 80% to about 40% of total exports.

The period from 1987 to 1992 was an exception to the Dutch disease phenomenon, when good times still led to outward-oriented policies. The success of the export-oriented industrialisation policy gave Indonesia the confidence to commit to the ASEAN FTA in 1991. It subsequently ratified various WTO commitments into Law No. 7/1994 and relaxed foreign investment restrictions when it was the chair of APEC – providing leadership for free trade and investment. This period is an example of deregulation and reform, even though Indonesia's economy was performing well. It is also an example of reforms that were shaped by international commitments. Despite these reforms, policies were mixed because many preferential policies and import monopolies remained.

It took the Asian financial crisis to remove most of the distortive policies. The crisis forced Indonesia to submit to an International Monetary Fund rescue package, under the fund's supervision. Major reforms were undertaken, such as the scrapping of special preferences for certain state-owned enterprises and business groups, the removal of import concessions, import deregulation, and the removal of various restrictions on foreign investment such as in the retail sector.

Since 2004, reforms have included the passage of the FDI law, simplification of already low tariffs, rationalisation of NTMs, streamlining of regulations, and improvement of customs procedures. The tariff-setting process under the inter-ministerial tariff team was improved, with clear evidence-based policymaking, and a similar attempt was introduced to increase transparency in the setting of NTMs. As part of the commitment to trade facilitation under the ASEAN Single Window, import procedures were simplified and standardised. However, since 2012, we have seen the return of protectionist measures – mainly through the increased use of NTMs, some of which are not consistent with the WTO and which have been taken to the WTO for dispute settlement. The percentage of imports subject to some form of restriction increased from around 20% to 48% (Ministry of Trade, Indonesia, 2018) of tariff lines from 2012 to 2018, even though some of those NTMs are valid for health and safety standards.

4 Indonesia's recent trade policy and globalisation

To reduce the reliance on imported inputs, as 50% of intermediate input and raw material is imported, Indonesia introduced a local content requirement (LCR) policy in the 1980s. However, the discriminative implementation of tariffs on the final product and intermediate input, and the government response to the LCR – without domestic supply-side support – have not led to an increase in local intermediate input production and have been counter-productive to investment flows. The LCR policy keeps Indonesia in the so-called 'hollow middle,'[12] as it is competitive in the production of raw materials and the assembly of manufactured products, but weak in producing intermediate inputs and machinery. The LCR is one type of NTM that Indonesia has implemented, i.e. in the automotive and electronic industries, which had to be eliminated in 1995 upon ratifying the WTO agreements. In recent times, Indonesia has tried to introduce the LCR in several sectors and manners on various occasions, e.g. LCRs for mobile phones in 2012.

As an alternative to implementing the LCR, the government should improve the quality standard of domestic local content and stimulate the local production of intermediate inputs by opening up FDI inflows to the production of intermediate inputs. If domestic producers can create high-quality intermediate input, producers will buy local intermediate inputs. To encourage investment in intermediate products, it is possible to use incentives rather than mandatory requirements. Currently, the shift in policy aims to increase the intermediate product supply from the domestic market, and recognises the need for supply-side supporting policy.

As a result, the ERP for final products has been decreasing (Marks, 2017; Widodo, 2008). The average nominal tariff fell during 1995–2008 in Indonesia, while the average ERP rate increased then decreased (Marks and Rahardja, 2012). The study by Marks and Rahardja also argued that whilst protection using tariffs has fallen, protection policy has shifted to the use of NTMs, which are less transparent, tend to be inconsistent, and are susceptible to rent-seeking activities.[13] Some examples can be found in the import of key food products such as rice and sugar, where import licensing procedures have become much more restrictive in the name of price stabilisation. In fact, prices rise – hurting the poor whilst benefiting importers, including the state-owned logistics agency and other state and private sector companies. Another example is the restrictions on imports of horticulture imports entering via certain ports for quarantine reasons, although the intention is to protect local fruits from imported fruits.

5 The impact of trade liberalisation on Indonesia's economy

5.1 Economic growth

Indonesia's gains from trade liberalisation, through open trade and investment policies, were reflected in the strong growth performance following deregulation from 1986 to 1997 (James, 2001). Indonesia increased exports in the primary and service sectors due to both backward and forward linkages, led by increased exports of manufactured products. Indonesia experienced increasing job creation in the primary sector because of the increase in primary product exports. The most significant impacts of globalisation were in export volume, terms of trade, export tax, import volume, and domestic income through increased FDI (Sofjan, 2017). The study by Sofjan found that changing the strategy from import substitution to export promotion was the essential factor that created positive impacts from globalisation on Indonesia's economic growth.

Empirically, Indonesia has experienced the benefits of globalisation since 1970, with an increase in GDP per capita of 40% after five years and 76% after 10 years (Billmeier and Nannicini, 2013). The study by Billmeier and Nannicini applied the synthetic control method to assess the impact of economic liberalisation on countries' GDP per capita. The time frame is after liberalisation, and they compared countries that liberalised and others that did not liberalise as synthetic control countries. They found that Indonesia's GDP per capita was 40% higher than counterfactual countries only five years after its first liberalisation in early 1970 and 76% higher after 10 years in 1980.

Wacker, Grosskurth, and Lakemann (2014) confirmed that trade liberalisation has increased both Indonesia's terms of trade and economic growth. This study showed that the country's terms of trade decreased at the beginning because the cost of trade liberalisation came immediately but increased afterwards when the benefits of trade liberalisation came. Empirically, the increasing trade balance always fosters economic growth.

5.2 *Productivity and labour*

The tariff reduction on inputs doubled the productivity level in comparison to the tariff reduction on outputs (Amiti and Konings, 2007). Their study used Indonesia's annual medium–large manufacturing survey and applied tariff rates from 1991 to 2001. They found that having a lower intermediate input tariff rate, compared to that of the final good, doubled firms' productivity against the case without tariff reductions. Amiti and Konings also found that having higher tariff rates for imported final products than for imported intermediate inputs led to an increase in Indonesia's ERP. The ERP policy increases a country's productivity if its local producers are stimulated to compete with the imported products.

Trade liberalisation increases one of the main sources of economic growth – productivity. Hayakawa and Matsuura (2017) calculated the impact of tariff rates on productivity using the simple dynamic simulation method, by comparing the actual and counterfactual scenarios of tariff rates. Their study proved that tariff reduction has improved intra-plant productivity. This reduction generated a significant impact on productivity, as seen in the increased quality of Indonesian products resulting from the reduction in input tariffs. This study adopted price as a proxy for quality – the higher the price of the products (in this case, apparel), the higher their quality. Hayakawa and Matsuura found that a reduction in input tariffs significantly affected product quality, while a reduction in output tariffs did not. A reduction in input tariffs would increase the import of higher-quality inputs. This increasing higher quality of imported products would support Indonesia to produce higher-quality final outputs.

Trade liberalisation also increases labour productivity (Kis-Katos and Sparrow, 2009). Their study investigated the impact of trade liberalisation on child labour in Indonesia by analysing geographical differences due to the trade policy of import tariff reduction at the district level from 1993 to 2002. They found that trade liberalisation generated a positive impact on the declining number of child workers, in particular those aged 10–15 years old. The strongest impact of import tariff reduction occurred on children with a low-skills background, older siblings, and those who work in rural areas. Kis-Katos and Sparrow showed that trade liberalisation opened more job opportunities for skilled workers, so the demand for unskilled child labour declined.

The positive impacts of trade liberalisation on competitiveness are affected by product quality, firm size, capacity, and strength (Narjoko and Urata, 2019). Their study adopted both developed and developing countries, including Indonesia. Rahardja et al. (2015) found that Indonesia's economic liberalisation benefited from the global economy since economic openness to trade improved Indonesia's competitiveness. This study showed that trade competitiveness increased through export promotion, distributor creation programmes, and intermediate input liberalisation, which supported Indonesia to engage with the global value chain and keep its economic growth sustainable.

Beaulieu and Pakrashi (2013) examined an econometric model to test the correlation between child labour force participation and WTO membership. They used panel data analysis for 94 countries with data from 1980 to 1999 and found that WTO membership had a negative correlation with child labour. In addition, the higher the price of rice, the higher the amount of child labour. Less restrictive rice import policies increased rice imports and reduced its price. This decreased the amount of child labour.

Reductions in the tariff rates of imported inputs resulted in increased participation of women in the labour force and a rise in work hours, but no significant effect on working men (Kis-Katos, Pieters, and Sparrow, 2018). The decreasing cost of imported inputs was transformed into increasing job creation for female workers, who had lower wage rates than male workers. Their study found that tariff reductions had a positive impact on the female-intensive sector, while the male-intensive sector dropped because they found that tariff rate reductions in Indonesia are more female-biased than skill-biased. Intensive female-labour participation sectors in Indonesia are textiles, clothing, and footwear (Pangestu and Hendytio, 1997). Kis-Katos, Pieters, and Sparrow (2018) also found that trade liberalisation declined Indonesia's marriage rates for women aged 20–29 and men aged 30–39 because it increases job opportunities for women and decreases subsequent marriages.

Labour market changes are gradual and hinder different groups of workers (Edmonds and Pavcnik, 2005). In the short run, employees are less flexible across industries, so tariff cuts benefit jobs in sectors that adopt a flexible labour market. In regions where labour is concentrated in sectors that are losing most of their protection from imports, tariff cuts create regional wage loss and unemployment in the short run (Hasan et al., 2012).

As for the comparison in reducing output and input tariffs, Hayakawa, Matsuura, and Takii (2017) found that reducing output tariffs created a lower impact than that of an input tariff reduction. They confirmed that the application of tariff discrimination between the final product and intermediate input would be beneficial for Indonesia's trade liberalisation. Such trade liberalisation, through the introduction of FTAs, has contributed to the rise in high-quality imported materials. The significant impact of the quality improvement of imported products creates spillover effects. Local suppliers benefit from the increased quality of products. The study of ERP confirmed that trade liberalisation of inputs is more beneficial than that of finished goods. This policy motivates firms to produce the final product in the domestic market rather than importing from abroad.

5.3 Poverty, inequality, and SMEs

Kis-Katos and Sparrow (2015) estimated the impact of trade liberalisation on the poverty line in Indonesia. They used regional poverty level data for 1993 and 2002 from 259 districts in Indonesia. They also used labour market data and found a decrease in poverty, particularly in districts with sectors that were more exposed to intermediate input tariff liberalisation. This study found that trade liberalisation of intermediate inputs by lowering import tariffs increases demand for low- and medium-skilled worker participation, and this is a driving factor for poverty alleviation effects.

In the long run, trade openness reduces poverty, income inequality (as measured by the Gini coefficient ratio), and open unemployment[14] in Indonesia (Agusalim, 2017). This study examined secondary data from 1978 to 2015 on import value, GDP, income per capita, open unemployment, and the poverty rate.[15] Agusalim argued that trade openness has a significant impact on poverty reduction in the long run. His impulse response function model showed that the poverty rate decreased in the first two years and recorded the most significant negative response in the fifth year. In the predicted error variance decomposition analysis, trade openness starts to have an impact in the seventh year, with the highest impact in the ninth year.

In terms of inequality, using data from developing countries and the Organisation for Economic Co-operation and Development (OECD) countries, Urata and Narjoko (2017) showed that globalisation reduces wage inequality gaps between developed and developing countries. This shows that globalisation enables economic convergence and equality between and amongst countries. Three essential factors leading to a decline in the wage inequality gap were found: the labour market, capital inflow, and policy reform – suggesting a direction and focus for government policy to improve human capital and establish a well-functioning and flexible labour market. Indonesia is experiencing rapid changes in its international trade and related policies as a consequence of its participation in numerous bilateral, global, and multilateral FTAs (Revindo and Gan, 2017). Free trade increases competition in the domestic market for SMEs through cheap imported goods and the growing presence of international enterprises. On the other hand, it provides an enormous opportunity for SMEs to export and venture abroad.

Sandee, Isdijoso, and Sulandjari (2002) concluded that the macroeconomic environment affected by international trade policy was an essential determinant for the stability of SME operations. They confirmed that, in the long run, the free trade system creates more advantages than burdens for SMEs.

Tambunan (2011) argued that SMEs could not be sustained without globalisation. He discussed the implications of domestic product scarcity on international trade liberalisation and how trade protection on imports of raw materials has generated difficulties for local SMEs. Several times in the 1980s and 1990s, metalworking SMEs in East Java had to close their businesses due to lack of raw materials. The raw materials needed to support Indonesia's metal industry have been imported from China due to the lack of domestic supply (Tambunan, 2007, 2008). Tambunan's studies confirmed that imported input availability due to trade liberalisation was important to support the SMEs' production process.

On the export liberalisation impact, Tambunan (2005) showed that most SMEs did not export directly, but through intermediate agents. He found no strong evidence that trade openness would hurt SMEs in the long run and no evidence that the AFTA of 1992 would be harmful to Indonesia's SMEs. Furthermore, a strong correlation between trade liberalisation and plant size was found by Takii (2014), suggesting that the larger the size of firms, the higher the usage of imported inputs and more orientation for exports. This proves that large companies have driven exports and imports in terms of value instead of small ones. Both Tambunan (2011) and Takii (2014) proved that globalisation is essential for firms of all sizes – small, medium-sized, and large – in Indonesia.

5.4 Trade impacts on tourism

Trade creates movement of people, which is indicated by the flows of foreign tourists. Sugiyarto, Blake, and Sinclair (2003) argued that globalisation and trade increase international tourism. They also found that tourism increases trade, as tourism increases demand in the domestic market. The depreciation of the rupiah against the US dollar has made tourism more competitive. Combined with the government's prioritisation of tourism, the improvement in infrastructure (e.g. airports), increased number of countries receiving visa exemptions, and enhanced promotion increase the number of foreign tourists and foreign currencies in Indonesia.

The continued growth of international tourism increases the country's international reserve and decreases its reliance on trade in goods. Sugiyarto, Blake, and Sinclair confirmed that tourism had become a major source of international reserves for Indonesia, whose tourism yield reached about $14 billion in 2018, up from $10 billion per year in the last five years. Tourism is Indonesia's only trade in services account with a positive net trade balance. Indonesia relies significantly on international tourism for its trade in services foreign exchange reserve. Data on Indonesia's trade balance show that the source of trade in services is tourism, as Indonesia's transportation, insurance, and banking services are always in deficit. International tourism, which contributes to trade in services, has become an essential factor of globalisation for Indonesia.

6 The economic impacts of foreign direct investment

6.1 Investment liberalisation and economic growth

Sinha and Sinha (2002) found a positive relationship between openness in trade-related investment and economic growth in Asia, including Indonesia. They found how trade influences investment and economic growth, and in turn contributes to higher technological advancement and savings. There are three connections between economic growth and globalisation from trade to investment. First, while industrialisation is crucial for economic growth and domestic supply is higher than domestic demand, then exports provide an outlet for the excess production and generate international reserve revenue (Colombatto, 1990). Second, export-led growth shows that exports lead to more technical progress and additional savings, which increases economic growth (Krueger, 1978). Economic growth improves a country's credit ratings, which increases foreign investment inflows. Third, export promotion policies improve total factor productivity (Balassa, 1978). All these trade competitiveness improvements increase investment incentives, including from abroad, i.e. FDI inflows.

Ramstetter and Sjöholm (2006) showed significant differences in revenue, productivity, and trade between multinational corporations (MNCs) and local plants. Evidence also suggested that MNCs do not appear to target high-wage industries or take over plants in Indonesia, but they increase the wage level. Ramstetter and Sjöholm produced substantial evidence that Indonesia had a significantly higher export preference for MNCs, since MNCs have created significant positive impacts and benefits in Indonesia in terms of higher wages, productivity, and exposure to export markets.

FDI has had a greater impact on economic growth than domestic investment (Okamoto and Sjöholm, 2005). In the first half of the 1990s, FDI was a driving force for growth in both employment and production. The presence of foreign firms is also likely to increase profitability in domestic firms through increased competitive stress and technological externalities. Sjöholm (1999) found these productivity spillovers in the Indonesian manufacturing sector. The contribution of foreign plants to the aggregate total factor productivity is relatively high, but the contribution to labour productivity is relatively low due to the high numbers of low-skilled workers. However, the foreign contribution to productivity growth has been substantial in some sectors (e.g. electronics and automotive) because of the availability of high-skilled workers.

Economic models of endogenous growth have been applied to examine the effect of FDI on economic growth through the transfer of technology. Khaliq and Noy (2007) examined the direct effects of FDI inflows on economic growth in different economic sectors using a fixed effects model with sectoral data of FDI inflows, collected from Indonesia's Investment Coordinating Board (BKPM) for 1997–2006. They found that FDI can promote economic growth through the creation of dynamic comparative advantages that lead to technology transfer. Investment from foreign countries also accelerates economic growth by strengthening human capital, the essential factor in research and development (R&D), while an increase in competition and innovation results in technological progress and increases productivity – thus promoting economic growth in the long run. It can accelerate economic growth either directly or through spillover effects. The effects of FDI on economic growth vary across sectors. From the BKPM data, the secondary sector (including the food and textile industry, paper and printing, machinery, chemical, plastic, rubbers, and metal industry) always had the highest annual and cumulative FDI throughout 1997–2006. On the other hand, the tertiary sector (e.g. electricity, gas and water, trade, hotels, construction, transportation, and communication) received lower FDI inflows than the secondary sector.

6.2 Investment policy, spillover effect of technological transfer, and technological progress

The Government of Indonesia responded to an economic slowdown in 1994 by announcing radical economic deregulation, including the liberalisation of investment policies (Kuncoro, 2014). The deregulation relaxed foreign ownership restrictions, including allowing 100% foreign ownership investment liberalisation in the manufacturing sector, in particular R&D. Kuncoro (2012) used a model that sets out the concept of a conditional input demand function, which allows labour productivity to have an impact on R&D. The author observed that less successful companies are less likely to engage in R&D operations

At the same time, the government introduced policies and regulations to protect the poor from possible adverse effects of FDI. The policies include the closure of specific sectors, industries, or activities to FDI; and restrictions on modes of entry. These aimed to prevent possible adverse effects of the presence of foreign firms on local SMEs. Some examples are batik and crafts, and small retail enterprises. Other policies include local content and subcontracting policies, aimed at reducing the import dependency of domestic industries and developing production linkages between FDI and local SMEs. Policies to protect labour include regional minimum wages aimed at guaranteeing reasonable labour income and worker consumption levels; and local community development programmes, which are required for foreign mining corporations.

The key factor in the spillover effect of FDI inflow in four ASEAN member states, including Indonesia, was the transfer of technology (Lee and Tan, 2006). In the case of Indonesia, FDI has both direct and indirect economic impacts. FDI has a direct impact on Indonesia's output. On the indirect impact, FDI also promotes Indonesia's output growth, which results from technology transfers. The technology transfers into Indonesia will dramatically increase the efficiency of production by domestic firms. Therefore, they will also increase trade activities – both export and import.

Wie and Pangestu (1994) examined the technological capabilities of the Indonesian garment, clothing, and electronics industries to show that Indonesian clothing manufacturers have formed strategic alliances with their Japanese counterparts to open a critical technology transfer stream. Likewise, business ties with foreign firms have been a significant channel of technology transfer for electronics firms, in particular consumer electronics and electronic components. Wie and Pangestu found that technology transfer in the textile industry was limited to the improvement of production capacity, though Japanese counterparts pursued significant, more advanced practices that could help local companies develop their technological capabilities – including pre-investment, plan execution, and technical changes in development and service.

Wie (2001) explained that the significant channels of technology transfer to Indonesia – including FDI, technological licensing agreements, capital goods imports, and involvement in world trade – have generally led to specific production capabilities in terms of developing local industrial technological capabilities.

Temenggung (2006) found a significant and robust increase in productivity in the Indonesian manufacturing industry over the entire period. She identified negative and significant spillovers during the pre-liberalisation period (1975–86) and neutral and significant spillovers during the post-liberalisation period (1987–2000). The study also found that the spillover effect differs across the two-digit ISIC industry, demonstrating that each economic sector experiences a different impact of the transfer of technology to local partners. This study used plant-level data from the unpublished manufacturing industry surveys (Survei Tahunan Perusahaan Industri Pengolahan) by Statistics Indonesia (BPS) from 1975 to 2000.

The spillover effect of FDI was reflected not only in the transfer of technology but also in technological progress, economies of scale, R&D expenditure, and transfer of knowledge and know-how (Suyanto and Salim, 2012). This study used two productivity measurement methods – the stochastic production frontier and the Malmquist productivity index – with data from 1988 to 2000, in investigating the spillover effects on firms' productivity.[16] The primary data source of this study was the annual survey of Indonesia's medium-sized and large manufacturing sector (Survei Tahunan Statistik Industri Indonesia) conducted by BPS. Suyanto, Bloch, and Salim adopted input–output table analysis for calculating FDI variables for downstream and upstream industries. Their findings confirmed that the spillover effects from FDI on productivity growth are derived from technical and scale efficiencies as well as from technology.

Based on a literature survey of the role of FDI in poverty alleviation, Tambunan (2005) argued that FDI may have positive effects on poverty reduction, mainly through three channels: (i) labour-intensive economic growth, with export growth as the most crucial engine; (ii) technological, innovation, and knowledge spillover effects from FDI-based firms on the local economy; and (iii) poverty alleviation government programmes or projects financed by tax revenues collected from FDI-based firms. Preliminary findings based on secondary data from Indonesia find some support for the role of FDI in poverty alleviation and consumption of the poor through labour-intensive export growth. Tambunan found that the implementation of an open-door policy in the New Order government proved that FDI could make significant contributions to economic development.[17]

7 Policy implications and recommendations

Indonesia experienced its worst net export performance in non-oil and gas exports in 2018. The trade surplus decreased significantly from $20.4 billion in 2017 to only $3.8 billion due to the 19.7% increase in imports, while exports only increased by about 6.2%. Part of the reason for the fall in exports was the decline in investment, which appears to be affected by the investment climate, including uncertainties resulting from the increase in the use of trade protection instruments through NTMs in Indonesia.

This paper shows how Indonesia has dealt with globalisation and the swings between outward- and inward-looking policy in various economic circumstances. To increase its exports, Indonesia must improve its supply-side competitiveness by supporting the manufacturing sector to be competitive and start producing higher quality intermediate goods that can compete with imports. Therefore, Indonesia has to commit to the AFTA agreement, and its expansion on the ASEAN Plus frameworks in the RCEP, as ASEAN plays a central role as the regional hub. For decades, Indonesia's liberalisation and protectionist measures were a reaction to global trends and declining productivity, without proper long-run liberalisation, with the strategic purpose of gaining the long-term benefits of trade and investment liberalisation.

This paper found that globalisation through trade liberalisation has led to a positive impact on Indonesia's economic growth, reducing wage inequality and the use of child labour, and increasing labour absorption, including women's participation in the labour market. In terms of trade, globalisation contributes to Indonesia's economic growth, productivity, structural economic transformation, SMEs, poverty alleviation, reduction in inequality, and enhanced trade in services such as tourism.

The investment liberalisation has had positive impacts on Indonesia's economic growth; and spillover effects from technology transfer, technological progress, know-how, and knowledge. These improve the role of SMEs and reduce the poverty level.

The impact of globalisation is dynamic and has had an overall positive impact in the long term, as shown through the trade and investment liberalisation channels. However, it has also created costs, which have impacted uncompetitive sectors through job losses (Baldwin, Mutti, and Richardson, 1980; Stiglitz, 2007; Dutt, Mitra, and Ranjan, 2009; Ranjan, 2012). Globalisation generates trade creation with other countries at the immediate cost of non-competitive local producers, while the benefit of globalisation through the investment creation comes afterwards.

The challenge for Indonesia is to ensure that it keeps the globalisation strategy focused on the long-term net positive benefits, while building a political and policy narrative to gain public support on this longer-term strategy. Indonesia also needs to focus on how to manage the immediate costs and transition (e.g. providing social safety nets), reskilling labour, adopting a good regulatory framework, and improving competitiveness (e.g. reducing the costs of doing business and improving the investment climate).

Lastly, Indonesia has to obtain the maximum benefit from globalisation at all levels of economic cooperation – global, regional, mega-regional, bilateral, and unilateral. It also needs to ensure consistency and make an effort to widen its markets, with the intention of allowing for more possibility of the trade and investment nexus, and the development of regional global value chains (Hidayat, Hidayat, and Hendrix, 2017; Nurika and Amaliyah, 2017; Sidharta and Nihaaiyyah, 2017). Indonesia must commit to globalisation consistently and, with the right strategy, can ensure it reaps net benefits.

Notes

1 According to the neo-classical model of economic growth, FDI only affects economic growth if it positively affects technology permanently (de Mello, 1997).

2 For instance, the cost of 50% tariff elimination in the United States (US) was around 4% of the resulting total gains (Baldwin Mutti, and Richardson, 1980). Workers bore 90% of this cost while employers bore the remaining 10%. Trade liberalisation in textiles, steel, and the automotive industry led to an estimated economic cost of around 1.5% of its total gain (de Melo and Tarr, 1992). The removal of subsidies and tariffs in the British footwear industry led to a low estimated cost of 0.5%–1.5% of total liberalisation gains (Takacs and Winters, 1991).

3 After the collapse of the economy and under the New Order era of President Suharto, the technocrats in government recognised the need to attract foreign investment to lift Indonesia out of its economic crisis and introduced Indonesia's first foreign investment law No. 1/1967, which adopted an 'open door policy,' as well as a parallel Domestic Investment Law in 1968.

4 In 2016, ASEAN began the implementation of the ASEAN Economic Community, the longest period of the liberalisation process from trade to investment. Based on the model of the European Union's regional economic integration, the process of integration began with the Free Trade Area (1957–67), followed by

the Customs Union or Economic Community (1967–87), the Common Market (1987–93), the Single Monetary Union (1993–99), and the Single Currency (1999–2002). The longest period was the Customs Union (20 years).

5 Liberalisation in Indonesia often required dealing with 'patron–client relationships' amongst members of former President Suharto's inner circle, who owned certain monopolies and private establishments backed by formal regulations (Pangestu, Rahardja, and Ing, 2015).

6 Economic growth is $\frac{\Delta Y_{it}}{Y_{it}} = \frac{(I_{it} - (\delta_{it} + n_{it} + \Delta E_{it} / E_{it})) + (X_{it} - M_{it})}{C}$; where Y is output; I is investment; n is population; E is productivity of labour; X is export; M is import; and C is incremental capital output ratio: additional unit of capital needed to increase an additional unit of economic growth.

7 King (2000), Robertson-Snape (1999), and Rock (2003) showed how the Indonesian economy can be sustained amid reform and economic-related liberalisation policy despite massive, systemic rent-seeking activities and corruption. Pincus and Ramli (1998) pointed out that the roots of the lack of preparation for the 1998 crisis were attributed to the series of policy errors in the name of economic liberalisation in the previous period.

8 See Bank Indonesia (2019).

9 'Sadli's Law' refers to the late Mohammad Sadli, Indonesian economist and Minister of Mining (1973–78), Minister of Manpower (1971–73), and Director of the University of Indonesia's think tank, LPEM-UI.

10 In this case, the Dutch disease refers to Indonesia's misallocation of subsidies and protectionism. Indonesia applied an import substitution policy, using tariff protection, instead of building the competitiveness of its supply side. The Dutch disease of the oil boom, moral hazard in subsidies, and misuse of the import substitution policy made economic liberalisation in Indonesia unsuccessful in improving domestic supply competitiveness. This stimulated rent-seeking activity and economic inefficiency in Indonesia.

11 Another example of such abuse of the trade liberalisation schemes was the exemption of import and luxury taxes for the national car company. This incurred the wrath of international automotive companies, as the holding group enjoyed the advantage of importing completely built-up cars.

12 Indonesia has a high comparative advantage in both raw materials and assembly but a low comparative advantage in producing intermediate inputs. The lack of comparative advantage in the middle is known as 'hollow middle' industry.

13 During the presidency of Susilo Bambang Yudhoyono, agricultural products became subject to restrictive permits – establishing a quota-based barrier that generated rent-seeking or misuse of the import quota for cows. This involved an Indonesian political party, whose leader was apprehended by the Indonesian Corruption Eradication Commission (KPK) for rent-seeking activity.

14 Open unemployment is the number of unemployed people divided by the number of people in the labour force.

15 In terms of dynamic time series tests, this study examined the vector error correction model (VECM). Before examining the VECM, it applied stationarity, optimal lag, stability, and cointegration tests. The VECM applies both short- and long-run modelling analysis, with the impulse response function and forecast error variance decomposition model, accordingly.

16 Test procedures such as Chow and Hausman were used to choose the appropriate model amongst the three competing models, i.e. the common or pooled effect, the fixed effect with least squares dummy variables, and the random effect of generalised least squares.

17 Tambunan (2005) adopted and adapted a linear regression method and data from the National Socio-Economic Survey (SUSENAS), an annual cross-sectional survey of households by the BPS for 1974–2002 for poverty analysis.

References

Agusalim, L. (2017), 'The Dynamic Impact of Trade Openness on Poverty: An Empirical Study of Indonesia's Economy', *International Journal of Economics and Financial Issues*, 7(1), pp.566–574.

Amiti, M. and J. Konings (2007), 'Trade Liberalization, Intermediate Inputs, and Productivity: Evidence from Indonesia', *American Economic Review*, 97(5), pp.1611–1638.

Balassa, B. (1978), 'Exports and Economic Growth: Further Evidence', *Journal of Development Economics*, 5(2), pp.181–189.

Baldwin, R., J. Mutti, and J.D. Richardson (1980), 'Welfare Effects on the United States of a Significant Multilateral Tariff Reduction', *Journal of International Economics*, 10(3), pp.405–423.

Bank Indonesia (2019), *Balance of Payments, Data on Current Account, Secondary Income.* Jakarta: Bank Indonesia. https://www.bi.go.id/en/publikasi/neraca-pembayaran/Pages/npitw419.aspx (accessed 1 December 2019).

BAPPENAS (2018), *Visi Indonesia 2045.* Jakarta: National Development Planning Agency.

Beaulieu, E. and D. Pakrashi (2013), 'Do WTO Members Employ Less Child Labour?' *Indian Growth and Development Review*, 6(1), pp.148–159.

Billmeier, A. and T. Nannicini (2013), 'Assessing Economic Liberalization Episodes: A Synthetic Control Approach', *The Review of Economics and Statistics*, 95(3), pp.983–1001.

Colombatto, E. (1990), 'An Analysis of Exports and Growth in LDCs', *Kyklos*, 43(4), pp.579–597.

Dick, H. (1979), 'Survey of Recent Developments', *Bulletin of Indonesian Economic Studies*, 15(1), pp.1–44.

Dix-Carneiro, R. (2014), 'Trade Liberalization and Labor Market Dynamics', *Econometrica*, 82(3), pp.825–885.

Dutt, P., D. Mitra, and P. Ranjan (2009), 'International Trade and Unemployment: Theory and Cross-National Evidence', *Journal of International Economics*, 78(1), pp.32–44.

Edmonds, E.V. and N. Pavcnik (2005), 'Child Labor in the Global Economy', *Journal of Economic Perspectives*, 19(1), pp.199–220.

Gnangnon, S. (2018), 'Multilateral Trade Liberalization and Economic Growth', *Journal of Economic Integration*, 33(2), pp.1261–1301.

Hasan, R., D. Mitra, P. Ranjan, and R.N. Ahsan (2012), 'Trade Liberalization and Unemployment: Theory and Evidence from India', *Journal of Development Economics*, 97(2), pp.269–280.

Hayakawa, K. and T. Matsuura (2017), 'Trade Liberalization, Market Share Reallocation, and Aggregate Productivity: The Case of the Indonesian Manufacturing Industry', *The Developing Economies*, 55(3), pp.230–249.

Hayakawa, K., T. Matsuura, and S. Takii (2017), 'Does Trade Liberalization Boost Quality Upgrading? Evidence from Indonesian Plant-Product-Level Data', *The Developing Economies*, 55(3), pp.171–188.

Hidayat, A., M. Hidayat, and T. Hendrix (2017), 'The Effect of Indonesia SMEs Participation in Global Value Chain to Enhance Competitiveness', in *A New Paradigm in Trade Governance to Increase Domestic Efficiency and to Strengthen Global Competitiveness*, The Proceeding of The International Conference and Call for Paper on Trade, 5–6th September 2017. Jakarta: Ministry of Trade, pp.207–238.

James, W. (2001), 'The Gains from Open International Trade and Investment in the Deregulation Era: Implications for Indonesia's International Economic Policy in the 21st Century', *ICSEAD Working Paper Series*, Vol. 2001–2006. Kitakyushu: International Centre for the Study of East Asian Development.

JETRO (2019), *2018 JETRO Survey on Business Conditions of Japanese Companies in Asia and Oceania*. Tokyo: Japan External Trade Organization. https://www.jetro.go.jp/ext_images/en/reports/survey/pdf/rp_firms_asia_oceania2018.pdf (accessed 19 May 2019).

Juoro, U. (1993), 'Financial Liberalization in Indonesia: Interest Rates, Money Market Instruments, and Bank Supervision', *ASEAN Economic Bulletin*, 9(3), pp.323–337.

Khaliq, A. and I. Noy (2007), 'Foreign Direct Investment and Economic Growth: Empirical Evidence from Sectoral Data in Indonesia', *Working Papers*, No. 200726, University of Hawaii at Manoa, Department of Economics.

King, D.Y. (2000), 'Corruption in Indonesia: A Curable Cancer?', *Journal of International Affairs*, 53(2), pp.603–624.

Kis-Katos, K. and R. Sparrow (2009), 'Child Work and Schooling Under Trade Liberalization in Indonesia', *Discussion Paper Series*, No. 8. Freiburg: University of Freiburg, Department of International Economic Policy.

Kis-Katos, K. and R. Sparrow (2011), 'Child Labor and Trade Liberalization in Indonesia', *The Journal of Human Resources*, 46(4), pp.722–749.

Kis-Katos, K. and R. Sparrow (2015), 'Poverty, Labor Markets and Trade Liberalization in Indonesia', *Journal of Development Economics*, 117, pp.94–106.

Kis-Katos, K., J. Pieters, and R. Sparrow (2018), 'Gender-Specific Effects of Trade Liberalization in Indonesia,' *IMF Economic Review*, 66, pp.763–793.

Kuncoro, A. (2012), 'Globalization and Innovation in Indonesia: Evidence from Micro-Data on Medium and Large Manufacturing Establishments', *ERIA Discussion Paper Series*, ERIA-DP-2012-09. Jakarta: Economic Research Centre for ASEAN and East Asia.

Kuncoro, A. (2014), 'Small and Large Firm Performance Gaps in Indonesia in the Era of Globalization: Evidences from Micro-Data on Manufacturing Establishments', in C.H. Hahn and D. Narjoko (eds.) *Globalization and Performance of Small and Large Firms*. ERIA Research Project Report 2013-3. Jakarta: Economic Research Centre for ASEAN and East Asia, pp.IX-1-IX-29.

Krueger, A.O. (1978), *Liberalization Attempts and Consequences*. New York: National Bureau of Economic Research.

Lee, H.H. and H.B. Tan (2006), 'Technology Transfer, FDI, and Economic Growth in the ASEAN Region', *Journal of the Asia Pacific Economy*, 11(4), pp.394–410.

Marks, S.V. (2017), 'Non-Tariff Trade Regulations in Indonesia: Nominal and Effective Rates of Protection', *Bulletin of Indonesian Economic Studies*, 53(3), pp.333–357.

Marks, S.V. and S. Rahardja (2012), 'Effective Rates of Protection Revisited for Indonesia', *Bulletin of Indonesian Economic Studies*, 48(1), pp.57–84.

de Mello, L.R. (1997), 'Foreign Direct Investment in Developing Countries and Growth: A Selective Survey', *The Journal of Development Studies*, 34(1), pp.1–34.

de Melo, J. and D. Tarr (1992), *A General Equilibrium Analysis of US Foreign Trade Policy*. Cambridge, MA: MIT Press.

Mattoo, A., A. Mulabdic, and M. Ruta (2019), 'Trade Creation and Trade Diversion in Deep Agreements', *Policy Research Working Paper*, No. 8206. Washington, DC: World Bank.

Ministry of Trade, Indonesia (2015), *Rencana Strategis Direktorat Jenderal Perundingan Perdagangan Internasional 2015–2019* (Strategic Plan of Directorate General of International Trade Negotiation). Jakarta: Ministry of Trade (Kemendag).

Ministry of Trade, Indonesia (2018), *Info Perdagangan* (*Trade Information*). Jakarta: Ministry of Trade (Kemendag).

Narjoko, D. and S. Urata (2019), 'Firm Adjustment to Trade Policy Changes in East Asia', *ADBI Working Paper Series*, No. 945. Tokyo: Asian Development Bank Institute.

Nurika, R.R. and R. Amaliyah (2017), 'Eco-Friendly Global Value Chain: How Indonesian SMEs Expand Their Business While Maintaining Sustainable Development', in *A New Paradigm in Trade Governance to Increase Domestic Efficiency and to Strengthen Global Competitiveness*, The Proceeding of The International Conference and Call for Paper on Trade 5th–6th September 2017. Jakarta: Ministry of Trade, pp.189–206.

OECD (2015), 'Trade in Value-Added: Indonesia', *OECD-WTO Trade in Value Added*, October. https://www.oecd.org/sti/ind/tiva/CN_2015_Indonesia.pdf (accessed 12 May 2019).

Okamoto, Y. and F. Sjöholm (2005), 'FDI and the Dynamics of Productivity in Indonesian Manufacturing', *The Journal of Development Studies*, 41(1), pp.160–182.

Otsuka, M., S. Thomsen, and A. Goldstein (2011, February), 'Improving Indonesia's Investment Climate', *OECD Investment Insights*, Issue 1. Paris: Organisation for Economic Co-operation and Development.

Pangestu, M. and M.K. Hendytio (1997), 'Survey Responses for Women Workers in Indonesia's Textile, Garment, and Footwear Industries', *Policy Research Working Paper*, No. 1755. Washington, DC: World Bank.

Pangestu, M., S. Rahardja, and L.Y. Ing (2015), 'Fifty Years of Trade Policy in Indonesia: New World Trade, Old Treatments', *Bulletin of Indonesian Economic Studies*, 51(2), pp.239–261.

Parikh, A. (2004), 'Relationship Between Trade Liberalization, Growth, and Balance of Payments in Developing Countries: An Econometric Study', *HWWA Discussion Paper*, No. 286. Hamburg: Hamburg Institute of International Economics (HWWA).

Permani, R. (2011), 'The Impacts of Trade Liberalisation and Technological Change on GDP Growth in Indonesia: A Meta Regression Analysis', *Global Economy Journal*, 11(4), pp.1–30.

Pincus, J. and R. Ramli (1998), 'Indonesia: From Showcase to Basket Case', *Cambridge Journal of Economics*, 22(6), pp.723–734.

Rahardja, S. et al. (2015), *Openness in Trade and Investment: Putting the Debate in Indonesia's Development Context – Executive Summary for Policy Note on Openness, Growth, and Productivity*. Washington, DC: World Bank.

Rajan, R. and R. Sen (2002), 'Singapore's New Commercial Trade Strategy: The Pros and Cons of Bilateralism', *CIES Discussion Paper*, No. 0202. Adelaide: Centre for International Economic Studies.

Ramstetter, E. and F. Sjöholm (2006), 'Multinational Corporations in Indonesia and Thailand: An Overview of Effects on Wages, Productivity, and Export', *East Asian Economic Perspectives*, 17(2), pp.78–102.

Ranjan, P. (2012), 'Trade Liberalization, Unemployment, and Inequality with Endogenous Job Destruction', *International Review of Economics and Finance*, 23, pp.16–29.

Ratnaike, Y. (2012), 'Is There an Empirical Link between Trade Liberalisation and Export Performance?' *Economics Letters*, 117(1), pp.375–378.

Revindo, M.D. and C. Gan (2017), 'Factors Influencing SMEs' Engagement in Direct Export Activities', *LPEM-FEBUI Working Paper*, No. 011. Jakarta: University of Indonesia, Faculty of Economics and Business.

Robertson-Snape, F. (1999), 'Corruption, Collusion and Nepotism in Indonesia', *Third World Quarterly*, 20(3), pp.589–602.

Rock, M.T. (2003), 'The Politics of Development Policy and Development Policy Reform in New Order Indonesia', *William Davidson Institute Working Paper*, No. 632. Ann Arbor, MI: University of Michigan, William Davidson Institute.

Sandee, H., B. Isdijoso, and S. Sulandjari (2002), SME Clusters in Indonesia: *An Analysis of Growth Dynamics and Employment Conditions.* Jakarta: International Labour Office.

Seng, T.S., R. Emmers, M.. Caballero-Anthony, A.. Acharya, B. Desker, and K.C. Guan (2002), A New Agenda *for the ASEAN Regional Forum*. Singapore: Institute of Defence and Strategis Studies – Nanyang Technological University.

Sidharta, H.E. and Z. Nihaaiyyah (2017), 'Strengthening Competitive Power Trading Through Improvement of National Logistics to SMEs Exports in Global Value Chain', in *A New Paradigm in Trade Governance to Increase Domestic Efficiency and to Strengthen Global Competitiveness*, The Proceeding of The International Conference and Call for Paper on Trade 5th–6th September 2017. Jakarta: Ministry of Trade, pp.151–160.

Sinha, D. and T. Sinha (2002), 'Openness, Investment and Economic Growth in Asia', *Indian Economic Journal*, 49(4), pp.90–95.

Sjöholm, F. (1999), 'Productivity Growth in Indonesia: The Role of Regional Characteristics and Direct Foreign Investment', *Economic Development and Cultural Change*, 47(3), pp.559–584.

Sofjan, M. (2017), 'The Effect of Liberalization on Export-Import in Indonesia', *International Journal of Economics and Financial Issues*, 7(2), pp.672–676.

Stiglitz, J. (2007), *Making Globalization Work*. New York: WW Norton & Co.

Sugiyarto, G., A. Blake, and M. Sinclair (2003), 'Tourism and Globalization: Tourism and Globalization', *Annals of Tourism Research*, 30(3), pp.683–701.

Suyanto, H.B. and R.A. Salim (2012), 'Foreign Direct Investment Spillovers and Productivity Growth in Indonesian Garment and Electronics Manufacturing', *Journal of Development Studies*, 48(10), 1397–1411.

Takacs, W.E. and L.A. Winters (1991), 'Labour Adjustment Costs and British Footwear Protection', *Oxford Economic Papers*, 43(3), pp.479–501.

Takii, S. (2014), 'Import Penetration, Export Orientation, and Plant Size in Indonesian Manufacturing', *ERIA Discussion Paper Series*, No. ERIA-DP-2014-17. Jakarta: Economic Research Centre for ASEAN and East Asia.

Tambunan, T. (2005), 'Economic Growth, Appropriate Policies and Poverty Reduction in a Developing Country: Some Experience from Indonesia', *South Asia Economic Journal*, 6(1), pp.59–78.

Tambunan, T.T. (2007), 'Trade and Investment Liberalization Effects on Small and Medium-Sized Enterprise Development: A Literature Survey and Case Study of Indonesia', in *Towards Coherent Policy Frameworks: Understanding Trade and Investment Linkages*, Studies in Trade and Investment, No. 62. Bangkok: United Nations Economic and Social Commission for Asia and the Pacific.

Tambunan, T. (2008), 'Trade Liberalization Effects on the Development of Small and Medium-Sized Enterprises in Indonesia: A Case Study', *Asia-Pacific Development Journal*, 15(2), pp.35–59.

Tambunan, T. (2011), 'The Impacts of Trade Liberalization on Indonesian Small and Medium-Sized Enterprises', *TKN Policy Paper*. Winnipeg: International Institute for Sustainable Development.

Temenggung, D. (2006), *Productivity Spillovers From Foreign Direct Investment: Indonesian Manufacturing Industry's Experience 1975–2000*. Canberra: Australian National University, Economics Division, Research School of Pacific and Asian Studies.

United Nations Department of Economic and Social Affairs, Population Division (2015), 'Trends in International Migrant Stock: The 2015 Revision'. https://www.un.org/en/development/desa/population/migration/data/estimates2/estimates15.asp (accessed 9 Sept. 2019).

Urata, S. and D. Narjoko (2017), 'International Trade and Inequality', *ADBI Working Paper Series*, No. 675. Tokyo: Asian Development Bank Institute.

Verico, K. (2017), *The Future of the ASEAN Economic Integration*. London: Palgrave Macmillan.

Verico, K. (Forthcoming a), *Review of Indonesia Manufacturing Sector*. Jakarta: Economic Research Institute for ASEAN and East Asia.

Verico, K. (Forthcoming b), 'Pertumbuhan Ekonomi Indonesia', *Buku ILUNI FEB UI*. Jakarta: Ikatan Alumni UI FEB/Alumnae Association of Faculty of Economics and Business, University of Indonesia.

Viner, J. (1950), *The Customs Union Issue*. New York: Carnegie Endowment for International Peace.

Wacker, K.M., P. Grosskurth, and T. Lakemann (2014), 'Terms of Trade, Foreign Direct Investment, and Development: A Case of Intra-Asian "Kicking Away the Ladder"?', *ADB Working Paper Series on Regional Economic Integration*, No. 122. Tokyo: Asian Development Bank Institute.

Warr, P.G. (1992), 'Comparative Advantage and Protection in Indonesia', *Bulletin of Indonesian Economic Studies*, 28(3), pp.41–70.

Widodo, T. (2008), 'The Structure of Protection in Indonesian Manufacturing Sector', *ASEAN Economic Bulletin*, 25(2), pp.161–178.

Wie, T.K. and M. Pangestu (1994), 'Technological Capabilities and Indonesia's Manufactured Exports', Revised Report for UNCTAD. *SAREC Project on Technological Dynamism and the Export of Manufactures from Developing Countries*. Jakarta: SAREC Project.

Wie, T.K. (2001), 'The Role of Foreign Direct Investment in Indonesia's Industrial Technology Development', *International Journal of Technology Management*, 22(5–6), pp.583–598.

World Bank (2019), *World Development Indicators.* Washington, DC: World Bank. https://data.worldbank.org/indicator/TM.TAX.MRCH.SM.AR.ZS?locations=ID (accessed 15 May 2019).

Wymenga, P.S. (1991), 'The Structure of Protection in Indonesia in 1989', *Bulletin of Indonesian Economic Studies*, 27(1), pp.127–153.

Ying, Y.-H., K. Chang, and C.-H. Lee (2014), 'The Impact of Globalization on Economic Growth', *Romanian Journal of Economic Forecasting*, XVII(2), pp.24–34.

5 The impact of economic globalisation on firm performance and the labour market: evidence from Japan

Keiko Ito

1 Introduction

The impact of globalisation on the economy and people's lives is attracting growing attention. In Japan, too, the economic impact of globalisation has been receiving significant interest, partly because there appears to be a link between the increase in trade and the overseas expansion of Japanese firms on the one hand and the prolonged sluggishness of the domestic economy on the other. In contrast to stagnant GDP growth, imports and exports and outward foreign direct investment (FDI) have increased, and as shown in Figure 5.1, the ratio of imports and exports and FDI to GDP has been rising sharply since the mid-1990s in Japan. Against this background, there is a burgeoning literature on the impact of globalisation – in particular, international trade and FDI– on productivity and the labour market. While the empirical results differ across studies to some extent, a broad picture regarding the major issues, especially in developed countries including Japan, has emerged. This can be summarised as follows.

First, in developed countries including Japan, macro-level structural changes have been widely observed. The share of workers in the manufacturing sector has declined dramatically, although the value-added share of manufacturing has remained relatively stable. While there are a number of reasons for this structural change, globalisation is regarded as one factor that is at least partly responsible. Second, underlying such macro-level structural changes, various micro-level effects of globalisation have been observed. One stylised fact is that firms engaged in international trade and direct investment tend to be more productive than non-internationalised firms (see, for example, Bernard and Jensen, 1999; Mayer and Ottaviano, 2008; and Wakasugi et al., 2011). The former outperforms the latter not only in terms of productivity but also in terms of various other performance indicators such as research and development (R&D) expenditure, patents, firm size, wage rates, and so on.

These changes are not necessarily bad for economic growth. The decline in manufacturing employment may accelerate economic growth if workers move towards fast-growing new industries. Moreover, if better-performing internationalised firms grow more and increase their shares in the economy, the efficiency of the economy overall is expected to be improved. The pro-competitive

DOI: 10.4324/9781003138501-5

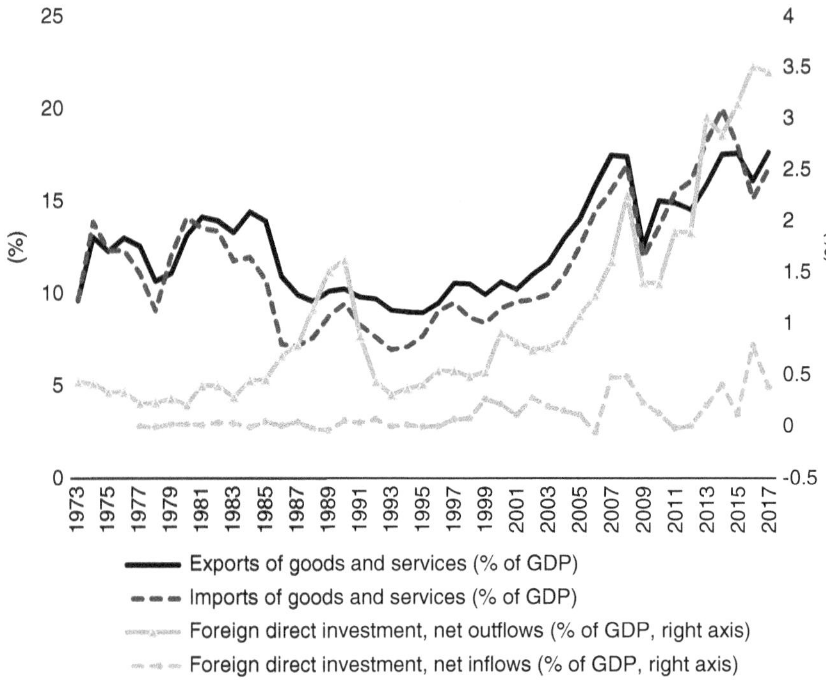

Figure 5.1 Value of Japan's Trade and FDI as a Share of GDP (%) FDI = foreign direct investment, GDP = gross domestic product.

Source: World Bank (2019), World Development Indicators 2019. Washington, DC: World Bank. https://databank.worldbank.org/source/world-development-indicators (accessed 19 May 2019).

effect of globalisation is likely to promote firms' efforts to improve productivity and develop new technologies, thereby increasing economic welfare.

Yet, in practice, a rise in anti-globalisation sentiment and protectionism can be observed across the world. One reason for the anti-globalisation sentiment is likely that the impact of globalisation is highly heterogeneous across firms and workers: globalisation creates winners and losers. As shown in Figure 5.2, in Japan for example, both the number and the share of workers in the manufacturing sector have been declining since the early 1990s (with the number falling by 4.8 million and the share by 7.2 percentage points from 1990 to 2012). On the other hand, the manufacturing share of real gross domestic product (GDP) has remained relatively stable, suggesting that labour productivity in manufacturing has been increasing relative to that in the service sector.[1] The figure also implies that many manufacturing workers lost their jobs and were forced to move into the service sector, where labour productivity is not increasing and pay is less likely to increase, while workers who stayed in the manufacturing sector, where labour productivity is increasing, are relatively well paid.

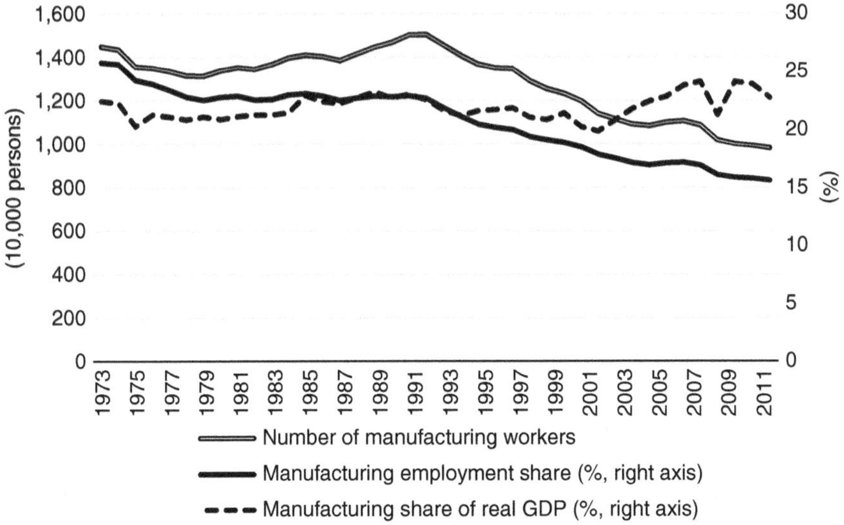

Figure 5.2 Employment and Value Added in the Japanese Manufacturing Sector.
Note: GDP = gross domestic product. Source: RIETI (2015) JIP J IP Database 2015. Tokyo: Research Institute of Economy, Trade and Industry. https://www.rieti.go.jp/en/database/JIP2015/index.html (accessed 1 April 2019).

Moreover, many previous studies suggest that although internationalised firms outperform others by a wide margin, the number of such firms is very small compared with the total number of firms. Furthermore, a large part of international trade is conducted by a very small number of top exporters (multinational firms in most cases). On the other hand, firms – particularly less productive ones – facing import competition from low-wage countries are more likely to exit or shrink, and workers employed in such firms or industries are likely to lose their jobs. Within an internationalised firm, labour demand tends to shift away from unskilled workers towards skilled workers as firms get more involved in the international division of labour via trade and FDI. Thus, in developed countries, while globalisation may benefit skilled workers, unskilled workers are more likely to be worse off. Therefore, many developed countries are facing the urgent policy issue of how to distribute the gains from globalisation so that everyone benefits.

Statistics in many developed countries, including Japan, show that (i) a huge productivity gap exists across firms and the gap seems to be persistent; (ii) manufacturing employment has been declining while employment in the services sector has been increasing; and (iii) labour demand has been shifting away from unskilled workers towards skilled workers, resulting in substantial wage gaps across workers. Although these changes are partly attributable to globalisation, technological change is another important factor. These two factors – trade and technology – are intertwined and affect firm performance and the labour market.

It is therefore important to note that it is extremely difficult to decompose the various changes into those resulting from globalisation and those caused by technological change.

This caveat notwithstanding, the aim of this paper is to derive the economic consequences of the expansion of international trade/investment with a focus on firm performance and the labour market, and to discuss the implications for policies to assist firms in their global activities and promote economic growth. The paper focuses primarily on evidence from Japan, mainly based on micro-data such as firm- or establishment-level data. In particular, the following three aspects of globalisation are examined: exports, imports, and FDI. Linked these three aspects, the impact of 'offshoring' – defined as both international in-sourcing (offshore production and imports from overseas affiliates) and international outsourcing (imports from non-affiliated foreign firms) – is also discussed. While international migration is another aspect of globalisation, this aspect is not covered in this paper, partly because of the lack of such studies for Japan.

The findings of many previous studies suggest that globalisation – such as increases in exports, imports, and FDI – to some extent create winners and losers amongst firms and workers. A widening gap in productivity and wages has been observed in many countries. However, previous studies also show that the magnitude of the impact that is directly attributable to globalisation is quite limited. Although the empirical evidence on Japan is more or less consistent with that on other developed countries, noteworthy observations for Japan are as follows. First, several empirical studies confirm a learning-by-exporting effect as firms tend to improve their productivity after they start exporting. However, such a learning effect is not always found for other countries. Second, increases in imports from China do not always have a significant negative effect on employment and value-added growth in Japan, which contrasts with results for the US and some European countries. A possible interpretation of the results for Japan is that they reflect a complementary relationship between Japan and China in global supply chains.

The findings for Japan suggest that both firms and governments should not take a negative approach towards globalisation. Rather, firms should invest in new technology and human capital to respond flexibly to the structural changes brought about by globalisation and technological change. The government should encourage investment in such intangible assets by firms that are striving to succeed in the global market.

The rest of the paper is organised as follows. The next section reviews the empirical evidence on the impact of globalisation on firm-level productivity and innovation. Turning to the labour market, Section 3 looks at the impact on employment, skill composition, and wages. Section 4 discusses the inter-industry impact of globalisation, while Section 5 concludes. Finally, the appendix provides a summary of key studies and their empirical findings on the impact of globalisation for Japan.

2 The impact of globalisation on firm productivity and innovation

Many previous studies show that firms engaged in international business are larger, more productive, and more innovative. Firms are also likely to improve their productivity after starting exporting and/or overseas production.[2]

2.1 Superior performance of internationalised firms

As numerous studies have shown, more productive firms that can pay the fixed cost required to start exporting/FDI are more likely to become exporters/ multinationals (selection effect), and such internationalised firms are more likely to improve their productivity by learning from international markets (learning effect). Internationalised firms, therefore, are expected to perform better than others because of these two effects. As for Japanese firms, many studies confirm that internationalised firms tend to be more productive than domestic firms (e.g. Kimura and Kiyota, 2006; Tomiura, 2007; and Wakasugi et al., 2011). For example, Wakasugi et al. (2011) showed that exporting firms' total factor productivity (TFP) is 38% higher than that of non-exporting firms. They also showed that multinational firms' TFP is 31% higher than that of non-multinational firms. Moreover, as predicted by Helpman, Melitz, and Yeaple (2004), firms engaged in both exporting and FDI show the highest productivity on average, followed by exporting firms and firms not engaged in exporting and FDI.[3] Furthermore, firms that invest in more regions tend to be more productive (Tanaka, 2012a).

The superior performance of internationalised firms can be explained by the selection effect and the learning effect. In the case of Japan, Kimura and Kiyota (2006) and Todo (2011a) confirmed that both effects raise the productivity of exporting and/or FDI firms. As shown in Figure 5.3, in the case of Japan, export starters tend to show higher productivity growth than firms that do not start exporting.[4] Although Wagner (2012) argued that previous studies on other countries did not always find a positive learning effect, in the case of Japan, many studies including the ones mentioned above, have found a positive learning effect. While firms are required to continuously improve their efficiency to survive competition in foreign markets, they can also learn foreign firms' best practices by entering foreign markets via exporting or FDI. They not only learn foreign competitors' marketing know-how and their products but also obtain feedback from foreign customers. As I will discuss in the next subsection, exporters tend to utilise such information obtained from foreign markets and develop their technological capability. Moreover, not only exporting but also importing may have a positive impact on firm productivity. By using cheaper and higher quality imported intermediate goods, firms may be able to be more cost-competitive and shift towards higher value-added processes. In the case of Japanese manufacturing firms, Hijzen, Inui, and Todo (2010) found that offshoring is likely to have a positive effect on productivity. While Ito, Tomiura, and Wakasugi (2011)

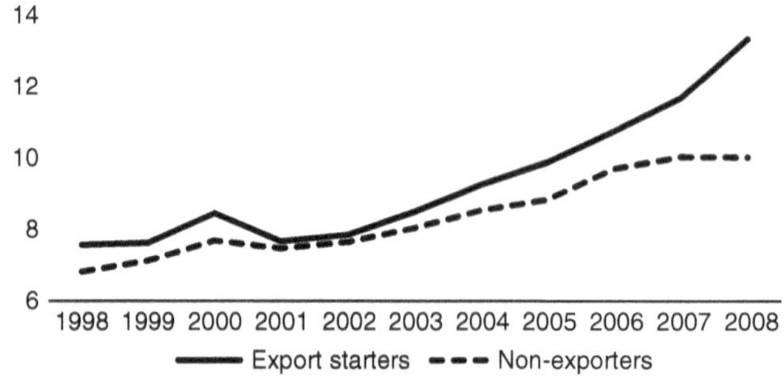

Figure 5.3 Average Labour Productivity of Export Starters and Non-Exporters.
Source: METI (2012), Figure 3-1-3-3 (a).
Notes: 1. The vertical axis shows the log of labour productivity. 2. Export starters are firms that started exporting in 2001.

also found a productivity enhancing effect of offshoring, their results indicate that only firms that offshore both manufacturing and service tasks enjoy an improvement in productivity and that the level of firms' engagement in offshoring matters more than whether or not firms engage in offshoring.

Turning to the selection effect, although some studies provide evidence of such an effect for Japan, Todo (2011a) pointed out that the impact of productivity on firms' decision to export is economically negligible in size. According to his estimates, when the log of TFP improves by 50%, the predicted probability that the average domestic firm becomes an exporter or an FDI firm increases by only 0.07%. Todo (2011b) argued that a significant number of high-productivity firms are not engaged in exporting and/or FDI. Todo (2011a) also pointed out that the exporting/FDI status of firms does not change easily. For example, more than 96% of non-exporters remain non-exporters the following year. The fact that only a few firms change their status over time implies that it is not easy to become an exporter or to expand overseas, even though firms' productivity is expected to increase after their status changes.

Why are some firms not engaged in international business even though they are productive? Possible reasons for the weak relationship between productivity and overseas expansion include a lack of information on foreign markets (information friction) and firms' risk-averse behaviour. For instance, Inui, Ito, and Miyakawa (2015) found that firms that have access to information on foreign markets via their main bank are more likely to start exporting. Todo and Sato (2014) found that firms with risk-tolerant and forward-looking managers are more likely to engage in international business. These studies suggest a need for policy support to potentially outward-oriented firms.

Although it is important to facilitate international activities by firms, particularly by promising and productive small and medium-sized enterprises, it is also widely observed in many countries that a large part of international trade is conducted by a very small number of internationalised firms. Wakasugi et al. (2011) showed that the largest 10% of exporters accounted for 92% of Japan's total exports (measured in value) and that this concentration ratio is comparable to that of the US and European countries. Similarly, Ito (2019) showed a huge gap in productivity between the top exporters and other exporters. Figure 5.4 shows the difference between the average productivity of exporting and non-exporting firms in the Japanese manufacturing sector. In the figure, exporters are further divided into four categories: top 10 exporters, permanent exporters, new exporters, and export exiters. The figure indicates that exporters as a whole are more productive than non-exporters (about 20% higher on average). It also shows that the top 10 exporters are much more productive than other exporters and that the average productivity of new exporters is not very high. It is well known that many export starters tend to stop exporting in a short period and it seems difficult for many new exporters to become permanent exporters (Inui, Ito, and Miyakawa, 2017). These findings suggest that another important policy issue is how to support new exporters to help them continue exporting to foreign markets in the long term to enjoy learning effects. For firms, one possible

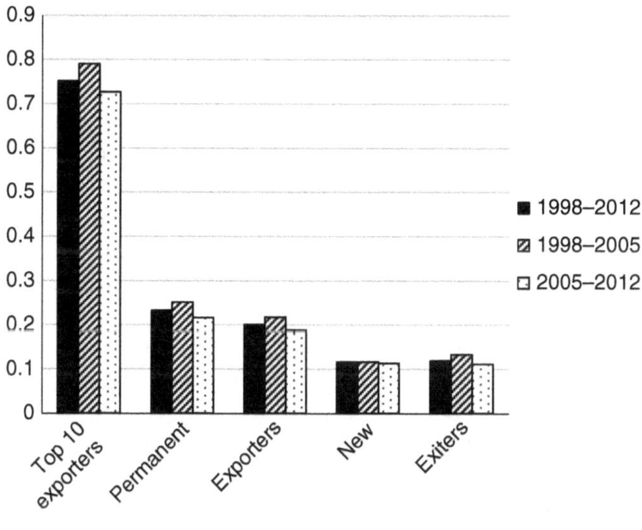

Figure 5.4 Difference in TFP between Exporters and Non-Exporters: Manufacturing Sector.

Source: Ito (2019), Figure 2 (b).

Notes: TFP = total factor productivity. 1. 'Top 10 exporters' denotes the 10 largest exporters in terms of export value. 2. 'Permanent' denotes firms exporting in at least three consecutive years, *t-1*, *t*, and *t+1*. 3. 'Exporters' denotes all exporting firms in year *t*. 4. 'New' denotes firms that did not export in year *t-1* but started exporting in year *t* and continued exporting in year *t+1*. 5. 'Exiters' denotes firms that exported in years *t-1* and *t* but stopped exporting in year *t+1*.

strategy might be to focus on niche markets; another might be to create transaction relationships with large global firms that help them to reduce the costs and risks involved in serving overseas markets. Reducing information frictions and facilitating risk management are areas in which the government could take some policy action.

2.2 Bidirectional causal relationship between innovation and internationalisation

Another issue that has been extensively investigated in the literature is the relationship between firms' decisions on exporting and on innovation. A substantial number of studies has shown a bidirectional causal relationship between firm innovation and export activity or complementarity between innovation and exporting (for empirical evidence on Japanese firms, see, for example, Ito and Lechevalier (2010) and Ito and Tanaka (2016)).[5]

While innovative firms are more likely to become exporters, firms serving international markets are also more likely to increase innovation activities because of knowledge spillovers from foreign competitors and partners as well as competitive pressures in those markets. Haneda and Ito (2014), employing the 'innovation accounting' framework proposed by Mairesse and Mohnen (2002), found that Japanese firms with R&D establishments abroad show the best innovation performance compared with all other types of firms. More specifically, although international activities do not necessarily raise the probability of innovation, i.e. whether a firm successfully develops a new product, new products tend to account for a much larger share of sales in the case of firms engaged in international activities. In other words, firms engaged in international activities are more likely to develop new products that sell well. Haneda and Ito (2014) suggested that information/knowledge obtained from international markets plays an important role in this context. This can be interpreted as an effect of learning from foreign markets.

Haneda and Ito (2014) also showed that a significant part of the higher innovation performance of internationally active firms can be explained by greater intra-firm knowledge spillovers, R&D intensity, perceived competitive pressure, and proximity to basic research. Highlighting the importance of knowledge spillovers from firms in foreign markets, Branstetter (2006) and Yashiro and Hirano (2010) argued that gathering information from foreign markets via exporting/FDI significantly raises firms' technological capabilities.

Also focusing on international knowledge spillovers, Ito et al. (2019) examined the relationship between patent applications by Japanese firms and their position in global value chains, which is measured using the Inter-Country Input–Output Tables of the Organisation for Economic Co-operation and Development. The authors assumed that industries with higher network centrality receive more knowledge spillovers because they are connected to more countries and industries. The study found that exporters in sectors that are more central in the forward linkage network (i.e. the downstream input linkage network) tend to file for more high-quality patents, as measured by the citation-weighted number of patent applications. Such exporters in sectors with higher forward centrality are interpreted as being key suppliers, and they tend to be more innovative. The finding suggests that the position within global value chains is another important factor determining the innovative capability of firms.

As suggested by Haneda and Ito (2014), competitive pressures may make firms more innovative. However, fierce competition potentially also dampens firms' investment in innovation activities, because market competition is likely to reduce firms' profits. Examining the innovation response of Japanese firms to intensified import competition from China during 1995–2010, Yamashita and Yamauchi (2020) found that firms that exported and/or imported filed for more patents in response to the increased import competition from China. However, Chinese import competition adversely affected the quality of innovation as measured by citations. While Chinese import competition did not have any significant impact on patent applications by domestic firms which are not engaged in exports/imports, it had a negative impact on their R&D expenditure.[6] Therefore, evaluating the impact of import competition from China on innovation output by Japanese firms is not straightforward. However, what seems safe to say is that the competition faced by firms engaged in international activities compels them to make greater efforts to innovate. Meanwhile, the negative impact on the quality of innovation (as measured by citations) is an issue that deserves further scrutiny in future research.

3 Globalisation and the labour market

Another hotly debated issue in many countries has been the impact of globalisation on employment and wages. In Japan, as shown above, the share of manufacturing workers has declined drastically since the early 1990s, when Japanese firms started expanding offshore production and increasing imports. Moreover, standard international trade theory predicts that trade liberalisation is likely to accelerate specialisation in capital- and skill-intensive production in developed countries, while unskilled labour-intensive production will be moved to developing countries. Therefore, for developed countries, increases in exports are likely to have a positive impact on demand for skilled workers on the one hand, and increases in imports are likely to have a negative impact on demand for unskilled workers on the other. Against this background, this section discusses the impact of imports and offshoring as well as exports on changes on domestic employment, wages, and the skill composition of workers.

3.1 Impact on domestic employment

Starting with the impact on domestic employment, several industry-level studies have examined the impact of imports and exports on employment in Japan. Using the decline in import prices as a measure of import competition, Tomiura (2003) found that import competition has a negative effect on domestic employment.

However, imports are only one side of the coin and often go hand in hand with increases in exports. This is shown by factor content analyses based on input–output tables, which highlight that globalisation increases not only imports but also exports, so that the negative impact of globalisation on domestic employment has been rather limited (see, for example, Sakurai [2014]).

In recent years, the rapid increase in imports from China has been blamed as a major cause of the decline in manufacturing employment in the US. For example, Autor, Dorn, and Hanson (2013) estimated that the increase in imports from China explains about a quarter of the decline in manufacturing employment in the US. However, using Japanese prefecture-level data, Taniguchi (2019) conducted a similar analysis to that of Autor, Dorn, and Hanson (2013) and found that in Japan an increase in imports from China is positively associated with manufacturing employment.[7] The reason for the positive impact of Chinese imports on employment in Japan is probably that industries importing from China increased their exports as well. The difference between Japan and the US potentially implies that Japanese imports from China are more likely to be complementary to, and not substitutes for, Japanese production and exports.

Studies based on firm-level data have also shown that the direct impact of globalisation on firm employment has been quite limited. Since increases in imports of intermediate inputs to a large extent are due to the expansion of overseas production by Japanese multinational enterprises (MNEs), Yamashita and Fukao (2010) examined the relationship between domestic employment and employment in overseas affiliates of Japanese manufacturing MNEs using parent–affiliate matched data. They did not find a statistically significant negative relationship. Meanwhile, following the research framework employed by Harrison and McMillan (2011), Kambayashi and Kiyota (2015) examined the effects of FDI on the domestic employment of Japanese manufacturing MNEs. They found that 'disemployment' (reductions in employment, especially in the manufacturing sector) in Japan is mainly driven by substitution between capital and labour rather than the reallocation of labour from Japan to overseas via FDI.[8] Ando and Kimura (2017) also found that Japanese multinational firms which expand their foreign operations tend to increase domestic employment, mainly in the form of boosting headquarters services, and concluded that the globalisation of corporate activities contributes to the expansion of domestic employment by boosting complementary activities at home.

These studies suggest that domestic workers were not perfectly substituted for foreign workers embodied in imported goods. By shifting operations at home towards higher value-added processes which are complementary to offshored lower value-added processes, Japanese firms have been trying to sustain domestic employment but the composition of worker skills and occupations may have been changed substantially. I will return to this point in the next subsection.

While the above studies have suggested that the overseas expansion of Japanese MNEs did not have a significant negative impact on the domestic employment of the MNEs themselves, it may have had a negative impact on the employment of domestic firms acting as suppliers to MNEs. Taking domestic supplier–customer relationships into account, Ito and Tanaka (2014) examined the relationship between the overseas expansion of Japanese MNEs and the employment of domestic suppliers of these MNEs. However, they did not find any negative relationship and instead discovered that the relationship tends to be positive. The finding suggests that domestic suppliers selling to MNEs that are expanding overseas do not reduce employment more than firms not selling to MNEs.

Summing up, the studies on Japan suggest that we cannot conclude that globalisation has a negative impact on domestic employment.[9]

3.2 Impact on skill composition

Globalisation is likely to have differential effects on the domestic demand for labour in terms of the skills that workers possess and the tasks in which they engage. In particular, this differential impact on labour demand is likely to increase wage gaps across workers. This is borne out in studies showing that globalisation negatively affects certain types of workers in certain regions and/or industries. Generally speaking, in developed countries, low-skilled workers tend to be worse off while high-skilled workers tend to be better off as a result of globalisation. This section provides a summary of research findings on such heterogeneous effects of globalisation on the labour market in Japan.

The rapid and worldwide advances in trade liberalisation and the development of information and communication technologies since the 1990s have dramatically reduced the cost of the international division of labour or fragmentation of production. In production fragmentation, unskilled labour-intensive processes are located in low-wage developing countries, while skilled labour-, capital-, and knowledge-intensive processes are located in developed countries. Unskilled labour-intensive processes or tasks are increasingly moved offshore or outsourced to developing countries.

Therefore, fragmentation is expected to increase the demand for skilled workers in developed countries, and many studies confirm that increases in imports of intermediate inputs are positively associated with an increase in the skill intensity of production in developed countries. Ito and Fukao (2005), following the framework employed by Feenstra and Hanson (1996), showed that imports of intermediate inputs, particularly imports of relatively low-tech intermediate inputs from Asian countries, have led to an increase in the share of skilled workers in Japan's manufacturing sector. Ito and Fukao (2005) estimated that nearly half of the increase in the skilled worker share in Japan's manufacturing sector from 1988 to 2002 is attributable to the increase in the intra-industry division of labour with Asian countries. Similarly, Ahn, Fukao, and Ito (2008) and Yamashita (2008) found a positive relationship between intermediate input imports from Asia and skill intensity in Japan. Further, Kiyota and Maruyama (2017) concluded that offshoring has increased the demand for high-skilled workers in Japan. Studies based on firm-level data have also found strong evidence that the expansion of the overseas production of Japanese MNEs has increased the skill intensity of production at home (e.g. Head and Ries, 2002; Hayakawa et al., 2013).[10]

On the other hand, Tanaka (2012b) found that the share of temporary workers dispatched from staffing companies tends to increase after a firm becomes a multinational, although the number of workers at home does not decline. This is an interesting finding and may imply that globalised firms tend to utilise more temporary workers, the number of which firms can flexibly increase or reduce in response to economic conditions and/or the speed of technological developments. This result suggests that, in addition to the demand for skilled workers, globalisation appears to increase the need for a more flexible workforce.

3.3 Impact on wages

The previous section has shown considerable evidence that globalisation has increased the demand for skilled workers more than for unskilled workers. This demand shift towards skilled workers in turn has implications for the wage gap between skilled and unskilled workers. In fact, it is now well known that the demand shift towards skilled workers has been larger and more significant within industries and within firms than between industries. Previous research has highlighted that the demand shift within industries and firms is attributable to skill-biased technological change and offshoring. For instance, one of the pioneering studies on the US, Feenstra and Hanson (1999), found that both skill-biased technological change and offshoring have contributed to the increased wage gap between skilled and unskilled workers in the US, although the impact of skill-biased technological change was larger than that of offshoring.

As for Japan, Sasaki and Sakura (2004) and Sakurai (2014) confirmed that the wage gap between skilled and unskilled workers has been increasing, albeit slowly, and that international trade (i.e. import competition and offshoring) have contributed to this increase in the wage gap to some extent. Although these two studies took different approaches, both concluded that the impact of offshoring was almost the same as, or slightly larger than, the impact of skill-biased technological change. Endoh (2018), analysing employer–employee-matched data for Japan, also found that offshoring has contributed to the widening of the wage gap.

However, the widening wage gaps at the macro level observed in many countries are because of a number of reasons, and the contribution of globalisation appears to be modest (Helpman, 2016). This is the conclusion suggested by, for example, Burstein and Vogel (2017), who estimated the impact of globalisation on the wage gap using a trade model and data for 60 countries around the world covering the period from 2005 to 2007. They measured the impact of trade by comparing the estimated wage gap in the case with international trade and without international trade (i.e. trade costs are infinity). They found that international trade increased the wage gap between skilled and unskilled workers by 5.1% on average, although the impact varied across countries depending on various country characteristics such as the trade openness and comparative advantage. For the US and Japan, the impact was about 2%. Burstein and Vogel (2017) as well as Burstein, Morales, and Vogel (2019) suggested that the magnitude of the impact of international trade depends on each country's trade share and the size of the elasticity of substitution across workers with different skills. Given the estimated trade shares and elasticity of substitution based on actual trade data, these studies confirmed that international trade impacted wage inequality but had only moderate effects.

As reviewed by Helpman (2016), various factors affect wage inequality, including labour supply changes, technological changes, firm and worker heterogeneity, and labour market frictions. While the impact of globalisation on wage inequality has been extensively investigated, incorporating these various factors, quantitative estimates produced so far have revealed that the effects of globalisation explain only a fraction of the actual rise in wage inequality. For example, Autor (2014) showed that the college wage premium in the US doubled from 48% in 1979 to 96% in 2012; i.e. in 2012, a college graduate earned 96% more than a high-school graduate. Thus, compared with the increase in the college wage premium, the impact of trade on the wage gap estimated by Burstein and Vogel (2017) is very small. On the other hand, in the case of Japan, Kawaguchi and Mori (2016) showed that the college wage premium decreased by 1 percentage point from 1986 to 2008.[11] Therefore, while the impact of trade on the wage gap may have been quite substantial in Japan, other factors, presumably the rapid increase in the supply of college graduates, appear to have more than offset the widening of the wage gap due to trade.

More recently, a growing number of researchers have suggested that the shift in labour demand is not actually from unskilled towards skilled workers. Rather, they argue, it is the demand for middle-skilled workers that is negatively affected by globalisation, while demand for low-skilled and high-skilled workers is increasing. The reason is that middle-skilled workers tend to engage in routine tasks that are easily computerised and/or offshored. On the other hand, non-routine cognitive analytical/interpersonal and non-routine manual physical tasks are not easily offshored, i.e. the 'offshorability' of such non-routine tasks is low. Therefore, such tasks tend to remain at home, and demand for high- and low-skilled workers engaged in these tasks has been increasing at home (e.g. Oldenski, 2012; Autor and Dorn, 2013; Becker, Ekholm, and Muendler, 2013; and Goos, Manning, and Salomons, 2014).

In the case of Japan, there are no rigorous analyses on the relationship between globalisation and labour demand at the detailed task level because of lack of data. However, employing factor content analysis using input–output tables and industry-level employment data, Tomiura, Wakasugi, and Zhu (2014) showed that Japan's net exports of routine tasks significantly decreased from 1995 to 2005. The finding suggests that globalisation has contributed to job polarisation in Japan. However, studies on European countries such as Becker, Ekholm, and Muendler (2013) and Baumgarten, Geishecker, and Görg (2013) argued that the effects of globalisation on wage gaps between workers engaged in different tasks are quite complex and depend on workers' educational attainment, skill types, the degree of task 'offshorability,' and the size and scope of firms' international activities.

In sum, many previous studies, including studies on Japan, show that globalisation has affected domestic employment, the composition of workers, and wage gaps across workers. More specifically, offshoring has shifted labour demand away from low-skilled and/or medium-skilled workers towards high-skilled workers, thereby increasing the wage gaps across different types of workers. However, relative to actually observed macro-level changes in employment and wages, it is generally believed that the direct impact of globalisation has been rather limited. Of course, it should be noted that it is difficult to perfectly separate out the impact of globalisation from other effects such as those caused by technological change (and, such as in the case of Japan, changes in the labour supply due to demographic changes).

4 Inter-industry impact of globalisation

The studies reviewed in the preceding sections have suggested that globalisation has not necessarily had a large negative impact on firm performance or the labour market. More globalised firms tend to be more productive and more incentivised to innovate, resulting in higher wages. Although globalisation has increased wage gaps across workers, the impact has been rather limited. However, most of the studies reviewed so far examine the direct impact of globalisation on the industries or firms involved and do not take inter-industry effects into account. While globalisation is likely to have a positive impact on 'better' (more internationalised and more innovative) firms and on 'better' (more skilled) workers, such effects may change the composition of activities and worker types within industries/firms. Moreover, even though the micro-level impact has been limited, it is possible that effects are amplified via inter-industry or inter-firm relationships, leading to significant structural changes such as the sharp decline in manufacturing employment shown in Figure 5.1 above.[12]

Therefore, by changing firms' behaviour and the composition of the workforce, globalisation may have accelerated structural changes. This section discusses the inter-industry effects of globalisation.

4.1 Servicification or changes in activities within manufacturing firms

One of the aspects related to the offshoring of production processes and tasks is the increased 'servicification' of manufacturing firms in many developed countries. Relatively low skill-intensive and routine task-intensive processes are easily offshored, and these processes tend to be the 'manufacturing' part of the supply chain. Therefore, manufacturing MNEs tend to move such manufacturing processes offshore and concentrate on high skill-intensive and non-routine task-intensive services at home. This is illustrated, for example, by a study by Ito and Ikeuchi (2017), who, using Japanese firm-establishment matched data, found that firms are more likely to shut down domestic establishments in more routine task-intensive industries after they became a multinational. They also found that establishments in non-routine task-intensive industries tend to show higher employment growth. While not all non-routine task-intensive industries are service industries, their study suggests that expansion abroad may have led to the restructuring of domestic activities and may to some extent have driven the 'servicification' of manufacturing firms and the economy overall.[13]

4.2 Propagation of the impact of increased imports from China across industries

In the US, some researchers such as Acemoglu et al. (2016) have argued that import competition from China has a significant impact on economy-wide employment when the indirect effects of globalisation through input–output linkages are taken into account. Acemoglu and his research group also examined how shocks in the form of increased imports from China propagate across industries via input–output linkages. For example, Acemoglu, Akcigit, and Kerr (2016) showed that increases in imports from China in an industry reduce value-added growth in upstream industries, although the impact on downstream industries is not significant.[14]

In the case of Japan, Fabinger, Shibuya, and Taniguchi (2017) examined the impact of increases in imports from China following the framework employed by Acemoglu, Akcigit, and Kerr (2016). Their results were somewhat different from those obtained by Acemoglu Akcigit, and Kerr (2016). That is, while the studies found a significant negative impact on upstream industries for both Japan and the US, increases in imports from China have a positive effect on value-added growth in downstream industries in Japan but no significant impact in the US. Therefore, while in the US increases in imports from China only have a negative impact, in the case of Japan they have a positive impact on downstream industries. While Fabinger, Shibuya, and Taniguchi (2017) did not investigate the reasons for this difference between Japan and the US, one possible interpretation is that the impact of imports differs depending on the relationship between imports and domestic production. That is, while Chinese imports likely are more complementary to domestic production in Japan, they are more likely to be substitutes in the US.

To illustrate this point, Figure 5.5 shows the value of trade between China on the one hand and the US or Japan on the other for different types of goods. The US has a trade deficit with China both in final and in intermediate goods, while Japan has a trade surplus with China in intermediate goods. This pattern suggests that Japan exports a substantial amount of intermediate goods to China, implying that Japan and China are more heavily involved in a division of labour between each other than the US and China. This difference between Japan and the US may explain the different results of the empirical studies on these two countries.

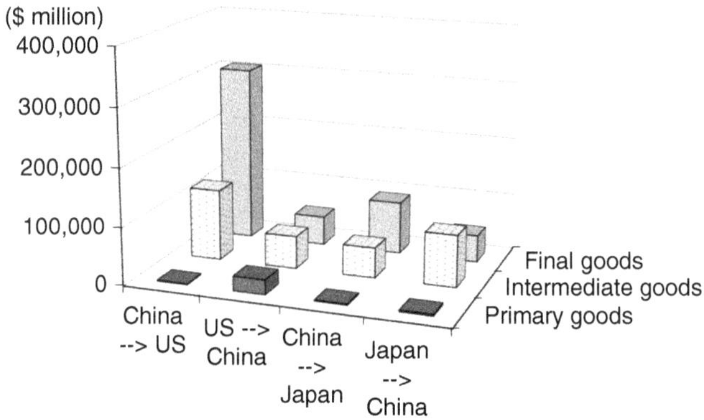

Figure 5.5 Value of China–US and China–Japan Trade by Type of Goods, 2016.
Source: RIETI (2015) RIETI Trade Industry Database 2017 (RIETI-TID2017). Tokyo: Research Institute of Economy, Trade and Industry. https://www.rieti.go.jp/en/projects/rieti-tid/ (accessed 17 January 2019).
Note: US = United States.

5 Summary and policy implications

This paper summarised the major findings of and arguments in the literature on the impact of globalisation on firm performance and the labour market, focusing on the case of Japan.

Similar to their counterparts in many other developed countries, Japanese firms that are engaged in international trade and FDI outperform other domestic firms. However, only a small number of firms is directly engaged in international business, while most firms operate only in the domestic market. A noteworthy observation for Japan is that several empirical studies confirm a learning-by-exporting effect, even though such a learning effect is not always found for other countries. Yet, there is a huge performance gap not only between exporters and non-exporters but also amongst exporters – such as between top exporters and new exporters. These findings suggest that providing support to firms trying to serve foreign markets could be an important way to improve the performance of the economy overall. Such support could take the form of policies to reduce information frictions and the risks involved in overseas business. Moreover, given that many studies show that international activities and innovation are complementary, it might be useful to devise packages that combine both policies to promote science and technology and policies to promote international trade.

As for the impact of globalisation on the labour market, many studies have shown that competition from imports as well as offshoring have shifted labour demand towards skilled workers, resulting in a widening of the wage gap between skilled and unskilled workers. However, although some types of workers, or workers in certain occupations or industries or regions, may be severely affected by globalisation, the contribution of globalisation to the widening wage gap is considered to be quite limited. Moreover, in the case of Japan, there is no strong evidence that increases in imports from China have significantly reduced domestic employment in industries and regions facing import competition from China, which differs from results for the US. The difference between Japan and the US potentially implies that imports from China are more likely to be complementary to domestic production in Japan, while they are more likely to be substitutes in the US.

The findings summarised in this paper suggest that many Japanese firms still have the potential to grow by learning from foreign markets and that Japanese firms and industries are likely to benefit from globalisation in the case where domestic production is complementary to imports from foreign countries. As for the impact of globalisation on the labour market, while some types of workers and firms do not enjoy significant benefits from globalisation, previous studies have shown that the magnitude of the impact that is directly attributable to globalisation is quite limited.

That said, it is possible that globalisation has accelerated structural changes in the Japanese economy. The share of manufacturing workers has shrunk dramatically, and more workers are now engaged in labour-intensive service industries, where labour productivity is relatively low. Looking ahead, it is likely that globalisation and technological change will be even more intertwined than they have been so far, meaning that both may have an even greater effect on firm performance and the labour market. This means that it is of the utmost importance for firms in Japan to invest in new technology and human capital to respond flexibly to the structural changes brought about by globalisation and technological change. However, various statistics indicate that Japan is lagging other developed economies in terms of investment in intangible assets such as organisational capital and human capital (see INTAN-Invest (2019) for the US and European countries and RIETI (2015) for Japan). Therefore, it may be useful to provide policy support to increase investment, particularly investment in intangible assets, by firms that are striving to succeed in the global market. Japanese firms need to continue investing in R&D, human capital, global production and distribution networks, new technology, etc., to benefit from the globalised economy. Amongst such investment, investment in human capital is of particular importance, as it helps workers respond to the structural changes brought about by globalisation and hence can help to address the growing anti-globalisation sentiment and protectionism mentioned at the outset.

Notes

1 Baily and Bosworth (2014) and Fort, Pierce, and Schott (2018) showed a similar trend for manufacturing in the United States (US).

2 There is a large body of literature on the relationship between globalisation and firms' performance. See previous literature reviews such as those by Greenaway and Kneller (2007); Wagner (2007, 2012); and Hayakawa, Machikita, and Kimura (2012).

3 Wakasugi et al. (2011) and many other studies have shown that firms engaged in international activities such as exporting and FDI are not only more productive but also outperform other firms in various other respects. For instance, such firms are larger, more R&D-intensive, more capital- and skill-intensive, and pay higher wages. As for the wage premium of exporters, Ito (2017) found that, after controlling for worker characteristics, the premium is much larger for smaller plants than for larger ones. On the other hand, Tanaka (2018) concluded that most of the wage premium of exporting and/or FDI firms can be accounted for by worker characteristics. These results may suggest that internationalised firms, particularly large internationalised firms, tend to employ more skilled workers, resulting in higher performance and higher wages.

4 The same study on which Figure 5.3 is based (METI, 2012) provided a similar figure comparing firms that started FDI (rather than exports) and firms that did not. The figure indicates that FDI starters similarly show higher productivity growth after starting FDI.

5 Regarding other countries, Damijan, Kostevc, and Polanec (2010), for example, examined the bidirectional causal relationship in the case of Slovenia.

6 Yamashita and Yamauchi (2020) employed a similar approach to that used by Bloom, Draca, and Van Reenen (2016) for European firms and by Autor et al. (2016) for US firms. While Bloom, Draca, and Van Reenen (2016) found a positive impact of import competition from China on patent applications by European firms, Autor et al. (2016) obtained the opposite result for US firms.

7 Studies for European countries (e.g. Dauth, Findeisen, and Suedekum, 2014; Balsvik, Jensen, and Salvanes, 2015; and Donoso, Martin, and Minondo, 2015) obtained results consistent with those of Autor, Dorn, and Hanson (2013) for the US.

8 Analysing data for US MNEs, Harrison and McMillan (2011) concluded that increases in offshoring by US MNEs reduced manufacturing employment at home, but the magnitude was very limited.

9 According to Wagner (2011), many studies on developed countries have found no statistically significant relationship between FDI and employment at home. Instead, several studies have found a positive relationship.

10 The definition of 'skilled' or 'unskilled' workers differs across studies. For instance, Ito and Fukao (2005) defined skilled workers as workers whose profession is classified as 'professional and technical' or 'managerial and administrative.' Meanwhile Ahn et al. (2008) and Kiyota and Maruyama (2017) defined 'skill' in terms of educational attainment, while Yamashita (2008), Head and Ries (2002), and Hayakawa et al. (2013) defined workers in terms of whether they are engaged in production or non-production activities and regard non-production workers as 'skilled' workers.

11 In contrast, for the US, Kawaguchi and Mori (2016) estimated that the college wage premium increased by 22 percentage points from 1986 to 2008.

12 In the case of other developed countries, there is some empirical evidence that offshoring and import competition have negatively affected the demand for middle-skilled workers in the manufacturing sector and have forced such workers into low-wage service jobs. See, for example, Ebenstein et al. (2014); Goos, Manning, and Salomons (2014); and Keller and Utar (2016).

13 Bernard, Smeets, and Warzynski (2017) and Crozet and Milet (2017) showed that the switch to the service sector or 'servicification' of manufacturing firms explains a significant part of the reduction of manufacturing employment and sales in Denmark and France, respectively.

14 In the case of the US, imports from China have a significant negative impact on overall employment because of both direct and indirect effects. Acemoglu et al.

(2016) estimated that about 2.0 million–2.4 million workers in the US manufacturing sector lost their jobs during 1999–2011 because of import competition from China.

References

Acemoglu, D., U. Akcigit, and W. Kerr (2016), 'Networks and the Macroeconomy: An Empirical Exploration', *NBER Macroeconomics Annual*, 30(1), pp.273–335.

Acemoglu, D., D. Dorn, G.H. Hanson, and B. Price (2016), 'Import Competition and the Great US Employment Sag of the 2000s', *Journal of Labor Economics*, 34(S1), pp.S141–S198.

Ahn, S., K. Fukao, and K. Ito (2008), 'Outsourcing in East Asia and Its Impact on the Japanese and Korean Labour Markets', *OECD Trade Policy Papers*, No. 65. Paris: Organisation for Economic Co-operation and Development.

Ando, M. and F. Kimura (2017), 'Job Creation and Destruction at the Levels of Intra-firm Sections, Firms, and Industries in Globalization: The Case of Japanese Manufacturing Firms', *RIETI Discussion Paper*, 17-E-100. Tokyo: Research Institute of Economy, Trade and Industry.

Autor, D.H. (2014), 'Skills, Education, and the Rise of Earnings Inequality Among the "Other 99 Percent"', *Science*, 344(6186), pp.843–851.

Autor, D.H. and D. Dorn (2013), 'The Growth of Low-Skill Service Jobs and the Polarization of the US Labor Market', *American Economic Review*, 103(5), pp.1553–1597.

Autor, D.H., D. Dorn, and G.H. Hanson (2013), 'The China Syndrome: Local Labor Market Effects of Import Competition in the United States', *American Economic Review*, 103(6), pp.2121–2168.

Autor, D., D. Dorn, G.H. Hanson, G. Pisano, and P. Shu (2016), 'Foreign Competition and Domestic Innovation: Evidence from U.S. Patents', *NBER Working Paper*, No. 22879. Cambridge, MA: National Bureau of Economic Research.

Baily, M.N. and B.P. Bosworth (2014), 'US Manufacturing: Understanding Its Past and Its Potential Future', *Journal of Economic Perspectives*, 28(1), pp.3–26.

Balsvik, R., S. Jensen, and K.G. Salvanes (2015), 'Made in China, Sold in Norway: Local Labor Market Effects of an Import Shock', *Journal of Public Economics*, 127, pp.137–144.

Baumgarten, D., I. Geishecker, and H. Görg (2013), 'Offshoring, Tasks, and the Skill-Wage Pattern', *European Economic Review*, 61, pp.132–152.

Becker, S.O., K. Ekholm, and M.A. Muendler (2013), 'Offshoring and the Onshore Composition of Tasks and Skills', *Journal of International Economics*, 90(1), pp.91–106.

Bernard, A.B. and J.B. Jensen (1999), 'Exceptional Exporter Performance: Cause, Effect, or Both?', *Journal of International Economics*, 47(1), pp.1–25.

Bernard, A.B., V. Smeets, and F. Warzynski (2017), 'Rethinking Deindustrialization', *Economic Policy*, 32(89), pp.5–38.

Bloom, N., M. Draca, and J. Van Reenen (2016), 'Trade Induced Technical Change? The Impact of Chinese Imports and Innovation, IT and Productivity', *The Review of Economic Studies*, 83(1), pp.87–117.

Branstetter, L. (2006), 'Is Foreign Direct Investment A Channel of Knowledge Spillovers? Evidence from Japan's FDI in the United States', *Journal of International Economics*, 68(2), pp.325–344.

Burstein, A. and J. Vogel (2017), 'International Trade, Technology, and the Skill Premium', *Journal of Political Economy*, 125(5), pp.1356–1412.

Burstein, A., E. Morales, and J. Vogel (2019) 'Changes in Between-Group Inequality: Computers, Occupations, and International Trade', *American Economic Journal: Macroeconomics*, 11(2), pp.348–400.

Crozet, M. and E. Milet (2017), 'The Servitization of French Manufacturing Firms: Outsourcing, Servitization, and the Future of Industry,' in L. Fontagné and A. Harrison (eds.) *The Factory-Free Economy: Outsourcing, Servitization, and the Future of Industry*. Oxford: Oxford University Press, pp.111–135.

Damijan, J.P., C. Kostevc, and S. Polanec (2010), 'From Innovation to Exporting or Vice Versa?', *The World Economy*, 33(3), pp.374–398.

Dauth, W., S. Findeisen, and J. Suedekum (2014), 'The Rise of the East and the Far East: German Labor Markets and Trade Integration', *Journal of the European Economic Association*, 12(6), pp.1643–1675.

Donoso, V., V. Martin, and A. Minondo (2015), 'Do Differences in the Exposure to Chinese Imports Lead to Differences in Local Labour Market Outcomes? An Analysis for Spanish Provinces', *Regional Studies*, 49(10), pp.1746–1764.

Ebenstein, A., A. Harrison, M. McMillan, and S. Phillips (2014), 'Estimating the Impact of Trade and Offshoring on American Workers Using the Current Population Surveys', *The Review of Economics and Statistics*, 96(4), pp.581–595.

Endoh, M. (2018), 'The Effect of Import Competition on Wages in the Japanese Manufacturing Sector', *Asian Economic Papers*, 17(1), pp.46–67.

Fabinger, M., Y. Shibuya, and M. Taniguchi (2017), 'International Influences on Japanese Supply Chains', *RIETI Discussion Paper*, 17-E-022. Tokyo: Research Institute of Economy, Trade and Industry.

Feenstra, R.C. and G. Hanson (1996), 'Globalization, Outsourcing, and Wage Inequality', *The American Economic Review*, 86(2), pp.240–245.

Feenstra, R.C. and G. Hanson (1999), 'The Impact of Outsourcing and High-Technology Capital on Wages: Estimates for the United States, 1979–1990', *The Quarterly Journal of Economics*, 114(3), pp.907–940.

Fort, T.C., J.R. Pierce, and P.K. Schott (2018), 'New Perspectives on the Decline of US Manufacturing Employment', *Journal of Economic Perspectives*, 32(2), pp.47–72.

Goos, M., A. Manning, and A. Salomons (2014), 'Explaining Job Polarization: Routine-Biased Technological Change and Offshoring', *American Economic Review*, 104(8), pp.2509–2526.

Greenaway, D. and R. Kneller (2007), 'Firm Heterogeneity, Exporting and Foreign Direct Investment', *The Economic Journal*, 117(517), pp.F134–F161.

Haneda, S. and K. Ito (2014), 'Modes of International Activities and the Innovativeness of Firms: An Empirical Analysis Based on the Japanese National Innovation Survey for 2009', *Economics of Innovation and New Technology*, 23(8), pp.758–779.

Harrison, A. and M. McMillan (2011), 'Offshoring Jobs? Multinationals and U.S. Manufacturing Employment', *The Review of Economics and Statistics*, 93(3), pp.857–875.

Hayakawa, K., T. Machikita, and F. Kimura (2012), 'Globalization and Productivity: A Survey of Firm-Level Analysis', *Journal of Economic Surveys*, 26(2), pp.332–350.

Hayakawa, K., T. Matsuura, K. Motohashi, and A. Obashi (2013), 'Two-Dimensional Analysis of the Impact of Outward FDI on Performance at Home: Evidence from Japanese Manufacturing Firms', *Japan and the World Economy*, 27(C), pp.25–33.

Head, K. and J. Ries (2002), 'Offshore Production and Skill Upgrading by Japanese Manufacturing Firms', *Journal of International Economics*, 58(1), pp.81–105.

Helpman, E. (2016), 'Globalization and Wage Inequality', *NBER Working Paper*, No. 22944. Cambridge, MA: National Bureau of Economic Research.

Helpman, E., M.J. Melitz, and S.R. Yeaple (2004), 'Export Versus FDI with Heterogeneous Firms', *The American Economic Review*, 94(1), pp.300–316.

Hijzen, A., T. Inui, and Y. Todo (2010), 'Does Offshoring Pay? Firm-Level Evidence from Japan', *Economic Inquiry*, 48(4), pp.880–895.

INTAN-Invest (2019), INTAN-Invest Database, Edition January 2019. http://www.intaninvest.net/intan-invest-data/download-data/ (accessed 7 April 2019).

Inui, T., K. Ito, and D. Miyakawa (2015), 'Overseas Market Information and Firms' Export Decision', *Economic Inquiry*, 53(3), pp.1671–1688.

Inui T., K. Ito, and D. Miyakawa (2017), 'Export Experience, Product Differentiation and Firm Survival in Export Markets', *The Japanese Economic Review*, 68(2), pp.217–231.

Ito, K. (2017), 'Wage Premium of Exporting Plants in Japan: Do Plant and Firm Size Matter?', *RIETI Discussion Paper*, No. 17-E-115. Tokyo: Research Institute of Economy, Trade and Industry.

Ito, K. (2019), 'Exporter Dynamics and Productivity Dispersion within Industry', *ERIA Discussion Paper*, No. 20. Jakarta: Economic Research Institute for ASEAN and East Asia.

Ito, K. and K. Fukao (2005), 'Physical and Human Capital Deepening and New Trade Patterns in Japan', in T. Ito and A. Rose (eds.) *International Trade in East Asia*. Chicago: University of Chicago Press, pp.7–49.

Ito, K. and K. Ikeuchi (2017), 'Overseas Expansion and Domestic Business Restructuring in Japanese Firms', *The Developing Economics*, 55(2), pp.75–104.

Ito, K., K. Ikeuchi, C. Criscuolo, J. Timmis, and A. Bergeaud (2019), 'Global Value Chains and Domestic Innovation', *RIETI Discussion Paper*, No. 19-E-028. Tokyo: Research Institute of Economy, Trade and Industry.

Ito, K. and S. Lechevalier (2010), 'Why Some Firms Persistently Out-Perform Others: Investigating the Interactions Between Innovation and Exporting Strategies', *Industrial and Corporate Change*, 19(6), pp.1997–2039.

Ito, K. and A. Tanaka (2014), 'The Impact of Multinationals' Overseas Expansion on Employment at Suppliers at Home: New Evidence from Firm-Level Transaction Relationship Data for Japan', *RIETI Discussion Paper*, No. 14-E-011. Tokyo: Research Institute of Economy, Trade and Industry.

Ito, B. and A. Tanaka (2016), 'External R&D, Productivity, and Export: Evidence from Japanese Firms', *Review of World Economics*, 152(3), pp.577–596.

Ito, B., E. Tomiura, and R. Wakasugi (2011), 'Offshore Outsourcing and Productivity: Evidence from Japanese Firm-level Data Disaggregated by Tasks', *Review of International Economics*, 19(3), pp.555–567.

Kambayashi, R. and K. Kiyota (2015), 'Disemployment Caused by Foreign Direct Investment? Multinationals and Japanese Employment', *Review of World Economics*, 151(3), pp.433–460.

Kawaguchi, D. and Y. Mori (2016), 'Why Has Wage Inequality Evolved So Differently Between Japan and the US? The Role of the Supply of College-Educated Workers', *Economics of Education Review*, 52(C), pp.29–50.

Keller, W. and H. Utar (2016), 'International Trade and Job Polarization: Evidence at the Worker-Level,' *NBER Working Paper*, No. 22315. Cambridge, MA: National Bureau of Economic Research.

Kimura, F. and K. Kiyota (2006), 'Exports, FDI, and Productivity: Dynamic Evidence from Japanese Firms', *Review of World Economics*, 142(4), pp.695–719.

Kiyota, K. and S. Maruyama (2017), 'ICT, Offshoring, and the Demand for Part-Time Workers: The Case of Japanese Manufacturing', *Journal of Asian Economics*, 48(C), pp.75–86.

Mairesse, J. and P. Mohnen (2002), 'Accounting for Innovation and Measuring Innovativeness: An Illustrative Framework and an Application', *The American Economic Review*, 92(2), pp.226–230.

Mayer, T. and G.I.P. Ottaviano (2008), 'The Happy Few: The Internationalisation of European Firms', *Intereconomics*, 43(3), pp.135–148.

METI (2012), *White Paper on International Economy and Trade 2012*. Tokyo: Ministry of Economy, Trade and Industry.

Oldenski, L. (2012), 'Export Versus FDI and the Communication of Complex Information', *Journal of International Economics*, 87(2), pp.312–322.

RIETI (2015), *Japan Industrial Productivity Database 2015 (JIP Database 2015): Investment and Capital Stock in Intangible Assets*. Tokyo: Research Institute of Economy, Trade and Industry. https://www.rieti.go.jp/en/database/JIP2015/index.html (accessed 7April2019).

Sakurai, K. (2014), 'Gurobaru-ka to Nihon no Rodoshijo: Boeki ga Chingin Kakusa ni ataeru Eikyo wo Chushin ni' (Globalization and the Japanese Labour Market: Focusing on the Impact of International Trade on Wage Gaps), *Bank of Japan Working Paper*, 14-J-5. Tokyo: Bank of Japan.

Sasaki, H. and K. Sakura (2004), 'Seizogyo ni okeru Jukuren Rodo he no Juyo Shifuto: Sukiru Henko-teki Gijutsu Shimpo to Gurobaru-ka no Eikyo' (The Demand Shift to Skilled Labor in the Manufacturing Sector: The Impact of Skill-Biased Technological Change and Globalization, *Bank of Japan Working Paper*, 04-J-17. Tokyo: Bank of Japan.

Tanaka, A. (2012a), 'Firm Productivity and the Number of FDI Destinations: Evidence from a Non-Parametric Test', *Economics Letters*, 117(1), pp.1–3.

Tanaka, A. (2012b), 'The Effects of FDI on Domestic Employment and Workforce Composition', *RIETI Discussion Paper*, No. 12-E-069. Tokyo: Research Institute of Economy, Trade and Industry.

Tanaka, A (2018), 'Why Do Exporters and Multinational Firms Pay Higher Wages? Evidence from Japanese Linked Employer–Employee Data', *Kyoto University Graduate School of Economics Discussion Paper Series*, No. E-17-013. Kyoto: Kyoto University.

Taniguchi, M. (2019), 'The Effect of an Increase in Imports from China on Regional Labor Markets in Japan', *Journal of the Japanese and International Economies*, 51, pp.1–18.

Todo, Y. (2011a), 'Quantitative Evaluation of the Determinants of Export and FDI: Firm-Level Evidence from Japan', *The World Economy*, 34(3), pp.355–381.

Todo, Y. (2011b), *Nihon Keizai no Sokojikara: Garyo ga Mezameru-toki* (*The Underlying Strength of the Japanese Economy: The Time When the Unrecognized Genius Arises from Sleep*). Tokyo: Chuokoron-Shinsha.

Todo, Y. and H. Sato (2014), 'Effects of Presidents' Characteristics on Internationalization of Small and Medium Firms in Japan', *Journal of the Japanese and International Economies*, 34, pp.236–255.

Tomiura, E. (2003), 'The Impact of Import Competition on Japanese Manufacturing Employment', *Journal of the Japanese and International Economies*, 17(2), pp.118–133.

Tomiura, E. (2007) 'Foreign Outsourcing, Exporting, and FDI: A Productivity Comparison at the Firm Level', *Journal of International Economics*, 72(1), pp.113–127.

Tomiura, E., R. Wakasugi, and L. Zhu (2014), 'Task Content of Trade: A Disaggregated Measurement of Japanese Changes', *Japanese Economic Review*, 65(2), pp.238–251.

Wagner, J. (2007), 'Exports and Productivity: A Survey of the Evidence from Firm-Level Data', *The World Economy*, 30(1), pp.60–82.

Wagner, J. (2011), 'Offshoring and Firm Performance: Self-Selection, Effects on Performance, or Both?', *Review of World Economics*, 147(2), pp.217–247.

Wagner, J. (2012), 'International Trade and Firm Performance: A Survey of Empirical Studies Since 2006', *Review of World Economics*, 148(2), pp.235–267.

Wakasugi, R., B. Ito, T. Matsuura, H. Sato, A. Tanaka, and Y. Todo (2011), 'Features of Japanese Internationalized Firms: Findings Based on Firm-Level Data', in R. Wakasugi (ed.) *Internationalization of Japanese Firms: Evidence from Firm-level Data*. Tokyo: Springer, pp.15–45.

Yamashita, N. (2008), 'The Impact of Production Fragmentation on Skill Upgrading: New Evidence from Japanese Manufacturing', *Journal of the Japanese and International Economies*, 22(4), pp.545–565.

Yamashita, N. and K. Fukao (2010), 'Expansion Abroad and Jobs at Home: Evidence from Japanese Multinational Enterprises', *Japan and the World Economy*, 22(2), pp.88–97.

Yamashita, N. and I. Yamauchi (2020), 'Innovation Responses of Japanese Firms to Chinese Import Competition', *The World Economy*, 43(1), pp. 60-80

Yashiro, N. and D. Hirano (2010), 'Anatomy of Learning-from-Exporting: Role of Foreign Knowledge Acquisition', *RIETI Discussion Paper*, No. 10-E-053. Tokyo: Research Institute of Economy, Trade and Industry.

Appendix

Table 5A.1 Recent Empirical Studies on the Economic Impact of Globalisation Focusing on Japan

Author(s) and date	*Findings*
1. Globalization and firm productivity	
Wakasugi et al. (2011)	Exporters/MNEs have higher TFP than non-exporters/non-MNEs.
Tanaka (2012a)	MNEs investing in more regions tend to be more productive.
Kimura and Kiyota (2006)	More productive firms tend to be exporters/MNEs (selection effect). Exporters/MNEs enjoy higher productivity growth (learning effect).
Todo (2011a)	Both the selection and learning effects are confirmed. However, the magnitude of the selection effect is economically negligible.
Todo (2011b)	There are a significant number of firms that do not export despite their high productivity.
Hijzen, Inui, and Todo (2010)	Offshoring has a positive effect on productivity.
Ito, Tomiura, and Wakasugi (2011)	Firms offshoring various tasks to various destinations enjoy higher productivity growth.
2. Exporting and firm characteristics	
Wakasugi et al. (2011)	The largest 10% of exporters account for 92% of Japan's total exports.
Ito (2019)	There is a huge productivity gap between the top exporters and other exporters.
Inui, Ito, and Miyakawa (2015)	Firms that have access to information on foreign markets via their main bank are more likely to start exporting.
Inui, Ito, and Miyakawa (2017)	Many export starters stop exporting in a short period. More R&D-intensive firms tend to survive in export markets for a longer period.
3. Innovation and internationalization	
Ito and Lechevalier (2010)	Firms engaged in R&D activities are more likely to improve their productivity after entering export markets.
Ito and Tanaka (2016)	Exporters engaged in R&D activities (either inhouse R&D or R&D outsourcing) are more productive than non-exporters and exporters with no R&D.
Haneda and Ito (2014)	New products tend to make up a much larger of sales for firms engaged in international activities than for domestic firms.
Branstetter (2006)	Japanese firms investing in the United States receive significant knowledge spillovers from US firms. In addition, US firms also receive knowledge spillovers from Japanese firms that have invested in the United States.

(*Continued*)

Table 5A.1 (Continued)

Author(s) and date	*Findings*
Yashiro and Hirano (2010)	Exporters that gather various kinds of information from foreign markets are more likely to succeed in technology upgrading and development of new products.
Yamashita and Yamauchi (2020)	Exporters/Importers tend to file for more patents in response to increased import competition from China.
Ito et al. (2019)	Exporters in sectors with higher network centrality tend to file for more high-quality patents.
4. Globalization and domestic employment.	
Tomiura (2003)	Import competition has a negative effect on domestic employment.
Sakurai (2014)	Factor-contents of trade estimation results suggest that the net impact of exports and imports on domestic employment is rather limited.
Taniguchi (2019)	Imports from China have a positive effect on manufacturing employment.
Yamashita and Fukao (2010)	There is no significant negative relationship between overseas employment by Japanese MNEs and their domestic employment.
Kambayashi and Kiyota (2015)	Manufacturing disemployment in Japan is not driven by the reallocation of labour from Japan to overseas via FDI.
Ando and Kimura (2017)	Japanese MNEs that expand overseas operations tend to increase domestic employment.
Ito and Tanaka (2014)	There is no significant negative relationship between employment by domestic suppliers and overseas expansion of their customers.
5. Impact on skill composition	
Ito and Fukao (2005)	Increases in imports of intermediate inputs increase the share of skilled workers in the Japanese manufacturing sector.
Ahn Fukao, and Ito (2008)	There is a positive relationship between intermediate input imports from Asia and skill intensity in Japan.
Yamashita (2008)	There is a positive relationship between intermediate input imports from Asia and skill intensity in Japan.
Kiyota and Maruyama (2017)	Offshoring increases the demand for high-skill workers in Japan.
Head and Ries (2002)	Expansion of overseas production of Japanese MNEs increases the skill intensity at home.
Hayakawa et al. (2013)	Expansion of overseas production of Japanese MNEs increases the skill intensity at home.
Tanaka (2012b)	The share of temporary workers dispatched from staffing companies increases after a firm becomes a multinational.

(*Continued*)

Table 5A.1 (Continued)

Author(s) and date	*Findings*
6. Impact on wages, etc.	
Sasaki and Sakura (2004)	Import competition and offshoring increase the wage gap between skilled and unskilled workers.
Sakurai (2014)	Import competition and offshoring increase the wage gap between skilled and unskilled workers.
Endoh (2018)	Offshoring increases the wage gap between skilled and unskilled workers.
Burstein and Vogel (2017)	International trade increases the wage gap between skilled and unskilled workers by 5.1% on average for 60 countries, but the impact cpcprintis is only approximately 2% in the case of Japan.
Tomiura, Wakasugi, and Zhu (2014)	Japan's net exports of routine tasks significantly decreased from 1995 to 2005.
7. Inter-industry impact of globalization	
Ito and Ikeuchi (2017)	Firms are more likely to shut down domestic establishments in more routine task-intensive industries after they became a multinational.
Fabinger, Shibuya, and Taniguchi (2017)	Imports from China have a negative effect on value added growth in upstream industries but a positive effect in downstream industries.

FDI = foreign direct investment, MNE = multinational enterprise, R&D = research and development, TFP = total factor productivity. Source: Author's compilation. MNE = Multinational Enterprises. R&D = Research & Development. TFP = Total Factor Productivity. FDI = Foreign Direct Investment. Source: Author's compilation.

6 Globalisation and economic development: Malaysia's experience

Cassey Lee

1 Introduction

Globalisation has historically played an important role in the emergence of Malaysia as a nation and its subsequent development. Almost every important aspect of globalisation involving trade, capital, labour migration, technology, and information flows has left deep imprints on Malaysia's economy and society. The nature and impact of globalisation, however, have changed over time. These changes include the economic transformation of an economy that was highly dependent on primary commodities (tin and rubber) into one driven by manufactured exports. Waves of migrant workers have also shaped the country into a multi-ethnic society especially since the nineteenth century. The openness of the country's economy in terms of trade and investment has also made it vulnerable to global economic shocks.

The goal of this paper is to examine the impact of globalisation on the Malaysian economy through the different phases of its development experience. This will include socio-economic development (poverty eradication and inequality), structural transformation (industrialisation and deindustrialisation), and vulnerability to external shocks (oil crises and financial crises). The paper will also discuss the country's domestic and external economic policies aimed at meeting domestic needs (affirmative action) and managing the effects of globalisation.

2 Globalisation and the formation of Malaysia

The formation of Malaysia as a nation is a useful starting point for analysing the impact of globalisation on the country. Globalisation played an important role in the economic and political history of Malaysia in the pre-colonial, colonial, and post-colonial (independence) periods. In the pre-colonial period from the fifteenth to the eighteenth century, the early states in Peninsular Malaysia such as Melaka and Penang grew as major entrepôts for intra- and inter-regional trade flows. The strategic locations of these port cities together with bountiful natural resources (gold, tin, forest products) in their hinterlands attracted successive and competing colonial powers from the West.

DOI: 10.4324/9781003138501-6

The Portuguese conquered and occupied Melaka in 1511. The Dutch wrested Melaka from the Portuguese in 1641 and it remained under their control until it was handed over to the British as part of the 1824 Anglo-Dutch Treaty.[1] Penang came into the possession of the British East India Company when the island was leased from Sultan Abdullah of Kedah in 1786. Melaka and Singapore came under the control of the British East India Company in 1864. Three years later, in 1867, the three entrepôt states became crown colonies (Straits Settlements) and their administration was shifted from Calcutta to London in 1867.

The British colonisation of the rest of Peninsular Malaysia (Malaya) began to take shape in the 1870–80s with the implementation of the Resident System in the states of Perak (in 1874), Selangor (1874), Negeri Sembilan (1887), and Pahang (1888).[2] Control over these states was subsequently centralised with the formation of the Federated Malay States in 1896. The other Northern Malay states of Perlis, Kedah, Kelantan, and Terengganu came under British control with the signing of the Anglo-Siamese Treaty in 1909. These states, together with Johor, became British protectorates and were collectively known as the Unfederated Malay States. Two other states on Borneo island, namely Sabah and Sarawak, became British protectorates by 1888. Thus, by the late nineteenth century, all of the states that are part of Malaysia today had come under British control.

British control was disrupted by the Japanese occupation during the Second World War from 1941 to 1945. In the aftermath of the war, administration of all of the states in Malaya was centralised under British control through the formation of the Malayan Union in 1946. Fierce opposition from the Malay community and Malay rulers led to the replacement of the Malayan Union with the Federation of Malaya in 1948. Malaya gained independence in 1957. In 1963, Singapore, Sabah, and Sarawak joined Malaya to form Malaysia. Two years later in 1965, Singapore exited Malaysia, and the polity of Malaysia has remained unchanged since then.

In summary, the amalgamation of states into the Federation of Malaysia can be seen as part of the globalisation process involving colonialisation and de-colonialisation. The political changes that took place during this process were accompanied by significant growth and structural change in the economy.

3 Trade, growth, and structural change

Since the country's independence in 1957 and over a period of about 50 years since then, Malaysia has developed to become an upper middle-income developing country. In 1960, the country's gross domestic product (GDP) per capita stood at $1,354 (in 2010 constant prices), around 10% of the GDP per capita of the United Kingdom. By 2017, Malaysia's GDP per capita reached $11,528, about 27% of the GDP per capita of the United Kingdom (Figure 6.1). How did Malaysia grow to become a middle-income country? Trade has clearly played an important role in the country's growth and development, as can be seen in the country's dependence on it.

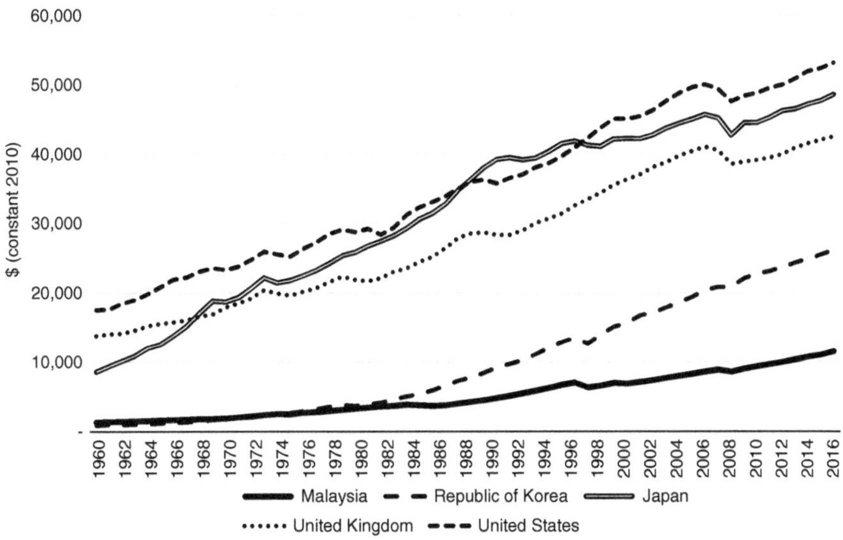

Figure 6.1 Gross Domestic Product Per Capita of Malaysia and Selected Developed Countries, 1960–2017.
Source: World Bank Open Data. https://data.worldbank.org (accessed 30 July 2019).

3.1 Pre-independence period

The Malaysian economy has always been very open. Even in the pre-independence period, the country's trade ratio (share of trade in GDP) ranged from 80% to 120% (Figure 6.2). In the post-independence period, Malaysia became even more open. The country's trade ratio rose from around 100% in the mid-1970s to a peak of 220% in 2000 (Figure 6.3). Thereafter, the country's trade ratio began to decline due to deindustrialisation. Despite this, the country's economy remains very open with a trade ratio of around 135%.

With trade as a major source of growth, the country did experience fairly high growth rates during the pre-independence period (Figure 6.4). However, economic growth during this period was very erratic. A major source of this instability was the importance of primary commodities such as tin and rubber as major sources of exports. These two commodities accounted for close to 80% of total exports during this period (Figure 6.5). Fluctuations in the prices of these commodities affected the country's economy.

Tin was an important industry in the late 1880s. Although tin had been mined in Malaya for hundreds of years, the discovery of tin in Perak in 1840 led to a rapid expansion of the industry through the mid-1890s. The tin industry also developed rapidly in other states, such as Selangor, Negeri Sembilan, and Pahang. The Second World War adversely affected tin production, but production recovered after the war, reaching a peak around 1970 and declining thereafter.

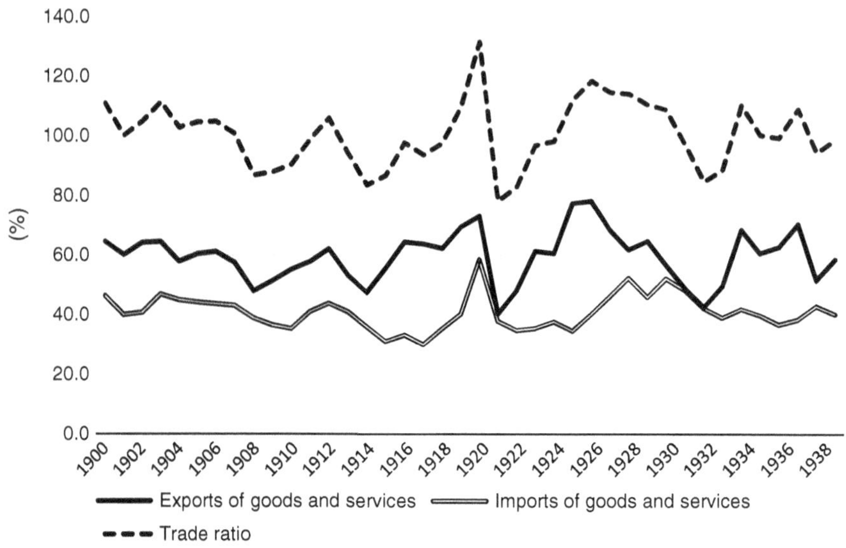

Figure 6.2 Share of Imports and Exports in Gross Domestic Product – Malaya, 1900–39.

Source: Economic History of Malaya. https://www.ehm.my/home (accessed 30 July 2019).

The decline in the importance of tin production and exports were offset by the rising importance of rubber exports, especially after the 1890s. The rubber industry grew rapidly in the states of Selangor, Perak, and Negeri Sembilan from 1905, but stagnated during the Japanese occupation and during the 1950s due to competition from synthetic rubber. However, the industry grew rapidly from the 1960s through the mid-1980s. The rubber industry only began to stagnate and decline after the mid-1980s (Figure 6.6).

3.2 Post-independence period

The subsequent decline of tin and rubber as sources of exports did not spell doom for the Malaysian economy in the post-independence years. Economic growth became more robust and less volatile in some periods. Although external global shocks such as the oil crisis in the 1970s and the Asian financial crisis in the 1990s did affect the Malaysian economy, it managed to maintain relatively robust growth during intermittent periods (Figure 6.7). For example, the average growth rate was 10% during 1988–96.

The relatively robust growth rates achieved in some periods in the post-independence era were made possible by the economic diversification strategies pursued and promoted by the Government of Malaysia. These strategies included

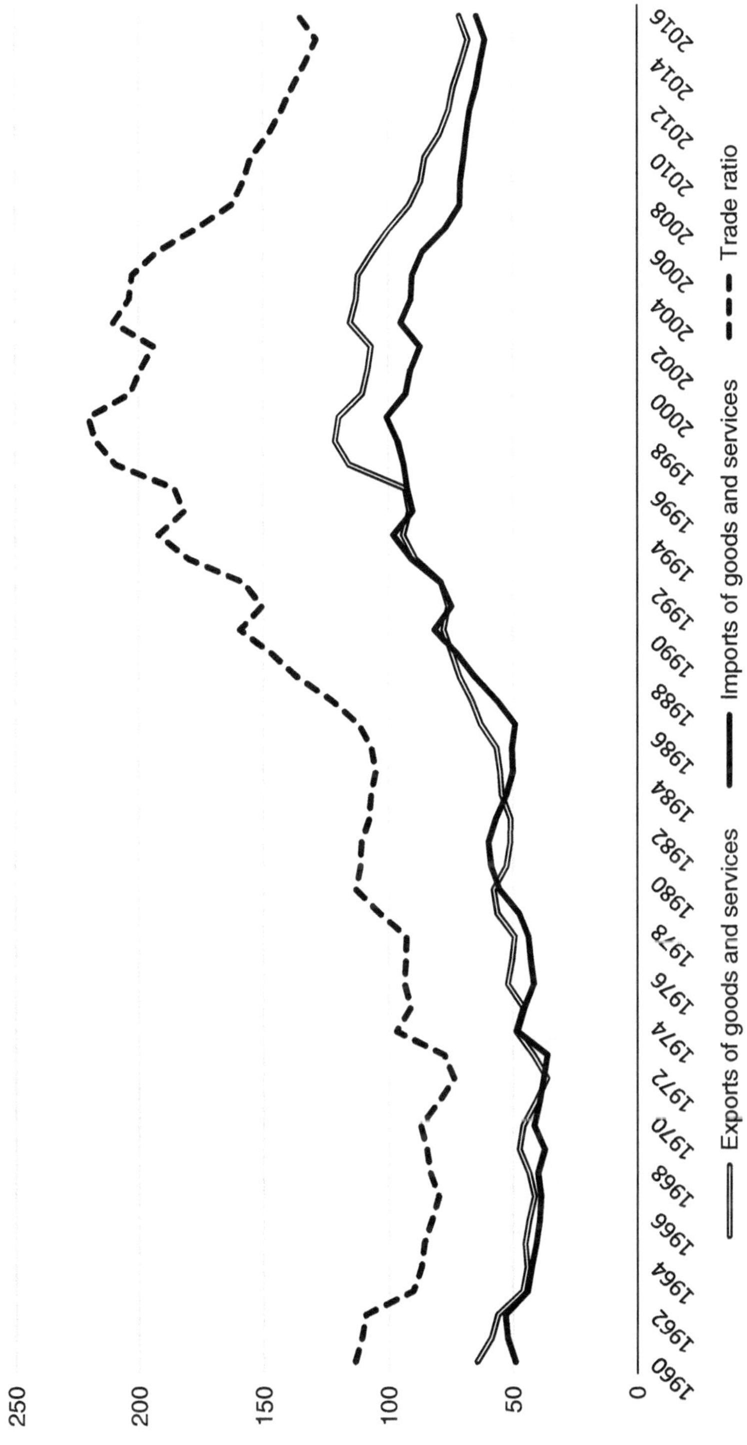

Figure 6.3 Share of Imports and Exports in Gross Domestic Product – Malaysia, 1960–2017.
Source: World Bank Open Data. https://data.worldbank.org (accessed 30 July 2019).

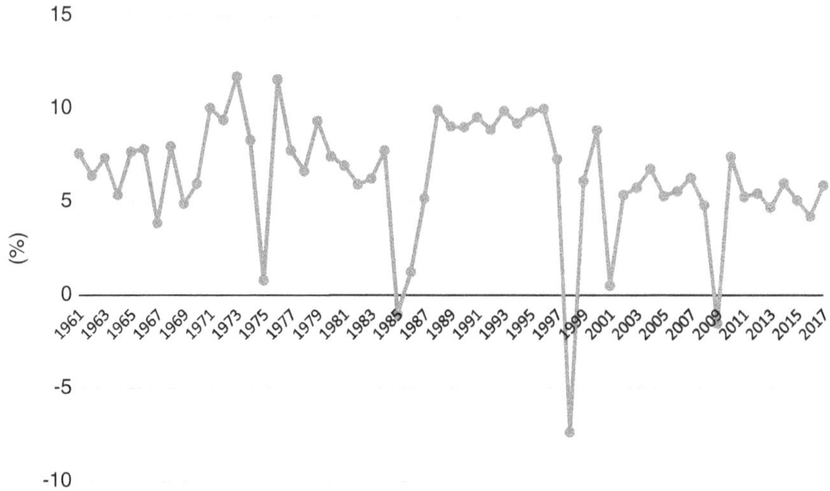

Figure 6.4 Annual Real Gross Domestic Product Growth – Malaya, 1901–39.
Source: Economic History of Malaya. https://www.ehm.my/home (accessed 30 July 2019).

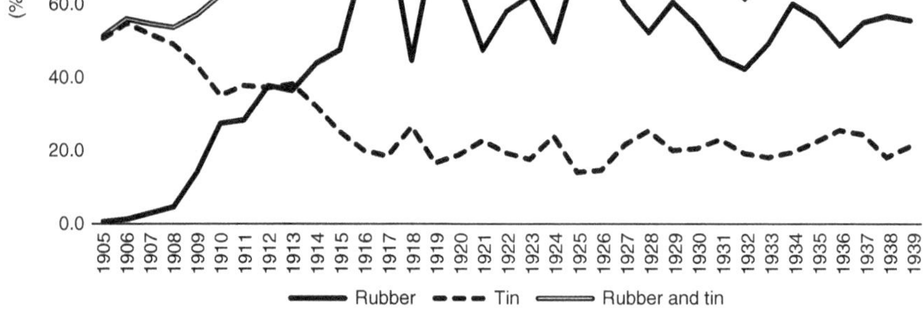

Figure 6.5 Malaya – Share of Tin and Rubber in Total Exports.
Source: Economic History of Malaya. https://www.ehm.my/home (accessed 30 July 2019).

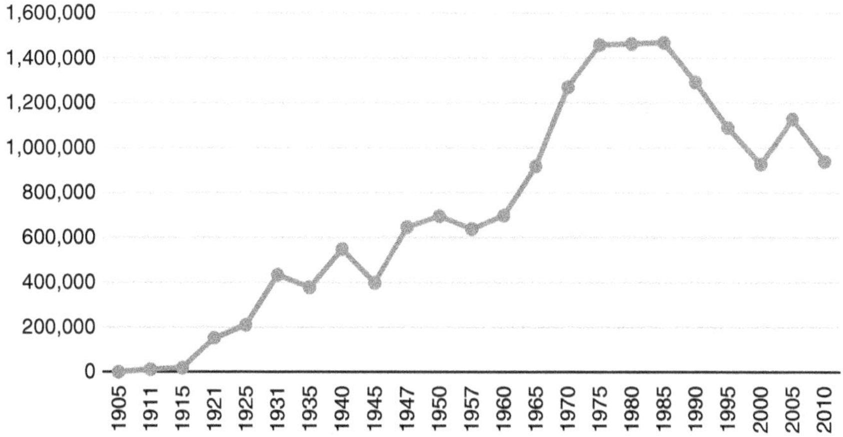

Figure 6.6 Rubber Production, 1905–2010 (tonnes).
Sources: Food and Agriculture Organization of the United Nations; Bruton (1992). *The Political Economy of Poverty, Equity and Growth: Sri Lanka and Malaysia*. Washington, DC: World Bank; Lim (1967). *Economic Development of Modern Malaya*. Kuala Lumpur: Oxford University Press.

Figure 6.7 Annual Real Gross Domestic Product Growth – Malaysia, 1961–2017.
Source: World Bank Open Data. https://data.worldbank.org (accessed 30 July 2019).

the promotion and development of the palm oil industry, petroleum and gas, and export-oriented manufacturing.

Historically, oil palms were first introduced into Malaya in the 1870s, but palm oil only became an important commercial crop between 1917 and 1960 (Rasiah, 2006). Palm oil production grew very rapidly starting in the 1970s partly due to the land development schemes implemented by the government (Figure 6.8). Even today, palm oil remains an important export, accounting for 7–9% of total exports.

Petroleum and gas have been important industries since the 1970s. The early phase of commercial oil exploration was undertaken during 1910–29 in Sarawak, but this was exhausted by 1973 (Adnan, 1982). Major discoveries in 1973 and 1974 off the coasts of Terengganu, Sabah, and Sarawak expanded the industry significantly. Liquefied natural gas became an important industry in the 1980s. The importance of crude oil and liquefied natural gas exports has fluctuated over the years (Figure 6.9). Fuel as a share of exports peaked at 32% in 1985 and 22% in 2013. In 2017, fuel as a share of exports was around 15%.

In the post-independence period, the most important structural change has been the rise of the manufacturing sector. Malaysia's export-oriented industrialisation strategy began in the 1960s. As a result, the manufacturing sector as a share of GDP has risen over time from 10% in 1960 to 31% in 1999 (Figure 6.10). A rapid expansion in manufacturing's role in the economy can be observed in two periods: 1963–80 and 1987–99.

Foreign direct investment (FDI) has been a significant driver of the rise of manufacturing. The first phase of export-oriented industrialisation was fuelled by FDI from the West. In the second phase, FDI in the late 1980s came primarily from Japan following the Plaza Accord. FDI as a share of GDP rose from 1.3% in 1987 to 8.7% in 1992 (Figure 6.11). However, since 1999, manufacturing's relative contribution to the economy has declined and this can also be seen from the trends in the sector's share of total employment (Figure 6.12). The country's

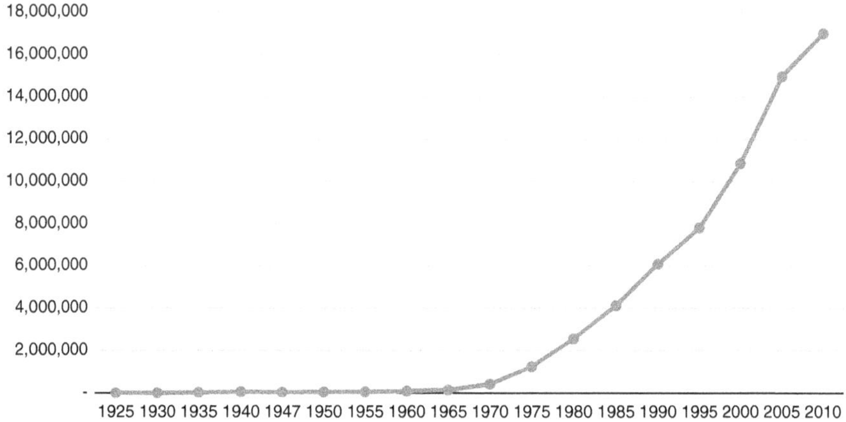

Figure 6.8 Palm Oil Production, 1925–2010 (tonnes).
Sources: Food and Agriculture Organization of the United Kingdom. http://www.fao.org/statistics/en (accessed 30 July 2019); Lim (1967),*Economic Development of Modern Malaya*. Kuala Lumpur: Oxford University Press; Malaysian Palm Oil Board. http://bepi.mpob.gov.my/index.php/en/statistics/production.html (accessed 30 July 2019).

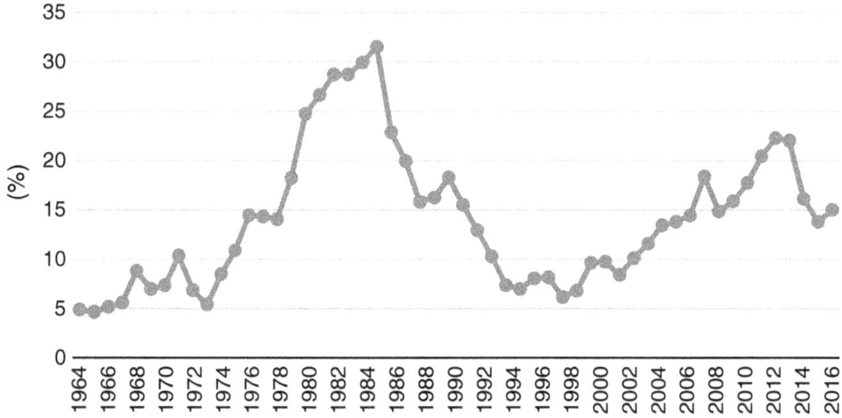

Figure 6.9 Fuel Exports (% of merchandise exports).
Source: World Bank Open Data. https://data.worldbank.org (accessed 30 July 2019).

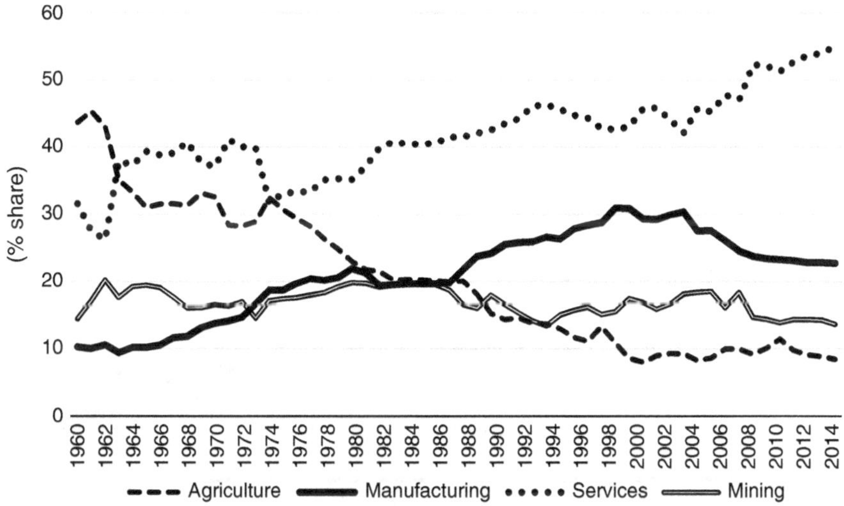

Figure 6.10 Structural Composition of Malaysia's Gross Domestic Product, 1960–2015.
Source: World Bank Open Data. https://data.worldbank.org (accessed 30 July 2019).

export structure has also changed over time (Figure 6.13). At its peak in 1999, the manufacturing sector accounted for some 80% of the country's total exports (Figure 6.14). However, the sector's share of GDP declined from 30% in 1999–2004 to about 22% in 2015. Thus, following a long period of

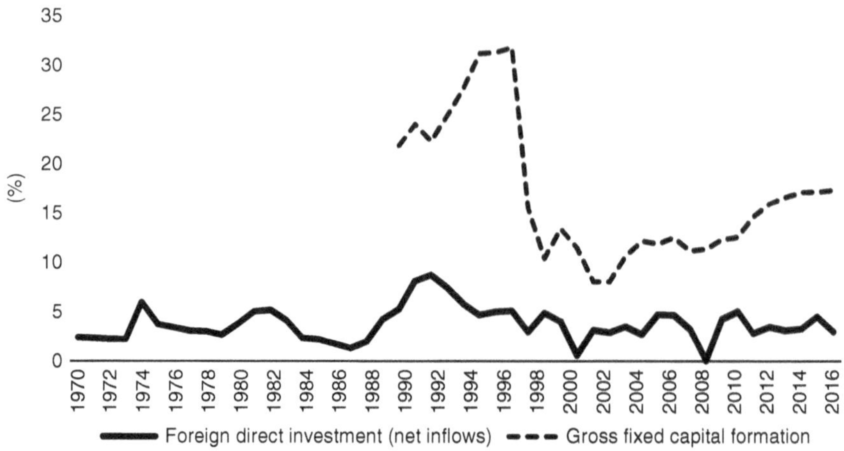

Figure 6.11 Foreign Direct Investment and Capital Formation as a Share of Gross Domestic Product.

Source: World Bank Open Data. https://data.worldbank.org (accessed 30 July 2019).

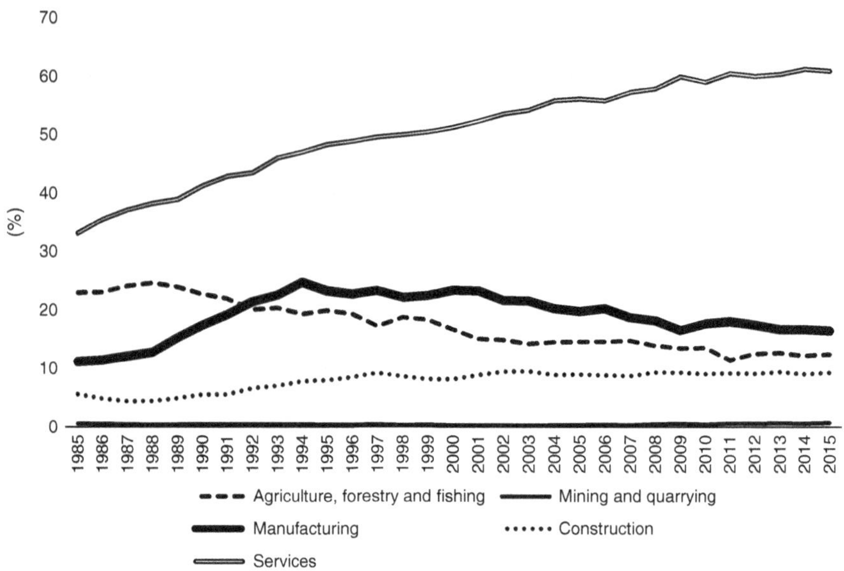

Figure 6.12 Sectoral Composition of Total Employment, 1985–2015.

Source: Department of Statistics. https://www.dosm.gov.my/v1/ (accessed 30 July 2019).

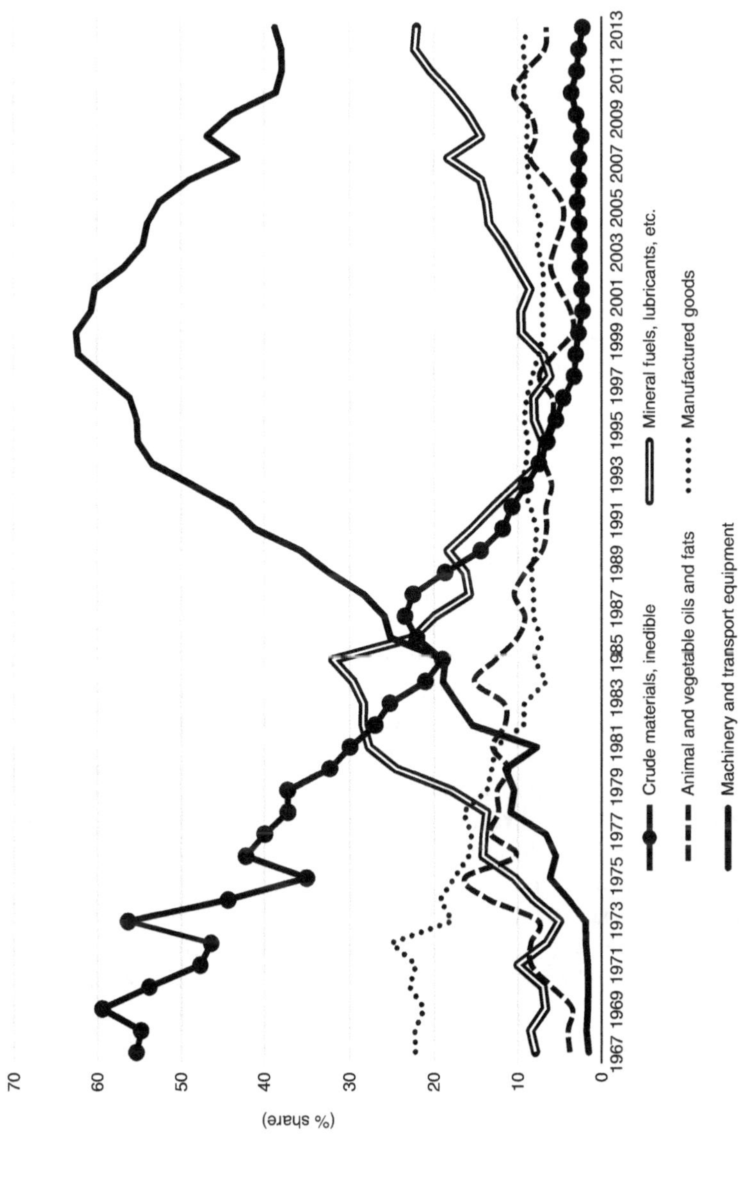

Figure 6.13 Major Export Products (% share of total exports).
Source: Department of Statistics. https://www.dosm.gov.my/v1/DOS (accessed 30 July 2019).

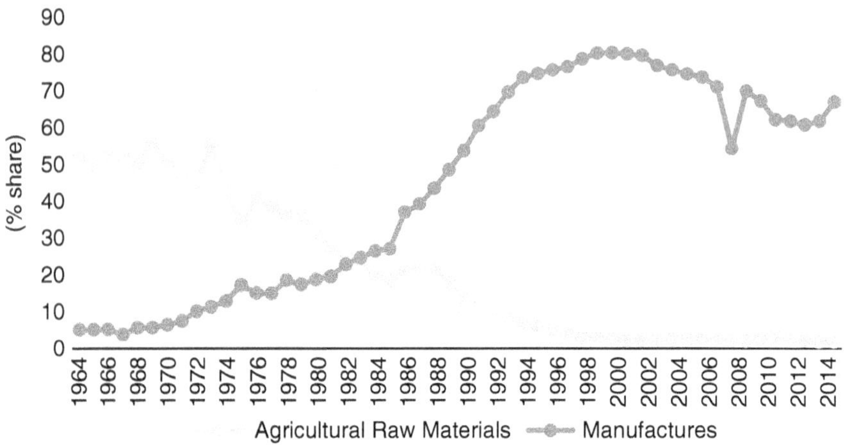

Figure 6.14 Agricultural and Manufactured Exports (% of total exports).
Source: World Bank Open Data. https://data.worldbank.org (accessed 30 July 2019).

industrialisation over a period of 40 years from around 1960 to 2000, the economy has been deindustrialising for close to 20 years since 1999/2000. This has been accompanied by the rise of the services sector's share of GDP (55% in 2015) and employment (60%).

3.3 Empirical studies on globalisation and economic growth

A number of time-series econometric studies on globalisation and economic growth in Malaysia have been carried out. In an early study using quarterly time-series data for the period 1970–94, Ahmad and Rashid (1999) found evidence of a stationary long-term relationship amongst exports, imports, and GDP. The study also found a feedback causal relationship between exports and economic growth for both manufacturing and agricultural exports.

Keong, Yusopa, and Khim-Sen (2003) used annual data for the period 1959–2000 to test the export-led growth hypothesis for Malaysia. The authors found that the hypothesis is valid for Malaysia in both the short and long term. The study also found that the growth rate is also positively affected by the growth rate of capital formation and imports.

Sulaiman and Saad (2009) used annual time series data for the period 1960–2005 to verify the positive relationship between exports and economic growth. The study also found a negative relationship between imports and economic growth.

In a more recent study, Makun (2017) used annual data for the period 1980–2013 to show that a positive and significant relationship exists between trade openness and growth. Furthermore, the effect of trade openness on growth is strengthened by human capital and good economic policies.

Overall, the empirical evidence on the relationship between exports and economic growth has been fairly robust across the different studies employing time-series econometrics. There is strong evidence that globalisation has a positive impact on economic growth in both the short and long term.

4 Impact of globalisation

Globalisation has impacted the Malaysian economy in many ways and through different mechanisms. This can be examined using different sources of information and data at various levels of aggregation. Section 4.1 discusses the empirical microdata literature on exporting, innovation, and productivity in the Malaysian manufacturing sector. Section 4.2 examines how trade and foreign labour have impacted Malaysia in terms of the country's demography and human capital over time. The impact of globalisation on poverty and inequality in Malaysia is discussed in Section 4.3. The openness of the Malaysian economy has also rendered it vulnerable to external economic shocks. This is discussed in Section 4.4. Finally, the relationship between globalisation and institutions (e.g. corruption) is discussed in Section 4.5.

4.1 Exporting, innovation, and productivity

Evidence on the role and impact of globalisation can also be derived from studies using microdata. In an early microdata study on the Malaysian manufacturing sector covering the period 2000–2001, Lee (2004) found that innovation is positively and significantly correlated with foreign participation. However, the same study showed that exporting may have a reverse relationship with innovation. This surprising result has been attributed to sampling limitations.

A study by Noor and Adam (2009), which used microdata from Malaysian manufacturing industries for the period 2000–04, found significant evidence of positive productivity spillovers to local firms in the same industry when foreign shareholding is used to measure foreign presence. Interestingly, the authors did not find any significant difference in labour productivity between wholly foreign-owned and locally owned establishments when foreign presence is proxied by employment share. In addition, both majority and minority foreign-owned establishments have significantly lower levels of labour productivity than locally owned establishments in Malaysia.

In a later study on productivity and exporting in the Malaysian manufacturing sector covering the period 1997–2004, Lee (2011a) found that the link between exporting and productivity is a weak. However, the paper presents stronger evidence that exporting is related to innovation.

Innovation by firms in the manufacturing sector can also be driven by their participation in the global economy through knowledge flows. Using firm-level manufacturing data covering the period 2002–04, Lee (2011b) provides some evidence that FDI and exporting are related to innovation activities such as training and acquisition of machinery, equipment, and software. However, the study also found that the links between innovative firms in Malaysia and other firms abroad in terms of cooperative activities are relatively weak.

Dogan, Nyen, and Yap. (2011) used a manufacturing micro panel data to examine the differences in productivity between exporters and non-exporters. Their study showed that exporters are more productive than are domestic-oriented establishments. Entrants to export markets were more productive than both the surviving domestic-oriented establishments (non-exporters) and, even more telling, surviving exporters. On the other hand, exiters from the export markets or 'export failures' were less productive than continuing exporters. Churning was also found to contribute to productivity growth in manufacturing due to entrants having higher productivity than exiters. In addition, the churning of exporters made larger contributions to productivity growth than churning amongst domestic-oriented firms.

Lee (2012) studied the dynamics of productivity and innovation using panel firm-level data from the manufacturing sector covering the years 2002 and 2006. The study provides some evidence for the existence of strong productivity premiums for continuing exporters (compared to non-exporters) and relatively weak productivity premiums for new exporters. There is also evidence of causality from exporting to innovation that supports the learning-by-exporting hypothesis in the case of Malaysia. It was also found that continuous exporters enjoy significant exporting premiums in terms of scale of production.

Another study by Lee (2013) examined the impact of globalisation on wage inequality at the firm level. The study used microdata collected by the Malaysian government covering the years 2002 and 2006 and the World Bank (covering the year 2006). The study found that there is a positive but weak relationship between average wage levels and exporting. There is also a positive relationship between trade liberalisation and wages, although this relationship is stronger for skilled workers. The employment of foreign workers also has a depressive effect on average wage levels for skilled workers.

Lee (2014) used manufacturing data for 2002 and 2006 to study the relationship between exporting and productivity across different firm sizes. The study affirmed the positive relationship between productivity and exporting. However, for larger firms, the productivity gap between exporters and non-exporters became less important, suggesting that the selection process for exporting is binding only for small firms.

Dogan, Nyen, and Yap (2017) used manufacturing microdata from 2000 to 2005 to analyse FDI spillover effects empirically. Their empirical findings are not very encouraging – horizontal spillovers from FDI are weak. In addition, backward and forward spillovers are found to be negative.

In a recent study, Chuah, Loayza, and Minh (2018) used microdata from three manufacturing censuses (2000, 2005, and 2010) to study the intra-sectoral reallocation of resources. In terms of globalisation, the authors found that export-oriented industries are generally more efficient at resource allocation.

These industries include the textile, wood products, and electrical and electronics industries. The authors also found that the productivity gap between Malaysia and the United States (US) has widened over time.

In summary, microdata studies on manufacturing do suggest that exporting is associated with higher productivity. The contribution of churning amongst exporting firms shows how such processes can contribute to economic growth. These findings are generally consistent with the theoretical and empirical literature in heterogeneous firms and trade (Melitz, 2003). There is also evidence supporting a positive relationship between innovation and exporting. These studies indicate that globalisation in the form of exporting is beneficial to firms in the manufacturing sector. However, there are weaknesses in the current state of export participation, including limited spillover effects and constraints on knowledge flows between subsidiaries based in Malaysia and their headquarters in more developed countries. Finally, even though there is a positive relationship between productivity and foreign ownership, this may not necessarily translate into a positive link between wages and exporting. This is due to excessive reliance on foreign labour with low skills and low human capital. This issue is explored further in the next section.

4.2 Trade, foreign labour, and human capital

Globalisation, in the form of trade and migration, has had a significant and long-term impact on Malaysia. In the pre-independence period under British colonial rule, the development of labour-intensive and trade-oriented industries such as tin and rubber necessitated the use of foreign labour. Between 1850 and 1930, the development of the tin industry brought about a massive migration of foreign workers from China into the tin mining areas in Malaya. Similarly, the advent and rapid growth of the rubber industry during 1911–31 saw the migration of workers primarily from South India.

The impact of migration went beyond the development of export-oriented primary commodities industries. The most important effect of the inflows of migrant workers in the 1850s to 1930s was the formation of a multi-ethnic society in Malaysia. While some migrant communities can be traced as far back as the fifteenth century, these earlier migrant communities were relatively small. The later waves of migrants into the tin and rubber industries were significantly larger to the extent that they subsequently altered the demographic composition of Malaysia. By 1947, the Chinese population in Malaya accounted for 38.4% of the total population (Table 6.1). The Indian community's share of total population peaked at 15% in 1921. Most of these migrant workers eventually became citizens of Malaysia. As a result of lower fertility rates amongst the Chinese and Indian communities in Malaysia, their population shares have declined over time. Despite this, Malaysia remains a multi-ethnic society. This has had important implications on the political economy of resource distribution in the country.

During the colonial period, one of the contentious elements in the Malayan Union (1846–1948) was the granting of citizenship and equal rights to migrant

Table 6.1 Census Population by Ethnic Group, Peninsular Malaysia, 1911–2010

Year	*Malays/Bumiputra*	*Population (number)* *Chinese*	*Indians*	*Others*	*Total*
1911	1,368,954	693,228	239,169	37,700	2,339,051
1921	1,568,588	855,863	439,172	43,068	2,906,691
1931	1,863,872	1,284,888	572,613	66,385	3,787,758
1947	2,427,834	1,884,534	530,638	65,080	4,908,086
1957	3,125,474	2,333,756	696,186	123,342	6,278,758
1970	4,663,284	3,117,896	933,250	66,298	8,780,728
1980	6,315,572	3,865,431	1,171,135	74,475	11,426,613
1991	8,433,826	4,250,969	1,380,048	410,544	14,475,387
2000	11,135,694	4,883,079	1,666,048	147,749	17,832,570
2010	13,735,752	5,509,302	1,892,322	130,205	21,267,581
		Population share (%)			
Year	Malays/Bumiputra	Chinese	Indians	Others	Total
1911	58.5	29.6	10.2	1.6	100.0
1921	54.0	29.4	15.1	1.5	100.0
1931	49.2	33.9	15.1	1.8	100.0
1947	49.5	38.4	10.8	1.3	100.0
1957	49.8	37.2	11.1	2.0	100.0
1970	53.1	35.5	10.6	0.8	100.0
1980	55.3	33.8	10.2	0.7	100.0
1991	58.3	29.4	9.5	2.8	100.0
2000	62.4	27.4	9.3	0.8	100.0
2010	64.6	25.9	8.9	0.6	100.0

Source: Economic History of Malaya. https://www.ehm.my/home (accessed 30 July 2019).

communities. In the aftermath of the nation's independence, children of migrants born in Malaya/Malaysia were automatically granted citizenship (the *jus soli* principle). However, the racial riots on 13 May 1969 proved to be a turning point in Malaysia. Thereafter, affirmative action policies were introduced to correct the economic imbalance across the different ethnic groups in Malaysia. The New Economic Policy (NEP) was introduced in 1970 both to eradicate poverty and to redress inter-ethnic economic imbalance.

The inter-ethnic economic imbalance is related to economic globalisation. The inflow of Chinese migrants in the late nineteenth century was mainly concentrated in modern sectors located in the more developed and urbanised states in Peninsular Malaysia. The Malay population was primarily agrarian and resided in less developed areas and states.

Thus, Malaysia's engagement in economic globalisation has had an impact on urbanisation and the spatial concentration of economic activities. In terms of urbanisation, the development of the tin industry during 1850–1930 brought about a massive migration of Chinese workers to the tin mining areas in three states, namely, Perak, Selangor, and Negeri Sembilan (Sidhu and Jones, 1981). The five largest cities during 1911–31 were Georgetown (Penang), Kuala Lumpur (Selangor), Ipoh (Perak), Melaka, and Taiping (Perak) (see Figure 6.15). With the

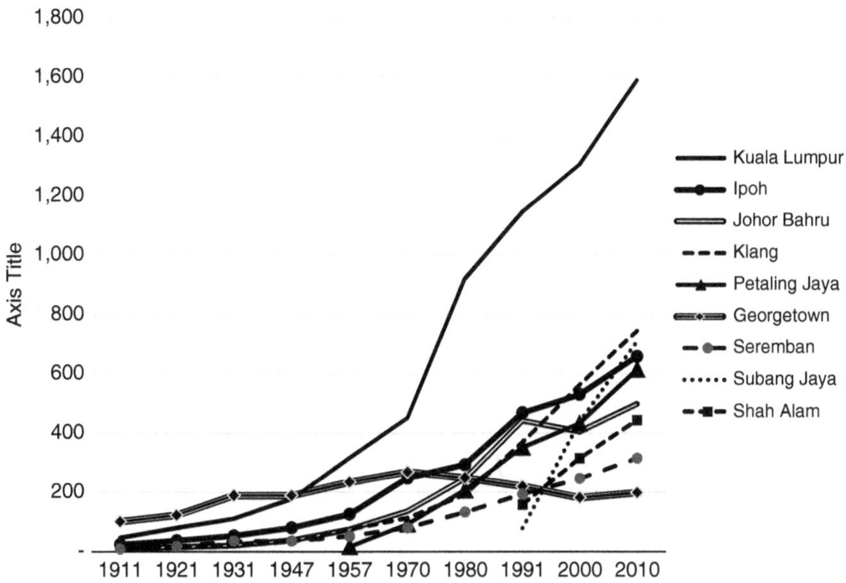

Figure 6.15 Size of Major Cities, 1911–2010 ('000 people).
Sources: Lim (1978), *The Evolution of the Urban System in Malaysia*. Kuala Lumpur: University of Malaya Press; Saw (2015), *The Population of Malaysia*, Second Edition. Singapore: Institute of Southeast Asian Studies; Department of Statistics, 2010 Population and Housing Census of Malaysia. https://www.dosm.gov.my/v1/ (accessed 30 July 2019).

exception of Melaka, these cities were mainly associated with tin mining activities. With the decline in mining, a few cities that relied on mining such as Georgetown (which was involved in the trading and shipping of tin) and Taiping declined in importance (Figure 6.16). For other cities, such as Seremban and Kuala Lumpur, the advent and rapid growth of the rubber industry (during the periods 1911–31 and 1947–80) and later palm oil likely mitigated the effects of the decline in the tin mining industry.

The rise of manufacturing since the 1960s also contributed to the growth of old cities (Ipoh and Johor Bahru) and the development of new ones such as Petaling Jaya and later, Shah Alam and Subang Jaya. The growth of these cities entailed inter-state migration that began to skew the population distribution across the Malaysian states (Table 6.2). The share of total population increased significantly in states with export-oriented manufacturing such as the state of Selangor.

Initially, the development of FDI-driven and export-oriented manufacturing did not entail the extensive use of foreign workers. However, by the early 1990s, the country began to experience labour shortages. This led to a rapid growth in the number of foreign workers in manufacturing, agriculture, and services for the

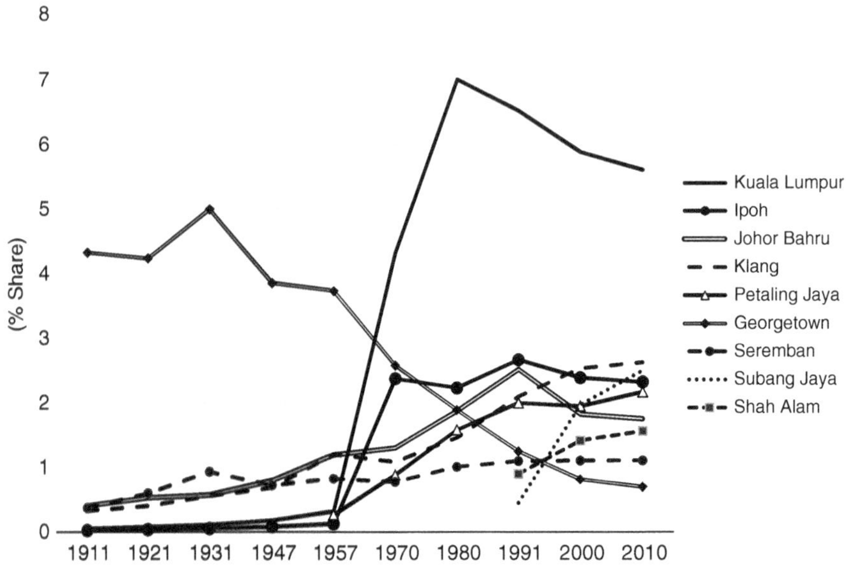

Figure 6.16 Major Cities' Share of Total Population, 1911–2010.
Sources: Lim (1978), *The Evolution of the Urban System in Malaysia*. Kuala Lumpur: University of Malaya Press; Saw (2015), *The Population of Malaysia*, Second Edition. Singapore: Institute of Southeast Asian Studies; Department of Statistics, 2010 Population and Housing Census of Malaysia. https://www.dosm.gov.my/v1/ (accessed 30 July 2019).

next 20 years. The dependence on foreign workers has increased across all states since the 1980s (Figure 6.17). Looking at the trends in foreign workers' share of total employment since the early 1980s, it can be seen that the share of foreign labour increased rapidly during two periods in particular: 1993–96, and 2009–13. The degree of dependence on foreign labour varied from state to state. The state of Sabah is especially dependent on foreign labour. Foreign workers account for some 40% of total employment in the state. Other states with significant dependence on foreign workers include Selangor (15%) and Kuala Lumpur (13%).

There are currently no data on foreign workers by sector in different states, but given differences in economic structure, foreign workers are likely concentrated in two sectors: (i) agriculture in Sabah and Sarawak; and (ii) manufacturing and services in Johor, Selangor, and KL. Agriculture and manufacturing are the two key sectors employing foreign labour (Figure 6.18).

One key concern with respect to the country's dependence on foreign workers is the relatively low human capital and skills associated with foreign workers compared to local workers. In 2015, only 5.7% of foreign workers had tertiary degrees whereas the corresponding figure for domestic workers exceeded 20% (Table 6.3).

Table 6.2 Distribution of Population by State in Peninsular Malaysia

State	*1911*	*1921*	*1931*	*1947*	*1957*	*1970*	*1980*	*1991*	*2000*	*2010*
Selangor	12.6	13.8	14.1	14.5	16.2	18.5	21.4	24.4	30.3	32.0
Perak	21.4	21.0	20.7	19.4	19.4	17.8	15.9	13.3	11.2	10.4
Johor	7.7	9.7	13.3	15.0	14.8	14.5	14.4	14.7	15.0	14.8
Kedah	10.5	11.5	11.3	11.3	11.2	10.5	9.9	9.2	9.0	8.7
Penang	11.1	10.1	9.0	9.1	9.1	8.8	8.2	7.6	7.1	6.9
Kelantan	12.2	10.6	9.6	9.1	8.5	7.8	7.9	8.3	7.1	6.8
Pahang	5.1	5.0	4.8	5.1	5.0	5.7	7.0	7.3	7.0	6.6
Negeri Sembilan	5.6	6.5	6.2	5.5	5.8	5.5	5.0	4.9	4.7	4.5
Terengganu	6.6	5.3	4.7	4.6	4.4	4.6	4.8	5.5	4.9	4.6
Melaka	5.3	5.3	4.9	4.9	4.6	4.6	4.1	3.6	3.4	3.6
Perlis	1.4	1.4	1.3	1.4	1.4	1.4	1.3	1.2	1.1	1.0
Total	100.0	100.0	100.0	100.0	100.0	100.0	100.0	100.0	100.0	100.0

Sources: Saw (2007), ***The Population of Malaysia***. Singapore: Institute of Southeast Asian Studies; (2015), *The Population of Malaysia*, Second Edition. Singapore: Institute of Southeast Asian Studies.

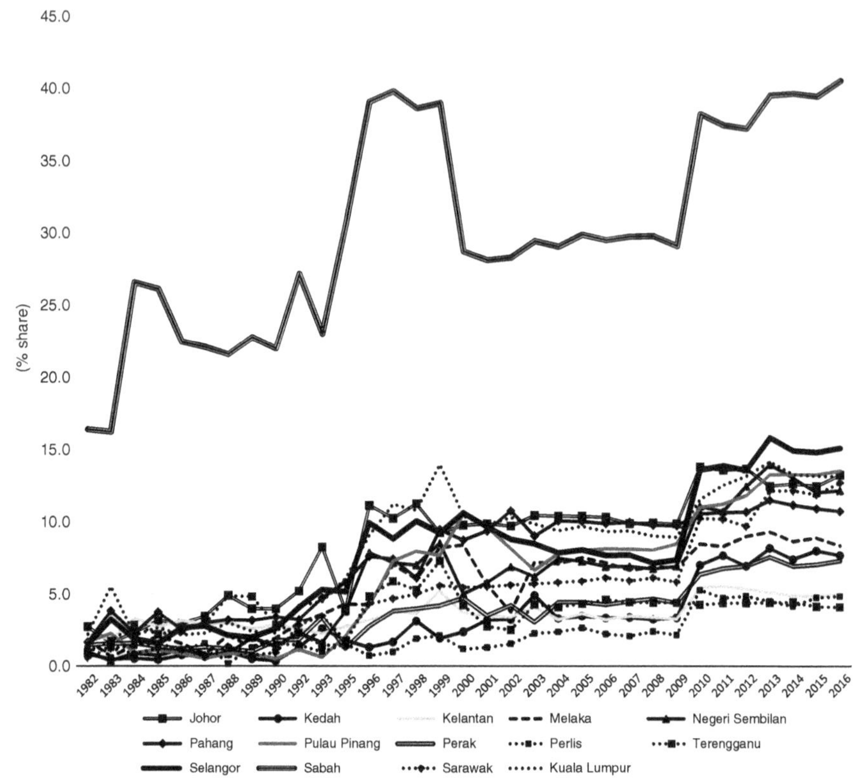

Figure 6.17 Foreign Workers' Share of Total Employment, 1982–2016.
Source: Department of Statistics, https://www.dosm.gov.my/v1/DOS (accessed 30 July 2019).

The World Bank (2012) estimated that in 2014 about 44% of foreign workers in Malaysia were employed in low-skilled elementary occupations. Only 5% of foreign workers in Malaysia have high-skilled jobs. Furthermore, sectors likely matter. Foreign workers in agriculture and construction may have lower human capital and skills than foreign workers in manufacturing and services. The proportion of foreign workers with no formal education (noedupct) or primary education (primarypct) is particularly high in states with large agriculture sectors such as Sabah and Sarawak (Figure 6.19).

Relatively cheap and low-skilled foreign labour helped sustain the country's manufacturing competitiveness in the 1990s; however, this later became an obstacle to efforts to upgrade the manufacturing and other economic sectors. The country's heavy dependence on low-skilled foreign workers has adversely affected productivity growth in all sectors in the economy. Access to cheap foreign labour could have disincentivised employers from upgrading their production technology (more capital intensive) and investing in human capital

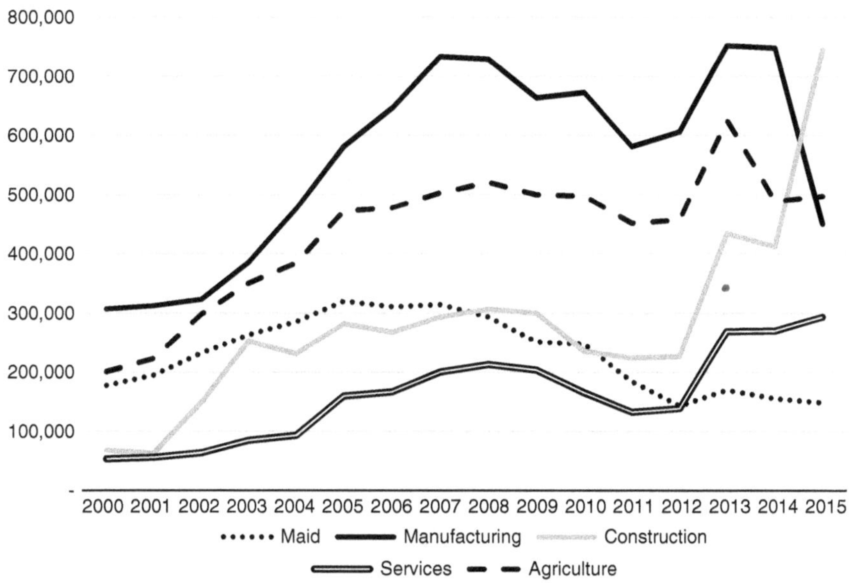

Figure 6.18 Number of Foreign Workers in Malaysia by Sector, 2000–15.
Source: Department of Statistics, https://www.dosm.gov.my/v1/DOS (accessed 30 July 2019).

Table 6.3 Labour Force by Educational Attainment, 2015

	Malay	*Chinese*	*India-ns*	*Others*	*Foreigners*	*Total*
No formal education	169.6	19.2	15.5	6.1	236.0	446.3
%	2.1	0.6	1.7	6.4	10.9	3.1
Primary	796.2	322.0	102.6	22.0	986.8	2,229.6
%	9.7	10.2	11.3	23.3	45.5	15.4
Secondary	4,584.2	1,856.1	526.3	46.9	823.1	7,836.6
%	56.0	58.9	58.0	49.7	37.9	54.0
Tertiary	2,642.4	956.7	263.3	19.4	123.5	4,005.4
%	32.3	30.3	29.0	20.6	5.7	27.6
Total	8,192.4	3,154.0	907.7	94.5	2,169.4	14,518.0
	100.0	100.0	100.0	100.0	100.0	100.00

Source: Department of Statistics. https://www.dosm.gov.my/v1/DOS (accessed 30 July 2019)

development. There is some evidence that the use of foreign labour could have weakened agglomeration economies related to human capital (Lee, 2018). Upgrading the country's manufacturing sector requires workers that are productive, innovative, and well-paid (World Bank, 2012).

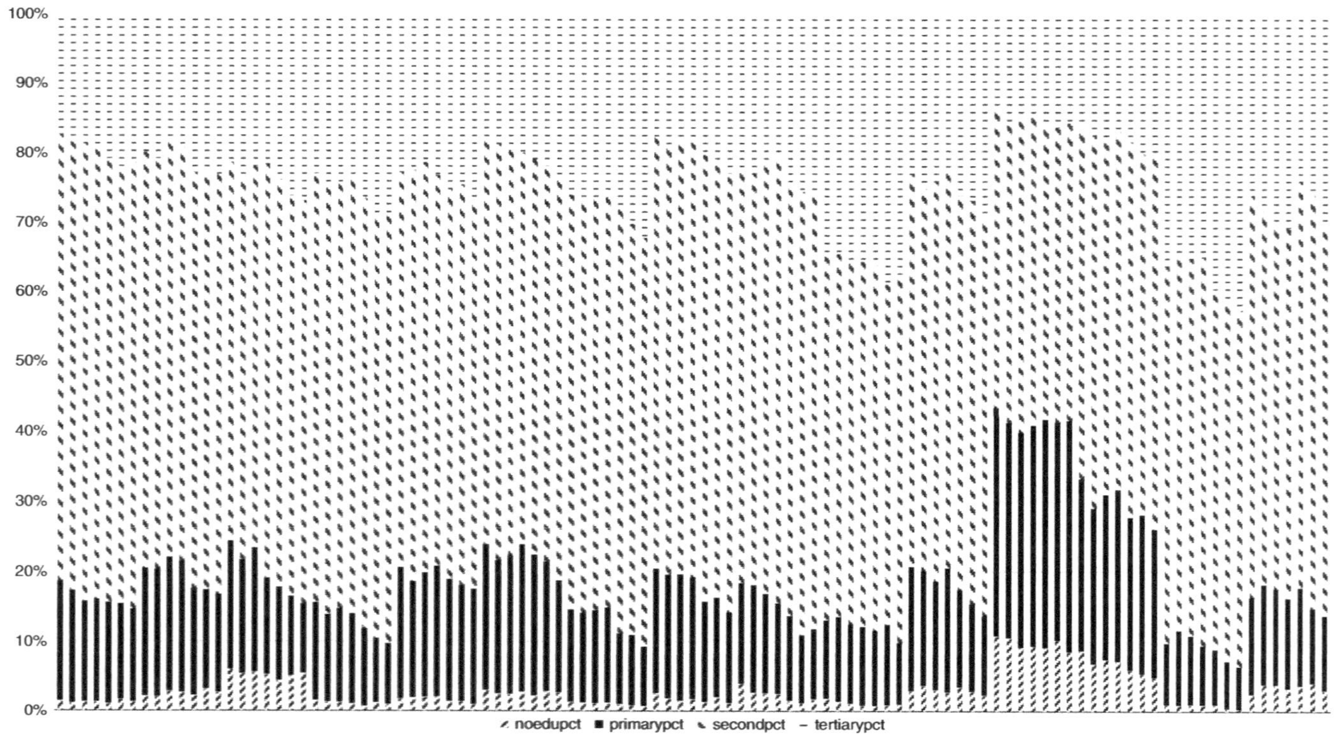

Figure 6.19 Education Composition of Workers by State, 2010–16 Note: noedupct = no education, primarypct = no primary education, secondpct = no secondary education, tertiarypct = no tertiary education.

Source: Department of Statistics. https://www.dosm.gov.my/v1/DOS (accessed 30 July 2019).

4.3 Poverty and inequality

Malaysia has made significant progress towards eradicating poverty since the 1970s. In 1970, close to 50% of the country's population were living below the poverty line. By 1997, the incidence of poverty had declined to about 11%. Even though the government implemented rural development programmes (such as the Federal Land Development Authority scheme) to eradicate poverty, the most important factor has been identified as the absorption of rural educated workers into higher income occupations in the industrial and services sectors (Ragayah, 2011). Thus, insofar as the country's manufacturing sector is export-oriented, globalisation has had a positive and indirect impact on the decline in the incidence of poverty in Malaysia.

Inequality in Malaysia as measured by the Gini ratio has declined over time since the 1960s (Figure 6.20). Significant reductions were achieved in the second half of the 1970s and remained relatively stable thereafter until further declines in the 2000s. A number of factors were identified, including improved salaries at the lowest levels in the public sector, a tight labour market, and income transfers to rural households (Ragayah, 2011). These last two factors are indirectly related to globalisation through employment and the income-generation effects of the export-oriented manufacturing sector. Figure 6.21

Despite the improvements in inequality, there is growing concern that the country's addiction to cheap foreign labour could have suppressed the wages of lower skilled workers in the labor market. A consequence of this could be worsening wage inequality. A few studies have examined these issues. Athukorala and Devadason (2012) provided industry-level evidence of the negative impact

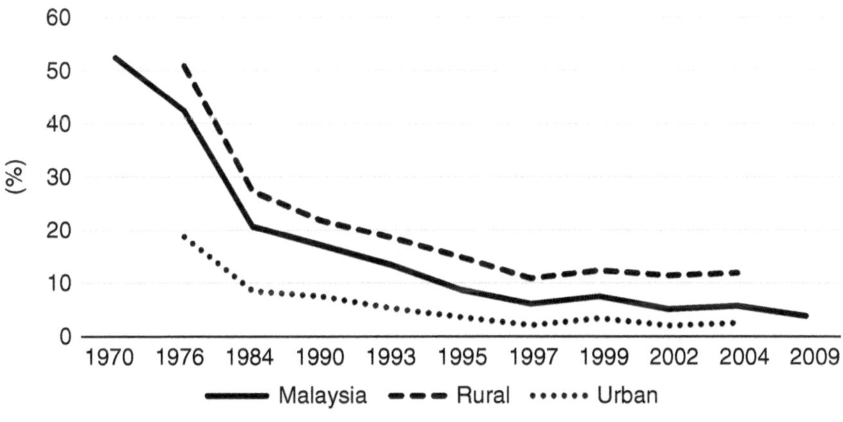

Figure 6.20 Incidence of Poverty in Malaysia, 1970–2009.
Sources: Ragayah (2011), 'Poverty and Income Distribution', in R. Rasiah (ed.) *Malaysian Economy*. New York: Oxford University Press; (2012), 'Poverty Eradication and Income Distribution', in H. Hill, T.S. Yean, and R.M. Zin (eds.) *Malaysia's Development Challenges*. London: Routledge.

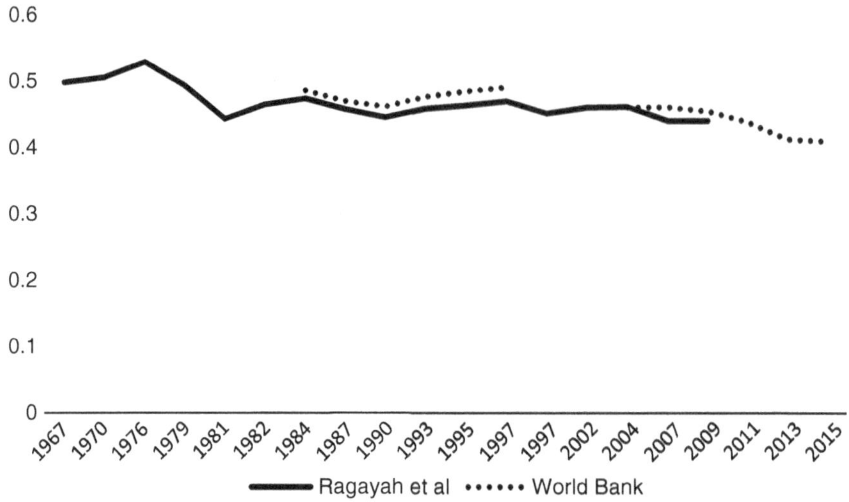

Figure 6.21 Gini Index Estimates.
Sources: Ragayah (2011), 'Poverty and Income Distribution', in R. Rasiah (ed.) *Malaysian Economy*. New York: Oxford University Press; (2012), 'Poverty Eradication and Income Distribution', in H. Hill, T.S. Yean, and R.M. Zin (eds.) *Malaysia's Development Challenges*. London: Routledge; World Bank Open Data. https://data.worldbank.org (accessed 30 July 2019).

of foreign workers on the wages of unskilled workers. This is borne out by the changes in average wage levels across occupational categories in the manufacturing sector during 2000–05.

There is also evidence that average wage levels have risen faster at the managerial, technical, and supervisory levels than for clerical, general, and production workers (Table 6A1). A more qualitative analysis was undertaken by Mohamad (2010) who argued that wage inequality worsened during 1995–2007 and that this might be due to industry-level effects and job characteristics. In another study, Said and Hamid (2011) argued that micro-level evidence based on household surveys points to decreasing demand for professional workers (rather than technical workers) due to changes in technology. All of these studies could also be capturing the effects of structural change, that is, deindustrialisation and the increasing prominence of the services sector. More recent data suggest that export-oriented manufacturing may be a less important source of job creation (Figure 6.22).

Finally, an important issue related to inequality in Malaysia is the inter-ethnic income and wealth distribution. Malaysia became a multi-ethnic society through the inflows of migrants into the tin and rubber industries in the late 19th to the early 20th centuries. In 1969, communal tensions following the general elections resulted in racial riots.

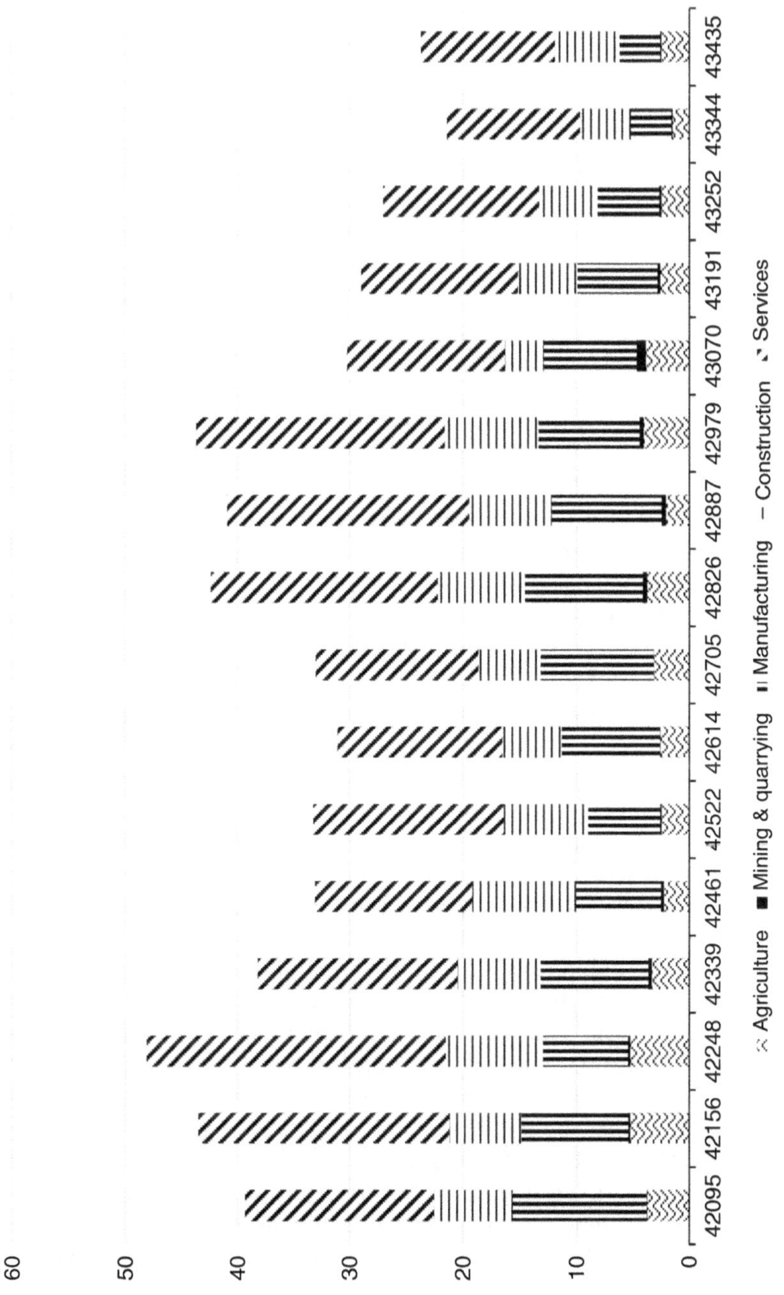

Figure 6.22 Jobs Created by Economic Activity, 2015–18.
Source: Department of Statistics. https://www.dosm.gov.my/v1/DOS (accessed 30 July 2019).

Table 6.4 Ownership of Share Capital in Listed Companies (%)

Group	*1970*	*1985*	*1990*	*2004*
Bumiputra	2.4	19.1	19.3	18.9
Chinese	27.2	33.4	45.5	39.0
Indians	1.1	1.2	1.0	1.2
Nominee companies	6.0	7.2	8.5	8.0
Foreigners	63.4	26.0	25.4	32.5

Source: Table 4.5 in Leete (2007), *Malaysia: From Kampung to Twin Towers*. Kuala Lumpur: Oxford Fajar.

The policy response to the riots was the NEP, a long-term strategic policy covering the period 1970–90 and aimed at addressing the root causes of the riots, namely, poverty and inequality. The two goals of the NEP were the eradication of poverty and achieving a more equitable inter-ethnic distribution of income and wealth. The policies for the NEP was subsequently extended under the New Development Policy (1991–2000) and the National Vision Policy (2001–10). In 2010, the New Economic Model covering the period 2011–20 was launched. The orientation of the New Economic Model differed from previous policies in that it attempted to depart from an affirmative action orientation to a more needs-based approach. However, this shift was not very successfully implemented due to concerns from the Bumiputra community regarding the erosion of their rights and special standing.

Several aspects of these NEP-type policies have implications for the country's engagement in globalisation. A key aspect of the implementation of NEP-type policies is the trusteeship model in which state-owned enterprises, government investment corporations, and government-linked corporations hold equity in large companies in key sectors on behalf of the Bumiputra community. These sectors include banking and transport. This strategy was aimed at ensuring that the Bumiputra community owned at least 30% equity in the modern sector (services and manufacturing). Another important aspect is public procurement in which some preferences were given to Bumiputra-owned companies. This was meant to support and nurture Bumiputra entrepreneurs.

More than 50 years after its implementation, the extent of corporate equity remains controversial. Though official data indicated that Bumiputra ownership in listed companies reached only 18.9% in 2004, a study undertaken by the Centre for Public Policy Studies and Asian Strategy and Leadership Institute suggest that the figure could be as high as 45% in 2005. In a more recent study, Gomez et al. (2017) estimated that the government's share in the companies listed on the Bursa Malaysia increased from 43.7% in 2011 to 47.1% in 2015. Much of the government-owned equity in the corporate sector is in the services sector. Menon and Ng (2017) have argued that state-owned enterprises or government-linked corporations crowded out private investment in 2007–11.

There are two important implications of government ownership and control in the services sector. The increasing importance of services in the Malaysian economy implies that the growth of the Malaysian economy is likely to be increasingly driven by productivity in the services sector. Furthermore, there are positive linkages between manufacturing productivity and services inputs (Lee, 2019). If productivity in the services sector is adversely affected by government ownership, this could have negative implications for the future growth of the Malaysian economy.

The significant presence of government ownership in the services sector and affirmative action in government procurement policies could be obstacles to the country's participation in the next generation of trade agreements. This is already an issue in Malaysia's guarded participation in recent trade agreements such as the Comprehensive and Progressive Agreement for Trans-Pacific Partnership. If Malaysia fails to liberalise its trade regime further, including its services sector, this could limit the country's ability to deepen its participation in the global value chain in manufacturing and services.

4.4 Openness and economic stability

The openness of the Malaysian economy has made it vulnerable to global economic shocks. This is one of the risks of economic globalisation. Since the country's independence in 1957, there have been four major global economic shocks that have had significant impacts on the Malaysian economy. These include (i) the Organization of Petroleum Producing Countries (OPEC) oil crisis (1973–74), (ii) the commodity crisis (1985–86), (iii) the Asian financial crisis (1997–98), and (iv) the global financial crisis (2008–09)

The impact of each of these shocks is summarised in Figure 6.23 and Table 6.5. The severity of the impact of each of these global economic shocks has varied. This is not surprising as the nature and sources of each of these shocks also differed.

The first shock, the OPEC oil crisis (1973–1974), was triggered by the actions of OPEC member countries. The oil embargo imposed by OPEC on the US and its allies essentially caused a severe oil shortage and a sharp increase in oil prices. This supply-side shock severely affected Malaysia, which had not yet fully developed its oil and gas sector.

The second shock, the commodity crisis (1984–85), was brought about by the high interest rate policy in the US in the early 1980s that weakened demand for primary commodities. This significantly affected Malaysia, which by this time had become a major exporter of both palm oil and, to a lesser extent, rubber and tin. The severity of this crisis was greater as it was more prolonged partly due to the country's inability to implement effective counter-cyclical policies because of fiscal constraints faced by the Malaysian government (Athukorala, 2010)."

The third shock was the Asian financial crisis (1997–98), which was triggered by Thailand's decision to devalue its currency following the Government of Thailand's decision not to peg the baht to the US dollar. This action unnerved

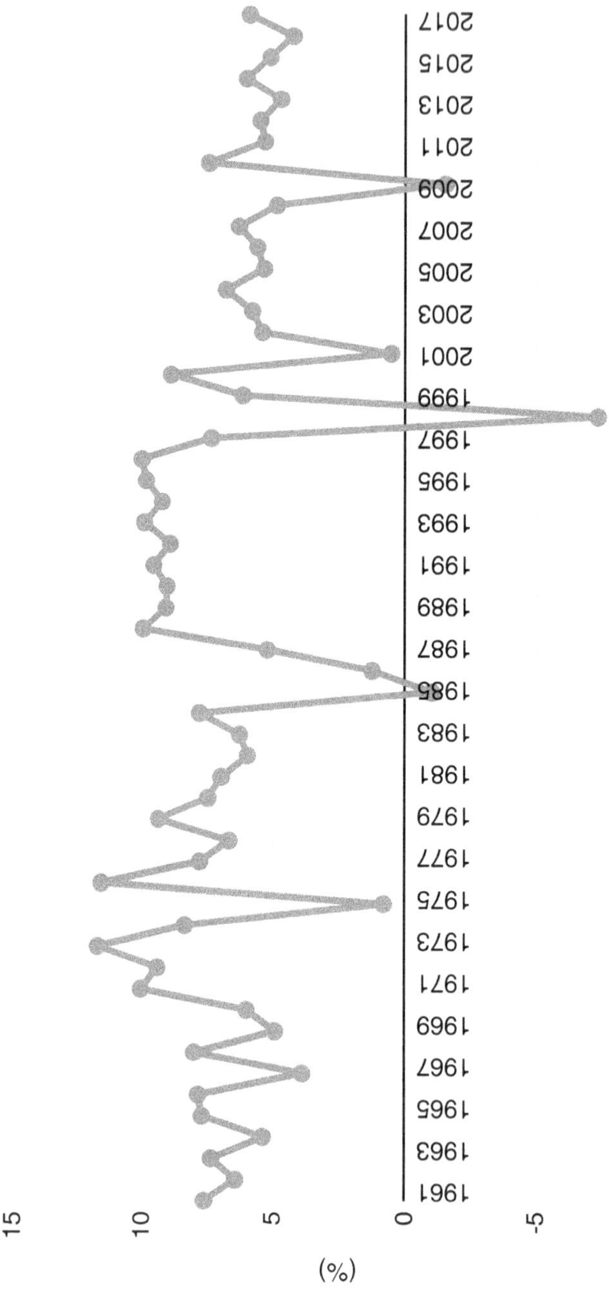

Figure 6.23 Annual Real Gross Domestic Product Growth – Malaysia, 1961–2017.
Source: World Bank Open Data. https://data.worldbank.org (accessed 30 July 2019).

Table 6.5 Impact of Global Economic Shocks on the Malaysian Economy

Period	*Event*	*Decline in economic growth (real GDP)*
1973–1974	OPEC oil crisis	8.3% (1974) → 0.8% (1975)
1985–1986	Commodity crisis	7.8% (1984) → -1.0% (1985)
1997–1998	Asian financial crisis	7.3% (1997) → -7.4% (1998)
2008–2009	Global financial crisis	4.8% (2008) → -1.5% (2009)

Source: World Bank Open Data. https://data.worldbank.org (accessed 30 July 2019).
GDP = gross domestic product, OPEC = Organization of the Petroleum Exporting Countries.

foreign investors, causing sharp withdrawals from equity markets in the region including Malaysia. This was accompanied by a speculative attack on the ringgit. The financial liberalisation in the 1990s was an important precursor to this crisis. Unlike the previous two crises, this crisis was primarily due to financial globalisation.

The fourth and more recent crisis, the global financial crisis (2008–09), was originally caused by the deterioration of sub-prime assets in the US, which subsequently led to systemic liquidity problems in the global interbank and credit markets. This brought about deleveraging activities and recessions in developed economies. Malaysia's exposure to this crisis was primarily through the weakened demand for the country's exports as well as the decline (following deleveraging activities) in foreign investments.

Given the different nature and impact of each of these economic crises, it is not surprising that the policy responses from the Malaysian government have been different (Athukorala, 2010). These policy responses depend on both external constraints (e.g. speed of global economic recovery) as well as internal constraints (e.g. socioeconomic policies and fiscal space). There are also intertemporal dependence and learning effects over time for policy makers. For example, the restructuring of the financial and corporate sectors in Malaysia during the aftermath of the Asian financial crisis strengthened the ability of the country's financial sector to cope with the effects of the global financial crisis.

In summary, the openness of the Malaysian economy made it vulnerable to global economic shocks. Prior to the 1990s, the crises were mainly transmitted through the trade sector; however, since liberalising its financial sector in the 1990s, the Malaysian economy became vulnerable to external shocks to both the trade and financial sectors.

4.5 Institutions

Institutions are today recognised as an important factor in economic growth (Acemoglu, Johnson, and Robinson, 2005). In the context of globalisation, institutions are also an important source of comparative advantage (Levchenko, 2007; Costinot, 2009). Within this literature, the traditional way of conceptualising institutions is in terms of the enforcement of contracts and property rights. In addition to these, the transaction costs of exporting and importing could also be affected by the quality of institutions. For example, rampant corruption in customs could increase importing and exporting costs. The implementation of trade facilitation measures could also be slowed as such measures could be perceived as reducing opportunities for corruption. Aside from transaction costs, the benefits of trade could also be reduced by corruption. For example, as a result of corruption, importers have to pay higher import costs that are then passed on to consumers. Corruption can also make it easier to smuggle goods into the country, resulting in the loss of government revenues.

In the case of Malaysia, there is a scarcity of empirical research on how trade is affected by problems related to the quality of institutions (e.g. corruption). There is anecdotal evidence but hardly any empirical quantitative studies on this issue.[3] Fortunately, the World Bank provides some statistics on the extent of corruption in relation to import licences (Table 6.6). Table 6.6 shows that the incidence of corruption (as measured by the percentage of firms expected to give gifts to obtain import permits) is fairly high in some industries in Malaysia, such as garments. Interestingly, the incidence of corruption amongst non-exporters is much higher than amongst exporters. However, firms with foreign ownership tend to experience a higher incidence of corruption compared to domestic firms.

The above statistics suggest that there is significant room for improvement in the area of corruption in trade-related activities. This topic is especially worth highlighting given the recent developments in Malaysian politics. One of the most significant events in Malaysia since the country's independence was the shock defeat of the ruling political party coalition, Barisan Nasional, in the 14th general election held on 9 May 2018. Prior to its defeat, Barisan Nasional had ruled the country continuously since 1957. A key reason for the end of Barisan Nasional's rule was the deterioration in institutions and governance in the country, which led to massive rent-seeking and corruption. A key item on the

Table 6.6 Globalisation and Incidence of Corruption in Malaysia, 2015

Subgroup level	*Percent of firms expected to give gifts to get an import license*
All	39.0
Food	24.6
Garments	74.6
Chemicals and chemical products	12.7
Electronics and communications equipment	34.0
Other manufacturing	38.4
Direct exports are 10% or more of sales	28.0
Non-exporter	47.9
Domestic	39.9
10% or more foreign ownership	49.3

Source: World Bank – Doing Business Data. https://www.doingbusiness.org/en/data (accessed 30 July 2019).

agenda of the new Pakatan Harapan government is institutional reforms, which are largely aimed at improving economic and political governance in Malaysia. These are likely to include reductions in the incidence of corruption in import and export activities. If such reforms materialise, Malaysia's competitiveness as an export-oriented manufacturing base and as a trading nation is likely to improve.

5 Conclusions

Globalisation has, without any doubt, had a very significant impact on Malaysia. The country's engagement in globalisation can be traced to the pre-independence period. This engagement – through trade and labour migration flows – helped shaped the country as it is today. The multi-ethnic nature of its society and its development into an upper middle-income economy were both driven by globalisation. The country's economic openness in terms of trade and investment brought about the development of an export-oriented manufacturing economy. Evidence from microdata research indicates that productivity and innovation are positively related to exporting in the manufacturing sector. However, these studies also indicate that there are weaknesses in terms of FDI spillovers and knowledge flows. Due to these problems, and possibly others, it is not surprising that premature deindustrialisation has been a problem since the late 1990s. This problem has been compounded by an over-dependence on low-skilled foreign labour. Extensive government ownership in the services sector to achieve affirmative action and wealth redistribution goals could also have limited the sector's potential contributions to economic growth. This could have adversely affected the productivity of the services sector and limited the country's participation in new regional trade agreements. One cost of engagement with the global economy is economic instability. All four major global economic crises in the post-war period have adversely affected the Malaysian economy. The transmission mechanisms of these crises have differed due to differences in the sources of these crises as well as changes in the Malaysian economy over time. Despite such risks from globalisation, disengaging from globalisation is not an option for the Malaysian economy due to its small size. From a policy perspective, better institutions and policy instruments are needed to cope with the risks arising from globalisation. Improvements in institutions are also likely to improve Malaysia's trade competitiveness further.

Notes

1 The Dutch ceded their control over Melaka to the British between 1795 and 1816 during the Napoleonic Wars (1795–1815).

2 Under the Resident System, state revenues were under the control of British advisors.

3 In a 2014 statement by customs, it was reported that RM1.67 billion worth of cigarettes and alcohol had been smuggled into Malaysia since 2011. See 'Corrupt

M'sian customs officers: Lavish lifestyle gave them away', *AsiaOne*, 7 September 2014.

References

Acemoglu, D., S. Johnson, and J. Robinson (2005), 'Institutions as a Fundamental Cause of Long-Run Growth', in P. Aghion and S.N. Durlauf (eds.), *Handbook of Economic Growth*, Vol 1A. Amsterdam: Elsevier B.V.

Adnan, M.A. (1982), 'Extractive Industries', in E.K. Fisk and H. Osman-Rani (eds.), *The Political Economy of Malaysia*. Kuala Lumpur: Oxford University Press.

Ahmad, Z.B. and S. Rashid (1999), 'Exports, Imports and Economic Growth in Malaysia: Empirical Evidence Based on Multivariate Time Series', *Asian Economic Journal*, 13(4), pp.389–406.Athukorala, P.-C. (2010), 'Malaysian Economy in Three Crises', *Working Paper*, No. 2010/12. Canberra: Australian National University, Arndt-Corden Department of Economics.

Athukorala, P.-C. and E. Devadason (2012), 'The Impact of Foreign Labor on Host Country Wages: The Experience of a Southern Host, Malaysia', *World Development*, 40(8), pp.1497–1510.

Brawley, M. (2009), 'Globalization', in K.A. Reinert, R.S. Rajan, A.J. Glass, and L.S. Davis (eds.), *Princeton Encyclopaedia of the World Economy*. Princeton, NJ: Princeton University Press.

Bruton, H.J. (1992), *The Political Economy of Poverty, Equity and Growth: Sri Lanka and Malaysia*. Washington, DC: World Bank.

Chai, H.-C. (1967), *The Development of British Malaya 1896–1909*, 2nd Edition. Kuala Lumpur: Oxford University Press.

Cho, G. (1990), *The Malaysian Economy: Spatial Perspectives*. London: Routledge.

Chuah, L.L., N. Loayza, and N.H. Minh (2018), 'Resource Misallocation and Productivity Gaps in Malaysia', *Policy Research Working Paper*, No. 8368. Washington, DC: World Bank Group.

Costinot, A. (2009), 'On the Origins of Comparative Advantage', *Journal of International Economics*, 77(2), pp.255–264.

Dogan, E., W.K. Nyen, and M. Yap (2011), 'Does Exporter Turnover Contribute to Aggregate Productivity Growth? Evidence from Malaysian Manufacturing', *World Economy*, 34(3), pp.424–443.

Dogan, E., W.K. Nyen, and M. Yap (2017), 'Vertical and Horizontal Spillovers from Foreign Direct Investment: Evidence from Malaysian Manufacturing', *Asian Economic Papers*, 16, pp.158–183.

Drabble, J.H. (2000), *An Economic History of Malaysia: The Transition to Modern Economic Growth*. London: Macmillan.

Fong, C.-O. (1989), *The Malaysia Economic Challenge in the 1990s: Transformation for Growth*. Singapore: Longman.

Gomez, T., T. Padmanabhan, N. Kamaruddin, S. Bhalla, and F. Fisal (2017), *Minister of Finance Incorporated: Ownership and Control of Corporate Malaysia*. London: Palgrave MacMillan.

Henderson, V. (2002), 'Urbanization in Developing Countries', *World Bank Research Observer*, 17(1), pp.89–112.

International Tin Research Institute (2011), 'Historical Trends in Tin Production', mimeo.

Jomo, K.S. (1990), *Growth and Structural Change in the Malaysian Economy.* London: Macmillan.

Keong, C.-C., Z. Yusopa, and V. Khim-Sen (2003), 'Export-Led Growth Hypothesis in Malaysia: An Application of Two-Stage Least Square Technique', mimeo.

Lee, C. (2004), 'The Determinants of Innovation in the Malaysian Manufacturing Sector: An Econometric Analysis at the Firm Level', *ASEAN Economic Bulletin*, 21(3), pp.319–329.

Lee, C. (2011a), 'Trade, Productivity, and Innovation: Firm-Level Evidence from Malaysian Manufacturing', *Journal of Asian Economics*, 22(4), pp.284–294.

Lee, C. (2011b), 'Knowledge Flows, Organization and Innovation: Firm-Level Evidence from Malaysia', in C.H. Hahn and D. Narjoko (eds.), *Globalization and Innovation in East Asia.* Economic Research Institute for ASEAN and East Asia (ERIA) Research Project Report, 2010(4), pp.370–409. Jakarta: ERIA.

Lee, C. (2012), 'Exporting, Productivity, Innovation and Organization: Evidence from Malaysia Manufacturing', in C.H. Hahn and D.A. Narjoko (eds.), *Dynamics of Firm Selection Process in Globalized Economies.* ERIA Research Project Report, 2011(3), pp.289–305.

Lee, C. (2013), 'Globalization and Wage Inequality: Firm Level Evidence from Malaysia', in C.H. Hahn and D.A. Narjoko (eds.), *Impact of Globalization on Labor Market.* ERIA Research Project Report, 2012(4), pp.197–231.

Lee, C. (2014), 'The Exporting and Productivity Nexus: Does Firm Size Matter?' Globalization and Performance of Small and Large Firms, in C.H. Hahn and D.A. Narjoko (eds.). ERIA Research Project Report, 2013(3), pp.225–248.

Lee, C. (2018), 'Agglomeration, Human Capital and Foreign Labour: The Case of Malaysia', mimeo.

Lee, C. (2019), 'Manufacturing Performance and Services Inputs: Evidence from Malaysia', *ISEAS Economics Working Paper*, Vol. no. 2018-2, pp. 1–24.

Leete, R. (2007), *Malaysia: From Kampung to Twin Towers.* Kuala Lumpur: Oxford Fajar.

Levchenko, A.A. (2007), 'Institutional Quality and International Trade', *Review of Economic Studies*, 74(3), pp.791–819.

Lim, C.-Y. (1967), *Economic Development of Modern Malaya.* Kuala Lumpur: Oxford University Press.

Lim, H.-K. (1978), *The Evolution of the Urban System in Malaysia.* Kuala Lumpur: University of Malaya Press.

Makun, K. (2017), 'Trade Openness and Economic Growth in Malaysia: Some Time-Series Analysis', *Foreign Trade Review*, 52(3), pp.157–170.

Malaysian Rubber Board (2016), *Natural Rubber Statistics 2016.* Kuala Lumpur: Malaysian Rubber Board.

Melitz, M. (2003), 'The Impact of Trade on Intra-Industry Reallocation and Aggregate Industry Productivity', *Econometrica*, 71(6), pp.1695–1725.

Menon, J. and T.H. Ng (2017), 'Do State-Owned Enterprises Crowd Out Private Investment? Firm Level Evidence from Malaysia', *Journal of Southeast Asian Economies*, 34(3), pp.507–522.

Mohamad, J. (2010), 'Wage Inequality and Trade Reforms in Malaysia', Paper presented at the International Conference on Applied Economics, Athens, Greece.

Nazrin, S. (2017), *Charting the Economy: Early 20th Century Malaya and Contemporary Malaysian Contrasts*. Shah Alam: Oxford University Press.

Noor, A.K. and R. Adam (2009), 'Productivity Spillovers from FDI in Malaysian Manufacturing: Evidence from Micro-Panel Data', *Asian Economic Journal*, 2(2), pp.143–167.

Perkins, D. and W.-T. Woo (2000), 'Malaysia: Adjusting to Deep Integration with the World Economy', in J.D. Sachs and K. Schwab (eds.), *The Asian Financial Crisis: Lessons for a Resilient Asia*. Cambridge, MA: Massachusetts Institute of Technology Press.

Ragayah, M.Z. (2011), 'Poverty and Income Distribution', in R. Rasiah (ed.), *Malaysian Economy*. New York, NY: Oxford University Press.

Ragayah, M.Z. (2012), 'Poverty Eradication and Income Distribution', in H. Hill, T.S. Yean, and R.M. Zin (eds.), *Malaysia's Development Challenges*. London: Routledge.

Rasiah, R. (2006), 'Explaining Malaysia's Export Expansion in Palm Oil and Related Products', in V. Chandra (ed.), *Technology, Adaptation and Exports*. Washington, DC: World Bank.

Rasiah, R. (ed.) (2011), *Malaysian Economy: Unfolding Growth and Social Change*. Kuala Lumpur: Oxford University Press.

Said, R. and K.H. Hamid (2011), 'The Effects of Occupational Differentials: Between or Within Industrial Effects', *International Journal of Economic Policy Studies*, 6, pp.83–97.

Saw, S.-H. (2007), *The Population of Malaysia*. Singapore: Institute of Southeast Asian Studies.

Saw, S.-H. (2015), *The Population of Malaysia*, 2nd Edition. Singapore: Institute of Southeast Asian Studies.

Sidhu, M.S. and G.W. Jones (1981), *Population Dynamics in a Plural Society: Peninsular Malaysia*. Kuala Lumpur: University of Malaysia Cooperative Bookshop Publications.

Sulaiman, M. and N. Md. Saad (2009), 'An Analysis of Export Performance and Economic Growth of Malaysia Using CoIntegraton and Error Correction Models', *Journal of Developing Areas*, 43(1), pp.217–231.

World Bank (2012), *Malaysia Economic Monitor: Modern Jobs*. Kuala Lumpur: World Bank.

Appendix

Table 6.A1 Malaysia – Population and Labour Market Indicators, 2000–2010

	2000	*2001*	*2002*	*2003*	*2004*	*2005*	*2006*	*2007*	*2008*	*2009*	*2010*
0–14 years	8,003	7,880	7,893	7,891	7,881	7,857	7,824	7,791	7,757	7,724	7,828
15–64 years	14,560	15,293	15,846	16,400	16,955	17,510	17,857	18,203	18,547	18,890	19,079
65+ years	932	950	989	1,029	1,069	1,110	1,151	1,193	1,236	1,282	1,427
Total population ('000)	23,495	24,123	24,727	25,320	25,905	26,477	26,832	27,186	27,541	27,895	28,334
Population growth rate (%)	2.5	2.6	2.5	2.4	2.3	2.2	1.3	1.3	1.3	1.3	1.6
0–14 years (%)	34.1	32.7	31.9	31.2	30.4	29.7	29.2	28.7	28.2	27.7	27.6
15–64 years (%)	62.0	63.4	64.1	64.8	65.5	66.1	66.6	67.0	67.3	67.7	67.3
65+ years (%)	4.0	3.9	4.0	4.1	4.1	4.2	4.3	4.4	4.5	4.6	5.0
Total population (%)	100.0	100.0	100.0	100.0	100.0	100.0	100.0	100.0	100.0	100.0	100.0
Labour force ('000)	9,556	9,699	9,886	10,240	10,346	10,413	10,629	10,890	11,028	11,315	11,517
Labour force participation (%)	65.4	64.9	64.4	65.2	64.4	63.3	63.1	63.2	62.6	62.9	62.7
Total employment ('000)	9,269	9,357	9,543	9,870	9,980	10,045	10,275	10,538	10,660	10,897	11,129
Unemployment rate (%)	3.0	3.5	3.5	3.6	3.5	3.5	3.3	3.2	3.3	3.7	3.4
Employment in manufacturing ('000)	2,174	2,184	2,069	2,131	2,023	1,989	2,083	1,977	1,945	1,807	1,880
Manufacturing employment share (%)	23.5	23.3	21.7	21.6	20.3	19.8	20.3	18.8	18.2	16.6	16.9
Growth in total employment (%)		0.9	2.0	3.4	1.1	0.7	2.3	2.6	1.2	2.2	2.1
Growth in manufacturing employment (%)		0.5	–5.3	3.0	–5.1	–1.7	4.7	–5.1	–1.6	–7.1	4.0

Source: Department of Statistics. https://www.dosm.gov.my/v1/DOS (accessed 30 July 2019).

7 Economic consequences of globalisation: case study of Thailand

Archanun Kohpaiboon and Juthathip Jongwanich

1 Introduction

The net benefits of economic globalisation are a subject of heated debate (Bhagwati, 2004; Wolf, 2005; Irwin, 2015).[1] Since the new millennium, anti-globalisation has grown stronger, reflecting cases where applied tariff rates have been raised, as well as non-tariff measures such as anti-dumping. In reality, economic globalisation has the potential to bring numerous benefits, making a systematic literature survey necessary.

Thailand was classified by Sachs and Warner (1995: Table 1) as always open since 1940, together with Barbados, Cyprus, Hong Kong, Malaysia, Mauritius, Singapore, and Yemen Arab Republic. This is supported by Thailand being one of the production hubs of multinational enterprises (MNEs) (Kohpaiboon, 2008; Kohpaiboon and Jongwanich, 2013). This would seem to run counter to Thailand's maintaining a relatively high tariff by regional standards. The un-weighted average tariff of Thailand is relatively high compared with six original ASEAN members. In addition, the story of Thai automotives is often claimed as a success of government intervention, local content requirements (LCRs), and high cross-border protection. Against this backdrop, the paper reviews empirical works using Thailand as a case study.

The paper is organised as follows: Section 2 presents policies regarding the global integration of the Thai economy, particularly regarding trade, foreign direct investment, and labour mobility. In Section 3, growth and industrial transformation are described in order to raise concerns about economic consequences of globalisation, which will be used for in-depth discussion in the following section (Section 4: Economic Consequences). Conclusions and policy lessons are in the final section.

2 Policies and global integration of Thailand

From 1960 onward, the Thai government has maintained a firm commitment to private sector industrialisation combined with prudent public investment in infrastructure. Influenced by the World Bank in the late 1950s, government

DOI: 10.4324/9781003138501-7

involvement shifted from direct production via state enterprises towards investment in public infrastructure required for economic development, such as electricity, water supply, and transportation facilities. The government virtually prohibited state participation in those commercial and industrial activities that might be expected to compete directly with private capital (Suehiro, 1989: 180).

This is associated with a 'market-friendly' approach towards foreign investors. There have not been any major policies preventing foreign investors from being involved in almost any business. This is especially true for the manufacturing sector, where foreign investors are usually guaranteed the same rights as domestic investors. There are guarantees against expropriation and nationalisation; further, the government permits remitting investment capital, profits, and other payments in any foreign currency. Despite the presence of capital control measures during the pre-1990 period, in practice, repatriation of foreign capital related to direct investment (e.g. investment capital, profit or dividends, interest and principal of foreign loans, royalties and payments on other obligations) has not been restricted (Suehiro, 1989: 179).

There have been restrictions on land ownership and hiring of foreign migrants by foreign investors. In general, according to the Land Code (1954), foreign-owned firms are not allowed to own land.[2] According to the Alien Occupation Law, passed in 1973 and amended in 1978, foreigners require a work permit. Such restrictions have not been prohibitive. They have not applied to foreigners who received investment privileges from the Thai Board of Investment (BOI). This restriction was abolished in 2000 for the manufacturing sector.

This trade policy regime influences firms' market orientation, as well as the speed of global integration of firms in Thailand. While Thailand also established the BOI to grant investment incentives and privileges to industries targeted by the government, its effectiveness remains unclear (Kohpaiboon, 2006a); at best, it has been complementary to the trade policy regime (Kohpaiboon, 2006; Kohpaiboon and Jongwanich, 2014).

Trade policy in Thailand heavily relies on tariff measures, whereas non-tariff measures (NTMs) and quantitative restrictions have been imposed on few products and agricultural items (World Trade Organization WTO, 2015).[3] The only exception was the automotive industries, which have been the main interest to the Ministry of Industry. There were government efforts that were first implemented in the mid-1970s (i.e. imposing local content requirement to carmakers) up to the new millennium (Kohpaiboon, 2006).

Between the 1960s and the mid-1980s, Thailand's escalating tariff structure was tilted towards the highest rate associated with finished products, as opposed to the lowest rate associated with raw materials. This structure was to promote an import-substitution strategy, with relatively high tariff levels, together with a cascading structure tending to alter relative prices in favour of producing goods for the domestic market, instead of targeting exports. The average unweighted most-favoured nation rate was 41.2% by 1986. As shown in Figure 7.1, the degree of openness, that is, the sum of export and import of goods and services as a percentage of gross domestic product (GDP), was around 40%–50%. To eliminate

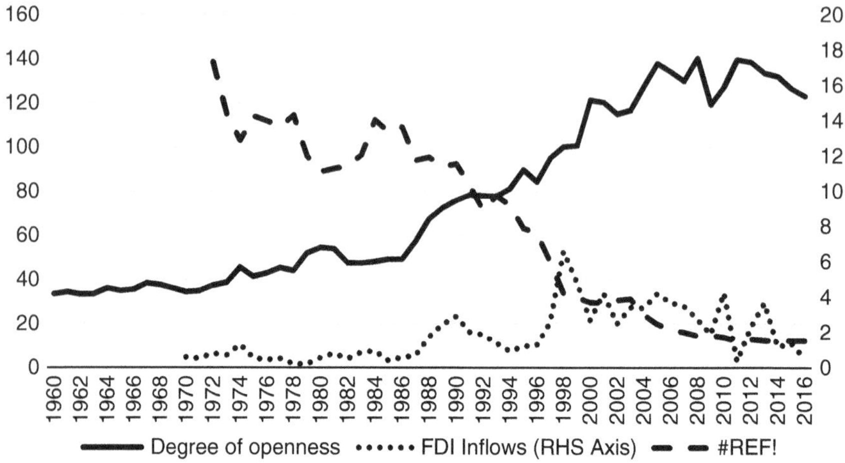

Figure 7.1 Global Integration of Thailand between 1960 and 2017.
Source: Degree of openness is from World Development Indicator whereas FDI inflows from.
Note: Unit = % of GDP. FDI = foreign direct investment.

excess supply in the domestic market, exports during this period were dominated by agricultural raw materials.

A similar pattern was observed with inflows of FDI, whose annual rates varied between US$100 and $400 million over the considered period, accounting for around 0.5% of GDP (Figure 7.1). FDI inflows were dominated by tariff-hopping ones (Kohpaiboon, 2006).

While tariff levels remained virtually unchanged with few exceptions from 1983 to the mid-1990s, various exemption schemes promoted Thailand as an export platform for multinationals (Kohpaiboon, 2006; Jongwanich and Kohpaiboon, 2007). By 1990, the average unweighted most-favoured-nation rate remained at around 40%. Domestic firms can be export-oriented and apply available exemption schemes in order to mitigate any of the adverse effects of input tariffs. The effectiveness of the exemptions was reflected by the declining tariff incidence and the percentage of tariff revenue to total imports, most noticeably between the mid-1980s and the early 1990s. These exemption schemes and one introduced by the BOI have been intensively used since then. As argued in Kohpaiboon and Jongwanich (2019), exemption schemes accounted for 45% of total imports in 2012.

As result, the degree of openness of Thailand increased dramatically, increasing to 89.8% in 1995. It was associated with influx of FDI inflows, whose annual rates rose more than fivefold to over US$2 billion and remained at roughly these levels over the next eight years. This is in line with Bhagwati's 1985 hypothesis that an export-oriented industrialisation (EOI) strategy is likely to both attract more FDI and promote its more efficient utilisation than import substitution.[4]

In the 1990s, when the Thai government experienced substantial improvements in its fiscal position, tariff reform was undertaken. In particular, tariff bands were cut from 39 to six (0%, 1%, 5%, 10%, 20%, and 30%). Nonetheless, there were substantial exemptions whose tariffs were greater than 30%. As a result, the simple tariff average dropped substantially from 40% in the mid-1980s to 17% in 1997. Tariff restructuring received renewed emphasis in the new millennium with an ambitious target of three tariff bands, i.e. 0%–1% for raw materials, 5% for intermediates, and 10% for finished products. It began in June 2003. The magnitude of such reduction was moderate and focused on intermediate tariffs. As a result, the average tariff dropped to 8.7% by 2011. Nonetheless, nearly one-fifth of tariff lines had rates greater than 20% in 2004–08 (Table 7.1).

By the standard of developing countries in the region, Thailand's tariff rate is relatively high (Table 7.2). In particular, the average tariff of Thailand was higher than Malaysia (5.3% in 2012), the Philippines (6.2% in 2011), and Indonesia (6.6% in 2012). The weighted average was much lower than the unweighted, implying that tariffs imposed on certain products are redundant. In some products such as vehicles and clothing, tariffs are still very high, that is, 30% and 80%, respectively. In addition, the tariff structure remains escalating in spite of the lower tariff protection.

In the new millennium, political attention and negotiating resources in Thailand have been shifted towards preferential trade agreements and bilateral free trade accords (FTAs). This was driven by various factors such as the slowdown in WTO liberalisation negotiations, and the political re-entry by Thaksin Shinawatra and his newly found political party Thai Rak Thai (Kohpaiboon and Jongwanich, 2019). As a result, there were 18 FTAs signed with partners including ASEAN members, Japan, Republic of Korea, China, Australia, New Zealand, India, Chile, and Peru, many of which have more than one FTA in effect. Note that only eight FTAs involve substantial tariff cuts, covering more than 80% of tariff lines and having been offered since 2010. These include the ASEAN Free Trade Area (now known as ASEAN Economic Community),

Table 7.1 Share of Four-Digit HS Categories of Applied Tariff Rates in Thailand, 1989–2008

Tariff Bands	*1989*	*1995*	*2002*	*2003*	*2004–08*
0	2.5	2.6	5.6	5.7	6.0
0.1–5	14.4	17.3	33.3	37.7	48.8
5.1–10	14.2	17.6	14.1	14.2	14.8
10.1–15	12.7	3.2	3.9	4.5	3.6
15.1–20	15.4	16.4	21.4	17.9	8.4
20.1–30	15.8	16	13.8	14.3	12.7
30–100	25	26.8	7.8	5.8	5.7

Source: Data for 1989 and 1995 from World Trade Organization (1990; 1995), respectively. Data for 2002–08 are from authors' compilation from official document provided by Ministry of Finance.

HS = Harmonized Commodity Description and Coding Systems.

Table 7.2 Weighted Average of Most-Favoured-Nation Tariff Rate of Selected Countries during 2010–12

Country (Year)	*Unweighted*	*Weighted*	*Agricultural Products*	*Non-agricultural Products*
Thailand (2011)	8.7	5.0	9.0	4.9
Vietnam (2010)	9.8	12.2	24.4	10.7
Singapore (2011)	0.0	0.0	0.0	0.0
Philippines (2011)	6.2	12.2	23.2	10.4
Myanmar (2011)	5.6	6.6	12.6	4.9
Malaysia (2012)	5.3	6.7	8.7	6.5
Indonesia (2012)	6.6	9.8	1.8	11.1
Lao PDR (2008)	9.7	13.6	19.3	12.6
Brunei Darussalam (2011)	2.5	1.7	0.0	2.6
Cambodia (2012)	10.9	12.0	14.7	11.1
Australia (2011)	2.8	3.8	1.6	3.9
New Zealand (2011)	2.0	2.7	1.9	2.8
China (2010)	9.9	8.6	21.5	7.4
India (2012)	13.3	9.4	48.6	7.7
Japan (2011)	3.0	2.1	7.0	1.3
Republic of Korea (2011)	11.2	9.6	34.1	5.6

Source: Author's calculation using most-favoured-nation tariff rates from the World Trade Organization.
Lao PDR = Lao People's Democratic Republic.

ASEAN–China FTA, the Thailand–Australia FTA, the Thailand–New Zealand FTA, the Japan–Thailand Economic Partnership Agreement, the ASEAN–Japan FTA, the ASEAN–Korea FTA, and the ASEAN–Australia–New Zealand FTA. In the other three FTAs (i.e. the Thailand–Peru FTA, the Thailand–Chile FTA, ASEAN–India FTA), substantial tariff cuts took place in 2015 and 2016 (Kohpaiboon and Jongwanich, 2019).

Interestingly, commitments made in these FTAs focus on goods market liberalisation. The commitments that Thailand made on other issues under these FTAs, except in the case of the ASEAN Economic Community, were rather weak and at most in line with WTO commitments. This is especially true for FTAs that Thailand has with developing country FTA partners. As argued in Kohpaiboon and Jongwanich (2019), Thailand was reluctant to offer tariff cuts in these FTAs in terms of product coverages and long-time schedules of implementation. On the import side, therefore, tariff cuts under FTAs might not induce any substantial trade enhancing effect from FTA partners to Thailand.

FTAs ensure firms in Thailand are not in a disadvantageous position with respect to accessing partner markets. This would maintain Thailand's attractiveness for export-oriented FDI. It seems that this strategy has been partially successful as the use of FTAs in terms of exports was highly concentrated between 2006 and 2015 (Jongwanich and Kohpaiboon, 2017; Kohpaiboon and Jongwanich, 2019). To a certain extent, it is a testament to the increasing openness of the Thai economy. Nonetheless, the evidence supporting the idea that the FTAs attracted FDI is rather weak. As shown in Figure 7.1, FDI as a percentage of GDP exhibited a downward trend from 2005 onward. In addition, there was no clear correlation between bilateral FDI inflows before and after signing FTAs in most of the partners documented in Kohpaiboon and Jongwanich (2019).

Until the new millennium, trade and FDI were the main driver of economic globalisation in Thailand. Since then, labour mobility has played an increasing role. In the past, Thailand was a net labour exporter, with many Thais working in the Middle East. Nonetheless, the number of these workers was rather small, as reflected in the negligible share of remittances in total export earnings from the 1970s to the 1990s. The tightening labour market in Thailand and the economic development gap with neighbouring countries in mainland Southeast Asia caused an influx of workers from elsewhere in the region (Figure 7.2). The number of total foreign workers in Thailand increased from 0.17 to 2 million between 2006 and 2017. Note that such official figures tend to be underestimated; for example, Bylander and Reid (2017) claimed the figure exceeded 4 million. This size is double the official figure, giving a rough size of the underestimation of the official figure.

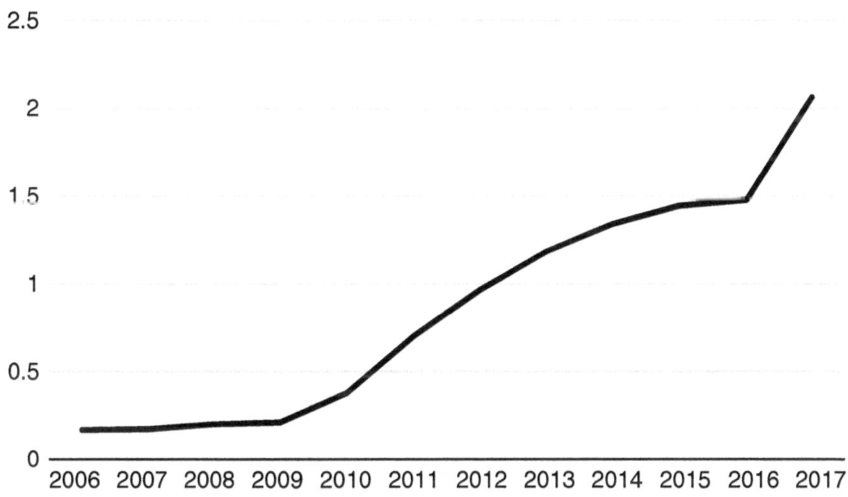

Figure 7.2 Number of Foreign Workers from 2006 to 2017.
Source: Author compilation from Department of Employment, Ministry of Labor, Thailand, available at https://www.doe.go.th/prd/alien/statistic/param/site/152/cat/82/sub/74/pull/sub_category/view/list-label.
Note: Unit = million workers.

Despite starting in the late 1980s, the policy stance of the Thai government has been clearer in the new millennium where the need for foreign workers was evident. The policy stance was shifted towards managing these workers while avoiding permanent settlement and any potential adverse effects, such as a rising demand for public services, a reduction in social cohesion, and other negative social effects. Hence, a new registration system was introduced in 2004. It is worth noting that under the new registration, firms are allowed to temporarily hire illegal foreign workers, but must bring them to be registered with the Ministry of Labor to identify their true nationality. While waiting for nationality identification to be completed, these workers are allowed to work at a given firm and in a given location (i.e. province). Nonetheless, illegal migrant problems remain as a result of regulatory cumbersome involving in nationality. Given the number of immigrants in Thailand, labour mobility will be another driver of economic globalisation for the next decade.

3 Growth and industrial transformation

From 1960 to 1985, the import substitution undermined the domestic incentive structure and favoured those industries over export-oriented ones. As a consequence, the Thai economy began to grow rapidly from the 1960s through the mid-1970s. The annual growth rate during the considered period averaged 7.5% (Figure 7.3). As expected, the share of the manufacturing sector to GDP rapidly increased from 11.6% in the 1950s to 14.2% and 18.6% during the 1960s and the first half of the 1970s, respectively (Figure 7.3).

As argued in Krueger (1992: 43–4), rapid expansion of import-substituting industries is typically short lived, after the easy opportunities (meeting domestic demand

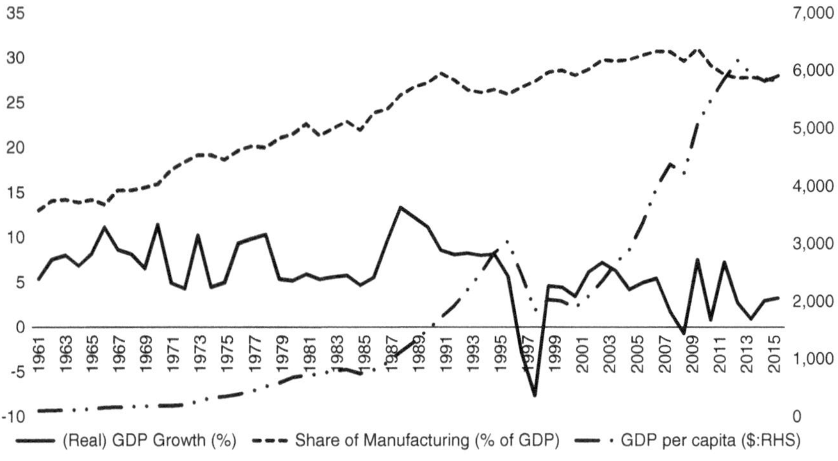

Figure 7.3 Growth and Industrialisation in Thailand.
Source: World Development Indicator database.
Note: GDP = gross domestic product.

in textiles, footwear, some food processing, and other light labour-intensive activities) are exhausted. In Thailand, the easy import substitution opportunities included textiles and clothing, transport equipment, basic metal industries, and chemical products. In the textile industries where there is a wide range of production technology involved, from capital-intensive, i.e. synthetic fibres, to labour-intensive, i.e. fabrics, production took place in the most labour-intensive segment, i.e. the shuttle-loom weaving industry (Suehiro, 1989; Kohpaiboon, 1995). Similarly, the Thai automotive industry began with local manufacture of bulky, simple, and quasi non-tradable parts, whereas it was heavily reliant on imports of complicated parts, especially engines (Kohpaiboon, 2006).

Since then, new import-substituting activities were associated with higher investment costs so that manufacturing growth bottomed out in 1985. The average annual growth of GDP dropped noticeably to 5% during the period 1981–85. The manufacturing share in the GDP remained more or less the same at around 22% between 1976 and 1985. Import-substituting industries did not contribute significantly to employment (Figure 7.3).

Between 1970 and 1985, manufacturing employment accounted for only 8.2% of total employment. The employment share of the manufacturing sector increased from 4.5% in 1970 to around 8.4% in 1975 and then remained more or less unchanged at this level during the following decade ending in 1985. Figure 7.4

Another undesirable consequence of pursuing an import substituting industrialisation strategy is that local manufacturing was heavily reliant on imported intermediate goods. Thus, the successive balance of payment deficits

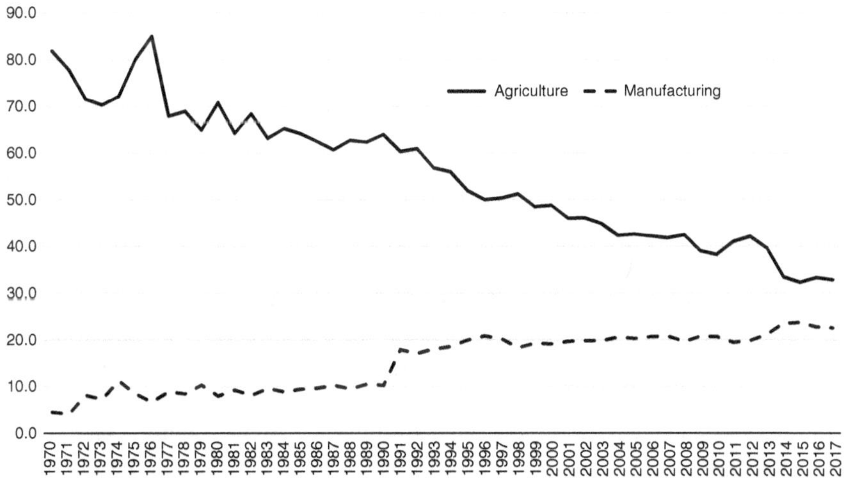

Figure 7.4 Employment Structure in Thailand from 1970 to 2017.
Source: World Development Indicator Database.
Note: Unit = % to GDP.

between the late 1970s and the early 1980s gradually caused the government to shift the industrialisation strategy to favour exports. As mentioned above, the main instrument was the tariff exemption scheme by BOI that partly mitigated the adverse impact of input tariffs on the international competitiveness of export-oriented industries (Suehiro, 1989: 270).

Two favourable factors in promoting exports of Thai manufacturing were interplaying. The first factor was a series of currency devaluations during the first half of the 1980s to improve external imbalances (Warr and Nidhiprabha, 1996: 206). In particular, the baht was devalued by around 36% in 1985. The second favourable factor was that East Asian investors were seeking an export base abroad to maintain their international competitiveness in labour-intensive products in the mid-1980s. The erosion of their home countries' international competitiveness was the outcome of wage increases and currency appreciation in the mid-1980s. In addition, the imposition and gradual tightening of quantitative restrictions by developed countries constrained certain labour-intensive exports, mostly textiles, garments, and footwear, from these East Asian exporters (Wells, 1986). In the electronics industry and other durable consumer goods industries, technological innovations began to allow these investors to slice up the value chain of their production, relocating labour-intensive segments rather than entire industries to benefit from cheap labour available abroad (Krugman, 1995).

As a result, manufacturers from Japan and the Northeast Asian Newly Industrialized Economies (NIEs) have become actively involved with outward direct investment and have established a regional network to strengthen their international competitiveness. Thailand was selected by these investors to be their labour-intensive export base and rapidly integrated into global production sharing (GPS) of multinationals around the world (Kohpaiboon, Jongwanich, and Kulthanavit, 2012; Kohpaiboon and Jongwanich, 2013).

After shifting towards an EOI strategy around the mid-1980s, the economy experienced a rapid growth. Manufacturing export growth increased from 11.1% in the first half of the 1980s to 40.5% and 18% during the periods 1986–90 and 1991–96, respectively. The average annual growth of manufacturing output jumped to 15.1% and declined slightly to 10.5% during the same periods, respectively (Figure 7.3). As a result, the share of the manufacturing sector in GDP increased from 22% in the first half of the 1980s to 27% in the decade ending in 1996. The annual economic growth rate between 1988 and 1996 averaged out at 9.3%. This was a classic example of the export-led growth phenomenon.

As documented in Kohpaiboon (2006), EOI began with labour-intensive manufacturing industries such as clothing, footwear, leather products, furniture, toys, jewels and gems, and electronics (Table 7.3). While capital-intensive industries figured prominently among the declining sectors, transportation equipment retained its share. The expansion of such labour-intensive manufactured products increased importance for the sector not only in terms of export earnings, but also in terms of employment absorption, with its share increasing to 13.6% and 15.1% in 1991–95 and 1996–2000, respectively, from around 8%

Table 7.3 Sectoral Composition of Thai Manufacturing, 1971–2017 (in %)

	1971–5	*1976–80*	*1981–5*	*1986–90*	*1991–5*	*1996–2000*	*2001–5*	*2006–10*	*2011–7*
Food and beverages	24.2	24.7	21.5	18.1	15.1	15.1	19.9	19.9	22.0
Tobacco	7.6	6.2	4.9	3.4	2.3	1.5	1.9	1.6	1.5
Textiles	12.2	13.1	10.7	10.9	8.7	7.2	6.6	4.5	3.1
Clothing	9.3	8.5	9.4	10.5	9.4	7.4	5.8	3.5	2.2
Leather, leather products, and footwear	2.2	1.8	2.2	3.4	3.5	3.4	2.0	1.4	1.1
Wood and wood products	3.5	3	2.6	1.8	0.7	0.3	1.1	1.0	1.1
Furniture and fixtures	1.4	1.5	2.7	2.9	2.2	1.1	1.2	1.0	0.9
Paper and paper products	1.3	1.5	1.6	1.4	1.5	2	2.1	1.7	1.4
Printing, publishing and allied industries	1.5	1.5	1.7	1.2	1.1	0.9	0.5	0.4	0.3
Chemicals and chemical products	3.6	3.4	3	2.9	2.7	4.6	5.9	7.0	8.1
Petroleum refineries and petroleum products	7.8	7.2	8.8	7	6.6	10.2	6.0	7.0	7.9
Rubber and plastic products	2.6	2.6	2.2	2.7	2.9	3.2	6.1	6.6	7.2
Non-metallic mineral products	3.9	4	5.1	5.4	5.9	5	5.0	4.2	4.0
Basic metal industries	2.1	2	2.1	1.7	1.7	1.4	3.0	2.5	1.8
Fabricated metal products	2.6	2	2.5	2.6	2.7	2.9	3.7	3.2	2.9
Machinery	2.8	2.8	3	4.1	6.5	9.3	3.5	4.1	4.2
Electrical machinery and supplies	1.8	2.6	3.7	5.1	8.6	11	4.1	4.0	4.7
Computer, electronic and optical products	n.a.	n.a.	n.a.	n.a.	n.a.	7.5	8.5	13.2	9.8
Transport equipment	7.2	8.3	8	8.1	9.5	6.3	8.5	8.9	10.8
Other manufacturing industries	2.5	3.1	4.5	6.8	8.4	7.3	3.5	3.5	4.0
Total value added	100	100	100	100	100	100	100	100	100

Source: National Economics and Social Development Board available at www.nesdb.or.th

during the period 1970–85 (Figure 7.3). Nevertheless, its performance in employment absorption seemed to be far from satisfactory. More than 50% of employed workers are still in the agricultural sector, whose income share is around 10%.

The high-growth performance ended in 1997 when the country experienced the financial crisis. The economic growth dropped dramatically to -1.4 and -10.5% in 1997 and 1998, respectively. The economy, nonetheless, recovered gradually and achieved an annual growth rate of 7% by 2003. The model simulation in Jongwanich (2007) pointed to the capital account opening that was speeded up in the early 1990s as the main cause of the 1997–98 crisis. It seemed inevitable that the boom fuelled by non-FDI capital inflows should not go on under a more flexible exchange rate regime.

Although the dramatic currency depreciation during the onset of the crisis should have been the catalyst for a manufacturing export boom, manufacturing exporters were restrained by the credit crunch in the financial sector. Until 1999, manufacturing export growth resumed. By contrast, FDI inflows increased rapidly after the currency depreciation, referred to as fire-sale FDI in Krugman (2000). Even though there was substantial merger and acquisition FDI during the onset of the crisis, greenfield FDI accounted for more than 50% of total inflows.

Since the Asian financial crisis, Thailand experienced a slight growth slowdown between 2000 and 2005. The annual growth rate during this period was around 5.3% on average. It has worsened since 2006, with both internal and external factors interplaying. These included political unrest starting in 2005, the sickness of King Rama IV from 2006 to 2016, the 2011 Great Floods, the deteriorating global situation (e.g. the global financial crisis beginning in 2008, Brexit, the European crisis, and the trade war between the US and China starting in 2018). Nonetheless, such a slow growth episode after the financial crisis is often claimed as the symbol of the middle-income trap in Thailand (e.g. Warr, 2011; Jitsuchon, 2012; Bisonyabut and Kamsaeng, 2015; Tangkitvanich and Bisonyabut, 2015; and World Bank, 2016). Many believe that it is an economic consequence of global integration of Thailand and that of the export-led growth model adopted through EOI strategy. As presented in the latest country's diagnostic report in 2016 by World Bank, causes of growth slowdown are listed below:

- Fail to sustain strong productivity-driven growth;
- Losing export competitiveness in labour-intensive manufacturing;
- Unsuccessful upgrading to sophistication of Thailand's medium and high-tech exports; and
- Limited FDI spillovers and slump of private investment (World Bank, 2016).

Whether the causes of growth slowdown listed are economically sound remains debatable, but these causes were well taken into Thailand's policy-making as reflected in the report prepared by Dr. Kanit Sangsubhan for Prime Minister in

17 November 2015 (Private Investment Promotion Working Group, 2015). This report resulted in the Thailand 4.0 Policy, the latest economic policy flagship of Gen Prayuth's administration (2014–the present) to transform the economy. In the plan, 10 industries are selected as new engines of growth. They are divided into two segments, five S-curved and five new S-curved industries. The former are existing industrial sectors, which will be improved through technological uptake. They include new-generation automotives, smart electronics, tourism, agriculture, and biotechnology. The latter are manufacturing robotics, medical hub, aviation and logistics, biofuels and biochemicals, and digital, all of which are slated to become significant long-term growth drivers.

To achieve the industrial transformation above, the Eastern Economic Corridor (EEC) special economic zone was established. The EEC straddles three eastern provinces – Chonburi, Rayong, and Chachoengsao – off the coast of the Gulf of Thailand and spans a total of 13,285 square kilometres. The government hopes to complete the EEC by 2021, turning these provinces into a hub for technological manufacturing and services with strong connectivity to its ASEAN neighbours by land, sea, and air. On 1 February 2018, the Thai parliament approved the law for trade and investment in the EEC. The government of Thailand expects US$43 billion of investment will be channelled into the EEC by 2021, from state funds, FDI, and through infrastructure development under a public–private partnership framework. An estimated 100,000 new jobs will be created as a result.

Despite the effort to target certain industries, there have not been any concrete policies to alter private sector industrialisation starting in the 1960s. To a large extent, the EEC project is similar to the Eastern Seaboard project launched in the mid-1980s, where investment incentives were offered to invite FDI, together with enlarging capability in supplying physical infrastructure services.

4 Economic consequences

As discussed in the previous section, debate on economic consequences of globalisation seems to be a recent phenomenon after the 1997–98 Asian financial crisis. In this section, the causes of growth slowdown mentioned in World Bank (2016) can be addressed in four aspects.

4.1 Trade and productivity

One favourable consequence of economic globalisation is that opening up to international trade could foster productivity growth. Productivity gains arising from the development of neoclassical international trade have been studied for several decades. Such gains are derived from resource reallocation from sectors in which the country has a comparative disadvantage to those in which it holds a comparative advantage driven by either technology, resource endowment, or both. This reallocation improves productivity at the aggregate level, despite the fact that individual firms' productivity remains unchanged. In addition, international trade can act as a channel for advanced technology developed elsewhere to be transmitted to a country in interest. Pioneered by Melitz (2003), firm heterogeneity suggests that international trade might have different effect in a given industry, driving better-performing ones to expand into larger markets, and stimulating resource reallocation. This, therefore, leads to productivity improvement, despite the fact that individual firms' productivity remains unchanged. The key inference is in favour of pursuing trade liberalisation.

The empirical studies examining the effect on trade liberalisation in Thailand were found in both aggregate and plant-level data analysis. The sample of the former includes Urata and Yokota (1994), Kohpaiboon (2003), Diao, Rattso, and Stokke (2006), and Phoonichaisuk (2010). Note that only Urata and Yokota (1994) directly addressed the effect of trade liberalisation on total factor productivity. Diao Rattso, and Stokke (2006) examined it by undertaking the model simulation. The other two studies empirically examined the effect of FDI on growth, with export–output being introduced as one of explanatory variables in the analysis. What the aggregate analysis points to is the net positive effect of trade liberalisation.

In the latter, empirical works examine the effect of trade policy through a productivity determinant equation in Thai manufacturing. They include Jongwanich and Kohpaiboon (2017) and Kohpaiboon and Jongwanich (2019). Despite having slightly different research focuses, both studies examine the effect of trade protection on productivity. Trade protection measured by changes in the lagged effective rate of protection at the industry level is one of the explanatory variables among the others. Note that Kohpaiboon and Jongwanich (2019) is a panel data analysis (from 2006 to 2016), whereas Jongwanich and Kohpaiboon (2017) is cross-sectional (using the 2011 industrial census). Both found empirical support for the positive effect of trade liberalisation on productivity.

There are two important findings from these studies. First, Jongwanich and Kohpaiboon (2017) showed that input and output tariffs should be treated separately in examining their impact on productivity. *Ceteris paribus,* lowering input tariffs potentially has at least two opposite effects: it allows firms to benefit in several ways enhancing their productivity, while also discouraging their efforts to improve productivity due to the increased level of effective protection. This necessitates caution when pursuing trade policy reform in not lopsidedly focusing on input tariffs while leaving output tariffs untouched. Even though input and output tariffs work differently in promoting firms' productivity, any trade policy reform process should take both input and output tariffs into consideration in ensuring trade is actually liberalised.

Secondly, as argued in Kohpaiboon and Jongwanich (2019), the negative effect of trade protection on productivity is enlarged by the highly concentrated domestic market, as measured by the Hirschman Herfindahl concentration index. This seems to be in line with the experience of Thai automotive industries where we observe water-in tariff, where the effectiveness of tariff protection on domestic price is deteriorated as a consequence of competition among firms.

Another empirical work is Kohpaiboon (2012b), which examined the import-as-a-market-discipline hypothesis in Thai manufacturing. The key finding suggests that international trade can act as a market discipline. Nonetheless, the net discipline effect is not found in all kinds of imported goods that would have it. In fact, the study also highlights how participating in the global production network, as well as outward market orientation, could play a key role to promote efficient use of scarce resources.

Another branch of literature focuses on exporting firms themselves. This is due to exporting firms often exhibiting higher productivity than locally oriented ones. Exporting firms must improve their production efficiency to overcome higher trade barriers and face different consumer tastes and tougher competition in international markets. In addition, exporting makes firms aware of potential innovations taking place aboard and they may assimilate these in order to improve their position in foreign markets (Greenaway and Kneller, 2007).

Such a finding is also found in empirical research of productivity determinants in Thai manufacturing (e.g. Jongwanich and Kohpaiboon, 2008; Kohpaiboon, 2012a; Kohpaiboon and Jongwanich, 2019). The finding is robust, regardless of the studying periods, the nature of the data (cross-sectional and panel) and how productivity is measured. All of these studies employed standard productivity determinant equations where the measure is the dependent variable. In all studies, explanatory variables include both firm- and industry-specific variables. The latter includes trade policy, producer production concentration ratio, and the presence of MNEs. Labour productivity is employed in Jongwanich and Kohpaiboon (2008) and Kohpaiboon (2012a) due to the cross-sectional nature of the data. In Kohpaiboon and Jongwanich (2019), Levinsohn and Petrin total factor productivity is used in the panel regression analysis. Export zero-one dummy and export propensity ratio at the plant level are used as alternative measure of exporting firms. In theory, the causality between export and productivity remains debatable, as it can be either firms learning from exports, learning to export, or both. Given the nature of plant-level data available in Thailand, the hypotheses cannot be empirically tested. Higher productivity found in the exporting firm could be explained by the propensity to commit product development R&D found in the inter-plant cross-sectional analysis in Jongwanich and Kohpaiboon (2015). This is to learn more about competing products and customer preference in the international market.

4.2 Export performance

Poor quality is one criticism made towards the export-led growth strategy Thailand has pursued since the mid-1980s. In particular, the claim is that Thailand is struggling to maintain competitiveness in labour-intensive manufacturing (World Bank, 2016). Interestingly, the claimed poor export quality does not seem to be consistent with actual export performance, as described below. Figure 7.5 reports the scatter plot between annual growth rate of GDP

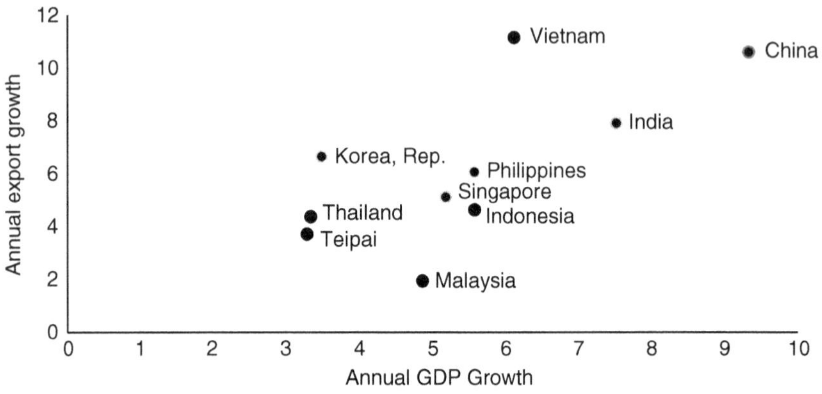

Figure 7.5 GDP-Export Nexus in Selected East Asian Economies between 2006 and 2016.

Source: World Development Indicator Database.

Note: GDP = gross domestic product.

and exports of selected Asian countries averaging out between 2006 and 2016. The figure is the average from 2006 to 2016.

Thailand's annual growth was the lowest (the horizontal axis). It was not the export performance indicated by the position on the vertical axis. In addition, the simple and rather straightforward indicators like the successively increasing share of Thai manufacturing exports in the world for the past two decades cast some doubt on the claim above (Figure 7.6). In particular, the share of manufacturing exports from Thailand increased from 0.8% in 1992 to 1.4% in 2016.[5]

The recent study by Jongwanich (2019) examined the relationship between export diversification, export margins, and economic growth at the industry level using Thailand as a case study during 2002–16. The key finding is that the effects of export diversification and margins on economic growth vary across industries. In particular, export diversification helps to boost growth only in some sectors, including electronics, automotives, and chemicals, plastic, and rubber; while in the processed food, textile, and apparel industries, specialisation matters more in promoting growth. Such findings point to the danger of overemphasising extensive margins, especially in terms of new products, in promoting economic growth in developing countries like Thailand, where they still play an important role in many industries.[6]

One side effect of exports is the vulnerability of the economy to external shocks. This seems to be a trade-off. This was empirically examined in Cheewatrakoolpong and Manprasert (2014) through the case of the global financial crisis. Trade in East Asia is still largely linked to the US, regardless of its relative importance as an export destination. The explanation is the growing importance of GPS in the region.

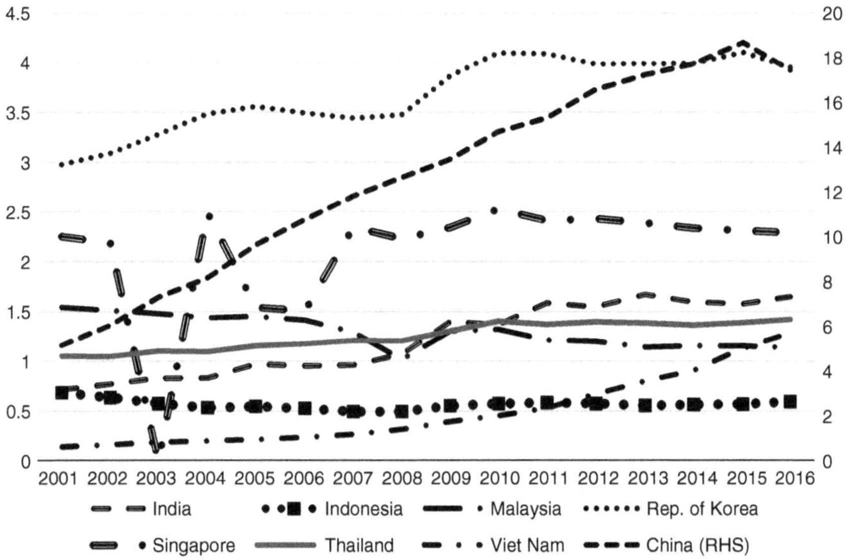

Figure 7.6 World Market Share of Manufacturing Products of Selected East Asia (%).
Source: UN Comtrade database.
1Note: Manufacturing product is defined as Standard International Trade Classification 5-8 net of 68.

Another concern is about the job quality created by the export-led growth strategy adopted (Mounier and Charoenloet, 2010; Rasiah, Cheong, and Doner, 2014; and Charoenloet, 2015). In particular, Charoenloet (2015: 136) argued that many job opportunities created under an EOI strategy are sub-contracting, and vulnerable to being retrenched in the presence of negative shocks. Nonetheless, the relation between economic globalisation and low job quality in these studies is based on interpretation from various years of national socio-economic surveys. It remains a wonder how the situation is taking place amid the rising real wage and the tightening labour markets. This points to the need for further research.

4.3 Foreign direct investment and its spillovers

The discussion above suggests that FDI plays an important role of global integration in Thailand. The entry of MNEs could affect the aggregate productivity of host investment-receiving countries. As MNEs are now widely regarded as the principle bearers of technology across international borders, their direct investment brings in not only capital but also production technology, managerial skills, international marketing channels and so on to host countries (Sjöholm, 1997; Borensztein, Gregorio, and Lee, 1998; Lipsey, 2000; Vernon, 2000). Their entry would be equivalent to adding highly productive firms and eventually affecting the overall productivity in host countries. This is widely known as the direct effect.

Indirectly, MNE presence could positively affect the productivity of locally non-affiliated firms in the host country. This is due to the fact that advanced technology that MNE affiliates bring with them could also generate a positive externality to the local firm. Technology is partially a public good in which owners cannot entirely prevent others from benefitting from it. Hence, locally non-affiliated firms could benefit to a certain extent MNE presence and experience productivity improvement. The positive externality is referred to as FDI/MNE productivity spillover (Blomström and Kokko, 1998). Though not the only gain from FDI, spillover is often argued as the most desirable benefit.

FDI spillover, nonetheless, does not always exist, depending on the type of FDI inflows (e.g. efficiency and/or market seeking), or the economic and policy environments in host countries.[7] Two factors are highlighted in the literature, namely absorptive capability and trade policy regime. Whether a local firm benefits from MNE presence depends on its knowledge-absorptive capability. The higher the absorptive capability, the greater the spillover the local firm in the host country can expect. Trade policy regime is another factor postulated in the literature.[8] Productivity spillover tends to be smaller, or possibly even negative, under a restrictive, import substitution regime compared with a liberalising, export promotion regime, simply because different trade policy regimes entice different types of FDI inflows. As in Bhagwati's hypothesis, FDI inflows enticed by import substitution tend to be market-seeking and are invested mostly in the industries where proprietary assets are important. This creates barriers to entry for local firms and thus constrains productivity spillovers. In contrast, export promotion is more conducive to generating favourable spillover effects because, under such a regime, FDI is mostly attracted to industries in which the country has comparative advantage, i.e. efficiency-seeking FDI. In such industries, local firms have a greater potential to catch up with foreign firms and achieve productivity improvement. (Table 7.4)

Recently, the empirical studies of FDI spillover literature point to linkages and backward ones in particular as other potential channels that advance technology associated with MNE affiliates could benefit local non-affiliates.[9] Spillovers through linkage channels are often referred to as vertical FDI, whereas the spillover mentioned above is horizontal. Many empirical works prefer vertical FDI spillovers because there would be mutual benefit that MNE affiliates and local suppliers can share. This is different from what we expect from the horizontal FDI spillovers, where MNEs would have an incentive to prevent information leakage to their competitors, including local enterprises, thereby reducing the possibility of the spillover taking place (Javorcik, 2004).

One consensus in the empirical research about the presence of MNEs in Thai manufacturing is that MNE affiliates are likely to be more productive than indigenous ones.[10] This finding is insensitive to model specification (trans-log vs. Cobb–Douglas production function), as well as the measure of productivity (total factor productivity vs. labour productivity). Interestingly, a finding

Table 7.4 Shares of FDI Inflows Classified by Home Country, 1970–2003 (in %)

	1970–5	*1976–80*	*1981–5*	*1986–90*	*1991–5*	*1996–2000*	*2001–05*	*2006–10*	*2011–15*	*2016–18*
Japan	22.8	15.8	19.2	41.1	15.1	23.1	26.0	31.1	41.4	49.4
US	39.6	16.5	20.7	10.3	11	17.7	7.5	3.9	17.9	4.0
EU	11.5	9	13.8	8.1	8.7	18.5	11.8	15.9	5.6	-6.8
NICs	10.5	18.1	15.3	22.3	22.7	12.2	7.6	5.4	10.7	20.7
Hong Kong	10	17.9	14.8	12.7	19	8.1	4.1	4.0	6.9	14.4
Taiwan	0.3	0	0.4	9	3.2	3.5	2.6	-0.1	0.9	4.3
Rep. of Korea	0.2	0.2	0	0.6	0.4	0.6	0.8	1.4	3.0	2.0
Others	15.6	40.6	30.9	18.3	42.5	28.5	47.1			
	43.7	24.5	32.7							
Total	**100**	**100**	**100**	**100**	**100**	**100**	**100**	**100**	**100**	**100**
Value of FDI Inflows ($million)	**115**	**285**	**508**	**1,456**	**3,437**	**5,525**	**8,017.66**	**9,454.21**	**9,042.35**	**4,820.83**

Source: Bank of Thailand, on-line database, available at www.bot.or.th.
EU = European Union, FDI = foreign direct investment, NIC = newly industrialized country, US = United States.

revealed in Jongwanich and Kohpaiboon (2015) is that MNE affiliates are less likely to commit to R&D investment. This is especially true for production technology and product development. Nonetheless, an MNE presence could affect R&D propensity and intensity of locally non-affiliated firms to do R&D, leading to product development and process innovation.

It is the MNE technology spillover that varies across industries. So far there are four systematic analyses examining FDI spillovers in Thai manufacturing, i.e. Kohpaiboon (2006), Kohpaiboon (2012a), Wongseree (2012), and Tantratananuwat (2015). Each of these uses different sets of plant-level data. Kohpaiboon (2006) uses the 1996 industrial census and undertook the cross-sectional inter-industry analysis (i.e. four-digit ISIC), whereas Kohpaiboon (2012a) and Wongseree (2012) are the panel data econometric analysis at the plant level, using the survey information by Office of Industrial Economics, Ministry of Industry. Note that Kohpaiboon (2012a) employs the panel data between 2001 and 2003, whereas Wongseree's 2012 analysis is based on that between 2001 and 2006. As documented in Kohpaiboon (2012a), the data quality of the survey noticeably deteriorated after 2004. Analysis in Tantratananuwat (2015) is plant-level cross-sectional, using the 2006 industrial census of Thai manufacturing. Only Kohpaiboon (2012a), Wongseree (2012), and Tantratananuwat (2015) examined both horizontal and vertical spillovers together. Kohpaiboon (2006) focused solely on horizontal spillovers.

The key finding from all studies but Wongseree (2012) nonetheless supports the role of trade policy. That is, advanced technology associated with MNE affiliates does not always spill over to the local plants operating in the same industry. The extent of spillovers depends on the nature of the trade policy regime. Only industries operating under a liberal trade policy regime experience positive horizontal FDI spillovers. Vertical FDI spillovers are found only when an assumption of identical horizontal ones is in place, as indicated in Kohpaiboon (2012a), Wongseree (2012), and Tantratananuwat (2015). This is what has been done in the existing literature (e.g. Javorcik, 2004; and Blalock and Gertler, 2008). When such an assumption is relaxed, as performed by Kohpaiboon (2012a) and Tantratananuwat (2015), neither backward nor forward spillovers are found.

This finding is important amid the growing protectionism sentiment. In particular, policymakers in many countries overclaimed the finding of spillovers through backward linkages and tried to pursue policy-induced linkages like local content requirements towards MNEs. As revealed in Kohpaiboon (2015) and Hill and Kohpaiboon (2017) through an in-depth case study of Thai automotive development, the conducive role of the backward linkage channel mentioned in the literature is a result of natural links that are driven by economic concerns and can be distorted by policy measures. The ability of the policy domain to forge linkages seems to be limited. Policy-induced linkages are not perfect substitutes for natural linkages. The *magnitude* of linkages is not a good proxy of the magnitude of vertical FDI spillovers. It is better to be measured by the *quality* of backward linkages, where actual participation between upstream and downstream firms is intensive based on common interest. Where quality is concerned, backward linkages driven by economic concerns, as well as motivated by capability of indigenous suppliers, are by far superior to those induced by policy measures.

In addition to productivity spillovers, two additional types were examined empirically in Thai manufacturing. They are those where MNE presence affects firms' decision to export and to commit to R&D, respectively. In particular, Jongwanich and Kohpaiboon (2008)[11] and Jongwanich and Kohpaiboon (2015) found evidence supporting a favourable effect of MNE presence on decision to export and R&D investment, respectively.

4.4 Upgrading

Upgrading plays a crucial role in promoting medium-to-long-term economic growth, as well as sustainable economic development. Nonetheless, prospects of a firm upgrading are related to at least two drivers of economic globalisation, i.e. labour mobility and trade, each of which is relevant for Thailand.

Labour mobility

As mentioned earlier, the labour market tightening and a continued increase in (real) wages since the new millennium resulted in an increase in unskilled foreign workers from neighbouring countries in mainland Southeast Asia in Thailand. The official estimates of these workers reached 2 million by 2017, but these far underestimated the actual totals. Thai governments have expressed a reluctance to allow an inflow of workers, unskilled labourers in particular, despite the demand from entrepreneurs. Among numerous social and economic consequences resulting from the import of unskilled foreign workers, one relates to the possible negative effects on the structural adjustment processes of organisations. In particular, when firms are allowed to hire unskilled foreign workers to support structural adjustment, they may eventually become reliant on them. Subsequently, their investments and other decisions could be made on the premise that labour costs will continue to be held down by migration. As a result, firms will remain at the low end of the value chain and rely on low wages as a key factor in competing on the world market. This would eventually retard upgrading.

Kohpaiboon, Jongwanich, and Kulthanavit (2012) undertook a systematic analysis using the Thai clothing industry as a case study. The analysis is based on in-depth interviews with 50 clothing firms in Thailand during November 2009–February 2010. This issue was revisited in Kohpaiboon and Jongwanich (2017), where a questionnaires approach was conducted during October–December 2015. Three sets of questionnaires were developed to address stakeholders, including 25 firms, 120 local workers, and 186 foreign workers. The point to be revisited is due to the changing situation in both labour-importing and -exporting countries. In the former, the policy stance of the Thai government has adjusted to managing, rather than preventing, the flow of these workers. Economic progress during 2010–15 in the latter countries, such as Cambodia, Lao People's Democratic Republic, and Myanmar, encouraged some foreign workers to return home to benefit from the increasing job opportunities at home. This may have been supported by an influx of FDI into the labour-exporting countries, especially Myanmar.

The key finding is that not all firms opt to hire unskilled foreign workers. All firms in both Kohpaiboon, Jongwanich, and Kulthanavit (2012) and Kohpaiboon and Jongwanich (2017) agreed in the interviews that they opted to employ foreign workers to keep their operations running smoothly, although this option incurs costs and uncertainty. Interestingly, firms employing foreign workers also used other options, such as improving productivity, exporting capital, and capital deepening (using capital to substitute for workers) to cope with labour shortages, indicating that they are not mutually exclusive and firms can use any or all of them to maintain performance.

There is no evidence of a causal relationship to indicate that employing foreign workers retards firms' productivity. Rather, we found the opposite. It is the well-performing firms that are in a better position to attract foreign workers and maintain production capacity. Struggling firms are less likely to be able to compete for, and therefore benefit from, foreign workers to enhance their capacity. The differences in company characteristics between firms that hire foreign workers and those that do not are clear. Between 2009 and 2010, those hiring unskilled foreign workers were likely to be relatively small, both in terms of employees and sales, and were typically struggling to maintain their profit margins; hence, they did not adequately invest in upgrading activities (Kohpaiboon, Jongwanich, and Kulthanavit, 2012). The situation slightly changed in 2015, when large firms started to compete with medium-sized firms for foreign workers (Kohpaiboon and Jongwanich, 2017).

The chance to access unskilled foreign workers at lower wages would not significantly deter process-based upgrading. The decision to employ foreign workers depends on other factors, such as policy uncertainty and the associated management problems, such as communication and worker cohesion, compared with the benefits of maintaining the production capacity. Upgrading decisions are largely influenced by global competition and multinational firms that govern production networks in particular.

The finding above is in line with that in Sriudomkajorn (2016), who examined the wage impact of these unskilled foreign workers. In particular, the growth of (real) wages in Thai manufacturing continued, even though there was an influx of foreign workers. Both an industrial census and a socio-economic survey were employed in Thailand to test the impact.

Participating in global production sharing (GPS)

As illustrated above, Thailand has long been engaged in GPS via MNEs. One undesirable consequence of GPS for developing countries is that as production processes are divided into separate stages and economically allocated, and relatively unskilled labour-intensive activities may be moved to developing countries in line with their comparative advantage, this would increase demand for unskilled workers as opposed to skilled ones. As a result, the wage gap between unskilled and skilled workers would tend to contract and it is likely for developing countries to be trapped into low-end segments of value chains. In other words, the prospect is bleak for developing countries' firms.

Nonetheless, the discussion above is carried out under the implicit assumption that there is a single production cone where there is no factor intensity reversal and firms in developed and developing countries face the same factor endowment vector. In reality, a number of studies point to such an assumption being rather restrictive (Leamer and Levinsohn, 1995; Feenstra, 2004; Leamer and Schott, 2005; Kiyota, 2012). Therefore, unskilled labour-intensive activities outsourced by firms in developed countries might require relatively skilled workers in developing countries for these activities to be performed. Therefore, it is possible that demand for skilled to unskilled workers increases in both developing and developed countries simultaneously, so that a wage gap persists as a result of GPS.

Empirical studies by Chongvilaivan and Thangavelu (2012), Kohpaiboon and Jongwanich (2014), and Kohpaiboon (2019) study this issue. Chongvilaivan and Thangavelu (2012) did not address the role of GPS itself; instead, outsourcing in their study is defined loosely as the arrangements whereby the physical and/or human resources related to a firm's production factors are administrated by outside providers. In Kohpaiboon and Jongwanich (2014), the issue was addressed through the effect of GPS on wage premiums, defined as the wage gap between unskilled and skilled workers using an inter-plant, cross-sectional 2011 industrial census of Thai manufacturing. In addition to plant- and industry-specific variables, the extent to which an industry participates in GPS is introduced as the explanatory variable to test the hypothesis.

In Kohpaiboon (2019), three industrial censuses of Thai manufacturing between 2006 and 2016 are used to perform the panel econometrics. In the analysis, the decision to hire workers is examined, i.e. how many blue-collar workers are hired, and their relative importance vis-à-vis total workers (a sum of white- and blue-collar workers). The extent to which an industry participates in the GPS is introduced to examine the effect on skill formation.

Despite differences in various aspects across these three studies, each points to the fact that the outsourced labour-intensive activities do not necessarily imply unskilled worker activities to developing countries. Evidence from Thai manufacturing supports developing countries opening up to international trade and participating in GPS. Mutual benefits from participating in the global production network remain to be shared between developed and developing countries.

Interestingly, in Kohpaiboon (2019), one interesting finding is that plants in GPS-intensive industries are likely to hire skilled workers all other things being equal. It does not mean that they tend to hire fewer unskilled ones; in fact, both unskilled and skilled workers complement each other. This would have an immense policy implication in managing flows of unskilled workers from neighbouring countries.

5 Conclusion and policy lessons

The paper reviews empirical works examining the effect of globalisation in Thailand. It begins with a policy discussion and how Thai economy is integrating into the global economy. Three drivers of economic globalisation are emphasised, i.e. international trade, foreign direct investment and cross-border labour mobility. The 2016 World Bank diagnostic report is used to address the current criticism made of globalisation's economic consequences.

The finding in the empirical studies points to globalisation and its potential to create favourable impacts on economic development. Opening up to international trade could promote Thai productivity and drive economic growth. Export-oriented firms exhibit higher productivity as opposed to locally oriented ones, and are more likely to invest in R&D and develop products. Export performance cannot be a source of the growth slowdown in Thailand since 2005. FDI inflows enticed by EOI strategies are large and likely to generate horizontal technological spillovers from foreign affiliates to indigenous ones within a given industry. The presence of vertical spillovers through the linkages was not a robust result. This is especially so in cases where the horizontal spillover is different across industries, instead of assuming it occurs homogenously.

Firms opted to employ foreign workers to keep their operations running smoothly, although this option incurs costs and uncertainty. There is no evidence of a causal relationship to indicate that employing foreign workers retards firms' productivity. Rather, we found the opposite. It is the well-performing firms that are in a better position to attract foreign workers and maintain production capacity. The chance to access unskilled foreign workers at lower wages would not significantly deter the decision to undertake upgrading, which is largely influenced by global competition and multinational firms that govern production networks in particular.

Participating in GPS does not necessarily mean the participating countries are trapped into the low end of the quality ladder. In fact, evidence from Thai manufacturing suggests the outsourced labour-intensive activities are not the unskilled-worker activities to developing countries. Even though plants in GPS-intensive industries are likely to hire skilled workers, all other things being equal, it does not mean that they tend to hire fewer unskilled ones. In fact, both unskilled and skilled workers complement each other.

Three policy lessons can be drawn from this paper. First, the Thai experience points to globalisation and its potential to create favourable economic impacts. This argues for further accelerating Thailand's push to be globally integrated. This is especially true for trade policy, which remains unfinished business in many developing countries. Such policy reluctance could retard productivity improvement.

Second, there are side effects as a consequence of globalisation, including economic vulnerability to external shocks and the possibility of creating inferior jobs by the export-led growth strategy outsourced. However, these can be mitigated by other policies such as strengthening the social safety net instead of deterring progress in economic globalisation.

Third, it seems that participating in GPS plays an important role in the global integration of Thailand due to the presence of mutual benefits shared between developed and developing countries. The outlook of GPS remains uncertain due to several structural changes in the world economy, some promoting it while others do not. The net effect is largely unknown, but unlikely to take place in disruptive manner. Hence, this would be another upcoming challenge for policymakers in Thailand, as well as other GPS participating countries to keep eye on it.

Notes

1 Henceforth, economic globalisation is at the centre of the following discussion and is referred to as globalisation for brevity.
2 Under the Thai–US Treaty of Amity and Economic Relations signed in 1966, US companies in Thailand are granted equal treatment to Thai companies. This permits 100% of US-owned companies to operate in sectors where other foreign companies are generally allowed a maximum ownership level of 49%. In addition, US companies are allowed to own land up to 10 rai, or 0.16 hectares, with an approval from the Ministry of Interior. The Land Code (1954) was amended in 1999 to relax this restriction. Since 1999, foreign investors regardless of nationality have been able to own up to four rai of land for residential purposes.
3 Arguably, the World Trade Organization (WTO) notification about NTMs might be underestimated due to underreporting. Based on the comprehensive database on NTMs from the United Nations Conference on Trade and Development's global database at trains.unctad.org., Ing, de Cordoba, and Cadot. (2016) suggested the opposite outcome. This is clearly beyond the current scope of this paper, but important to further research topics.
4 See cross-sectional, inter-country empirical evidence in Balasubramanyam, Salisu, and Sapsford (1996).
5 Interestingly, when focusing only on developing countries, the slightly declining trend of Thailand's manufacturing export share was observed from 2000 to 2014. In particular, the share dropped from 3.6% in 2000 to 2.9% in 2014. Note that this seems to be a common trend amongst developing East Asia as a result of the rapid expansion of manufacturing exports from China and Vietnam. Nonetheless, the declining trend of Thai manufacturing is less when compared to other developing East Asia economies. Data are available upon request.
6 Extensive margin refers to a situation where a country exports to new destinations, new products, or both, whereas intensive margin is that where a country exports the same product to the export destination.
7 See the recent survey in Crespo and Fontoura (2007).
8 See a comprehensive review about the role of trade policy in conditioning on gains from FDI in Kohpaiboon (2006).
9 See, for example, Rodríguez-Clare (1996), Markusen and Venables (1999), Javorcik (2004), Lin and Saggi (2004), Blalock and Gertler (2008).
10 For example, see Kohpaiboon and Jongwanich (2019).
11 Jongwanich and Kohpaiboon (2008) employed the 1996 industrial census, whereas Jongwanich and Kohpaiboon's 2012 analysis is based on the 2006 industrial census. Estimation in the former is based the limited dependent variable technique (i.e. Logit and Probit estimation). In the latter, Heckman's two steps were used.

References

Balasubramanyam, V.N., M.A. Salisu, and D. Sapsford (1996), 'Foreign Direct Investment and Growth in EP and IS Countries', Economic Journal, 106 (434), 92–105.

Bhagwati, J . (2004), *In Defense of Globalization*. New York: Oxford University Press.

Bisonyabut, N. and C. Kamsaeng (2015), *Local Innovation Vital to Sustain Growth*. Bangkok: TDRI Insight. Tdri.or.th/en/tdri-insight/local-innovation-vital-to-sustain-growth

Blalock, G. and P.J. Gertler (2008), 'Welfare Gains from Foreign Direct Investment through Technology Transfer to Local Suppliers', *Journal of International Economics*, 74(2), pp.402–421.

Blomström, M. and A. Kokko (1998), 'Multinational Corporations and Spillovers', *Journal of Economic Surveys*, 12, pp.247–277.

Borensztein, E., J.D. Gregorio, and J.W. Lee (1998), 'How Does Foreign Direct Investment Affect Economic Growth?', *Journal of International Economics*, 45(1), pp.115–135.

Bylander, M. and G. Reid (2017), 'Criminalizing Irregular Migrant Labor: Thailand's Crackdown in Context', Migration Information Source, October. https://www.migrationpolicy.org/article/criminalizing-irregular-migrant-labor-thailands-crack-down-context

Charoenloet, V. (2015), 'Industrialization, Globalization and Labour Force Participation in Thailand', *Journal of the Asia Pacific Economy*, 20(1), pp.130–142.

Cheewatrakoolpong, K. and S. Manprasert (2014), 'Trade Linkages and Crisis Spillover', *Asian Economic Paper*, 13(1), pp.84–103.

Chongvilaivan, A. and S.M. Thangavelu (2012), 'Does Outsourcing Provision Lead to Wage Inequality? New Evidence from Thailand's Establishment-level Data', *Review of International Economics*, 20(2), pp.364–376.

Crespo, N. and M.P. Fontoura (2007), 'Determinant Factors of FDI Spillovers: What Do We Really Know?', *World Development*, 35(3), pp.410–425.

Diao, X., J. Rattso, and H. Stokke (2006), 'Learning by Exporting and Structural Change: A Ramsey Growth Model of Thailand', *Journal of Policy Modeling*, 28, pp.293–306.

Feenstra, R. (2004), *Advanced International Trade: Theory and Evidence*. Princeton, NJ: Princeton University Press.

Greenaway, D. and R. Kneller (2007), 'Firm Heterogeneity, Exporting and Foreign Direct Investment', *Economic Journal*, 117(517), pp.134–161.

Hill, H. and A. Kohpaiboon (2017), 'Policies for Industrial Progress, Not Industry Policy: Lessons from Southeast Asia', in L.Y. Ing and F. Kimura (eds.), *Production Networks in Southeast Asia*. New York, NY: Routledge, pp.202–224.

Ing, L., S. de Cordoba, and O. Cadot (2016), *Non-Tariff Measures in ASEAN*, United Nations Conference on Trade and Development (UNCTAD) and Economic Research Institute for ASEAN and East Asia, Jakarta.

Irwin, D. (2015), *Free Trade Under Fire* (4th edition). Princeton, NJ: Princeton University Press.

Javorcik, B.S. (2004), 'Does Foreign Direct Investment Increase the Productivity of Domestic Firms? In Search of Spillovers through Backward Linkages', *American Economic Review*, 94(3), pp.605–627.

Jitsuchon, S. (2012), 'Thailand in a Middle-income Trap', *TDRI Quarterly Review*, 27(2), pp.13–20.

Jongwanich, J. (2007). *Capital Mobility, Exchange Rate Regimes, and Currency Crisis.* New York: Nova Science.

Jongwanich, J. (2019), 'Export Diversification, Margins and Economic Growth at Industrial Level: Evidence from Thailand', Presentation at Transforming Economies – For Better Jobs UNU–WIDER Development Conference in partnership with UNESCAP, 11 September, Bangkok.

Jongwanich, J., & A. Kohpaiboon (2007). 'Determinants of Protection in Thai Manufacturing,' *Economic Papers*, 26(3), 276–94.

Jongwanich, J. and A. Kohpaiboon (2015), 'Multinational Enterprises, Exporting and R&D Activities in the South', *Thailand and the World Economy (Formerly Thammasat Economic Journal)*, 33(2), pp.1–54.

Jongwanich, J. and A. Kohpaiboon (2017), 'Trade Protection and Firm Productivity: Evidence from Thai Manufacturing', *Developing Economies*, 55(2), pp.130–157.

Kiyota, K. (2012), 'A Many-cone World?', *Journal of International Economics*, 86(2), pp.345–354.

Kohpaiboon, A. (2003), 'Foreign Trade Regime and FDI-growth Nexus: A Case Study of Thailand', *Journal of Development Studies*, 40(2), pp.55–69.

Kohpaiboon, A. (2006a), 2006a. Multinational Enterprises and Industrial Transformation: Evidence from Thailand, Cheltenham: Edward Elgar.

Kohpaiboon, A. (2006b), 'Foreign Direct Investment and Technology Spillover: A Cross-industry Analysis of Thai Manufacturing', *World Development*, 34(3), pp.541–556.

Kohpaiboon, A. (2008), 'Multinational Enterprises and Export of the Developing Country: Analysis of Thai Manufacturing', *Thailand and the World Economy (Formerly Thammasat Economic Journal)*, 26(3), pp.1–40.

Kohpaiboon, A. (2012a), 'Vertical and Horizontal FDI Technology Spillovers: Evidence from Thai Manufacturing', in S. Urata, C. Hahn, and D. Narjoko (eds.), *Economic Consequences of Globalization: Evidence from East Asia*. New York: Routledge–ERIA Studies in Development Economics, pp.148–168.

Kohpaiboon, A. (2012b), 'Imports-as-Market-Discipline Hypothesis: Evidence from the Thai Manufacturing Sector', in S. Urata, C. Hahn, and D. Narjoko (eds.), *Economic Consequences of Globalization: Evidence from East Asia*. New York: Routledge–ERIA Studies in Development Economics, pp.190–212.

Kohpaiboon, A. (2015). *FTAs and Supply Chains in the Thai Automotive Industry in ASEAN and Regional Free Agreements.* edited by C. Findlay, Routledge, pp. 229–255.

Kohpaiboon, A. (2019), 'Hiring Skill Workers in Global Production Sharing: Evidence of Thai Manufacturing Plants', Policy Report submitted to Human Resource Institute, Thammasat University, Bangkok.

Kohpaiboon, A.(2020). 'Industrial 4.0 of Thailand', ISEAS Policy Brief, Singapore.

Kohpaiboon, A. and J. Jongwanich (2013), 'International Production Network, Clusters and Industrial Upgrading: Evidence from Automotive and Hard Disk Drive Industries', *Review of Policy Research*, 30(2), pp.211–239.

Kohpaiboon, A. and J. Jongwanich (2014), 'Global Production Sharing and Wage Premiums: Evidence from the Thai Manufacturing Sector', *Asian Development Review*, 31(2), pp.141–164.

Kohpaiboon, A. and J. Jongwanich (2017), 'Structural Adjustment and International Migration in the Thai Garment Industry: Re-visit', in *Rethinking Migration Governance in the Mekong Region: From the Prospective of the Migrant Workers and Their Employers.* ERIA Research Project Report No.19, Jakarta. http://www.eria.org/uploads/media/FullReport_RPR_FY2017_19.pdf

Kohpaiboon, A. and J. Jongwanich (2019a), 'Effectiveness of Industrial Policy on Firm's Productivity: Evidence of Thai Manufacturing', Research submitted to Economic Research Institute of ASEAN and East Asia (ERIA), Jakarta.

Kohpaiboon, A. and J. Jongwanich (2019b), 'The Use of FTAs: the Thai Experience', in L.Y. Ing, M. Richardson, and S. Urata (eds.), *East Asian Integration: Goods, Services and Investment.* New York: Routledge, pp.114–142.

Kohpaiboon, A., J. Jongwanich, and P. Kulthanavit, (2012), 'Structural Adjustment and International Migration: An Analysis of the Thai Clothing Industry', *Oxford Development Studies*, 40(2), pp.231–260.

Krueger, A.O. (1992), *Economic Policy Reforms in Developing Countries.* Oxford, United Kingdom: Basil Blackwell.

Krugman, P. (1995), 'Growing World Trade: Causes and Consequences', *Brookings Papers on Economic Activity*, 25th Anniversary Volume, Vol. 26, pp.327–377.

Krugman, P. (2000). 'Fire-sale FDI,' in E. Sebastian (ed). Capital Flows and the Emerging Economies: Theory, Evidence, and Controversies, Chicago: University of Chicago Press, pp. 43–58.

Leamer, E. and J. Levinsohn (1995), 'International Trade Theory: The Evidence', in G. Grossman and K. Rogoff (eds.), *Handbook of International Economics Vol. 3.* Amsterdam: Elsevier.

Leamer, E. and P. Schott (2005), 'The Rich (and Poor) Keep Getting Richer', *Harvard Business Review*, 83(4), p.20.

Lin, P. and K. Saggi (2004), 'Multinational Firms, Exclusivity, and the Degree of Backward Linkages', *Kiel Institute for the World Economy (IFW) Working Papers 1250.* Kiel: IFW.

Lipsey, R.E. (2000), 'Inward FDI and Economic Growth in Developing Countries', *Transnational Corporations*, 9(1), pp.67–95.

Markusen, J. and A. Venables (1999), 'Foreign Direct Investment as a Catalyst for Industrial Development', *European Economic Review*, 43, pp.335–356.

Melitz, M.J. (2003), 'The Impact of Trade on Intra-Industry Reallocations and Aggregate Industry Productivity', *Econometrica*, 71(6), pp.1695–1725.

Mounier, A. and V. Charoenloet (2010), 'New Challenges for Thailand: Labour and Growth after the Crisis', *Journal of Contemporary Asia*, 40(1), pp.123–143.

Phoonichaisuk, A. (2010), 'FDI–Growth Nexus: Evidence of Thailand', MA Thesis, Faculty of Economics, Thammasat University.

Private Investment Promotion Working Group (2015), '10 Target Industries: New Engine of Growth', Report submitted to Prime Minister, 17 November. https://thaipublica.org/wp-content/uploads/2015/11/BOI_kanit.pdf (in Thai).

Rasiah, R., K.C. Cheong, and R. Doner (2014), 'The Southeast Asian Experience with the Asian and Global Financial Crises', *Journal of Contemporary Asia*, 44(4), pp.572–580.

Rodríguez-Clare, A. (1996), 'Multinationals, Linkages, and Economic Development', *American Economic Review*, 86(4), pp.852–873.

Sachs, J. and A. Warner (1995), 'Economic Reform and the Process of Global Integration', *Brookings Papers on Economic Activity*, 1(25th Anniversary), pp.1–95.

Sjöholm, F. (1997), '*R&D*, International Spillovers and Productivity Growth', Lund Economics Studies, No. 63. Lund: Lund University.

Sriudomkajorn, P. (2016), 'Foreign Workers in Thai Manufacturing: Trends, Patterns, and Implications for Domestic Wages', MA Thesis, Thammasat University, Bangkok.

Suehiro, A. (1989), *Capital Accumulation in Thailand, 1855–1985*. UNESCO. Tokyo: The Center for East Asian Cultural Studies.

Tangkitvanich, S. and N. Bisonyabut (2015), 'Toward High-Quality Growth: Thailand's Challenges and Opportunities in the Next Three Decades', *TDRI Quarterly Review*, 30(1, March), pp.3–15.

Tantratananuwat, P. (2015), 'Vertical and Horizontal FDI Technology Spillovers in Thai Manufacturing: Does Measurement Matter?', MA Thesis, Thammasat University, Bangkok.

Urata, S. and K. Yokota (1994), 'Trade Liberalization and Productivity Growth in Thailand', *Developing Economies*, 32(4), pp.444–459.

Vernon, R. (2000), *In the Hurricane's Eye: The Troubled Prospects of Multinational Enterprises*. Cambridge: MIT Press.

Warr, P. (2011), 'A Nation Caught in the Middle-Income Trap', *East Asia Forum Quarterly*, (October–December), pp.4–6. https://www.eastasiaforum.org/2011/12/18/thailand-a-nation-caught-in-the-middle-income-trap/

Warr, P.G. and B. Nidhiprabha (1996), *Thailand's Macroeconomic Miracle: Stable Adjustment and Sustained Growth*. Kuala Lumpur: Oxford University Press.

Wells, L.T. Jr. (1986), 'Investment Incentives: An Unnecessary Debate', *TNC Reporter*, 22(Autumn), pp.12–16.

Wolf, M. (2005), *Why Globalization Works*. New Haven: Yale University Press.

Wongseree, S. (2012), 'Foreign Direct Investment and Local Firm Productivity: Evidence from Thailand', Doctoral Dissertation, University of Tennessee, Knoxville.

World Bank (2014), *Preserving Stability and Promoting Growth*. Washington, DC: World Bank. http://documents.worldbank.org/curated/en/256651468248662652/pdf/East-Asia-Pacific-economic-update-April-2014-preserving-stability-and-promoting-growth.pdf

World Bank (2016), 'Thailand: Getting Back on Track: Reviving Growth and Securing Prosperity for All (A Systematic Country Diagnostic), November 10.

World Trade Organization (WTO) (2015), *Trade Policy Review – Thailand*. Geneva, Switzerland: WTO.

8 The economic consequences of globalisation in the United States

Peter A. Petri and Meenal Banga

1 The globalisation debate

In 1999, Merrill Lynch, a leading wealth manager in the US, took out full-page ads in major US newspapers to celebrate the era of globalisation: 'The World Is 10 Years Old. It was born when the Wall fell in 1989.' The ads argued that the 'spread of free markets and democracy around the world is permitting more people everywhere to turn their aspirations into achievements. And technology, properly harnessed and liberally distributed, has the power to erase not just geographical borders but also human ones.'

The current era of globalisation began in the 1970s, when the share of trade in world output was around 10% (Figure 8.1). Globalisation accelerated in the 1980s, when the share of world trade in output surpassed historical records, eventually climbing to about 25% by 2009. Since then, the trade share of GDP has flattened. For reasons ranging from trade policy to technological changes and the maturation of international supply chains, trade intensity is not likely to rise as fast in the future as it did in recent decades.

The unprecedented rise in global interdependence has been very productive. World GDP growth, which hovered in the 2% per year range in the 1970s and early 1980s, doubled to reach the 4% range before the global financial crisis. Growth spread to the world's largest countries and lifted more than a billion people out of extreme poverty. New global supply chains brought emerging, trade-oriented economies into the network of global expansion. However, the fragility of rapid, interdependent growth also became apparent. In 2008, Merrill Lynch succumbed to the global financial crisis. Meanwhile, criticism of the distributional effects of globalisation, particularly in advanced countries, intensified as Piketty (2015) and others brought inequality and wage stagnation to the forefront of public debate.

The chief concern in the US is that the economy is delivering a disproportionate share of gains to the wealthiest few. According to Census data, from 1970 to 2018 the median US household income rose from $50,545 to $63,179, or by 0.46% per year, while that of the top 5% of households rose from $192,603 to $416,520, or by 1.62% per year (Semega et al., 2019). In 1970, a high-income household earned 3.8 times as much as the median household, but this

DOI: 10.4324/9781003138501-8

Figure 8.1 Value of Exported Goods as a Share of Gross Domestic Product.
Source: Fouquin and Hugot (2016).
Note: GDP = gross domestic product.

ratio had grown to 6.6 by 2018. Still more extreme contrasts emerged between richer and poorer households, and amongst subgroups by levels of education. In turn, inequality may have contributed to other trends such as withdrawal from the labour force, increased mortality and morbidity, and political polarisation. These trends are not direct results of globalisation, but they are often attributed to trade in popular discussions.

This paper attempts to dissect the consequences of globalisation. Rather than offering new research, it reviews the extensive literature on these issues, including about 20 studies with significant influence on the debate. These studies span three subfields: the overall gains from trade, adverse labour market trends and the causal effects of trade, and the results of changes in trade policy.

- Studies on the overall effects of globalisation suggest large gains. Although these results are important to our analysis, this review is relatively brief since the findings reflect familiar theoretical ground and its empirical results broadly agree on the magnitude of gains from trade.
- Studies of US labour market data reveal significant adverse trends, which include extreme cases of very harmful effects. Yet globalisation is only one of several factors that appear to be at work, including technological progress, demand shifts, and diverging, unrelated trends in economic activity across sectors and locations.
- Studies of specific policy changes have findings broadly consistent with those of the first two areas of research – that the overall effects of increased trade have been positive. However, these gains coincided with adverse labour market trends that were most likely attributable to other factors.

The adverse side effects of globalisation require policy attention, but the evidence suggests that erecting trade barriers is a poor response. For one thing, past trade changes have already resulted in adjustments that cannot be reversed without imposing further costs on workers and consumers. Better approaches will focus on making workers more productive through education and mobility, and distributing the gains from globalisation more equally through fiscal policies.

Section 2 of this paper examines the gains from globalisation. Section 3 addresses developments in labour markets. Section 4 surveys the ex-post effects of the North American Free Trade Agreement (NAFTA) and permanent normal trade relations (PNTR) with China. Section 5 concludes.

2 The gains from globalisation

The case for economic integration is well known, and recent empirical estimates suggest substantial benefits from global trade and deeper integration by groups of countries. Strong anecdotal evidence supports this positive view – in addition to relieving extreme poverty in developing countries, interdependence enables consumers to enjoy unprecedented variety, quality, and availability of goods and services everywhere.

Federico and Tena-Junguito (2016) estimated that the increase in the share of world trade in GDP since the 1950s has added about 5 percentage points to world income (Figure 8.2). Given world GDP of $85 trillion in 2018, the incremental benefits from trade since the 1950s represent about $4.3 trillion of world income. Globalisation has also stimulated flows of capital, technology, and talent, further raising incomes and improving well-being.

Additional studies suggest that the US has benefited from globalisation even more than the rest of the world. In a multi-study review, Bradford, Grieco, and Hufbauer (2005) concluded that advances in globalisation from 1947 to 2003 added $0.8 trillion–$1.5 trillion, or 11%–14%, to the US GDP of $11 trillion in 2003. Extrapolating these estimates to 2018 GDP suggests that changes in economic interdependence since 1947 added $2.2 trillion–$4.0 trillion to US GDP in 2018, or 11%–19% of 2018 GDP of $20.5 trillion.[1]

Moreover, these benefits do not seem to have been exhausted. Bradford, Grieco, and Hufbauer (2005) surveyed estimates which suggest that further liberalisation of policy barriers could almost double these benefits. Despite controversies over the distribution of benefits from trade, the overall gains from globalisation for the US are so ubiquitous and widely accepted amongst economists that few have focused on refining or updating their magnitudes since Bradford's study. This contrasts with a much more active and voluminous body of research on how economic openness affects growth in developing economies.

Nevertheless, important related findings by Bernard et al. (2003) highlighted the determinants of productivity at the firm level. They found that exporting firms are much more productive than domestically focused firms, which in turn are more productive than firms vulnerable to import competition. Based on these results and the Eaton-Kortum trade model, they then simulated shifts from current levels of US openness to autarky. They found that these shifts would lead to productivity losses, accounting for 9% of the output of an average US producer. This estimate is within the range, in percentage terms, of those referenced above by Federico and Tena-Junguito (2016) and Bradford, Grieco, and Hufbauer (2005), although the three studies rely on very different methodologies.

Unlike many smaller economies, the US is less dependent on globalisation for finding new technologies and competitive challenges, or for accessing large markets and varieties of inputs. However, the US does benefit from globalisation through a different, important channel. Global supply chains enable US producers to concentrate on their most productive tasks while shifting less efficient tasks elsewhere. An early study of US offshoring found that outsourcing service tasks had significantly positive effects on the productivity of US firms, although offshoring of material inputs less so (Amiti and Wei, 2009). With recent data and a broader definition of supply chains, Constantinescu, Mattoo, and Ruta (2019) showed that embedding foreign value added in production generally increases productivity across US sectors, especially in industries producing exports. Results from Formai and Vergara Caffarelli (2016) confirm these findings, demonstrating that the results appear mainly in 'fragmentable' sectors, i.e. industries where supply chains are easily divided into tasks.

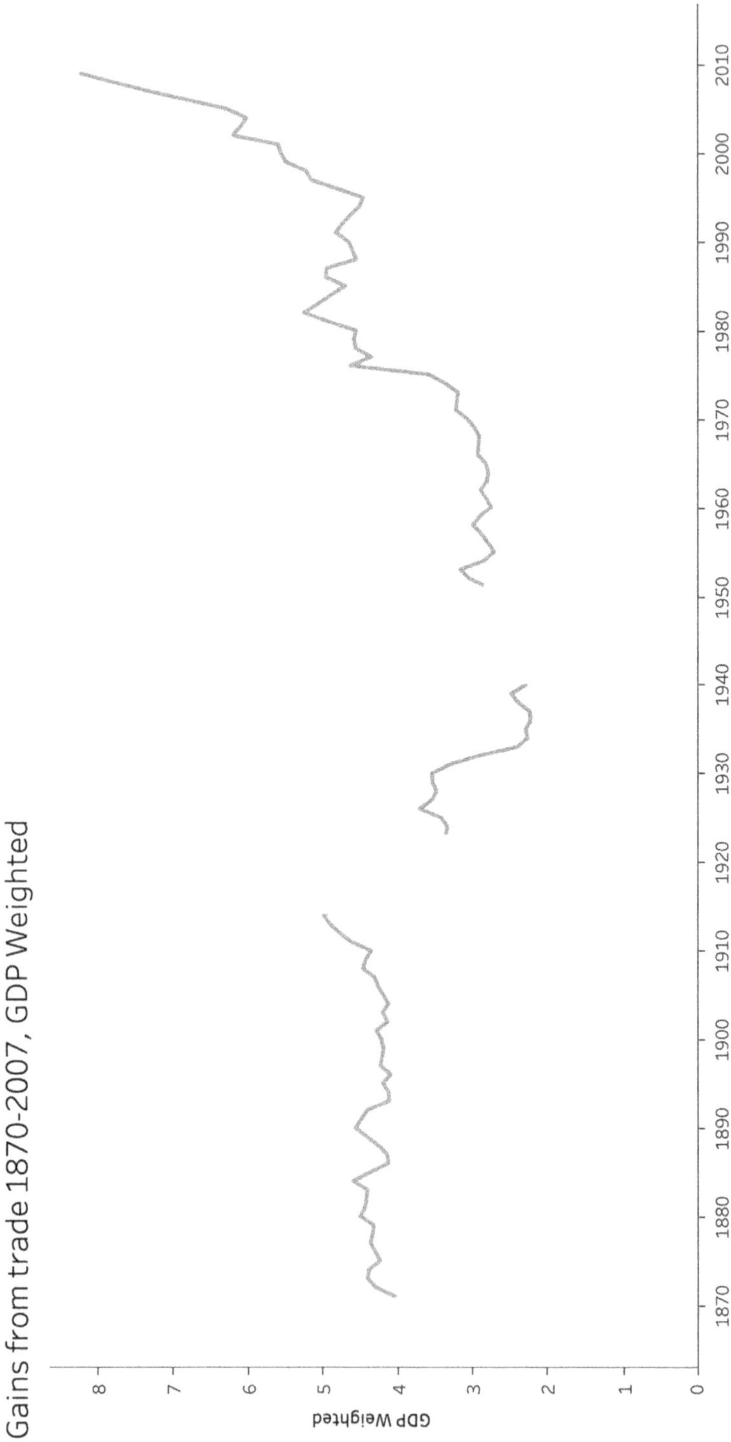

Figure 8.2 Gains from Trade, 1870–2007 (GDP weighted).
Source: Federico and Tena-Junguito (2016).
Note: GDP = gross domestic product.

Finally, globalisation has enormously benefited US innovation – a rapidly expanding sector of the US economy. These gains appear through channels ranging from the inflow of ideas and money to attracting talent. Global markets also increase returns on ideas, which are non-rival products. Several indicators suggest that these benefits are very large. 65% of the world's 25 most valuable public companies are technology companies, and 82% of the total market capitalisation of these companies consists of US tech firms (Forbes, 2019). In addition, 55% of US 'unicorns' (start-ups worth $1 billion or more) were founded by immigrant entrepreneurs and more than 80% of these companies also had immigrants as key managers (Anderson, 2018). Such connections provide US companies with an unparalleled edge in penetrating global markets. The US benefits especially well from new technology markets – including those in information technology and biotechnology – since these often have winner-take-all profit distributions. Strong US capital markets reinforce these advantages and attract venture capital from across the world.

Regrettably, aside from rare exceptions such as Clausing (2019), the general US public discussion does not fully recognise these benefits. Yet it would be difficult to imagine life in the US without imported food, steel, garments, electronics, or cars. Equally, highly productive US firms such as JP Morgan, Boeing, Intel, Facebook, and Johnson & Johnson could not easily replace export markets for airplanes, online platforms, pharmaceuticals, financial products, movies, higher education, or agricultural products. Precisely because trade is so ubiquitous, the debate takes its positive effects for granted. Few US consumers fully appreciate how imports affect what they spend and exports affect where they work. At the same time, those who experience job losses, whether due to automation or trade, see very personal costs. As theory anticipates, the debate focuses primarily on those costs.

3 Globalisation and labour market effects

Labour market effects, which have dominated recent critiques of globalisation in the US, focus on unemployment, wage inequality, and other concerns such as low labour force participation rates. Some critics argue that more trade, say due to trade liberalisation, causes trade deficits, which in turn cause unemployment. Some studies find significant impacts from trade on unemployment under specific circumstances, such as large, rapidly emerging threats for declining industries in some localities. However, there is no convincing evidence that trade increases unemployment in a long-term, economy-wide context.

Other critics focus on the effects of low-wage competition on wage growth and wage inequality in the US. There is considerable evidence that wage inequality has increased over time, but the causes are less clear. Trade may have contributed to increased inequality – as a high-wage country, the US tends to import products from countries with lower wages – but the evidence mainly points to technological change rather than import competition as the source of pressure. Nevertheless, given the implications of inequality, there is an urgent need for understanding the mechanisms that account for it and countering their effects. The gains from trade likely exceed – potentially by orders of magnitude – the costs of fighting inequality attributable to trade, but unfortunately effective policies have yet to be deployed.

3.1 Unemployment

The simplest and most frequent argument made is that globalisation, i.e. keeping US markets open, has created trade deficits which in turn have led to US job losses. To President Trump and others, the case is self-evident: imports replace jobs while exports create them. As the US opened its markets, its trade deficits rose as other countries 'stole' its jobs.

However, there is no logical link between economic openness and a trade deficit, or between a trade deficit and unemployment. Trade deficits are determined by the excess of national savings over investment. Unless a trade shock – say, tariff reductions – affects these variables,[2] the deficit will not change. (For example, even if imports decrease, other adjustments will lead to a similar fall in exports.) Even when trade deficits change, employment tends to be unaffected. Employment is determined by demographic and macroeconomic forces that automatically, or sometimes with a nudge from policy, restore normal employment levels.

In fact, *high* trade deficits usually correlate with *low* unemployment (Figure 8.3). This is not a causal relationship – changes in both variables are due to changes in economic activity. A strong economy generates investment demand by more than it increases savings – and thus generates labour market pressures that reduce unemployment. That is why, given continuing robust economic growth, the US trade deficit has grown by 24%, from $502 billion in 2016 to $622 billion in 2018 (US Census Bureau, 2019), while unemployment has fallen to record levels, despite unprecedented tariffs mistakenly imposed to reduce the trade deficit.

Nevertheless, some studies have suggested long-lived unemployment in specific locations because of unusual trade shocks. Autor and colleagues (2013b, 2016, reviewed in detail below) found serious and persistent consequences from some trade shocks as they interact with multiplier effects in local economies. In those cases, production displaced by imports results in additional job losses in local firms which depend on selling their goods to displaced manufacturers and their workers. Because these effects reinforce the trade shocks, adjustment is slow and costly. Such costs are concentrated in communities where adjustment options are limited.

3.2 Wage inequality

Americans have come to believe the social contract underlying the US market-oriented economic system: hard work will generate steady improvements in the standard of living. However, the data suggest that this expectation is no longer reliably met. Household incomes have grown substantially only at the top, and

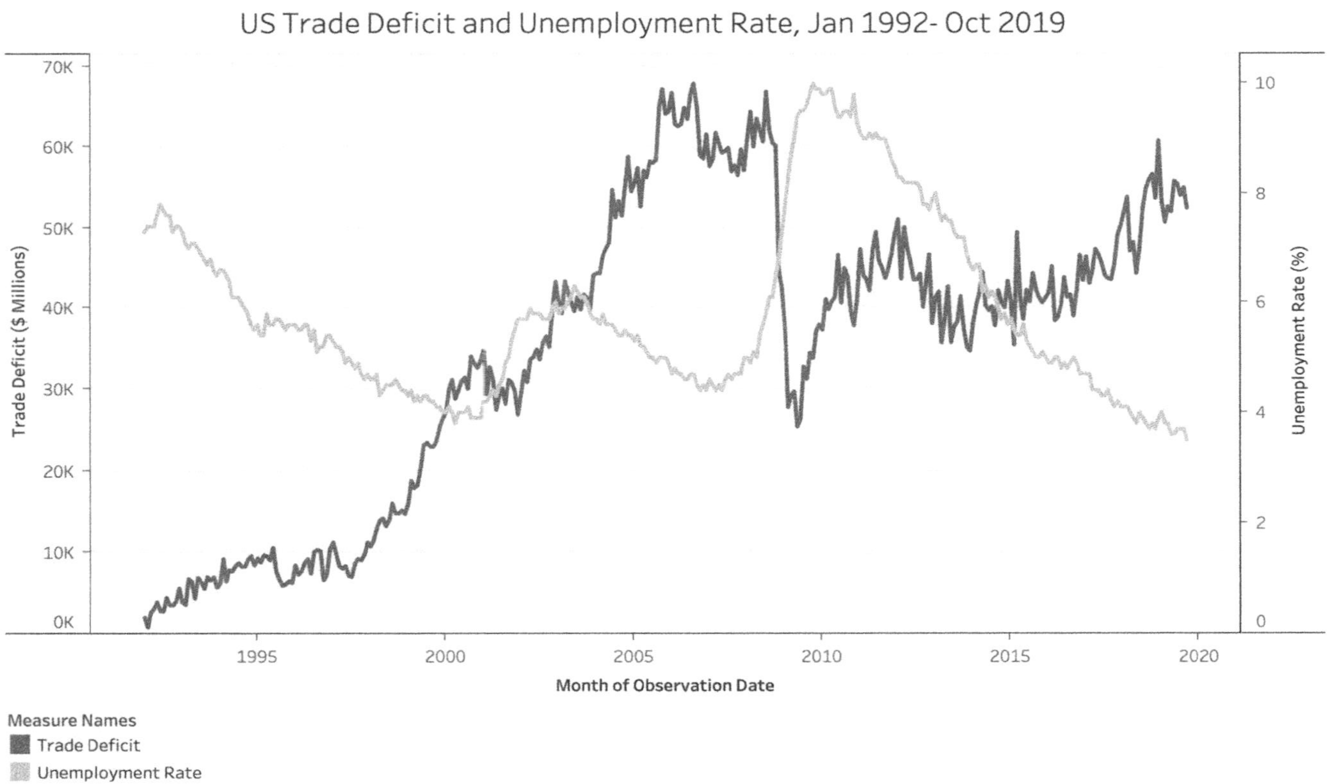

Figure 8.3 US Trade Deficit and Unemployment Rate, January 1992–September 2019.
Source: Trade Deficit: US Bureau of Economic Analysis and US Census Bureau, Trade Balance: Goods and Services, Balance of Payments Basis [BOPGSTB], retrieved from FRED, Federal Reserve Bank of St. Louis; https://fred.stlouisfed.org/series/BOPGSTB (accessed 1 December 2019), Unemployment rate: US Bureau of Labor Statistics, Unemployment Rate [UNRATE], retrieved from FRED, Federal Reserve Bank of St. Louis; https://fred.stlouisfed.org/series/UNRATE (accessed 1 December 2019).

real wages for many workers have stagnated for decades. Figure 8.4 shows starkly divergent trends for wages sorted by education, which diverge especially significantly for male workers (Autor, 2014). Male workers with a post-college education saw their real wages rise in the last four decades. Those with just a college education earned about the same real wage in 2012 as in 1973, and those with less-than-college education generally earned less.

The data leave little doubt that wage inequality is increasing. Inequality is also increasing amongst women, but they have generally done better than men in recent decades. These trends appear to date back to the 1970s, at about the beginning of the rise of global interdependence, but well before the recent emergence of China as a major trading power. Over time, they have cumulatively led to large wage gaps and increasing political concern. As explored below, the mechanisms driving wage inequality could include trade, technological change, and trends in the structure of demand.

3.3 Declining labour force participation and other effects

The slow recovery of US employment after the global financial crisis was due in part to a decline in labour force participation after 2008. A popular explanation

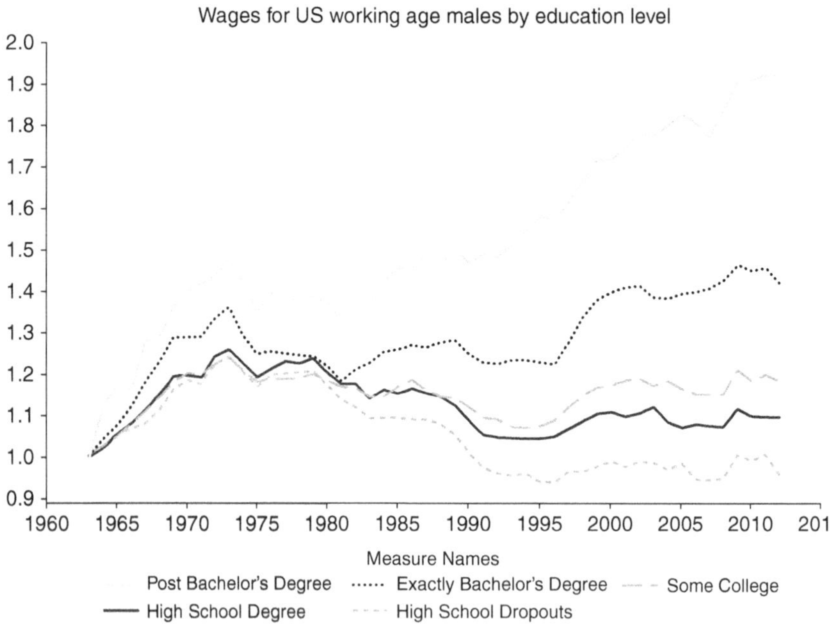

Figure 8.4 Wages for US Working Age Males by Education Level.
Source: Autor (2014).
Note: Based on weekly earnings data from the US Current Population Survey for working age adults who worked at least one week during the year.

was that stagnating wages at the low end of the distribution discouraged workers from re-entering the labour force even when jobs became available. Diminished labour force participation is partly explained by population aging and the end of a sharp rise in women entering the workforce. In 2018 and 2019, labour force participation rates have begun to rise again, without a significant narrowing of wage gaps. This suggests that pure market demand for labour, rather than growing wage gaps, was the principal driver of participation trends. Sustained growth in demand appears to draw even marginal workers back into the labour force.

In popular discussion, bleak wage and job quality trends are also often linked to dramatic declines in the well-being of some US workers. In a widely cited study, Case and Deaton (2017) found that increases in all-cause mortality rates rose steadily from 1998 to 2015 – a period roughly coinciding with the labour market effects considered here – for white, non-Hispanic Americans without a college degree. These rates included increases in drug overdoses, suicides, and alcohol-related disease. Yet direct links to labour market results are very difficult to find – the authors could not find statistical connections between contemporaneous resources, stagnating incomes, and mortality. They instead proposed that explanations lie in cumulative disadvantages – in labour market, health, and other outcomes – from one birth cohort to the next. They believe that these disadvantages may have been building steadily for whites with low education levels, leading to current mortality trends.

3.4 Mechanisms which cause inequality

Given the important social and economic role of wage inequality, we next examine the potential drivers of recent trends, including trade, technological change, and changes in product demand. We review major mechanisms that appear to be driving wage inequality as a step towards understanding the role of globalisation as a cause.

Trade and offshoring. There are good reasons to expect that trade will increase wage inequality. Since the US has plentiful endowments of capital relative to labour, increased trade generally raises the return to capital and lowers the return to labour. Since capital includes human capital, the wages of educated workers may then rise relative to those with limited skills. In addition to trade, offshoring – the relocation of production abroad by domestic firms – has been specifically blamed for adverse labour market effects, since domestic firms may be more effective than foreign firms in producing abroad to exploit endowment differences. Improved logistics and communications also enable companies to break production into smaller tasks and import a growing share of components from abroad. For example, car manufacturers have increasingly lengthy supply chains that typically include locating significant parts of production abroad.

Technological change. Research on technological change has focused on the possibility of job polarisation – the growth of low- and high-skilled jobs coupled with a decline in middle-skilled jobs (Goos and Manning, 2003). The result may be a loss of careers that once provided reasonable incomes without a college-level education. Traditional manufacturing is one source of such jobs and explains the preoccupation of President Trump and other policymakers with aiding the manufacturing sector. There is indeed evidence of polarisation, but its causes could include several drivers.

Autor (2014) noted that tasks which are difficult to automate are those that demand flexibility, judgment, and common sense. These include two categories: 'abstract' tasks that require extensive problem solving and include professional, technical, and managerial occupations; and 'manual' tasks that require situational adaptability and personal interactions, which include service jobs such as food preparation and health assistance. While these types of jobs are relatively safe from automation, middle-skilled jobs with routine tasks are often exposed. Figure 8.5 shows that, from 1979 to 2012, changes in the occupational distribution did support the polarisation hypothesis. The decline in middle-skilled jobs was especially significant in the 2007–12 sub-period.

Trade or offshoring may aggravate this polarised pattern. The production of tradable products, such as manufactures, tends to require high-skilled or middle-skilled jobs. For an advanced economy, such as that of the US, this means increasing high-skilled employment for sophisticated export industries and reducing middle-skilled employment in less sophisticated import-competing industries. Meanwhile, as the share of demand grows in non-tradable service industries, demand will increase in low-wage service occupations. Thus, the polarising effect of technological change on job markets is reinforced by trade specialisation in sophisticated products.

Superstars. Data show that the wages of the highest paid workers have risen especially fast in the US. This may be because workers at the high end of the distribution are generally well educated, but the correspondence is not perfect – Mark Zuckerberg, Bill Gates, and Jan Koum all failed to finish college. Highly compensated workers may be successful less because of their education and more because they become 'superstars' in markets that produce 'winner take all' returns (Rosen, 1981).

In winner-take-all sectors, best performers may be only slightly more productive than the next best, but will still capture a large share of total returns. Some examples include sports and entertainment stars, as well as senior managers of large corporations. Superstar markets emerge with technologies that expand the scale of markets, as for example through wide access to audio or video broadcasts. Superstar markets may also emerge when scale economies or network externalities eliminate competition – for example, in retail markets such as those dominated by Walmart or Amazon.

Although the earnings of superstars are rooted in technology, inequality is aggravated by the large markets created by international economic integration. Ebenstein, Harrison, and McMillan (2015) argued that superstar effects originate not in ordinary channels of trade, but in new channels that reflect the improved tradability of services. They found little evidence for classic channels of globalisation in goods and services in superstar returns – it is the interplay of

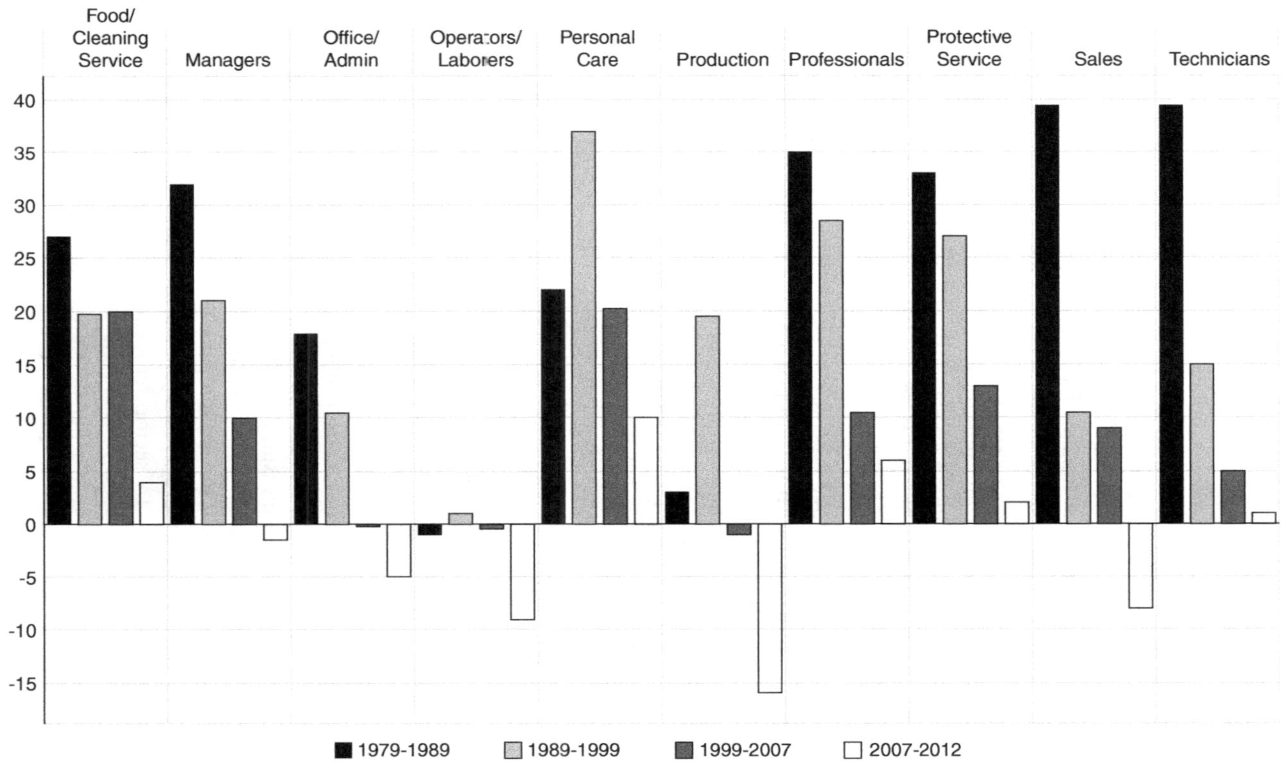

Figure 8.5 Change in US Employment by Occupational Category.
Source: Autor (2015).
Note: Based on data from the American Community Survey, 2006–08 and 2012. Employment is measured as full-time equivalent workers in non-agricultural employment in the United States.

technologies and market sizes (made possible by economic integration) that explains dramatically rising wage differentials in some occupations and industries.

3.5 Is globalisation to blame?

Few estimates are available for separating the relative importance of trade and productivity effects. One recent study of the decline in US manufacturing employment suggested that technological changes have been much more important (Hicks and Deveraj, 2017). Table 8.1 shows that total manufacturing employment declined by 5,647,700 workers from 2000 to 2010. Net import increases explained 13.4% of this change, while productivity improvements accounted for 87.8%. (Together, these causes explained 101.2% of job losses; the extra 1.2% is due to jobs created by an increase in demand.) Thus, the shares of trade and technology were 13.2% (=13.4/101.2) and 86.8% (=87.4/101.2), respectively, of manufacturing job losses from 2000 to 2010. This was when US net imports were rising rapidly due to China's accession to the World Trade Organization (WTO) and the explosion of the US trade deficit. While no similar calculations are available for wage inequality, one might expect effects on those measures to be broadly similar.

Econometric evidence on how trade policy affects wage inequality is sparse. A review of seven studies by Deardorff and Hakura (1994) reported that the effects of liberalisation episodes on the wage distribution ranged from substantial to nil. Slaughter (1998) reviewed nine additional studies and also reached mixed conclusions. Recent work (Haskel et al., 2012) has continued to find mixed results. A third study by Baldwin and Cain (2000) used a general equilibrium approach to analyse how changes in trade affect wages, and found that trade alone could not account for observed wage inequality effects. They argued that growing inequality must be the result of alternative forces, including education-biased technical change, and a growing supply of educated labour compared with unskilled labour.

Ebenstein, Harrison, and McMillan (2015) found, however, that globalisation may have significantly affected US wage inequality. They argued that previous studies missed this effect because they examined wage differentials across industries rather than occupations. They viewed a worker's occupation as the locus of exposure to international competition, since it is harder for workers to switch occupations than industries (Kambourov and Manovskii, 2009a, 2009b). They therefore regressed wages on measures of offshoring and trade with annual data from 1983 to 2008. They first ran regressions for wages on offshoring and trade for various industrial sectors. They then repeated the analysis using various occupations and found that these regressions do not fit nearly as well for industries as they do for occupations. In sector regressions, the offshoring and trade coefficients were typically close to zero and insignificant, while in occupational regressions they were larger and generally significant with the expected sign. Further, they found that exposure to offshoring and trade with high-income

Table 8.1 Trade and Productivity Effects in Manufacturing

Sector	*Production Change per Worker*	*Actual Job Losses*	*Job Losses due to Trade*	*Job Losses due to Productivity*	*Job Gains due to Demand*
All manufacturing	67.5%	5,647,700	13.4%	87.8%	1.2%
Durable goods manufacturing	82.9%	3,737,200	12.3%	88.2%	0.5%
Wood products	47.0%	274,900	14.4%	81.9%	–3.6%
Non-metallic mineral products	6.5%	177,000	12.8%	90.4%	3.2%
Primary metals	39.1%	248,500	–3.3%	76.7%	–26.7%
Fabricated metal products	8.9%	478,200	6.9%	97.7%	4.5%
Machinery	39.9%	447,400	0.8%	99.6%	0.4%
Computer and electronic products	350.3%	694	18.8%	117.7%	36.5%
Electrical equipment, appliances, and components	57.3%	233,700	19.0%	88.1%	7.1%
Transportation and motor vehicles	64.1%	716,500	5.5%	85.5%	–9.0%
Furniture and related products	5.6%	327,700	40.2%	81.1%	21.3%
Miscellaneous manufacturing	62.2%	140	21.7%	76.7%	–1.6%
Non-durable goods manufacturing	48.5%	1,910,500	12.3%	90.0%	2.3%
Food and beverage and tobacco products	23.1%	119,200	4.3%	96.8%	1.1%
Textile and textile product mills	22.4%	345,200	9.5%	97.6%	7.0%
Apparel, leather, and allied products	45.9%	370,500	44.6%	58.5%	3.1%
Paper products	13.0%	210,300	1.7%	93.2%	–5.0%
Printing and related activities	54.1%	319	–2.1%	101.8%	–0.3%
Petroleum and coal products	41.0%	9,100	13.3%	77.1%	–9.6%

(*Continued*)

Table 8.1 (Continued)

Sector	*Production Change per Worker*	*Actual Job Losses*	*Job Losses due to Trade*	*Job Losses due to Productivity*	*Job Gains due to Demand*
Chemical products	52.8%	186,500	1.4%	101.1%	2.5%
Plastics and rubber products	30.4%	351,100	7.4%	100.5%	7.9%

Source: Hicks and Deveraj (2017).
Notes: Based on calculations from United States Census Bureau. Motor vehicles and transportation sectors are aggregated because of incomplete data.

partners raises an occupation's wages, while exposure and trade with low-income partners depresses wages.

Ebenstein, Harrison, and McMillan (2015) also studied labour force participation. They hypothesised that people who worked in the 'glory days' of US manufacturing would find wages depressed due to globalisation and would not find them attractive enough to stay in the labour force. Their regressions, however, did not show reduced labour force participation. Only exposure to offshoring to China had the expected negative effect – perhaps because it was a larger and more sudden shock. They also found that technological factors, including the use of computers and capital intensity, were significantly associated with declining labour force participation.

In summary, the evidence suggests that technological change had a much larger effect on employment in different industry sectors than globalisation. However, studies which attempt to tease out the relative effects of these drivers on wage inequality have shown mixed results.

4 The effects of trade policy changes

Most trade deals involve political controversy in the US, typically pitting labour-oriented Democrats against business-oriented Republicans. In the usual resolution, a centrist wing of the Democratic party sides with Republicans to ensure the passage of an agreement. This was the case with the Uruguay Round agreement; NAFTA; the granting of PNTR to China; and bilateral trade agreements with Chile, the Republic of Korea (henceforth, Korea), and Colombia, amongst others. More recently, however, this calculus has been upended by the shift in the position of the Republican party under President Trump, perhaps to court older, white workers in the centre of the country who have been historically employed in manufacturing. This new anti-trade faction has made it unusually difficult to defend the traditionally liberal trade policies of the US.

Controversies over old agreements have also resurrected. Two significant agreements are prominent in the debate: NAFTA (which the President re-negotiated as the US–Mexico–Canada Agreement) and PNTR for China. President Trump has indicated his displeasure with both.

4.1 NAFTA

Although NAFTA has been in effect for a quarter century, estimates of its benefits are difficult to pinpoint since the economic results of NAFTA countries are attributable to many forces. However, trade amongst NAFTA countries has increased substantially, suggesting greater specialisation and the development of more competitive industries in each country.

Caliendo and Parro (2015) estimated the benefits of NAFTA with a rigorous modern empirical model. They found welfare increases of 0.08% for the US, 1.31% for Mexico, and –0.06% for Canada. When applied to 2018 GDP levels, these ratios represent annual gains of $16.4 billion, $15.2 billion, and –$1.0 billion for the three countries. (Canada had a free trade agreement with the US before NAFTA, so its losses with NAFTA may represent trade diversion to Mexico.) However, these estimates are likely to be too low, since they only considered tariff changes and ignored other important changes in non-tariff barriers and the certainty of regional trade and investment rules.

Hufbauer, Cimino-Isaacs, and Moran (2014) provided theoretically less rigorous but empirically very thorough estimates based on increased trade amongst NAFTA economies. They calculated the incremental trade effect as actual post-NAFTA trade minus trade that would have taken place due to GDP growth alone. They then calculated welfare gains as a share of trade gains, finding annual gains of $127 billion for the US, $170 billion for Mexico, and $50 billion for Canada. These estimates are likely too high, since only a fraction of trade growth beyond GDP-related growth can be attributed to NAFTA. Hufbauer, Cimino-Isaacs, and Moran (2014) also noted the following:

- The shift in bilateral trade between Mexico and the US – from a $5 billion surplus in 1994 to a $45 billion deficit in 2013 – cannot be attributed to NAFTA, since it was the result of greater US energy imports due to the changing energy position of the US, and large opposite shifts in the Mexican and US global trade deficits.
- Only 5% of US job dislocations in the years following NAFTA can be attributed to NAFTA; of these workers, only one-fifth became unemployed and eligible for Trade Adjustment Assistance. Nevertheless, NAFTA was a small part of the US job churn,[3] which typically involves 4 million US workers every year.
- Trade with Mexico likely increased, rather than depressed, US wages, given observations on wages paid in newly created export jobs and jobs replaced by

import competition. US firms also became more competitive vis-à-vis third countries.

In addition, NAFTA had important political objectives. The US wanted a positive partnership with its largest neighbour; corruption and leftist ideologies had long marred this relationship. Mexico's political system gradually modernised and its relations with the US improved. Polling has shown that the share of Mexicans trusting the US more than doubled from 2004 to 2016, and then collapsed abruptly after President Trump took office (Las Américas y el Mundo (n.d.) survey conducted by the Centro de Investigación y Docencia Económicas (CIDE)).

The US also wanted to stimulate Mexican development to reduce disparities that caused political tensions and immigration pressures. For a variety of reasons that have little to do with trade policy, NAFTA did not succeed in substantially accelerating Mexican growth, but progress was made on modernising the Mexican economy. Meanwhile, immigration decreased substantially, with the apprehension of illegal migrants on the US southern border falling from 1.6 million per year in 2000 to about 400,000 in 2018 (US Customs and Border Protection, n.d.). This falloff had multiple causes, including changes in Mexican demographics, rising US unemployment, and improved border controls.

NAFTA increased the interdependence of its members and thus had positive effects on the region's economy. There is little evidence that it affected US labour markets negatively, and it almost certainly helped to improve US–Mexico relations. Auto industry representatives are especially supportive, arguing that diverse regional production capabilities made the US much more competitive with Japan, Korea, and potentially China in the long run.

4.2 *Permanent normal trade relations with China*

The effects of the US conferral of PNTR on China and its subsequent accession to the WTO in 2001, frequently described as the 'China shock' in the research literature, are more ambiguous. PNTR did not change the tariffs applied by the US to Chinese goods, since US imports from China had been subject to normal tariffs reserved for WTO members since the 1980s. However, China's normal trade relations rates had to be renewed annually in an uncertain and politically contentious process. Without renewal, tariffs would have jumped to high rates set by the Smoot-Hawley Tariff Act of 1930. PNTR reduced uncertainty for Chinese exporters serving the US.

The importance of PNTR is confirmed by the growth of US–China trade: from 2000 to 2007, Chinese exports to the US increased from $122 billion to $330 billion, at an average rate of 15% per year (US International Trade Commission, 2019). This increase explains a substantial part of the globalisation benefits estimated in Section II. In addition, China's entry into mainstream world markets led to a greater reliance on markets at home and a larger role in the international governance system. Until relatively recently, PNTR was viewed as a critical step in paving the way to the fuller integration of China in the world economic system.

The implications for US labour markets are framed by two research contributions. Pierce and Schott (2014) examined the growth of US imports from China after China's admission to the WTO, based on the hypothesis that these increases reflect the reduction in uncertainty over tariffs. Autor, Dorn, and Hansen (2013b) examined the effects of import increases on employment and wages in the localities exposed to imports. Their main findings are that local labour market effects are substantial and persistent.

Pierce and Schott (2014) used the gap between the Smooth–Hawley tariffs and the PNTR rates as a measure of the uncertainty that China's accession to the WTO eliminated. This tariff gap is large: in 1999, US PNTR tariffs averaged 4% while non-PNTR tariffs averaged 36%. The authors showed that in sectors where the tariff gap was initially large, and hence uncertainty was sharply reduced by the PNTR, US imports increased and US employment decreased. They further confirmed the causal role of PNTR by showing that pre- and post-PNTR trade evolved quite differently in high-tariff-gap and low-tariff-gap industries. After PNTR, employment fell sharply in high-tariff-gap industries, but remained relatively constant in low-tariff-gap industries.

Pierce and Schott (2014) also concluded that PNTR was an unexpected shock: it mattered for trade and employment, yet its effects could not be detected significantly before China was admitted to the WTO (using data with annual frequency). This finding is consistent with Autor et al. (2103b), using the 'China shock' as an explanatory variable in analysing the effects of imports.

The most influential contributions to the employment debate have come from Autor and colleagues (2013b, 2016) who argued that the economics profession has seriously underestimated the difficulty of adjusting to trade shocks. Their econometric approach focused on the surge in US imports from China following PNTR, and estimated the response of different US 'commuting zones'[4] to exposure to imports from China over several decades. Exposure was measured using data on the sectoral structure of a commuting zone and on corresponding imports from China, using an instrumental variable to represent the import shock in each commuting zone.

The central regressions show how several labour market variables react to the exposure of commuting zones to imports from China. The results show that a $1,000/worker increase in a commuting zone's exposure reduces its employment by 0.75%. Additional controls (the share of manufacturing in commuting zone employment and the share of routine occupations in employment) in this equation matter, but only reduce the employment effect by one-third. In addition, a commuting zone's exposure to the China shock does not lead to significant out-migration, but it does lead to both unemployment (about one-quarter of the effect) and lower labour force participation (about three-quarters of the effect). Somewhat surprisingly, wage regressions show no significant changes in manufacturing wages due to exposure, and decline only in non-manufacturing sectors. Finally, exposure raises the commuting zone's government transfer payments and reduces its household income.

An important criticism of the work of Autor and his colleagues is that it focuses only on imports, even though PNTR is also likely to have increased incentives for US firms to export to China and other markets. These activities will have generated jobs. However, since these endogenous export effects are not related to the import exposure of a commuting zone, they do not show up in the regression results of Autor and colleagues.

Feenstra and Sasahara (2017) used a methodology like Autor, Dorn, and Hanson (2013b) to add export exposure effects to the regression analysis. Applying their coefficients to actual trade values in 1991–2011, they found that import exposure resulted in about 4.22 million job losses for the US as a whole, while export exposure generated about 4.24 million job gains. Although US manufacturing experienced significant employment losses during this period, they concluded that this was associated with factors such as technological progress rather than trade. The results suggest a somewhat unexpected positive geographic correlation between import losses and export gains: commuting zones with high percentages of employment losses due to imports are also likely to have a higher percentage of employment gains due to exports. This explains how local labour markets reached equilibrium even in the absence of strong mobility across regions. However, this correlation weakened in the more recent decade of their analysis (2001–11).

In sum, ex-post studies of trade policy changes offer several results. Criticisms of NAFTA (unemployment in the US, wage depression, and illegal immigration) do not appear justified. Some large predicted adjustments, including the predicted 'giant sucking sound'[5] of an investment exodus to Mexico, did not materialise. Some large predicted benefits also failed to materialise, especially an acceleration of Mexican growth. Benefits on a more modest scale appear to have been realised, however, and NAFTA probably made US manufacturing more competitive by giving it better access to the North American production base. The case of PNTR for China produces more mixed evidence. Overall welfare gains were probably substantial, but some negative labour market effects may have been underestimated.

5 Concluding remarks

Globalisation has accelerated in recent decades and has had a large, positive impact on the US, the world economy, and many developing countries. At the same time, globalisation has faced intense criticism for adverse side-effects on employment and wages. Interestingly, in the US, both the political left and right claim focus on these negative results. The studies reviewed in this paper offer empirical evidence on these issues, but even more importantly confirm the large benefits associated with trade.

Nevertheless, the economic as well as political costs of worsening distributional trends are substantial and demand urgent solutions. These solutions will have to be based on creative and sophisticated ways of mitigating adverse trends. Even if technological change and international economic integration have 'caused' adverse labour market trends, it does not follow that the erection of barriers against them is a useful solution.

The drivers of economic progress – technological innovations; falling communication and transport costs; new opportunities to connect ideas, investments, and markets – have yielded large benefits in the past and will likely continue to do so in the future. Even if trade growth slows, the economic forces connecting countries are not likely to retreat. Meanwhile, technological change seems to be accelerating. In this period of rapid change, economic shocks and policy confusion are inevitable. The critical challenge is to sustain the positive aspects of economic change while designing policies to overcome its negative side-effects.

Notes

1 This calculation assumes that gains are proportional to changes in the share of trade in US GDP. This ratio increased from 10.7% in 1947 to 22.4% in 2003 and 27.8% in 2018. Thus, the incremental gain from 1947 to 2018 was 17.1/10.7 = 1.46 times that of the gain from 1947 to 2003. These results are further scaled by the ratio of 2018 to 2003 GDP (=1.87).

2 This discussion abstracts from possible short-run, transitional links between trade shocks and savings.

3 The turnover in firms' staff as existing employees leave and new ones are hired.

4 A commuting zone is a geographic area used in population and economic analysis.

5 US presidential candidate Ross Perot's phrase for what he believed would be the negative effects of NAFTA.

References

Amiti, M. and S.-J. Wei (2009), 'Service Offshoring and Productivity: Evidence from the US', *The World Economy*, 32(2), pp.203–220.

Anderson, S. (2018), 'Immigrants and Billion-Dollar Companies', *NFAP Policy Brief*. Washington: National Foundation for American Policy.

Autor, D. (2014), 'Skills, Education, and the Rise of Earnings Inequality Among the "Other 99 Percent"', *Science*, 344(6186), pp.843–851.

Autor, D. (2015), 'Why Are There Still So Many Jobs? The History and Future of Workplace Automation', *Journal of Economic Perspectives*, 29(3), pp.3–30.

Autor, D.H., D. Dorn, and G.H. Hanson (2013a), 'Untangling Trade and Technology: Evidence from Local Labor Markets', *NBER Working Paper Series*, No. 18938. Cambridge, MA: National Bureau of Economic Research.

Autor, D.H., D. Dorn, and G.H. Hanson (2013b), 'The China Syndrome: Local Labor Market Effects of Import Competition in the United States', *American Economic Review*, 103(6), pp.2121–2168.

Autor, D., D. Dorn, and G.H. Hanson (2016), 'The China Shock: Learning from Labor Market Adjustment to Large Changes in Trade', *IZA Discussion Paper Series*, No. 9748. Bonn: Institute for the Study of Labor (IZA).

Baldwin, R.E. and G.G. Cain (2000), 'Shifts in U.S. Relative Wages: The Role of Trade, Technology, and Factor Endowments', *The Review of Economics and Statistics*, 82(4), pp.580–595.

Bernard, A.B., J. Eaton, J.B. Jensen, and S. Kortum (2003), 'Plants and Productivity in International Trade', *American Economic Review*, 93(4), pp.1268–1290.

Bradford, S.C., P.L.E. Grieco, and G.C. Hufbauer (2005), 'The Payoff to America from Global Integration', in C.F. Bergsten (ed.), *The United States and the World Economy: Foreign Economic Policy for the Next Decade*. Washington, DC: Peterson Institute for International Economics, pp.65–109.

Caliendo L. and F. Parro (2015), 'Estimates of the Trade and Welfare Effects of NAFTA', *The Review of Economic Studies*, 82(1), pp.1–44.

Case, A. and A. Deaton (2017), 'Mortality and Morbidity in the 21st Century', *Brookings Papers on Economic Activity*, 82(1, Spring), pp.397–443.

Clausing, K. (2019), 'The Progressive Case Against Protectionism: How Trade and Immigration Help American Workers', *Foreign Affairs*, 98(6), pp.109–121, November/December.

Constantinescu, C., A. Mattoo, and M. Ruta (2019), 'Does Vertical Specialisation Increase Productivity?', *The World Economy*, 42(8), pp.2385–2402.

Deardorff, A.V. and D.S. Hakura (1994), 'Trade and Wages – What Are the Questions?', in J. Bhagwati and M. Kosters (eds.), *Trade and Wages: Leveling Wages Down?* Washington, DC: American Enterprise Institute Press, pp.76–107.

Ebenstein, A., A. Harrison, and M. McMillan (2015), 'Why Are American Workers Getting Poorer? China, Trade and Offshoring', *NBER Working Paper Series*, No. 21027. Cambridge, MA: National Bureau of Economic Research.

Federico, G. and A. Tena-Junguito (2016), 'A Tale of Two Globalizations: Gains from Trade and Openness 1800–2010', *CEPR Discussion Papers*, No. 11128. London: Centre for Economic Policy Research.

Feenstra, R.C. and A. Sasahara (2017), 'The "China Shock", Exports and U.S. Employment: A Global Input-Output Analysis', *NBER Working Paper Series*, No. 24022. Cambridge, MA: National Bureau of Economic Research.

Forbes (2019), 'The World's Largest Public Companies'. Available at: https://www.forbes.com/global2000/list/ (accessed 25October2019).

Formai, S. and F. Vergara Caffarelli (2016), 'Quantifying the Productivity Effects of Global Sourcing', *Bank of Italy Working Papers*, No. 1075. Rome: Bank of Italy.

Fouquin, M. and J. Hugot (2016), 'Back to the Future: International Trade Costs and the Two Globalizations', *CEPII Working Paper*, No. 13. Paris: Centre d'études prospectives et d'informations internationales (CEPII).

Goos, M. and A. Manning (2003), 'Lousy and Lovely Jobs: The Rising Polarization of Work in Britain', *The Review of Economics and Statistics*, 89(1), pp.118–133.

Haskel, J., R.Z. Lawrence, E.E. Leamer, and M.J. Slaughter (2012), 'Globalization and U.S. Wages: Modifying Classic Theory to Explain Recent Facts', *Journal of Economic Perspectives*, 26(2), pp.119–140.

Hicks, M.J. and S. Deveraj (2017), *The Myth and the Reality of Manufacturing in America*. Muncie, IN: Ball State University Center for Business and Economic Research.

Hufbauer, G.C., C. Cimino-Isaacs, and T. Moran (2014), 'NAFTA at 20: Misleading Charges and Positive Achievements', *Policy Brief*, No. 14-13. Washington, DC: Peterson Institute for International Economics.

Kambourov, G. and I. Manovskii (2009a), 'Occupational Mobility and Wage Inequality', *The Review of Economic Studies*, 76(2), pp.731–759.

Kambourov, G. and I. Manovskii (2009b), 'Occupational Specificity of Human Capital', *International Economic Review*, 50(1), pp.63–115.

Las Américas y el Mundo (n.d.), *Poll.* Mexico City: Centro de Investigación y Docencia Económicas (CIDE). Available at: https://www.lasamericasyelmundo.cide.edu/en/inicio (accessed 25February2019).

Pierce, J.R. and P.K. Schott (2014), 'The Surprisingly Swift Decline of U.S. Manufacturing Employment', *CESifo Working Paper Series*, No. 4563. Munich: Center for Economic Studies and Ifo Institute (CESifo).

Piketty, T. (2015), 'Capital in the Twenty-First Century', *American Economic Review*, 105(5), pp.48–53.

Rosen, S. (1981), 'The Economics of Superstars', *American Economic Review*, 71(5), pp.845–858.

Semega, J., M. Kollar, J. Creamer, and A. Mohanty (2019), *Income and Poverty in the United States: 2018 – Current Population Reports.* Washington, DC: United States Census Bureau.

Slaughter, M.J. (1998), 'International Trade and Labour-Market Outcomes: Results, Questions, and Policy Options', *The Economic Journal*, 108(450), pp.1452–1462.

US Census Bureau (2019), 'U.S. Trade in Goods and Services – Balance of Payments (BOP) Basis'. Available at: https://www.census.gov/foreign-trade/statistics/historical/gands.pdf (accessed 25September2019).

US Customs and Border Protection Agency (n.d.), 'Fiscal Year Southwest Border Sector Apprehensions (FY 1960 - FY 2019)'. https://www.cbp.gov/sites/default/files/assets/documents/2020-Jan/U.S.%20Border%20Patrol%20Total%20Apprehensions%20%28FY%201925%20-%20FY%202019%29.pdf

US International Trade Commission (2019), 'USITC DataWeb'. Available at: https://dataweb.usitc.gov/ (accessed 25October2019).

9 Economic consequences of trade and investment liberalisation: the case of Vietnam

Thanh Tri Vo, Duong Anh Nguyen, and Thien Thi Nhan Do

1 Introduction

Since it initiated Doi Moi (Renovation) in 1986, Vietnam has embarked on bold and comprehensive economic reforms. A key pillar of reforms is economic integration, to reduce at-the-border and behind-the-border barriers to trade and investment. Economic integration has broadened opportunities through access to foreign investment and foreign markets, adaptation to international trade rules, deeper participation in global value chains, amongst others. By 2018, however, economic integration attempts largely focused on liberalisation of trade and investment. Deeper liberalisation attempts in labour mobility, environmental standards, competition policy, amongst others, were more evident only in high-quality free trade agreements (FTAs) such as the Comprehensive and Progressive Agreement for Trans-Pacific Partnership (CPTPP),[1] European Union (EU)–Vietnam FTA (EVFTA), amongst others. Whilst ensuring sustainable benefits from furthering economic integration remains a priority,[2] whether such benefits will continue to be realised is the subject of growing inquiry.

This paper reviews the literature and statistics on Vietnam's socio-economic performance during 2000–18, then draws out implications for policy reforms to leverage the benefits of economic integration. The paper will refrain from analysing the contribution of policies such as those on labour, land, and the environment to socio-economic performance.

Section 2 briefly overviews the process of trade and investment liberalisation in Vietnam. Section 3 provides background information on Vietnam's socio-economic performance during 2000–18. Section 4 reviews the literature on major impacts of trade and investment liberalisation on the economy. Section 5 recommends policy changes.

2 Overview of trade and investment liberalisation in Vietnam

Since Doi Moi, Vietnam has gradually opened the economy to foreign trade and investment. Economic integration had four milestones.

DOI: 10.4324/9781003138501-9

First, Vietnam joined the Association of Southeast Asian Nations (ASEAN) in 1995 and the ASEAN Free Trade Area in 1996. By August 2019, Vietnam was signatory to an array of FTAs under the ASEAN Plus framework. At the end of 2015, Vietnam joined the ASEAN Community. As of August 2019, Viet Nam had been active in negotiating the Regional Comprehensive Economic Partnership (RCEP), between ASEAN and China, the Republic of Korea (henceforth, Korea), Japan, Australia, New Zealand, and India.

Second, Vietnam negotiated and signed the Vietnam–United States (US) bilateral trade agreement in 2000, which induced Vietnam to prepare for regional FTA-based integration and the World Trade Organization (WTO) process and gave Vietnam better access to the US, its largest export market, implying improved competitiveness relative to other major exporters.

Third, Vietnam became a member of the WTO in January 2007. The greatest pressures under the WTO are related to institutional reforms and the service sector (CIEM, 2013). To fulfil its WTO commitments, Vietnam had to amend or promulgate many laws, ordinances, and decrees related to domestic institutional regulations.

Fourth, since 2008, Vietnam has focused on bilateral and plurilateral FTAs. It negotiated and/or signed, amongst others, the Economic Partnership Agreement with Japan and FTAs with the EU, Chile, Korea, and the Eurasian Economic Union. Whilst the Trans-Pacific Partnership Agreement (TPP), signed in 2016, could not proceed due to the US's withdrawal, Vietnam signed the CPTPP in March 2018 and ratified it in November 2018. Figure 9.1

3 Overview of Vietnam's socio-economic performance in 2000–18

This section focuses on gross domestic product (GDP), trade, investment, macroeconomic stability, and social aspects.

3.1 Gross domestic product

The dramatic opening of the economy undoubtedly contributed to rapid GDP growth and explosion of trade from the early 1990s until 2008 (Abbott, Bentzen and Tarp, 2009). In 1998–1999, Vietnam experienced the first bitterness resulting from economic integration as its growth was arrested by the Asian financial crisis. Because economic integration was modest, the effect of the crisis came later for Vietnam than for other more integrated economies (Tran 1999). Growth recovered momentum in 2000 and the country experienced its fastest growth, from 6.8% in 2000 to 7.1% in 2007 (Figure 9.2).

Soon after optimism was induced by WTO accession, GDP growth began to slow: 5.7% in 2008 and 5.4% in 2009, with a short-lived recovery to 6.4% in 2010 and deceleration in 2011–12. GDP growth has been recovering since 2013, however, reaching 6.7% in 2015, 6.8% in 2017, and 7.1% in 2018.

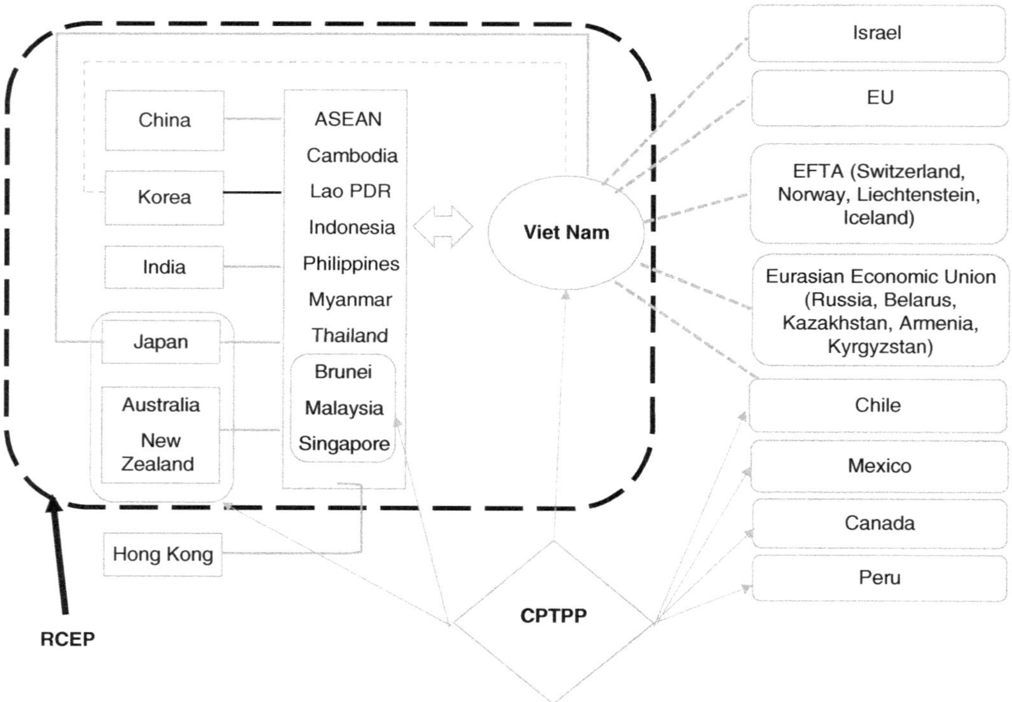

Figure 9.1 Vietnam's Free Trade Agreements.
Source: Authors.
Note: ASEAN= Association of South East Asian Nations; CPTPP= Comprehensive and Progressive Agreement for Trans-Pacific Partnership; EFTA= European Free Trade Area; EU= European Union; Lao PDR= Lao People's Democratic Republic; RCEP= Regional Comprehensive Economic Partnership.

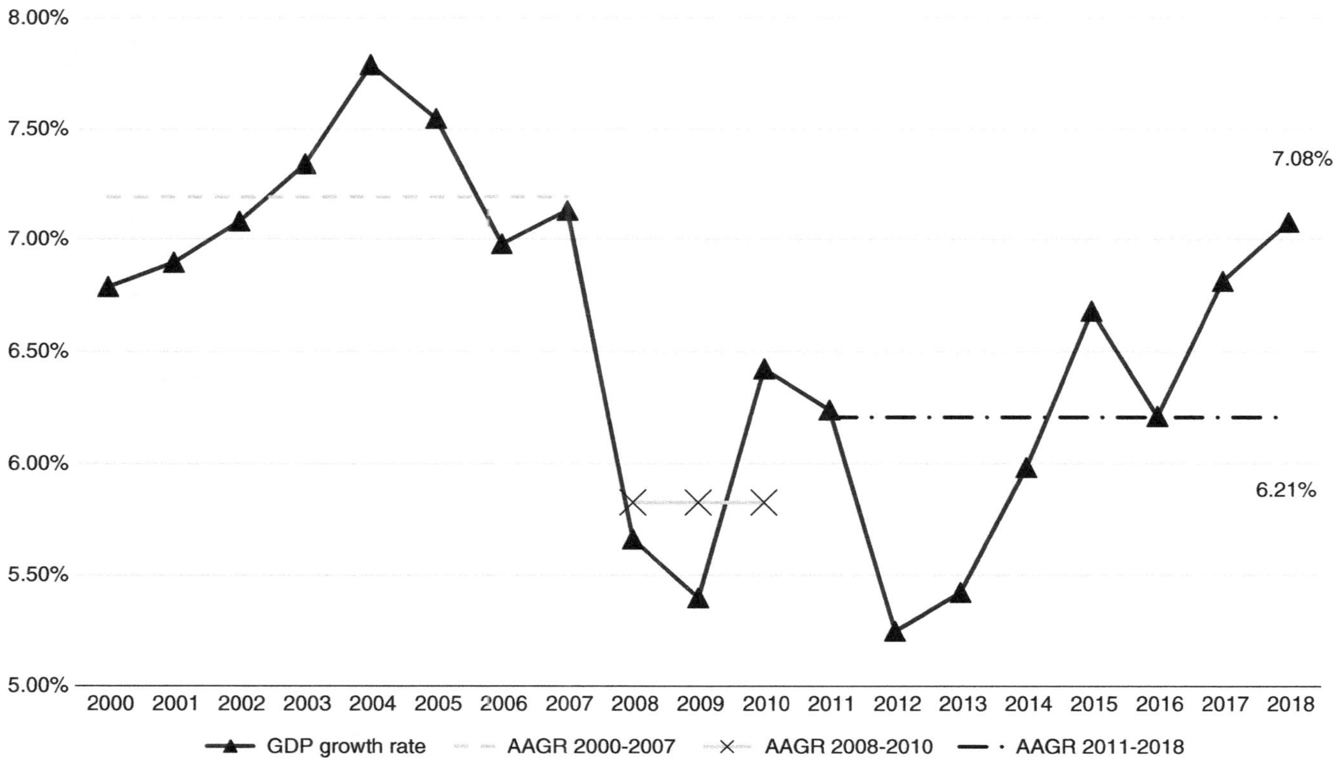

Figure 9.2 Gross Domestic Product Growth Rate, 2000–18, Vietnam.
Source: Authors, calculated from General Statistics Office of Viet Nam data.
Note: AAGR = average annual growth rate, GDP = gross domestic product.

3.2 Trade

Following WTO accession, trade increased almost continuously, except in 2009 (Figure 9.3), in value and percentage of GDP. In 2017, the sum of exports and imports reached around 200% of GDP, higher than in 2007 (154%) and 2000 (111%). Merchandise exports grew on average by more than 19.4% a year during 2000–06. Exports weakened sharply in 2009 amidst the global financial crisis but rebounded strongly in 2010.

The growth of imports clearly overwhelmed the increase in exports shortly after WTO accession (CIEM, 2013). Consequently, the trade deficit widened to over US$18.0 billion in 2008, compared with US$14.2 billion in 2007 and US $5.1 billion in 2006. After the global financial crisis, import growth decelerated and the trade deficit contracted to US$9.8 billion in 2011.

The years since 2012 exhibited different patterns of export and import growth. Export growth gradually recovered to 21.9% in 2017 and 13.2% in 2018 (CIEM 2018, 2019) whilst import growth has been generally slower. During 2012–18 (except 2015), Vietnam enjoyed a trade surplus, with a record level of US$6.8 billion in 2018 (Figure 9.3).

Export growth seems to be largely and consistently contributed by foreign-owned enterprises. The linkage between foreign-invested enterprises and local counterparts improved slowly. Therefore, export activities had to rely significantly on imported inputs (Vo et al., 2017). Table 9.1

The technology intensity in exports and imports improved over time (Table 9.2). The share of high-technology products in exports rose remarkably from 5.6% to 37.7% over 17 years. However, various export products still depended heavily on technology and/or imported materials, so the content of domestic value added was small (Truong et al, 2011; Tran et al., 2011; Vo et al., 2017; Ministry of Planning and Investment, 2018).

The key markets accounted for the lion's share of Vietnam's exports, which averaged 78.46% in 2002–07 and 77.29% during 2011–18 (Table 9.3). Notable increases in export share can be seen in the cases of China and Korea.

Similarly, the total share of imports from major markets ranged from 75.84% in 2008–10 to 79.89% in 2011–18 (Table 9.4). In 2011–18, China ranked first amongst seller of Vietnam's imports, followed by Korea and ASEAN. Notably, the Vietnam– Korea FTA has significantly induced imports from Korea since 2016 and diverted imports from other countries (CIEM, 2018, 2019).

3.3 Investment

Foreign direct investment (FDI) inflows have increased since 2001 but boomed only after Vietnam joined the WTO (Figure 9.4). Registered FDI capital exploded from 2007 to 2010, seemingly unaffected by the global recession of 2008–09. Since 2011, Vietnam has experienced a down cycle in registered foreign investment but the figure is still larger than in the pre-WTO period.

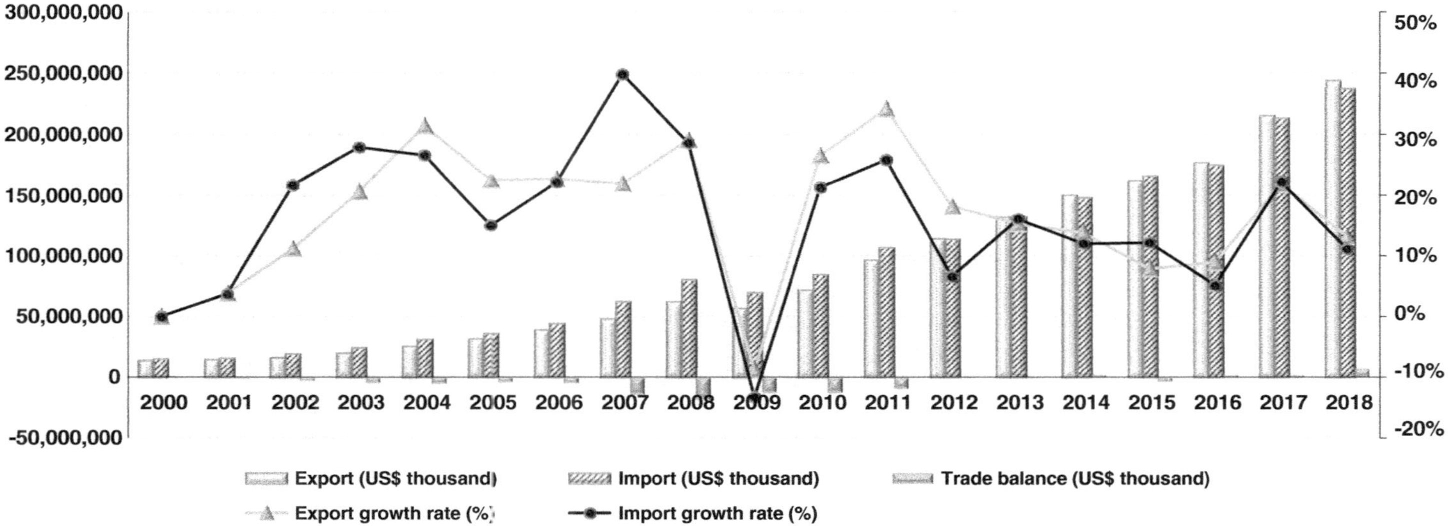

Figure 9.3 Exports and Imports, 2001–18, Vietnam.

Source: General Statistics Office of Viet Nam, Trade Map, and authors' calculation.

Note: Exports, imports, and trade balance are shown on the left-hand axis, and export and import growth rate are shown on the right-hand axis.

Table 9.1 Exports and Imports by Ownership, Vietnam

	Share (%)		*Growth Rate (%)*	
	2008–10	*2011–18*	*2008–10*	*2011–18*
Exports	100	100	14.3	16.4
FDI enterprises	*48.5*	*65.5*	*7.0*	*22.4*
Domestic enterprises	*51.5*	*34.5*	*22.8*	*8.3*
Imports	100	100	11.7	13.7
FDI enterprises	*39.0*	*57.1*	*19.6*	*18.3*
Domestic enterprises	*61.0*	*42.9*	*6.9*	*8.9*

Source: Authors' calculations based on data from the General Department of Viet Nam Customs and the General Statistics Office of Viet Nam.
FDI = foreign direct investment.

Implemented FDI capital exhibited important changes after WTO accession. Whilst implemented FDI was relatively modest until 2006, it went up to US$10 billion–US$12 billion per year during 2007–13. Implemented FDI then increased continuously, reaching US$19.1 billion in 2018. The share of FDI in gross investment increased from 14.9% in 2007 to 23.4% in 2018.

FDI was initially concentrated in oil and gas exploitation or construction, then moved rapidly to light and heavy industries. FDI was predominant in services; transportation and telecommunications; construction; and real estate (hotels and tourism, offices and apartments, infrastructure) (Tran and Dinh, 2013). Of the 76 countries and territories with investment projects in Vietnam in 2018, the top 5 in terms of registered capital are in Asia (Japan, Korea, China, Singapore, and Hong Kong), accounting for 74.5% of total registered capital (CIEM, 2019).

3.4 Macroeconomic stability

After WTO accession, Vietnam gradually learned to systematically ensure macroeconomic stability. In 2007 and early 2008, Vietnam was still inexperienced in dealing with the impacts of price hikes in international markets as well as in managing huge inflows of capital (Vo and Nguyen, 2009; CIEM, 2010, 2013). Bold and comprehensive measures to control inflation were identified in early 2008 but quickly replaced by policies to prevent economic downturn in the fourth quarter of 2008 – just 2 months after inflation peaked (CIEM, 2011, 2010b; Vo, 2015). As high inflation returned in 2011 after economic stimulus, Vietnam realised that it required bolder and more consistent measures to stabilise the macroeconomic environment in line with economic restructuring (CIEM, 2013, 2018, 2019). Inflation started to go down starting in 2012. In general, inflation has been more stable since 2012 than during 2007–11 (Figure 9.5).

Government budget revenues have been increasing continuously. During 2007–18, inflation-adjusted budget revenues rose by 6.9% per annum on average. The tax base was significantly improved, particularly in 2007–11

Table 9.2 Exports and Imports Classified by Technology-Intensity Level, Vietnam

	2000		*2017*		*2000*		*2017*	
	Export value (US$ million)	*Export share (%)*	*Export value (US$ million)*	*Export share (%)*	*Import value (US$ million)*	*Import share (%)*	*Import value (US$ million)*	*Import share (%)*
High technology	807	5.6	81,139	37.7	1,883	12.0	64,084	30.1
Medium technology	624	4.3	18,450	8.6	4,942	31.6	49,929	23.4
Low technology	3,562	24.6	64,112	29.8	2,864	18.3	33,254	15.6
Primary products	6,969	48.1	28,800	13.4	1,000	6.4	24,733	11.6
Resource-based products	888	6.1	12,603	5.9	3,238	20.7	23,721	11.1

Source: Authors' compilation based on the World Integrated Trade Solutions database.

Table 9.3 Export Structure and Export Average Growth Rates, by Major Destination, Vietnam

Exports	*Share (%)*			*Growth Rate (%)*		
	2002–07	*2008–10*	*2011–18*	*2002–07*	*2008–10*	*2011–18*
ASEAN	16.12	15.34	11.69	21.24	8.52	11.49
China	8.92	9.37	13.00	17.05	28.54	23.26
European Union 28	18.56	16.55	18.15	19.21	7.77	17.68
Japan	13.33	11.73	9.05	15.92	8.26	11.79
Republic of Korea	2.34	3.63	6.01	20.50	35.49	24.81
United States	19.17	19.57	19.39	45.50	12.12	16.25
Total	78.46	76.19	77.29			

Source: General Statistics Office of Viet Nam, Trade Map, and authors' calculations.

Table 9.4 Import Structure and Import Average Growth Rates, by Major Destination, Vietnam

Imports	*Share (%)*			*Growth Rate (%)*		
	2002–07	*2008–10*	*2011–18*	*2002–07*	*2008–10*	*2011–18*
ASEAN	25.44	21.14	15.03	24.99	1.04	8.61
China	15.78	22.44	27.74	41.16	16.71	15.82
European Union 28	8.27	7.56	6.39	21.84	7.36	10.24
Japan	11.02	10.50	8.66	18.97	13.36	9.77
Republic of Korea	9.68	10.19	17.47	18.93	22.25	21.88
United States	2.82	4.01	4.61	26.69	30.51	16.42
Total	73.01	75.84	79.89			

Source: General Statistics Office of Viet Nam, Trade Map, and authors' calculations.

(CIEM, 2013). The ratio of budget revenues to GDP, however, increased slightly from 20.5% in 2000 to 26.6% in 2008, then fell to 25.6% in 2018. Revenues from trade accounted for a smaller share in budget revenues (Table 9.5). Vietnam then had to rely more on other domestic taxes, particularly corporate income tax (Nguyen, Tran, and Le, 2018).

Vietnam has been running a prolonged budget deficit. Budget expenditures have kept expanding and remained in excess over budget revenues. Total expenditures (adjusted for inflation) rose on average by 5.8% per annum in 2007–18. The ratio of budget expenditures to GDP climbed from 28.7% in 2005 to 32.0% in 2007, then trended downwards to 29.1% in 2018. Vietnam has provided an increasing share of expenditures from the

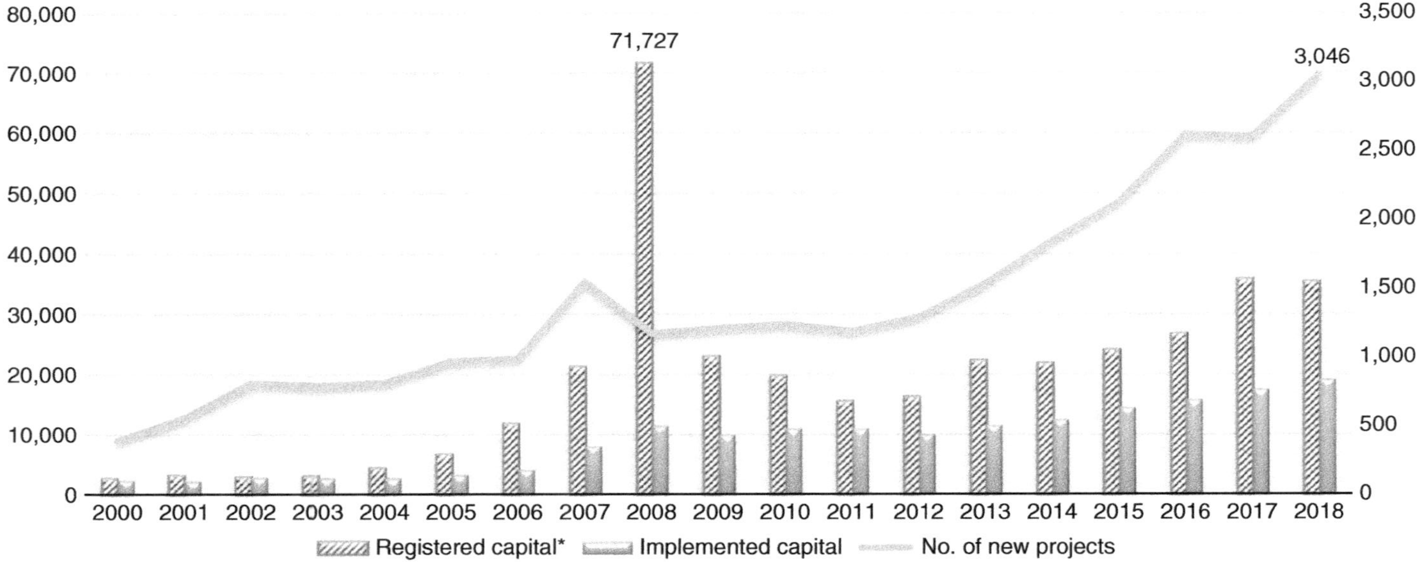

Figure 9.4 Foreign Direct Investment Inflows, 2000–18, Vietnam (US$ million) * Including adjusted capital for licensed projects and capital for buying shares.

Source: General Statistics Office of Vietnam.

Note: Registered capital and implemented capital are shown on the left-hand axis and the number of new projects is shown on the right-hand axis.

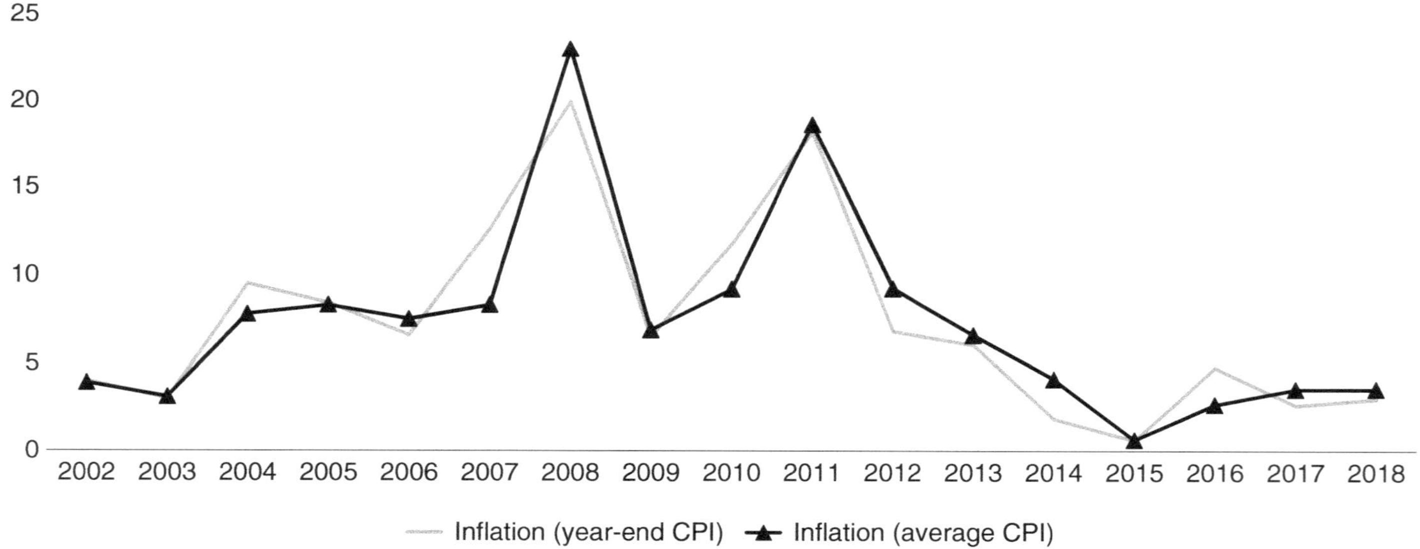

Figure 9.5 Inflation Rates, 2002–18, Vietnam (%).
Source: General Statistics Office of Viet Nam.
Note: CPI = consumer price index.

Table 9.5 Structure of Budget Revenues, 2000–18, Vietnam (%)

	2000	*2007*	*2008*	*2009*	*2010*	*2011*	*2015*	*2016*	*2017*	*2018*
Revenues from trade	20.9	19.1	21.2	23.2	22.2	21.6	17.0	15.5	15.4	13.9
Revenues from crude oil	25.9	24.4	20.8	13.4	11.8	15.3	6.8	3.6	3.8	4.0
Proceedings from land	3.1	10.7	9.1	9.6	9.5	8.4	8.6	11.4	12.0	10.8
Personal income tax	2.0	2.3	3.0	3.1	4.5	5.3	5.7	5.9	6.1	7.2
Other revenues	48.1	43.4	45.9	50.6	52.1	49.4	62.0	63.5	62.6	64.1

Source: Authors' calculations from data of the General Statistics Office of Viet Nam and the Ministry of Finance.
Note: As of May 2019, Vietnam had finalised budget figures up to 2016. Figures for 2018 are from the first estimate by the Ministry of Finance.

state budget for education and training, health, and pension and social security. Table 9.6

3.5 Social aspects

With a human development index (HDI) of 0.694 in 2017, Vietnam is in the high average group, ranking 116th out of 189 countries (similar to its rank in 2016). Vietnam still lags behind other Asia-Pacific countries. In 1990, Vietnam's HDI was 8.1%, lower than the average of the East Asia-Pacific region; this gap decreased to 4.7% in 2008 but had widened to 5.3% by 2017, arguably because other countries in the region were achieving better results in human development, especially in education (United Nations Development Programme UNDP, 2018).

Education is one sector where Vietnam has achieved the most impressive success in reaching the Millennium Development Goals (MDGs). The literacy rate reached 98.1% in the 15–35 age group and 96.83% in the 15–60 age group, according to the Ministry of Education and Training report on academic year 2015–16. Vietnam also participated in the Programme for International Student Assessment (PISA) test and scored higher than predicted by the country's income level (Glewwe et al., 2017).

Vietnam continues to reduce poverty. As of 2018, the poverty rate was 6.8%, lower than for 2006 (15.5%), but income inequality has been widening, partly because of high economic growth over the past 2 decades. The large increase in inequality was seen at the beginning of the 2000s and declined only marginally in the course of the decade (Multilateral Trade Assistance Project MUTRAP, 2015a). The Gini index declined from 37 in 2002 to 35.3 in 2016 following the removal of tariff protection. Figure 9.6

Table 9.6 Structure of Budget Expenditures, Final Account, 2005–18, Vietnam (%)

	2005	*2007*	*2008*	*2009*	*2010*	*2011*	*2015*	*2016*	*2017*	*2018*
Development investment	30.2	28.1	26.4	32.3	28.2	26.5	20.1	24.6	25.0	26.8
Expenditure on education and training	10.9	13.5	11.8	12.4	12.1	12.6	15.9	14.7	14.8	14.8
Expenditure on health	2.9	4.1	3.2	3.5	3.9	3.9	6.0	4.0	5.8	5.7
Expenditure on pension and social security	6.8	9.2	8.2	9.0	9.9	9.9	10.3	9.2	9.0	7.5
Other expenditures	49.3	45.2	50.4	42.9	46.0	47.1	47.7	47.5	45.4	45.2

Source: Authors' update from Nguyen, Tran, and Le (2018).

Note: As of May 2019, Vietnam had finalised budget figures up to 2016. Figures for 2018 are from first estimate of Ministry of Finance.

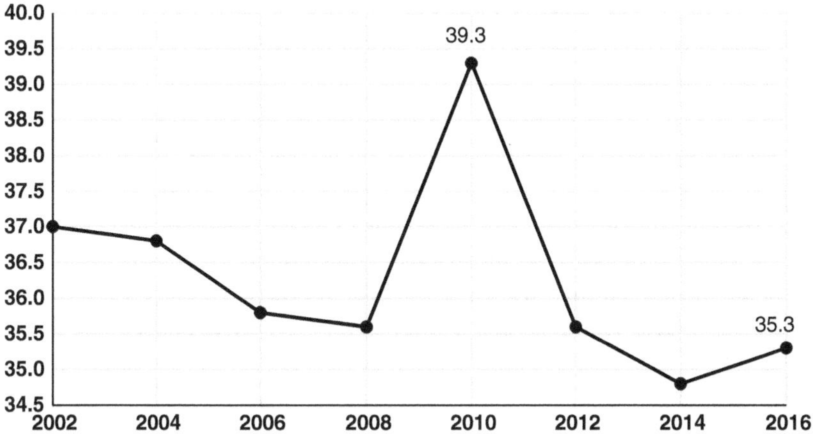

Figure 9.6 Vietnam's Gini Index.
Source: Knoema.

The Global Gender Gap Index 2017 ranked Vietnam 69th out of 144 countries, whilst the United Nations Development Programme (UNDP) Gender Inequality Index gave Vietnam a score of 0.304. Vietnam was ranked 97th out of 144 countries in terms of female ratio in political system (Vietnamnet, 2018). The gender pay gap still exists in many areas (World Bank, 2018b).

4 Major impacts of trade and investment liberalisation on Vietnam's economy

The literature on impacts of trade and investment liberalisation on Vietnam's economy is extensive. The assessments are ex ante and ex post, and qualitative and quantitative. This section surveys the economic and social aspects of the assessment results.

4.1 Economic impacts

The literature on economic impacts often focuses on imports, exports, real wages, employment, investment, and tariff revenues. Various quantitative studies also examine welfare, a measure of real income, to see expected and real improvements due to trade and investment liberalisation. This paper surveys only impacts on welfare, trade, and investment.

Vietnam's impressive GDP growth performance in 2007 was affected by internal and external factors. First, the implementation of a series of important WTO accession commitments to open the internal market has helped Vietnam offer a more predictable business environment for trade and foreign investment (CIEM, 2010, 2013). Second, after Vietnam joined the WTO, enterprises have benefited from a lower cost of accessing and expanding to international markets, whilst enjoying more equal treatment in trade and dispute settlement. Such lower costs have resulted from domestic economic reforms parallel to negotiation for WTO accession since 2000. This effect was observed by Roland-Holst et al. (2002) and ex-post confirmed by Vo and Nguyen (2009). Third, Viet Nam continued to appeal to foreign investment thanks to sustained political and socio-economic stability (CIEM, 2010, 2013).

Following the optimism induced by WTO accession, GDP growth slowed largely because of (i) the rapid and drastic impact of the global financial crisis and economic downturn as Vietnam's economic integration deepened (CIEM, 2013), and (i) the lagged effect of tightening macroeconomic policies to curb inflation in the first half of 2008 (CIEM, 2013; Vo and Nguyen, 2009). In the fourth quarter of 2008, Vietnam had to change its policy stance to prevent economic downturn. Economic growth then exhibited a short-lived recovery in 2010 to 6.4% due to massive fiscal stimulus: the stimulus package of 8.7% of GDP helped increase GDP growth rate by only 1.0–1.5 percentage points (CIEM, 2011).

Since 2011, Vietnam has embarked on consistent macroeconomic stabilisation (Vo, 2015; CIEM, 2013), which enables domestic economic restructuring in line with FTA negotiation and implementation. Vanzetti et al. (2011) estimate from various Global Trade Analysis Project simulations that FTAs with China, Japan, and Korea would provide the greatest potential gains in absolute terms for Vietnam, whereas FTAs with Australia, New Zealand, and India would generate little. The benefits from all ASEAN FTAs with Viet Nam in 2012 were estimated at 3% of the 2007 base national income. Nevertheless, GDP growth decelerated in 2011–12 and only recovered in 2013, reaching 6.7% in 2015, 6.8% in 2017, and 7.1% in 2018. Whilst this recovery was largely due to reforms in the domestic business environment (CIEM, 2018, 2019), it should be noted that market and investor confidence also rose due to Vietnam's preparation for mega FTAs (TPP/CPTPP, EVFTA, and RCEP). In light of this, Vietnam's growth potential can be improved after 2019, with FTAs being instrumental.

Various studies attempt to quantify the benefits of new-generation FTAs on Vietnam's economy, all using computable general equilibrium models. Nguyen et al. (2014) estimate that welfare gains from RCEP may amount to US$227 million–US$2,239 million. Baker et al. (2017) document expected gains from the EVFTA of US$3.2 billion in 2020, US$6.7 billion in 2025, and US$7.2 billion in 2030 compared with the baseline. The World Bank (2018a) estimates that the CPTPP may increase Vietnam's GDP in 2030 by 1.1% under the modest scenario and by 3.5% under the productivity-enhancing scenario. A caveat: all ex-ante quantitative studies before WTO accession underestimated the impact of institutional changes and capital flows induced by integration attempts (CIEM, 2013). Such underestimation may be inherent in the literature on impacts of new-generation FTAs (e.g. Vo, 2015, World Bank, 2018b).

Post-reform economic growth was accompanied by trade liberalisation reforms that led to an explosion in international trade (Abbott and Tarp, 2012; CIEM, 2013). Nguyen et al. (2018) use constant market share decomposition to show that enhanced competitiveness, as measured by the residual, accounted for around 65.1% of the export increase in 2014 relative to 2006. This share is significantly higher than corresponding figures for 2004–07 (Vo and Nguyen, 2011) and for 2006–10 (Nguyen et al., 2018). Thanks to various FTAs, including the TPP/CPTPP and EVFTA, and domestic business environment reforms since 2016, export growth recovered to 21.9% in 2017 and 13.2% in 2018 (CIEM, 2018, 2019).

However, Vietnam's export growth post-WTO fails to compensate for several issues. First, export growth seems to be largely and consistently contributed by foreign-owned enterprises, whilst domestic enterprises have failed to take advantage of integration-induced export opportunities (Vo and Nguyen, 2011; CIEM, 2015; World Bank, 2015; Nguyen et al., 2018; CIEM, 2019). The enhanced competitiveness explained by Nguyen et al. (2018) appears to be largely induced by the presence of major foreign-invested enterprises. The ability of domestic firms to move up in global value chains is limited, trapping them in low value-added production stages (World Bank, 2016b). Second, the linkage between foreign-invested enterprises and local counterparts improved slowly. Whilst motorcycles and electronics, amongst a few other products, have enhanced the capacity of local supporting industries, most sectors still have poor linkages between foreign and local firms (Ministry of Planning and Investment, 2018). Such poor linkages have led to only modest improvement in the domestic value-added content of exports (Tran et al., 2011; Vo et al., 2017). Third, despite the range of FTAs, the use of preferential treatment under them is limited and the extent of FTA utilisation has not significantly improved (Vo and Nguyen, 2015; WTO Center, 2019).

The export structure is shifting from traditional sectors, where Vietnam enjoyed comparative advantage, towards new ones, whose comparative advantage is still unknown (CIEM, 2013, 2017, 2019). Exports continue to shift away from raw materials and towards manufacturing and processing (Truong et al., 2011; Nguyen et al., 2014; Nguyen et al., 2017).

Whilst adding much-needed capital, foreign investment has boosted exports. Using macroeconomic data and error-correction models, Nguyen et al. (2018) and Vo and Nguyen (2011) show that a rise in implemented FDI disbursement tends to increase exports, and the increase is larger in the long term than in the short term. The greater long-term impact is due to FDI spillover effects on exports of other domestic enterprises. In the same manner, when additional employment generated indirectly by FDI in domestic firms is included, we should find an even greater contribution of FDI to total employment.

Linkages between FDI and domestic firms remain weak. Transfer of technology and knowledge by FDI to the nearly 1,500 enterprises in Vietnam was limited at the sectoral level (United Nations Industrial Development Organization UNIDO, 2012). FDI enterprises mainly depend on imported intermediate goods and raw materials, whilst linkages with domestic supply chains were not established (Multilateral Trade Assistance Project MUTRAP, 2015b;Ministry of Planning and Investment, 2018). Newman et al. (2013) claim that domestic firms had more productivity spillovers from joint ventures than wholly foreign-owned firms, yet such spillovers are unexplained in the sense that they cannot be attributed to real technology transfers between firms. However, it seems that the WTO and FTAs fail to encourage foreign firms to enhance linkages with domestic counterparts: the finding by Newman et al. (2013) appears to differ from the significant spillover effect during 2003–07 found by Hoang and Pham (2010).

Vietnam's exports exhibited high complementarity with import demand of major markets such as ASEAN, EU, Japan, Korea, the US, and China (Truong et al., 2011; Nguyen et al., 2014; CIEM, 2016). Some argue that high export concentration in selected markets is risky and propose that Vietnam diversify its export markets (Truong et al., 2011; CIEM, 2016). The wide range of FTAs since 2010 clearly reflects that approach. However, whilst creating trade, the new FTAs also significantly divert Vietnam's exports (e.g. World Bank, 2018a). Notable increases in export shares can be seen in the cases of China and Korea (Table 9.3).

Until 2011, the increase in imports was mainly due to (i) income effect as consumers had higher income (Vo and Nguyen, 2009; CIEM, 2010; CIEM, 2013); and (ii) higher demand for imported spare parts and materials for exports (Vo et al., 2017; Tran et al., 2011). Using an error-correction model, Truong et al. (2011) estimated that WTO accession led to a short-term increase of import growth by almost 2.4 percentage points and a long-term increase by 3.4 percentage points. Amongst the key reasons for slower import growth since 2011 were economic restructuring and control of public investment to help stabilise the macroeconomic environment, which reduced import demand (Nguyen et al., 2017). Besides, Vietnam had become better at using more non-tariff measures, which had the effect of reducing imports (Vo et al., 2017; Nguyen et al., 2019).

The boom in registered capital of FDI can be partly attributed to improved confidence of investors in Vietnam's post-WTO growth potential (Vo and Nguyen, 2011; CIEM, 2013). From 2011 onwards, Vietnam experienced a down cycle in registered foreign investment, but the figure is still larger than in the pre-WTO period. More important, implemented capital was stable until 2013 and has increased steadily since 2014 due to (i) increasing opportunities for foreign investors from FTAs with Vietnam (CIEM, 2015, 2018); and (ii) efforts by the government, ministries, and localities to improve the investment and business environment (CIEM, 2018, 2019).

The studies using ex-ante and ex-post quantitative analyses of impacts on the economy are subject to several limitations. These analyses have to assume that any agreement will be implemented as designed, but non-tariff measures may prevent further meaningful liberalisation in implementing existing and future FTAs (Nguyen et al., 2014). Some tariff peaks may be prohibitive, which may cause the overstatement of projected gains from tariff reform. Finally, the ex-post studies, however technically rigorous, could not entirely separate the impacts of trade and liberalisation from those due to other policies within Vietnam.

Nguyen et al. (2014) identify several limitations of the computable general equilibrium model employed in various studies (such as Nguyen et al. 2014, World Bank 2018a, Baker et al. 2017). First, some changes in production and consumption behaviours are assumed to be automatic responses to tariff changes (and thus relative prices), whilst some practical factors that may affect FTA utilisation are ignored. Second, the model can hardly incorporate impacts of institutional improvement and foreign capital flows. Third, the scenarios are useful to the extent that they help focus on the impacts of FTAs, whilst the actual non-trade policy settings may not be entirely consistent with such scenarios.

4.2 Social impacts

Whilst contributing to economic development, deeper economic integration made way for social progress by (i) enhancing economic opportunities and (ii) increasing people's capacity to use them (Vo and Nguyen, 2006;United Nations Development Programme UNDP, 2006). Vietnam, however, still has a bigger human development gap relative to other countries in the region, which have made more progress, especially in education (United Nations Development Programme UNDP, 2018).

Vietnam continues to reduce poverty even as it deepens economic integration. Well before WTO accession, the Centre for International Economics (2002, cited in Abbott et al., 2009) documented the beneficial effects of trade liberalisation on poverty under all scenarios, the results being valid for poverty incidence and poverty gap. Following WTO accession, poverty reduction progressed even with upward adjustment of the national poverty line (Vo, 2014; CIEM, 2013; Nguyen, Tran, and Le, 2018). Still, the new-generation FTAs may contribute to more sustainable reduction of poverty. Compared with the traditional quantitative analyses that rely only on macroeconomic variables, recent studies have utilised household data to simulate impacts at the micro level. Using macro–micro simulation, the World Bank (2018a) projects that CPTPP may help reduce the number of poor people (at the poverty line of US$5.50/day) by 0.5 million in 2030 compared with the baseline. Using a similar method, Baker et al. (2017) shows that the potential impacts of EVFTA on the poverty rate are favourable but not sizeable: 197,000 people may escape poverty in 2030 thanks to implementation of the agreement, compared with the baseline.

Amongst the reasons for progressive poverty reduction is the continued provision of social security after WTO accession. When hit by the global financial crisis, Vietnam incorporated a substantial social security programme to help disadvantaged groups. The programme includes unemployment insurance, preferential treatment for vulnerable groups, social relief, and support to the poor under government fiscal stimulus packages, amongst others (CIEM, 2010; Vo, 2014). Contingent support against climate change and natural disasters has been ensured by the state and other organisations such as ActionAID International Vietnam (Nguyen et al., 2011). Even though government revenues from trade have decreased, budget expenditures on education, health, and social security have not been pruned (Le et al., 2016).

Using micro data in macro–micro simulation, the literature shows that new FTAs such as CPTPP and EVFTA may contribute to income inequality. Baker et al. (2017) project a modest increase of the Gini index in 2020, followed by a fall in 2025 and then a rise again in 2030 in the case of EVFTA implementation compared with the baseline scenario. Such results, however, assume that there will be no effect from the reaffirmation of Vietnam and the EU of International Labour Organization conventions and declarations on the rights of workers.

Whilst the gender pay gap still exists in many areas (World Bank, 2018b), Vietnam can hope that it will narrow. Female labour may be paid more than men in such areas as food, manufacturing, textiles, apparel, beverages and tobacco, motor vehicles and transport equipment, minerals, sugar, and other crops (Baker et al., 2017).

5 New liberalisation context and policy recommendations

5.1 New liberalisation context

a. International context

First, international economic integration continues, albeit on a bumpier road. Whilst the Doha Development Agenda has stalled, FTAs may liberalise trade and investment but also challenge and destabilise the multilateral trading system. WTO statistics as of September 2019 show that there were 481 notifications by members, including of 302 regional trade agreements remaining in force. Some large-scale FTA agreements have been concluded (such as the EU–Japan FTA, US–Canada–Mexico Agreement, CPTPP), are under negotiation (such as the RCEP), or are under consideration (such as the Asia-Pacific FTA).

Second, the world and especially Asia-Pacific have yet to encounter traditional and nontraditional risk. Territorial disputes occur not only on land but also on the sea. Competition for and cooperation on power and water resources are complicated and affect world supply and prices. Adjustments in food security policy in some economies may lead to hunger and poverty in the region and the world in the absence of a concrete and collaborative framework for inclusive growth.

Third, the global and regional value chains span many countries and economies, especially in Asia–Pacific and particularly Southeast Asia (Baldwin, 2016; Iliuteanu, 2016; Ing and Kimura, 2017; West, 2018; World Bank, 2019). The establishment and development of industry clusters and chains give rise to intense competition in the context of globalisation (Donahue et al., 2018). The division of labour is more intensive and production restructuring is shifted from developed to developing countries to utilise cheap labour in production segmentation that is labour-intensive (for example, from China and Thailand to other countries in Southeast Asia [Intercedent Asia Pte Ltd, 2017]).

Fourth, handling the contagion effect or interaction between economies becomes complicated in the context of international integration. The instability and internal economic problems of Vietnam's partners (such as public debt and institutional restructuring in Europe, economic downturn in Japan and China) can cause an array of problems. Protectionism is increasing significantly in a number of economies, including Vietnam's major economic partners (Productivity Commission, 2017; Pacific Economic Cooperation Council PECC, 2018). The trade war between the US and China has cast further doubt on the prospects of the global economy and trade (International Monetary Fund IMF, 2019).

Fifth, the fourth industrial revolution has achieved technological breakthroughs in many core areas such as information and communication technology, energy, and transportation. Traditional large-scale production can take advantage of economies of scale. Cheaper production costs per unit can be achieved because the industrial revolution produces many products that meet specific demand, such as 3D printing, and develops new materials (World Economic Forum, 2017). Participation or non-participation in the industrial revolution can significantly affect the comparative advantage of countries, including Vietnam.

b. Domestic context

First, Vietnam has become a middle-income country. With the rise of a middle-income class (Berrou et al., 2018; Swedish Trade & Invest Council, 2018), consumer behaviour and demand for industrial products can be changed. Specifically, demand for high-quality products increases. Consumers are not only interested in the quality of a commodity but also in the services related to it.

Second, the macroeconomic environment was significantly more stable in 2016–18 than in 2011–15 (CIEM, 2018, 2019). Vietnam has more favourable conditions to implement reforms, especially of the microeconomic foundation. Vietnam needs to restructure the economy to shift growth towards improving quality, efficiency, and competitive capacity (CIEM, 2019).

However, the space to manipulate macroeconomic policy is more limited than before 2010. The space to conduct trade policy in support of domestic stakeholders is smaller in the context of FTAs (Vo et al., 2015). Public and government debts are close to their ceilings, increasing interest payments from the state budget and restricting capacity to borrow (CIEM, 2015, 2019). The ability to cope with adverse changes in the domestic economy depends to a large extent on whether Vietnam can retain and increase the space to conduct macroeconomic policies (Nguyen et al., 2019).

Third, Vietnam is quickly leaving the 'golden demographic structure.' Labour growth is on a significant downwards trend. Ageing in Vietnam is fast (Nguyen, 2016; World Bank, 2016a). Vietnam may risk falling into the 'middle-income trap' (PwC, 2017) and find it difficult to escape from the economic paradigm that has relied heavily on cheap and low-tech labour.

Fourth, Vietnam needs to focus on improving enterprises' competitiveness. Competitiveness in some traditional products is either slowly improving or significantly degraded. Development of competitive capacity in new products is still slower than expected. Many enterprises lack the patience, vision, aspiration, initiative, and motivation to participate in regional and global value chains.

Fifth, natural resources are being gradually depleted, whilst efficiency of use has not increased significantly. Negative impacts on the environment, especially climate change due to economic development and urbanisation, are becoming more noticeable. Changes in production conditions and the environment have negative effects on agriculture development and food security.

Sixth, Vietnam should tackle the risks of integration failure. Pressure from integration becomes more apparent when Vietnam has to remove tariffs on industrial products from ASEAN and as provided by FTAs with other countries. Utilising export preferences in partners' markets is not easy if Vietnam does not meet the rules of origin and other aspects such as labour standards, environmental protection, and corporate social responsibility. Without a strong supporting industry, Viet Nam risks losing opportunities to participate in industrialisation (Ministry of Planning and Investment, 2018).

5.2 Policy recommendations

First, notwithstanding deeper economic integration, Vietnam can do more than just depend solely on the global trade environment (Vo et al., 2017). Effective economic integration requires more than just efforts by firms to enhance their competitiveness; instead, the government of Vietnam should assume an equivalent role in accelerating reforms for a more favorable business environment. Unnecessary regulatory burden on business activities should be reduced and transparency and regulatory and policy predictability increased, which should go beyond streamlining non-tariff measures.

Policies to enhance competitiveness, especially to promote FDI, should be implemented. Measures to selectively attract FDI inflows should be enforced[3] whilst sudden changes (even reversals) of capital flows, especially short-term ones, should be managed. Cost-effective hard and soft infrastructure should be developed to reduce the cost of production and doing business.

Second, Vietnam should leverage the learning effect in post-WTO trade policy, particularly in identifying and penetrating fast-growing markets and regions. Strategic analysis of potential markets and regions is essential. Whilst such strategic analysis – however rigorous – cannot be error-free, the extent and cost of errors can be minimised with meaningful consultation with the business community, including foreign investors. Deepening trade relations with existing partners via new, higher-quality FTAs will generate more value for Vietnam.[4]

The design of FTAs and their harmonisation requirements should be determined beforehand irrespective of whether the arrangements will deliver ex-post benefits or not. Path dependence should be carefully considered. The benefits of FTAs may be reversed if commitments under them are inconsistent or developed without sequential consideration.

Third, information on the broad international economic integration agenda and on the content of each FTA before it is completed and signed should be disseminated. The relevance and timeliness of information are even more important as international and regional economic integration become more uncertain. More active dissemination of information will help ensure that the government gains the trust of the business community, which has a practical policy-relevant perspective.

Notes

1 Vietnam started implementing the CPTPP on 14 January 2019.
2 Reaffirmed in Resolution 06-NQ/TW by the Steering Committee of the Communist Party of Vietnam in November 2016.
3 Such selective attraction cannot violate WTO rules and principles (especially the most-favoured nation principle). Whilst allowing FDI in a range of sectors, Vietnam should encourage it in strategic, priority industries.
4 For an impact assessment of RCEP on Vietnam's economy, see Nguyen et al. (2014).

References

Abbott, P. and F. Tarp (2012), 'Globalization Crises, Trade and Development in Vietnam', *Journal of International Commerce, Economics and Policy*, 03(01), 1240006. World Scientific Publishing Co. Pte. Ltd.

Abbott, P., J. Bentzen, and F. Tarp (2009), 'Trade and Development: Lessons from Vietnam's Past Trade Agreements', *World Development*, 37(2), pp.341–353.

Baker, P., D. Vanzetti, T.L.H. Pham, C.T. Tran, T.X.T. Nguyen, and A.D. Nguyen (2017), Impact Assessment EU–Vietnam FTA. Activity EU-2, funded by Mutual Trade Assistance Project (MUTRAP).

Baldwin, R. (2016), 'GVC Revolution and Trade Policy'. https://piie.com/system/files/documents/baldwin20160614ppt.pdf (accessed 23 May 2019).

Berrou, J.P., M. Clement, F. Combarnous, D. Darbon, K.S. Le, and E. Rougier (2018), 'Should We Call It Middle Class?' Economic and Political Stakes of the Middle Income Group Expansion in Vietnam', *AFD Research Papers Series*, No. 2019-94, Agence Française de Développement.

CIEM (2010), *Comprehensive Evaluations of Vietnam's Socio-Economic Performance 3 Years after Accession to the WTO.* Ha Noi: Finance Publishing House.

CIEM (2011), *Viet Nam's Economy in 2010.* Ha Noi: Finance Publishing House.

CIEM (2013), *Comprehensive Evaluations of Vietnam's Socio-Economic Performance 5 Years after Accession to the WTO.* Ha Noi: Finance Publishing House.

CIEM (2015), *Macroeconomic Report for Q4 and 2014.* Ha Noi: Finance Publishing House. English and Vietnamese.

CIEM (2016), *Macroeconomic Report for Q4 and 2015.* Ha Noi: Finance Publishing House. English and Vietnamese.

CIEM (2018), *Macroeconomic Report for Q4-2017.* Ha Noi: Finance Publishing House. English and Vietnamese.

CIEM (2019), *Macroeconomic Report for Q1-2018.* Ha Noi: Finance Publishing House. English and Vietnamese.

Donahue, R., J. Parilla, and B. McDearman (2018), 'Rethinking Cluster Initiatives'. Brookings Institute. https://www.brookings.edu/wp-content/uploads/2018/

07/201807_Brookings-Metro_Rethinking-Clusters-Initiatives_Full-report-final.pdf (accessed 23 April 2019).

General Department of Vietnam Customs (2018), 'Statistical Data'. https://www.customs.gov.vn/Lists/ThongKeHaiQuan/Default.aspx (accessed February 2019). Vietnamese.

General Statistics Office of Vietnam (GSO) (2018), *Statistical Data*. Ha Noi: GSO. www.gso.gov.vn (accessed February 2019). Vietnamese.

Glewwe, P., H.A. Dang, J. Lee, and K. Vu (2017), 'What Explains Vietnam's Exceptional Performance in Education Relative to Other Countries?' *Analysis of the 2012 and 2015 PISA Data*. https://www.apec.umn.edu/sites/apec.umn.edu/files/pisa_vn4.pdf (accessed 22 May 2019).

Grossman, G.M. and A.B. Krueger (1991), 'Environmental Impacts of North American Free Trade Agreement', *Discussion Papers in Economics*, No. 158. Princeton, NJ: Woodrow Wilson School of Public and International Affairs.

Hoang, V.T., and T.H. Pham (2010), 'Chapter 7: Productivity Spillovers from Foreign Direct Investment: The Case of Vietnam', in C.H. Hahn and D. Narjoko (eds.), *Causes and Consequences of Globalization in East Asia: What Do the Micro Data Analyses Show?* Jakarta: Economic Research Institute for ASEAN and East Asia.

Iliuteanu, M.A. (2016), 'Deepening and Expanding Global Value Chain Participation across Asia and Europe'. http://www.eria.org/Deepening_and_Expanding_GVC_Participation.pdf (accessed 12 February 2019).

Ing, L.Y. and F. Kimura (2017), *Production Networks in Southeast Asia*. New York: Routledge Publishing House.

Institute of labour Science and Social Affairs (ILSSA) (2018), *Labour and Social Trends in Viet Nam 2012–2017*. Hanoi: Labour Publishing House.

Intercedent Asia Pte Ltd (2017), *Asia Corporate Strategy Assessment: 10 Trends in Corporate Strategic Planning for the Asian Region*. https://www.roihu.com/wp-content/uploads/2017/05/Tekes-Asia-corporate-strategy-assessment.pdf (accessed 23 May 2019).

International Monetary Fund (IMF) (2019), *World Economic Outlook Update: A Weakening Global Expansion*. Washington, DC: IMF.

Knoema. https://knoema.com/atlas/Viet-Nam/GINI-index (accessed 3 April 2019).

Le, M.S., T. Singh, and D.T. Nguyen (2016), *Trade Liberalisation and Poverty: Vietnam Now and Beyond*. New York, NY: Routledge Publishing House.

Ministry of Planning and Investment (2018), 'Đánh giá tình hình các doanh nghiệp sản xuất sản phẩm phụ kiện đầu vào cung cấp cho các doanh nghiệp đầu tư nước ngoài tại các tỉnh/thành phố trực thuộc Trung ương' [An Assessment of Suppliers of Inputs for Foreign-Invested Firms in Cities, Provinces directly under the Central Government, Report to the Government of Viet Nam]. Vietnamese.

Multilateral Trade Assistance Project (MUTRAP) (2015a), 'Assessing the Socio-Economic Preparedness of Vietnam Towards ASEAN Economic Community'. Activity: ICB-1.

Multilateral Trade Assistance Project (MUTRAP) (2015b), 'Assessing the Impacts of the Regional Comprehensive Economic Partnership on Vietnam's Economy'. Activity: ICB-8.

Newman, C., J. Rand, T. Talbot, and F. Tarp (2013), 'Technology Transfers, Foreign Investment and Productivity Spillovers: Evidence from Vietnam'. http://www.ciem.org.vn/Portals/1/CIEM/IndepthStudy/TCS12_Technology_Transfer_Final.pdf (accessed 22 May 2019).

Nguyen, A.D. (2018), 'Efforts to Foster Vietnam-Japan Investment Cooperation since 2008'. Presentation at the Annual CIEM–Toshiba International Foundation Workshop on Deepening Bilateral Cooperation After 10 Years of Vietnam–Japan Economic Partnership Agreement, Ha Noi, 15 November.

Nguyen, A.D., T.H. Dinh, T.N.T. Do, and T.T. Vo (2019), 'Non-tariff Measures in Viet Nam', in H.T.T. Doan and S. Rosenow (eds.), *Non-tariff Measures in ASEAN – An Update*. Jakarta: Economic Research Institute for ASEAN and East Asia (ERIA), pp.207–233.

Nguyen, A.D., T.Q. Le, B.M. Tran, and H.T. Nguyen (2011), 'Review of Country Strategy Paper for 2006–2010 of ActionAID International Vietnam'. Report for ActionAID International Vietnam.

Nguyen, A.D., D.C. Nguyen, T.T. Vo, B.M. Tran, T.H. Pham, and H.L. Le (2017), 'Việt Nam tham gia các hiệp định thương mại tự do mới: Một số yêu cầu cải cách thể chế thương mại và đầu tư' [Impacts of New-Generation FTAs and Institutional Reforms in Vietnam]. Funded by the Australian Department for Foreign Affairs and Trade project, Restructuring for a Competitive Vietnam. Vietnamese.

Nguyen, A.D., B.M. Tran, and M.A. Le (2018), 'Viet Nam VNMOD v1.0 (2012–17)'. Southmod Project Country Report. https://www.wider.unu.edu/sites/default/files/Publications/Report/PDF/SOUTHMOD-Viet-Nam-2018-V1.0.pdf (accessed 6 November 2019).

Nguyen, A.D., D. Vanzetti, R. Trewin, T.H. Dinh, T.H. Vu, and X.S. Le (2014), 'Assessing Impacts of Regional Comprehensive Economic Partnership on Vietnam's Economy. Activity: ICB-8 (Output 3)'. Funded by the Mutual Trade Assistance Project (MUTRAP).

Nguyen, A.D., T.T. Vo, and T.N.T. Do (2018), 'Vietnam's Exports After Joining the WTO'. Unpublished paper.

Nguyen, B.N. (2018), 'The Transition Process of Vietnam's Trade Policy from Closed Economy to "Servicification" Economy', *Studia i Prace WNEiZ US*, 53, pp.295–310.

Nguyen, D.C., A.D. Nguyen, B.M. Tran, T.H. Dinh, H.L. Le, and T.H. Pham (2019), 'Giải pháp tăng cường sức chống chịu của nền kinh tế Việt Nam' [Measures to Improve Economic Resilience of Viet Nam]. Report for Aus4Reform Project. Vietnamese.

Nguyen, H. (2017), 'Vietnam Macro – Analysis of BOP', *Viet Capital Security*. https://www.vcsc.com.vn/userfiles/others/MacroThougtPiece--20170531.pdf (accessed 5 January 2018).

Nguyen, T.H. (2007), 'The Impact of Globalisation on Higher Education in China and Vietnam: Policies and Practices'. Presented at a conference, Education in a Changing Environment, University of Salford, 12–14 September.

Nguyen, T.H. (2009), *Marketization of Higher Education in Vietnam in the Era of Neoliberal Globalization: Policy and Practice*. Master's thesis. Burnaby, Canada: Simon Fraser University.

Nguyen, T.T.A. (2005), *Impact of FDI on Economic Growth in Vietnam*. Hanoi: Science and Technics Publishing House. Vietnamese and English.

Nguyen, V.H. (2016), *Population Aging in Vietnam*. (accessed 2 February 2019) https://wapes.org/en/system/files/vietnamp2g3.pdf

Pacific Economic Cooperation Council (PECC) (2018), 'State of the Region 2018–2019'. https://www.pecc.org/resources/regional-cooperation/2584-state-of-the-region-2018-2019 (accessed 05 March 2019).

Petri, P.A. and L.K.P. Phan (2015), *Viet Nam Bets on Trade: The Implications of the TPP, EVFTA and RCEP Agreements.* Hanoi: United Nations Development Programme.

Productivity Commission (2017), 'Rising Protectionism: Challenges, Threats and Opportunities for Australia'. Research paper.

PwC (2017), 'Spotlight on Vietnam: The Leading Emerging Market'. October. https://www.pwc.com/vn/en/publications/2017/spotlight-on-vietnam.pdf (accessed 02 January 2018).

Roland-Holst, D., F. Tarp, V.A. Dinh, T.T. Vo, L.H. Pham, & H.M. Dinh (2002). 'Vietnamas Accession to the World Trade Organization: Economic Projections to 2020', Discussion Papers in Economic Policy Analysis, No. 0204.

Swedish Trade & Invest Council (2018), 'Capturing the Vietnamese Consumer Market'. *Business Sweden.* https://www.business-sweden.se/contentassets/c53a2f46ff1441d4adbe1f0da140a5ad/vietnam-consumer-goods-point-of-view.pdf (accessed 17 April 2019).

Trade Map. http://www.trademap.org/Bilateral_TS.aspx (accessed 28 February 2019).

Tran, B.M., T. Bui, Q.L. Trinh, and V.C. Hoang (2011), 'Ước tính hàm lượng nhập khẩu trong xuất khẩu phục vụ công tác hoạch định chính sách kinh tế ở Việt Nam' [Estimating the Import Content of Exports to Support Policies in Viet Nam]. Ministerial research project. Vietnamese.

Tran, D.T. (1999), 'Impact of the Regional Crisis on the Vietnamese Economy'. http://ismea.org/ASIAlist/Tran-Dinh-Thien.html (accessed 23 April 2019)

Tran, T.A.D. and T.T.B. Dinh (2013), 'FDI and Growth in Vietnam: A Critical Survey', *Journal of Economics and Development*, 15(3), pp.91–116.

Truong, D.T., T.T. Vo, T.G. Bui, V.C. Phan, T.D. Le, A.D. Nguyen, and S.A. Pham (2011), 'Tác động của cam kết mở cửa thị trường trong WTO và các hiệp định thương mại tự do đến hoạt động sản xuất, thương mại của Việt Nam và các cơ chế hoàn thiện cơ chế điều hành xuất nhập khẩu của Bộ Công Thương giai đoạn 2011–2015' [Impacts of Commitments on Opening the Market under WTO and other Free Trade Agreements on Vietnam's Production and Trade Activities and Mechanism to Improve Import and Export Management Scheme of the Ministry of Industry and Trade in 2011–2015]. Report for Multilateral Trade Assistance Project (MUTRAP). Vietnamese.

United Nations Commodity Trade Statistics Database (UN Comtrade) (2017), 'Metadata & Reference, Commodity List'. https://comtrade.un.org/db/mr/rfCommoditiesList.aspx (accessed February 2019).

United Nations Development Programme (UNDP) (2006), *South-East Asia Regional Economic Integration and Cooperation Deepening and Broadening the Benefits for Human Development.* Colombo: UNDP Regional Centre.

United Nations Development Programme (UNDP) (2018), 'Human Development Indices and Indicators: Viet Nam's 2018 Statistical Update'. https://www.vn.undp.org/content/dam/vietnam/img/undp-vn-hdr-stats-2018.pdf (accessed 6 November 2019).

United Nations Industrial Development Organization (UNIDO) (2012), 'Viet Nam Industrial Investment Report 2011 – Understanding the Impact of Foreign Direct Investment on Industrial Development'. https://www.unido.org/sites/default/files/2012-08/VIIR%20print_0.pdf (accessed 12 May 2016).

United Nations Economic and Social Commission for Asia and the Pacific (UNESCAP) (2015), 'Global Value Chains and Interconnectedness of Asia–Pacific

Economies'. In *Asia Pacific Trade and Investment Report 2015*, pp.103–138. https://www.unescap.org/sites/default/files/Chapter%207%20-%20GVCs%20in%20the%20Asia-Pacific.pdf (accessed 18 May 2019).

Vanzetti, D., R. Trewin, J. Cassing, D.T. Truong, L.H. Pham, A.D. Nguyen, and Q.L. Le (2011). 'Impact Assessment of Free Trade Agreements on Vietnam's Economy', Activity Code FTA-HOR. Multilateral Trade Assistance Project (MUTRAP).

Vietnamnet (2017), 'Illegal Waste Imports Difficult to Control, Manage: Agencies'. https://english.vietnamnet.vn/fms/environment/192031/illegal-waste-imports-difficult-to-control--manage--agencies.html (accessed 25 February 2019).

Vietnamnet (2018), 'Vietnam Expects High-quality FDI Inflows After CPTPP Ratification'. https://english.vietnamnet.vn/fms/business/213125/vietnam-expects-high-quality-fdi-inflows-after-cptpp-ratification.html (accessed 18 February 2019).

Vietnamnet (2018), 'Vietnam Makes Great Strides in Promoting Gender Equality'. https://en.vietnamplus.vn/vietnam-makes-great-strides-in-promoting-gender-equality/143585.vnp (accessed 6 November 2019).

Vietnamnews (2017), 'State Budget Reform Will Be a Testing Process'. http://vietnamnews.vn/economy/418748/state-budget-reform-will-be-a-testing-process.html#LAieUwrk7SPR5T4X.99 (accessed 18 February 2019).

Vo, T.T. (2012), 'Achieving an Efficient AEC by 2015: A Perspective from Vietnam', in S.B. Das (ed.), *Achieving ASEAN Economic Community 2015: Challenges for Member Countries and Businesses*. Singapore: Institute of Southeast Asian Studies, pp.161–177.

Vo, T.T. (2014), 'Making Growth Inclusive: The Case of Vietnam'. Unpublished report for the United Nations Economic and Social Commission for Asia and the Pacific. December.

Vo, T.T. (2015), 'In the Midst of Global Economic Uncertainties: Vietnam's Experience since WTO Accession', in S. Chirathivat, C. Sabhasri, and A. Chongvilaivan (eds.), *Global Economic Uncertainties and Southeast Asian Economies*. Singapore: ISEAS–Yusof Institute, pp.123–147.

Vo, T.T. (2015), 'Vietnam's Perspectives on Regional Economic Integration', *Journal of Southeast Asian Economies*, 32(1), pp. 106–124.

Vo, T.T. (2016), 'Country Paper for Viet Nam'. Unpublished report for the United Nations Economic and Social Commission for Asia and the Pacific. February.

Vo, T.T. and A.D. Nguyen (2009), 'Vietnam after Two Years of WTO Accession: What Lessons Can Be Learnt', *ASEAN Economic Bulletin*, 26(1), pp.15–35.

Vo, T.T. and A.D. Nguyen (2011), 'Revisiting Exports and Foreign Direct Investment in Vietnam', *Asian Economic Policy Review*, 6, pp.112–131.

Vo, T.T. and A.D. Nguyen (2015), 'Survey of FTA Utilisation in Viet Nam', in L.Y. Ing and S. Urata (eds), *The Use of FTAs in ASEAN: Survey-based Analysis*. Jakarta: Economic Research Institute for ASEAN and East Asia, pp.271–300.

Vo, T.T. and T. Nguyen (2006), 'Vietnam Human Development 1999–2004: What the Current Data Show?' Unpublished report for the United Nations Development Programme. English and Vietnamese.

Vo, T.T., A.D. Nguyen, and T. Bui (2017), 'Trade in Value Added: The Case of Viet Nam', in L.Y. Ing and F. Kimura (eds), *Production Networks in Southeast Asia*. New York: Routledge Publishing House, pp.183–201.

Vo, T.T., A.D. Nguyen, and B.M. Tran (2017), 'Non-tariff Measures in Viet Nam', in L.Y. Ing, S. Fernandez de Cordoba, and O. Cadot (eds), *Non-tariff Measures in ASEAN*. Jakarta: Economic Research Institute for ASEAN and East Asia, pp.155–167.

Vo, T.T., A.D. Nguyen, B.M. Tran, T.H. Dinh, and D.B. Le (2015), 'Impacts of Current and Proposed FTAs and BITs on Vietnam's Long-Term Development Goals: A Case Study of Food Processing and Electronics Manufacturing Sectors'. Report for ActionAID International Vietnam. July.

VOV (2018), 'Vietnam's GDP Growth Rate in 2018 Highest in 11 Years'. https://english.vov.vn/economy/vietnams-gdp-growth-rate-in-2018-highest-in-11-years-389676.vov (accessed February 2019).

West, J. (2018), 'Global Value Chains in the Asia–Pacific'. https://asiancenturyinstitute.com/international/1439-global-value-chains-in-the-asia-pacific (accessed 12 January 2019).

World Bank (2015), *Taking Stock: An Update on Vietnam's Recent Economic Developments*. Washington, DC: World Bank.

World Bank (2016a), 'Tiếp bước thành công – Nhóm ưu tiên tăng trưởng toàn diện và bền vững' [Moving Forward – Priority for Inclusive and Sustainable Growth]. http://documents.worldbank.org/curated/en/199441476437862446/pdf/108348-VIETNAMESE-PUBLIC-VietnamSCDfinalVNOct.pdf (accessed 23 April 2019).

World Bank (2016b), *Vietnam 2035. Towards Prosperity, Creativity, Equity, and Democracy*. Washington, DC: World Bank.

World Bank (2018a), *Economic and Income Distribution Impacts of the Comprehensive and Progressive Agreement for Trans-Pacific Partnership: The Case of Viet Nam*. Hanoi: World Bank. English and Vietnamese.

World Bank (2018b), 'Gender Gap in Earnings in Vietnam: Why Do Vietnamese Women Work in Lower Paid Occupations?'. http://documents.worldbank.org/curated/en/685791521537975174/pdf/124438-BRI-19-3-2018-11-16-51-EAPVietnamBriefWEBv.pdf (accessed 2 May 2019).

World Bank (2019), *World Development Report 2020: Global Value Chains – Trading for Development*. Washington, DC: World Bank.

World Economic Forum (2017), *Impact of the Fourth Industrial Revolution on Supply Chains*. Geneva: World Economic Forum.

World Integrated Trade Solution (WITS). (2019). http://wits.worldbank.org/WITS/WITS/Default-A.aspx?Page=Default (accessed February 2019).

WTO Center (2019), 'Tỷ lệ tận dụng C/O ưu đãi theo các hiệp định thương mại của Việt Nam qua các năm' [Use of Preferential C/O in Viet Nam's FTAs Over Time]. Vietnamese. www.trungtamwto.vn/download/18449/Bang%20tan%20dung%20uu%20dai%20FTAs%20qua%20tung%20nam%20-%20VN%20(updated%202018).pdf (accessed 22 May 2019).

Yen Hai (2015), 'Điểm mới trong Luật Đầu tư và Luật Doanh nghiệp' [New Content in the Investment Law and Enterprise Law]. http://baotintuc.vn/kinh-te/diem-moi-trong-luat-dau-tu-va-luat-doanh-nghiep-20150624173730816.htm (accessed 2 May 2019). Vietnamese.

Index

Note: *Italicized* page numbers refer to figures, **bold** page numbers refer to tables

For Product Safety Concerns and Information please contact our EU representative GPSR@taylorandfrancis.com
Taylor & Francis Verlag GmbH, Kaufingerstraße 24, 80331 München, Germany

www.ingramcontent.com/pod-product-compliance
Lightning Source LLC
LaVergne TN
LVHW021122300926
849160LV00010B/828
9780367686680